National Economics

Muxi Lin · Taiyan Huang

National Economics

A Systematic and Theoretical Framework

中国财经出版传媒集团
经济科学出版社
Economic Science Press

Springer

Muxi Lin
National Economic Academy
Liaoning University
Liaoning, China

Taiyan Huang
School of Economics
Renmin University of China
Beijing, China

Translated by
Yanfeng Huang
Jinan, China

ISBN 978-981-96-9617-8 ISBN 978-981-96-9618-5 (eBook)
https://doi.org/10.1007/978-981-96-9618-5

Jointly published with Economic Science Press
The print edition is not for sale in the Mainland of China. Customers from the Mainland of China please order the print book from: Economic Science Press.

This Springer imprint is published by the registered company Springer Nature Singapore Pte Ltd.
The registered company address is: 152 Beach Road, #21-01/04 Gateway East, Singapore 189721, Singapore

Preface

This is a *National Economics* written by Chinese scholars, grounded in China's national conditions and development practices, exploring the movement and regularity of China's national economic system. It aims to delve into new situations and issues, reveal new characteristics and laws, distill and summarize the research achievements of China's national economics development practices, elevate practical experience to systematic national economics theory, and contribute Chinese wisdom to promoting the construction of national economics.

The movement of China's national economic system follows both the general laws of national economic system movement and unique special laws specific to China, which exhibit several important characteristics:

The first is the research object of National Economics. Defining the research object of national economics as "the movement and regularity of the national economic system" is a major feature of this book. The "national economic system" mentioned here is a macro system, a composite system composed of the state, the people, and the market, a network system composed of multiple sectors, regions, and links, and a comprehensive system consisting of four types of reproduction: material products, population, spiritual culture, and natural environment. It is also an open and dynamic system. This is partly determined by China's special national conditions, and another important reason is that "concentrating efforts to accomplish major tasks" is an important characteristic of China's economic development, with unparalleled institutional advantages. Under this system, various resources can be effectively integrated and concentrated to achieve major goals of economic and social development.

The second is the national economic development strategy. The national economic development strategy is also known as the national economic and social development strategy or national strategy. The practice of China's national economic development has proven that strategic issues are fundamental to the Party and the country. The emergence of the Chinese miracle mainly lies in the accurate strategic judgment, scientific planning, and taking proactive measures by the Party and the country. Therefore, they have continuously overcome difficulties and setbacks in socialist industrialization and the Chinese path to modernization, fully exerting their overall, long-term, and guiding role. Currently, China is moving towards the Second Centenary Goal, advancing the socialist modernization led by the Communist Party of China, the modernization of a country with a huge population, the modernization of common prosperity for all people, the modernization of coordinated material and spiritual civilization, the modernization of harmonious coexistence between humanity and nature, and the modernization of following the path of peaceful development, promoting the national rejuvenation on all fronts through a Chinese path to modernization.

The third is the national economic planning. Guiding economic and social development with medium- and long-term planning is an important way for China to govern and administer the country. China's national economic planning primarily consists of five-year plans. These plans are phased deployments and arrangements of the socialist modernization strategy during the planning period, mainly systematically clarifying the intentions of national strategies. They serve as a grand blueprint for economic and social development and represent the institutional arrangement of national economic governance with the most Chinese characteristics. Their long duration, long preparation and implementation, and strong execution can be regarded as another miracle in the world. Practice has proved that medium- and long-term development planning can not only fully leverage the decisive role of the market in resource allocation but also better leverage the role of the government. It is particularly noteworthy that the tripartite coordination, mutual connection, and interaction of development strategies, development plans, and annual plans provide Chinese experience for implementing strategic governance and planning governance.

The fourth is the national economic governance. National economic governance, also known as national economic management or macroeconomic governance, is an important component of national governance. Promoting the modernization of national economic governance is a crucial aspect of advancing the modernization of the state governance system and capacity. It is an objective requirement for building a high-level socialist market economy and an important support for realizing the Chinese path to modernization. China's national economic governance not only possesses general characteristics of macroeconomic governance but also exhibits significant features that align with Chinese practices in terms of governance ideas, objectives, methods, and theories, thus constituting an important content of the research in this book.

The Chinese version of this book has been recognized as the first National Excellent Textbook, a National Planning Textbook, and a National Quality Textbook, marking it as a significant achievement in the national "Double First-Class" initiative and key disciplines. The English version of this book also serves as an attempt to facilitate communication with international scholars and readers.

April, 2025

Muxi Lin
Liaoning, China

Taiyan Huang
Beijing, China

Translation Team

Translator: Huang Yanfeng
Proofreaders: Wang Lu, Che Yanqiu

Contents

Chapter 1
Introduction: Research Objects and Methodology of National Economics

National Economics studies the national economic system (hereinafter referred to as NES) movement and its laws, specifically the strategies, planning, macro-adjustment, and micro-regulation, etc., aiming at the coordinated and sustainable development of the national economy.

National Economics is instrumental in shaping the discipline of economics in China. It facilitates the market's decisive role in resource allocation, enhances the government's capacity in macroeconomic management, modernizes the national economic governance system and capabilities, and propels China's reform, opening-up, and economic development.

1.1 Research Objects

1.1.1 NES Is the Starting Point of National Economic Research

Considering the characteristics of the discipline and China's economic reality, we define NES as the starting point of National Economics and the NES movement and laws as its research objects.

Based on systems theory, NES encompasses multiple dimensions.

First, NES is such a giant system that the traditional methods are not sufficient for analyzing a system with complex structures, functions, and numerous elements. National Economics should be regarded as an interconnected and integrated system and organism instead, so as to achieve overall coordination and holistic effects.

Second, NES is a complex system consisting of the state, the people, and the market. The term "national" in Chinese has the connotation of both the state and the people because all the actions taken by the state are ultimately for the people,

M. Lin and T. Huang, *National Economics*,
https://doi.org/10.1007/978-981-96-9618-5_1

and all the development of the state is people-centered, i.e., from the people, for the people and by the people. In other words, National Economics mainly studies how to promote the people's overall development via the development of the state. In the socialist market economy, the development of the state and the people is inseparable from the market. The movement of the system is based on the movement of market economy through which the market allocates the resources more efficiently, and the government plays a better role. The national economic governance is also based on the market. Nevertheless, starting and ending points of National Economics, from the logical point of view, are how to promote national economic development (NED) by observing the laws of the market, and how to promote the coordinated and sustainable development of the state and the people by using multiple means and playing the dual roles of market and government. These issues are at the heart of National Economics research.

Third, NES is a network composed of interconnected sectors, regions and links. It is a compound of multiple sectors and regional economic subsystems; an economic complex composed of all links of social reproduction, interconnected rather than disjointed or simply combined. Furthermore, social reproduction is an integrated process consisting of production, distribution, exchange, and consumption. National Economics studies the NES movement and its laws from a holistic perspective, taking into account the interrelation, interconnection, and interaction of various sectors, regions, and links of NES, and the impact of subsystems on the whole system.

Fourth, NES consists of four types of reproduction. The primary production activity of human beings is to produce and reproduce material goods, people's relations forming in production, exchange, distribution, and consumption. Meanwhile, reproduction also refers to population reproduction, the survival and breeding of humans, from which the reproduction of spiritual and cultural products ensues. The natural environment impacts the economic system, too. Therefore, NES is not limited to material reproduction but a comprehensive system with other three types of reproductions: the reproductions of population, natural environment, and spiritual and cultural reproduction. It is also an integrated compound of the economy, the population, the society, and the nature. Thus, it is a higher level of an integrated system.

Fifth, NES is open and dynamic. In the context of economic globalization, the economic development of any country is bound to be linked with the external environment in various ways and become an integral part of the entire global economy. China, in particular, is a large developing country and has become the world's second-largest economy. That means NES in question is not closed but open, not static but dynamic and active in reform and innovation. Its distinctive openness and dynamics enrich the disciplinary study and create a large space for the discipline.

Starting from NES helps us to view national economy from the whole system and has vital theoretical and practical significance.

Theoretically, it is conducive to a more profound understanding of the intricate economic phenomena and the nature of the movement of the system. As the national economy involves various sectors and regions, as well as industries, finance, international trade, etc., all these subsystems impacting the movement of whole system, taking National Economics as a giant system can help grasp its relationship with other subsystems and differentiate it from other disciplines of economics.

Practically, it is conducive to comprehensive, strategic and forward-looking analysis of the NES movement, finding countermeasures, promoting deeper reform and openness. After the global financial crisis, the international economy is becoming complicated and changeable, characterized by sluggish growth and insufficient momentum. More countries are turning to China's economic development. Under the new economic normal, people are increasingly interested in the overall performance of China's NES and its macro economy, thus providing a great opportunity for National Economics to better serve the economy by studying the NES movement.

1.1.2 The Research Objects of National Economics Are the NES Movement and Its Laws

As mentioned above, NES is a multi-objective, giant, open, and dynamic system encompassing various sectors, regions, links, layers and subsystems. So how do we study such a vast system with complicated structures and factors? The reason we take NES as the research object lies in the indisputable link between the national economy and that of the globe in the context of economic globalization. For the smooth operation and national economy and better macroeconomic benefits, not only the economic system but the other systems of population, society, and nature are all at play. The NES movement is targeting not only the growth and growth rate of the economic aggregates, but also the improved quality and the optimized structure. It is targeting for the overall development of people in essence rather than things. Therefore, the main aspects and factors are our focuses when analyzing the NES movement and its laws.

1.1.2.1 National Economic System

NES is the object of study, and the premise and foundation for analysis. Three aspects should be studied to discover the laws of its movement.

The first is the totality of NES, in order to understand and address the correlations among all aspects, links, and levels of NES. To a certain extent, it means properly handling the relationship between National Economics and other disciplines.

The second is its structure, especially the structures closely related to the NES movement, such as the industrial, regional, and urban–rural structures within NES structure.

The third is its environment. Analyzing the NES movement (i.e., integrated four types of reproduction) as well as the international economic environment is an indispensable part of National Economics. The NES movement cannot be separated from the international economic environment. National economic governance aims to achieve coordinated economic and social development, realize the harmonious coexistence of population, resources, and environment, i.e., achieving scientific, integrated, and sustainable development. At the same time, the concepts of "innovative, coordinated, green, open, and shared development" must be established to seek the coordination of the four reproductions and the five-sphered development concepts.

1.1.2.2 The NES Movement

The movement of NES is not only an essential part of the study of National Economics, but also national economic governance. The four aspects, namely the NES movement in general, demand impetus, supply thrust, and cyclical fluctuations, are to be analyzed.

The first is the general analysis of the NES movement, specifically on how the total output or supply is generated, how the total demand is formed and how changes in demand affect output. It also studies the equilibrium between total supply and demand. The focuses are the totality of the economy and the static equilibrium between total supply and demand.

The second is demand impetus and management of NES movement, focusing on three major demand drivers: investment, consumer, and net export demands, the so-called troika of economic growth. It is commonly used in the national economic analysis where aggregate demand and structure of demand are involved. The impact of the exchange rate on the balance of social supply and demand will also be taken into account, as it significantly impacts the balance of payments.

The third is supply thrust for the NES movement and supply-side structural reform. It primarily studies the relationship between the NES movement and various supplies, including labor, capital, technology, institutions, and natural resources such as land. The supply-side structural reform will also be analyzed regarding the current China's economy.

The fourth is cyclical fluctuations in the NES movement. The primary analysis is its presence, causes, and transmission mechanism, as well as the inflation and deflation in China from 1978 to the present and their causes, in order to provide a theoretical basis and first-hand account for analyzing macroeconomic adjustment.

1.1.2.3 National Economic Development Strategy and Planning

National economic development strategy and planning are the essential components of National Economics. Analyses are done into two categories:

One is the national economic development strategy, focusing on:

- its implication, basic features, and primary functions;
- its system, classifications, and roles;
- its selection and formulation;
- major development strategies determined by China.

The other is the national economic planning, focusing on the implications, characteristics, and functions of the national economic planning, its relationship with development strategies, the national economic planning and its indicator system, the complication of the national economic plan.

1.1.2.4 National Economic Governance

It defines the governance objectives, macro-adjustment, and micro-regulation for the national economy.

1.2 Research Methodologies

1.2.1 Theoretical Analysis of the National Economy

The main task is to analyze the NES movement and its laws by means of modern economic theory and its methods, such as political economics, macroeconomics, industrial economics, public finance, finance, international trade, population resource environment economics, comparative economics, new institutional economics, and regulatory economics.

1.2.2 Quantitative Analysis of the National Economy

It refers to applying economics, mathematics, and statistics to the quantitative analysis of national economy, i.e., the overall and average levels, growth rates, changing trends, and fluctuation patterns of macroeconomic indicators, such as total output, intermediate inputs, added value, gross domestic product (GDP), gross national income (GNI), total social supply, total social demand, total consumption, gross investment, economic growth, employment, overall price level, tax rates, interest rates, and exchange rates, so as to understand the whole picture of the economic development.

1.2.3 Analysis of the National Economic Structure

The quantitative analysis is conducted on the economic structure, i.e., the relationship between indicators or variables of the national economy, aiming to understand the interdependence between them from a macroscopic perspective. Standard quantitative analysis tools include elasticity, multiplier, and input–output analysis. Macroeconomic, industrial, regional, investment, and consumption structure are also part of the quantitative analysis of the structure, conducted on all the constituents of the national economy in temporal and spatial dimension.

1.2.4 Static vs. Dynamic Analysis of National Economy

Static and dynamic are relative; the distinction between the two is made primarily for analysis purpose. For example, when the equilibrium between total demand and supply is analyzed, it appears static because the complex changes between and within the two are temporarily abstracted. it is both static and dynamic when the mechanism is concerned through which changes in total demand affects total social output; it is typically dynamic when analysis is conducted on economic growth rate, business cycle, inflation, and deflation, and the specific application of macroeconomic adjustment policies are typical dynamic analyses.

1.2.5 Comparative Analysis of the National Economy

Comparative analysis is widely used in research, and the national economy is no exception. In the context of economic globalization, comparison between nations always apply in analyzing the NES and its subsystems systems. For instance, the comparison between the post-reform period and the pre-reform period, different stages during the reform, the different connotations of the reform and opening up, and economic development.

1.2.6 Case Study of National Economy

Based on the system theory, the NES, its subsystems, and branch systems can be regarded as cases. For instance, NES is a case relative to the economic system; China's national economy is a case relative to the world economy; and rural and urban reform is a case relative to China's economic reform. Moreover, each step taken in the urban reform can also be considered a case. Case studies help to find the commonality through individuality within the NES movement; the characteristics identified help us to better under how national economy develops and fluctuates.

Part I
National Economic System

Chapter 2
Overview of National Economic System

2.1 Components of National Economic System

According to systems theory, the national economy is a giant system of complex structure, integrated functions, diverse objectives, and intricate influencing factors. It consists of a series of closely linked elements or subsystems.

2.1.1 A Socioeconomic Complex of Interdependent Sectors

The national economy contains various sectors. According to the classification of China's statistics department, there are 20 economic sections, 95 divisions, 396 groups, and 913 classes. It should be noted that with economic development and technological progress, industries will continue to emerge as new members of NES, such as industries of information technology, biotechnology, aerospace, new materials, new energy, knowledge, network, creativity, animation, and high-end, etc. This demonstrates the extreme complexity of the structure of NES.

NES is not merely a combination but an integration of many sectors. Although each sector and industry, as components and subsystems of NES, has its scope of activities, characteristics, and independent functions, they are not isolated but interdependent and interconnected, through direct and indirect links. The function of the system is primarily determined by the structure of the system, among which industrial structure is the most important. Therefore, various industrial sectors are to cooperate, coordinate and advance synchronously, and eventually realize the optimization of industrial structures.

M. Lin and T. Huang, *National Economics*,
https://doi.org/10.1007/978-981-96-9618-5_2

2.1.2 A Complex of Regional Economies

All activities of the various national economic sectors take place in regions within a specific space; a national economic system, when viewed spatially includes various interconnected regional economic subsystems of the regions.

There are two ways to classify regional economies. The first is to divide the national economy into several zones based on the existing administrative structures and taking into account the factors of politics, economy, ethnic group, culture, and history; these zones are subdivided into levels of provinces, cities, counties and townships.

The second is to divide the national economy into several economic zones based on economic collaboration and linkages, such as the Yangtze River Delta Economic Zone, Pearl River Delta Economic Zone, Beijing-Tianjin-Hebei Economic Zone, and the Eastern, Western, Central, and Northeast Economic Zones.

Regional economies take place in a specific geographical location and environment. Their developments and performance can vary considerably for a variety of reasons.

The first is the difference in natural conditions. For example, the climate, topography, geomorphology, and soil in each region vary, as do mineral resources, energy, forests, grasslands, arable land, water areas, wildlife, plants, and their roles in regional economic activities.

The second is the difference in socioeconomic conditions, including the economic base, the level of development, the transport conditions, the market conditions, the scientific and educational development, and the like.

The third is the difference in technical and management factors, including the levels of production technology and processes, scientific and technological development as well as management capacity, the skills and literacy of the workforce, and the ability to develop and utilize various resources.

These three aspects work together to influence regional economic development.

As a component of NES, the regional economy is relatively independent. It is a microcosm of the national economy, composed of various sectors. But it is not a closed system but an open one, and it cannot and should not be self-contained. Therefore, homogenous economic structures or development models should be avoided. Instead, each region should start from its actual conditions, and draw on its comparative advantages. The regional division of labor and development orientation should be determined, develop characteristic economies and competitive industries, as well as forming their unique industrial system. Ultimately, the interdependence and complementarity of advantages between regions will be achieved.

2.1.3 An Economic Complex in which the Components of Reproduction Are Correlated and Restricted

Reproduction is the cyclic activity of the entire economy. Social reproduction is an organic integrity consisting of interlinked activities of production, distribution, exchange, and consumption.

Production is the starting point and dominant force in social reproduction, the basis for the existence and development of human society, and the fundamental economic practice of human beings. Food, clothing, housing, and supplies are life necessities and make up varied demands. Production must continue uninterruptedly, providing various materials and services to meet people's demands.

Distribution is the allocation of the material goods and social wealth created by society over a certain period (e.g., a year). Production determines the quantity and quality of distribution; its fairness, rationality, and effectiveness affect people's initiatives, and in turn affect production.

Exchange is the intermediary link between production and consumption. In the market economy, people exchange goods through markets based on equivalent value. The smooth flow of goods, the fairness of transactions, the breadth and depth of market exchange, and the modes of distribution all contribute to or hinder exchanges.

Consumption is the destination of social reproduction. In order to survive, improve lives, and pursue a higher level of overall human development, human beings generate all kinds of needs and maintain continuous consumption. Production determines consumption in a certain sense, and consumption also plays a vital role in guiding production.

Each of the four segments—production, distribution, exchange, and consumption—has a unique role, but they are interdependent and mutually affected, forming an inseparable entirety of social reproduction. The process of social reproduction in essence is that of the NES movement, displaying the intrinsic links between the various stages of production and revealing such key issues of national economic activities as the total social production and demand, fair distribution, and the organization of market activities, instrumental to the effective organization of operating NES.

2.1.4 A Combination of the Four Types of Reproduction

The reproduction of material goods is the basis of social production. However, knowledge and technology have become the main drivers of economic and social progress. As people's demand for spiritual culture is rising and becoming an indispensable part of life, the reproduction of spiritual culture is bound to increase synchronously with that of material goods. Production and reproduction concern human beings, too, as they are the agents of economic activity. Moreover, the ecological environment provides the space where human beings live and where NES operates, thus posing another type of reproduction. Sustainable development can be achieved if these four types of reproduction—population, material products, spirit and culture, and natural ecological environment reproductions—coordinate with and promote each other, and the four systems, made up of these reproductions, namely the population, economic, social, and natural ecological systems, coordinate with each other at a higher level.

2.1.5 A Network of Multi-level Economic Activities

2.1.5.1 NES Is the Integration of Three Levels of Economic Activities

National economic activities take place at different interlinked sectors, regions, links, and levels. The national economy can be divided into three basic levels: macroeconomy, mesoeconomy, and microeconomy. The macroeconomy focuses on the movement of the national economy. It is researched by reflecting the aggregates of the total economic activity, such as aggregate supply, aggregate demand, gross investment, total consumption, the total amount of banknotes issued, aggregate fiscal expenditure, and overall price level, as well as their structural changes. The microeconomy focuses on the economic behavior of individuals, households, and enterprises in the market. Its main objects include the production activities of enterprises, their technological development and product selection, their operation and sales activities, their investment and income distribution, the business behavior of individual operators, their personal consumption and investment behavior. Finally, the mesoeconomy between macroeconomy and microeconomy refers mainly to the regional and urban economies. Unlike macroeconomics, mesoeconomics focuses on regional economies. Instead of studying the productivity distribution and coordinated development between regions, it mainly studies how regions develop. For a country as vast as China, with a large population and huge differences between regions, it is essential to open up a new area between macroeconomics and microeconomics, i.e., studying mesoeconomics. Macroeconomic activities cannot be studied in isolation from the analysis of the microeconomic and mesoeconomy, nor can mesoeconomic and microeconomic activities be studied in isolation from the broader macroeconomic environment.

2.1.5.2 Enterprises Are the Essential Elements of NES

The agent of microeconomic activity is mainly enterprises, whose production and operation activities are the basis of national economic activities. It is mainly reflected in the following three aspects.

First, enterprises are agents of social production and construction, as well as economic entities that directly provide products and services. Therefore, developing societal productivity and creating material wealth are carried out ultimately by enterprises. Without the production and operation of enterprises, there will be no national economy nor economic strength, let alone the improvement of people's lives, nor the country's wealth and strength.

Second, enterprises constitute the cells of the national economy and are bound to have various ramifications for the national economic organism. The vitality of enterprises is directly related to the competitiveness of the national economy. The efficiency and profits of enterprises are directly related to those of the national economy. Furthermore, their independent innovation capacity is directly related to that of the whole country; their technology and management level are directly related to the level and quality of the national economy.

Third, enterprises are the micro-foundation for macro-adjustment. Macroeconomic adjustment is conducted on a macro level but has its roots at the micro level. Only when enterprises become the true players of the market economy and economic entities that operate independently, i.e., pursuing their interests and taking risks, with the ability to self-proliferate and self-restrain, can they react and adjust promptly to the market and macro-adjustment signals. Macro-adjustment must be combined with micro-flexibility.

2.1.5.3 The Macroeconomy Is the Overall Environment in which the Microeconomy Operates

First, creating an excellent macroeconomic environment for enterprises. The main task of macroeconomy lies in achieving a balance between economic aggregates and structures, ensuring the healthy and stable operation of the national economy, and securing coordinated and sustainable development of the economy, society, resources, and the environment. All these endeavors contribute to a sound macroeconomic environment for the regular operation of enterprises.

Second, providing necessary guidance to microeconomic activities. Starting from the requirement of overall coordination, action should be taken to stimulate the enthusiasm, initiative, and creative spirit of enterprises through reform so that the inherent potentials and energy can be released and the social productivity can be raised; in the meantime, millions of enterprises should be guided into an orderly track, their behavior being regulated through macro-adjustment, systems, policies, and statutes, so that enterprises and the entire economy can operate in order and in line with healthy, stable and sustainable development.

Third, creating an internationalized business environment for enterprises. (i) It has to strive for a broad space where all enterprises can give full play to their potential, vitality, and creativity, and entrepreneurs can give full play to their talents through deepening reforms. (ii) It has to refine the market mechanism and create a fair environment for enterprises to enjoy equal rights and compete. (iii) It has to raise their awareness of innovation, stimulate them to innovate independently. (iv) It has to create an environment with solid infrastructure and convenient services for enterprises.

Fourth, aligning microeconomic activities with the overall objectives of macroeconomic adjustment. It is indisputable that enterprises aim to gain profits. However, the government, as the body of macroeconomic adjustment (i.e., regulator), must also bring the behaviors of enterprises into line with the overall will and interests of society. In the course of economic development, such issues of people's livelihood are priorities as social equity, welfare, social security, and employment.

2.1.5.4 Raising Efficacy of the Mesoeconomy

Taking regional economy as an example, its outstanding roles are demonstrated as follows.

First, regions are an important platform for various economic activities. In general, the economic activities of various sectors and industries are carried out in a certain space or within a certain geographical area. Regions have an irreplaceable role in many economic activities, for example, organizing and implementing activities directly related to people's lives, such as public transport, municipal facilities, water supply, heating, landscaping, and housing construction. Likewise, only regions or cities can organize in sectors of primary and secondary education, health care, business and consumer services, and environmental improvement.

Second, regions are the essential links in the macro-adjustment system. Centralized and hierarchical controls are necessary for an effective macroeconomic adjustment system. However, it's almost impossible for the activities of the national economy, such a complex multi-level system, to conduct centralized control. A hierarchical control system is necessary to equip each level with the ability to control so that timely and effective adjustment can be made to accommodate changes in situation and newly emerging issues. All these endeavors are conducive to the functioning of macro- adjustment and conformity to the overall adjustment for a coordinated and effective national economy.

Third, regions are essential objects of macro-adjustment. The regional economy plays a vital role in national economic activities and has certain economic authority and financial resources according to the principle of decentralized management and tax distribution system. Therefore, it is an important task for national economic macro- adjustment to oversee regional economic activities and balance the relationship between the whole and its components.

Fourth, regional economy is an intermediate link between the macroeconomy and microeconomy: on the one hand, the major macroeconomic policies and decisions are to be implemented by regions; on the other hand, performance of enterprises in production and operation can be known by the regions promptly, making it possible for regions to help them in solving problems and providing better services. Regions serve as a bridge and link between macroeconomic adjustment and microeconomic invigoration.

Fifth, the regional economy is essential in reforming the economic system and transforming economic development mode. All changes in institutions and development modes are continuous processes of exploration and innovation. Almost all significant reforms are first pilot in regions and gradually promoted on a larger scale after gaining mature experience. In a certain sense, regional pilots are indispensable for the success of China's reform.

2.2 Nature of National Economic System

2.2.1 *Objective-Oriented*

As an intricate giant system, the national economy carries multiple objectives.

First, balancing between speed, quality, efficiency, and structural optimization to continuously improve economic development, thus achieving high-quality and rapid development of the national economy.

Second, coordinating the national economic aggregates on the basis of maintaining a reasonable and moderate economic growth rate; balancing between aggregate supply and demand to avoid dramatic economic fluctuations and shocks, thus ensuring stable and rapid development of the national economy.

Third, pursuing long-term sustainable development so that economic development is compatible with the capacity of the natural ecological system, thus the economy, population, society, resources, and environment can be coordinated.

Fourth, achieving mutual promotion and cooperation between economic development and social progress. Therefore, it is necessary to start from the overall system and balance between the development of urban and rural areas, regions, economy and society, human and nature, and domestic development and opening up.

Fifth, pursuing people-centered comprehensive development, the ultimate goal of national economic development. Ultimately, Economic development is for people to solve their livelihood problems and practical difficulties, meet their diversified needs, continuously improve their living quality, and eventually achieve free and comprehensive development of people. Thus, the talents, wisdom, and creativity of hundreds of millions of people have been fully unleashed, aiming at sustainable economic and social development.

2.2.2 *Integrity*

NES is an organic assembly of various interdependent and interrelated subsystems. Each subsystem or component has unique functions and relative independence. But it is dependent on the system, otherwise its independent functions and roles become rootless. Therefore, a deep understanding of the system's integrity is of great practical significance. As the national economic activities become increasingly complicated, the interdependence and mutual constraints among the components of NES are becoming increasingly remarkable, calling for increased adaptability and coordination between components.

2.2.3 Relevance

The national economy is a multi-sectoral, multi-regional, multi-linked, and multi-level system, with subsystems and constituent elements intricately intertwined. The functioning of NES can only be improved by understanding the correlation between the components, their interactive, interdependent, restrictive and mutually reinforcing relationship, and by constructing a mechanism which is coordinated, organized, flexible and efficient. This leads to forming a rational structure with benign interaction and organic integration.

2.2.4 Openness

NES is an open system and operates in a specific environment, constrained by and linked to it in various ways. The natural ecological environment, social and human environment, political environment, and international economic environment constitute its operating environment.

According to systems theory, the outer system that a system is placed in makes its environment. From a global perspective, a country's national economy is a part of the world economy and involved with it. Therefore, NES interacts with its environment in many aspects:

First, the carrying capacity and constraints of the environment on national economic activities. The ecological environment accommodates economic activities and people's livelihood. However, the proven reserves of natural resources are limited and cannot be exploited without restraint. In this regard, economic activities should be designed based on the carrying capacity of the natural environment and for minimal impact on the environment.

Second, the conditions, including the advantages and disadvantages furnished by the environment should be studied. Better and faster development of the national economy can be achieved by avoiding unfavorable conditions and tapping into favorable conditions, such as favorable natural conditions, the stable and positive political environment, opportunities provided by the favorable international economic environment.

Third, the positive impact of national economic development on the environment should be studied to improve the environment where the economic activities take place and make it more favorable for development. For example, economic development is the basis of social progress, while social progress is both the purpose and the condition for promoting economic development. Therefore, it's a practical approach to advance social progress and develop science, education, and culture while the economy is developing, and in turn, the people's quality and the quality and development of the national economy will be further improved.

2.2.5 *Dynamics*

Dynamics is a part of the national economic operation.

2.2.5.1 The NES Movement Is the Process of Social Reproduction

NES movement comprises the continuous cycle of social reproduction: production, distribution, exchange and consumption. Therefore, analysis of the NES movement as the process of reproduction includes how to organize production efficiently, distribute reasonably, exchange effectively, and organize and guide consumption actively; moreover, the activities of the various links should be studied to understand how they are articulated and organized, and how to improve the capacity of accumulation and development, to realize a virtuous cycle of reproduction.

2.2.5.2 The NES Movement Is Continuously Upgrading Process

The national economy movement is not a repetition but a continuously developing and upgrading process. This can be understood from the history of human socioeconomic development, from the industrialization and informatization. Starting from the textile industry and the invention of the steam engine, new industrial sectors such as coal, iron and steel, machinery, light industry, petroleum, and electric power emerged, resulting in the constant evolution of the industrial structure. In particular, starting from the middle of the twentieth century, the wave of technological revolutions has promoted the rapid development of science and technology. The key to upgrading of industries and the national economy as a whole lies in the continuous innovation of science and technology, injecting vitality through the transformation of traditional industries by advanced technology and industrialization by informatization. These efforts will profoundly impact China's production technology, industrial structure, and national economic system, leading to the upgrading of products and industries, and in turn the healthier development of national economy and social development. The continuous improvement of the national economic movement is the process of continuous modernization.

2.2.5.3 The NES Movement Is the Unification of Material and Value Movement

At the stage of social product production, the products' physical form is unified with the value form, and the process of material production coincides with its value production. Therefore, if all the links keep expenditures within their income limit, the total value and physical goods may be balanced. However, enterprises and governments may invest excessively in real life, i.e., beyond their paying capacity, causing credit inflation or financial overdrafts and, in turn, aggregate demand expansion, and imbalance between aggregate demand and supply. In this context, the national economic operation should be analyzed dynamically to observe the flow and channels of its material and value movements, and the capital and commodity flow of each link, getting a full picture of the national economy and the ins and outs of its imbalance. The monetary and fiscal policies, the main checks to regulate the aggregate supply and demand should be adjusted properly for a mutually coordinated macro-adjustment portfolio of policy instruments.

2.2.6 *Initiative*

As a science of economics, National Economics cannot only study national economic growth and various economic phenomena but also the people behind the complex economic phenomena, such as their purposes, pursuits, motives, behaviors, ideas, propensities, and preferences. In this way, we can discover the regularity of economic activities and understand the in-depth cause-and-effect relationship in the process of economic operation.

2.2.6.1 National Economic Activities Are People's Purposeful and Motivated Activities

Specific purposes and motives drive people to engage in economic activities. However, they are fundamentally aimed at meeting people's changing and growing needs, including survival, development, enjoyment, as well as material, spiritual and cultural needs. Therefore, studying people's needs and their motives, and the changes in people's needs are the starting point for vigorous development of the national economy.

2.2.6.2 People's Ideology Governs National Economic Activities

The so-called ideology is people's basic judgment and thinking pattern in long-term social and economic life. For example, the outlook on development involves the basic understanding of why development is pursued, what type of development is pursued, and how to develop. The practice has fully proved that ideas and culture are the soul of economic activities, an essential driving force for the development of the national economy and the source of the initiatives of NES. In a certain sense, the outstanding achievement of China's reform and opening up in the past 40 years is the outcome of ideological emancipation, the continuous and profound changes in people's ideology.

2.2.6.3 NES's Potential and Vitality Lie in People's Vitality and Creativity

People are decisive in economic and social development, and human resources are the most important among resources. The main characteristics of human resources are (i) renewable, (ii) subjective and initiative, (iii) intelligent potential, (iv) developable, and (v) social. Life is limited, but wisdom is infinite. In fact, each person has vast potential for talent and wisdom. The problem lies in deepening the reform and incentive mechanisms and giving full play to their motivation and initiative to tap their potential, then transforming them into real productivity, so that the national economic organism is full of vigor and vitality. The vitality of enterprises lies in the vitality of people, and that of the national economy lies in the full play of people's wisdom and intelligence. In the process of economic and social development, the primary factor determining the development of an enterprise, a region, or a country lies not only in the capital and equipment but mainly in people's talent, wisdom, creativity, initiative, and their ability to harness capital and advanced equipment.

2.2.6.4 National Economic Activities Are Organized Activities of People

Economic activities are not individual but collective activities of people, carried out through certain organizations, such as families, enterprises, groups, or temporarily formed groups. National economic activities, on the other hand, are a massive multi-level organizational system. Organization is a collection of people and a process of integration, i.e., the fusion and cohesion of many individuals into a group, forming a new force, group awareness and culture, thereby impacting organizational behaviors.

NES is a huge multi-layered organization, it is also a collection of people. Therefore, it is necessary to foster the group awareness of the members, to improve their scientific literacy, culture, civility and ethics, to encourage their involvement in the national economy and sense of identification with the overall goals, and to enhance the national cohesiveness, creativity, pride, and self-confidence. Furthermore, it is also necessary to cultivate the enterprising, pioneering and innovative spirit of the nation, and foster harmonious interpersonal relationships and social and humanistic environment. All these constitute the soft power of the nation and source for improving the national economy performance and raising international competitiveness.

2.2.7 *Adjustment*

The adjustment hereby mainly refers to the macro-adjustment of NES. Macroeconomic adjustment is the effective control of NES according to economic control theory and based on the analysis of its movement using contemporary scientific methods.

2.2.7.1 Objectives Are the Standard of Adjustment

Adjustments always revolve around specific goals and standards. In general, the goals of macroeconomic adjustments mainly include economic growth, stable prices, full employment, and balanced payments. Under the new economic normal, efforts should also be made to improve the quality and efficiency of economic growth, share the fruits of economic growth with all the people, and improve ecological and environmental quality.

2.2.7.2 Information Feedback Is the Soul of Adjustment

In the NES movement, a national economic information system, in parallel with the movement of tangible materials, reflects the state of national economy operation, and constantly carries out information feedback. It transmits the information output from the system reflecting the operating status of the national economy back to the input, thus reacting to the system's input and ultimately impacting the system's operation. Information feedback includes positive and negative feedback. Positive feedback plays a reinforcing role for the original economic behaviors. In contrast, negative feedback suppresses the original economic behaviors, identifies problems and deviations, and corrects the system behaviors. Therefore, information feedback is the basis for economic control, and its efficiency, sensitivity, accuracy, and quality are directly related to the efficiency and efficacy of the macroeconomic adjustment.

2.2.7.3 Application of Macroeconomic Adjustment Tools

Policy instruments must be carefully selected and combined for macro adjustment, based on the national medium- and long-term development objectives and the aggregate supply and demand pattern. A policy system should be formed based mainly on fiscal and monetary policies, coupled with industrial, regional, investment, consumption, and price policies. The organic combination of policy instruments can form synergy and finally achieve the overall macro-adjustment objectives. Concurrently, feed-forward, process, and feedback control are coordinated to improve the result of macroeconomic adjustment.

2.3 Function and Operation Mechanism of National Economic System

2.3.1 Function of System Conversion

As a multifunctional system, the primary function of a NES is system conversion, i.e., converting system input into system output. Economic benefits accrue when the system output is greater than the system input, which is the primary purpose of studying the conversion function and the fundamental issue of economic activities. Therefore, converting NES from input to output should aim at achieving maximum output with minimum input and creating a national economic system that adapts to the requirements of the ecological environment and meets the diversified needs of the market, society, and citizens.

2.3.1.1 Integrating Resources

Due to the prolonged predatory exploitation of natural resources, excessive and low-efficiency consumption, traditional economic and social development has depleted many resources. Moreover, due to the overexploitation of resources and the misuse of production technology, the ecological environment has been seriously damaged. Development relying on large amounts of resource input at the expense of the environment can no longer be sustained and future development can only rely more on technological innovation and knowledge updating. In fact, technology and knowledge have increasingly become major driving forces of economic and social development. The innovation-driven development, rather than resource-driven, will significantly improve resource use efficiency and total factor productivity. Therefore, as the driving force is shifting, innovation should be targeted to shape a mode of leading-edge development that relies more on innovation and first-mover advantages.

2.3.1.2 Optimizing the Links of System Conversion

The tasks mainly include:

First, optimizing the structure. As a component of NES, the interdependence and correlation of structures are directly related to the nature and function of the whole system. Structure defines the function. The healthier the system structure is, the better the system functions.

Second, optimizing the system conversion and development modes. To this end, economic development modes should be reshaped, and organization and management of NES should be shifted from extensive development to intensive development, with efforts to reduce consumption and costs, and improve economic efficiency and benefits.

Third, optimizing the system operation. It mainly refers to moving from a vicious cycle to a virtuous one, including the virtuous cycles of speed, quality, efficiency, production, life, ecology, economy, society, science, and technology. People can secure all-round development only when the three virtuous circles achieve mutual coordination and unity.

2.3.1.3 Coordinating System Output with the Environment

In a certain sense, the system output is the output to the environment, so it must adapt to the environment and form a benign interaction where the system output evolves with and keeps abreast of the environment and coordination is achieved between the market environment, the natural environment, and the overall environment of the world economy. The output of NES is the aggregate economic strength and total outcome of national economic development, which is bound to have various connections with the world economic system. Therefore, it should be adaptable to the requirements of opening up to the outside world and the general trend of global economic development. It should also promote better and faster development of the national economy through the far-ranging exchanges of materials, energy, and information.

2.3.2 Function of System Coordination

NES is a vast, complex and intertwined system. Therefore, uncoordinated, imbalanced, and disharmonious occurrences are unavoidable during its operation. Such disorder often affects and hinders the system's proper function. Therefore, one of the prominent issues is to ensure the effective operation of NES by continuous coordination, mainly the coordination between system components, development goals, economic interests, between the economy, society, the population, resources and the environment, and between domestic economic development and international economy.

2.3.3 Function of Overall Optimization

It is mainly through systemic coordination that the overall optimization of NES is achieved. Therefore, the way the system elements are connected and combined is directly related to the system's overall function. However, the system's function is not simply a mixture of the functions of the constituent elements but their coordination and combination. Therefore, a well-structured and coordinated system will produce a newer and more adequate superposition of functions, and then create the "one plus one is greater than two" effect or synergistic effect of overall optimization.

2.3.4 *Function of Innovation*

2.3.4.1 Mechanism of Innovation

As an economic system, NES itself has the function of self-development, self-sublimation, and self-creation and has the inherent mechanism of promoting innovation. It is mainly reflected in three aspects: (i) The traction of the market demand. With the economic and social development and the continuous improvement of people's living standards, the demand grows, diversifies and personalizes, thus requiring continuous innovation. (ii) The pressure of market competition. In the face of fierce market competition from home and abroad, each enterprise and economic organization can only survive and grow in the competition through innovating. (iii) The thrust of innovative personnel. The innovative personnel are talents with a strong sense and ability of innovation who stand at the frontier of their fields, constantly explore and create new technologies and knowledge. Therefore, the emergence of a group of innovative talents is essential for promoting innovation.

2.3.4.2 The Focuses of Innovation

The first is technological innovation. At the macro level, it changes the economic development mode, optimizes the industrial structure, and improves the overall quality and development of the national economy.

The second is institutional innovation. It mainly refers to establishing new institutions through the reform of economic system to inject vitality and stimulate innovation of people and enterprises.

The third is management innovation. Technological innovation is also regarded as organizational management. Technological innovation requires management innovation, and management innovation promotes technological innovation. They are inseparable and mutually reinforcing.

The fourth is ideological and cultural innovation. Innovative thinking, philosophy, and culture are the driving forces behind innovative activities. Facing the changing tide of the times, enterprises, industries, and the entire national economy must constantly innovate.

2.3.4.3 Innovation System of the National Economy

The innovation system of the national economy must be enterprise-based, market-oriented and talent-driven. Critical technologies that restrict economic and social development must be taken as the priority. Innovation and application of scientific advances should be encouraged by deepening the science and technology system reform, integrating science and technology resources, promoting cooperation among industries, universities, and research institutes, establishing robust legal system, policy system, incentive mechanism, and fostering favorable market, and social and humanistic environment.

2.3.5 Function of Self-Adjustment

Self-adjustment function is intrinsic only in the economic organism, maintaining the regular operation of NES and coordinating its progress according to the predetermined goals. The NES movement is driven by its own intrinsic dynamics and also has adjustment and coordination functions, which are closely integrated. The dynamics is the driving force of developing the national economy and source of vitality and vigor, reflected in three-level pursuits: (i) the pursuit of social members' needs for subsistence as well as spiritual and cultural needs; (ii) the pursuit of sound systems, institutions, and social environment; and (iii) the intrinsic pursuit of self-generated and self-perfection from enterprises, the combination of which constitute the driving force for the overall development of the national economy.

Self-adjustment function refers primarily to the self-adjustment mechanism of the market economy. The market mechanism is the unity of the mechanisms of price, supply and demand, and competition. However, it is not omnipotent and market fails occasionally, entailing macroeconomic adjustments by the state or the government. The macro-adjustment mechanism is based on the information feedback from the movement of NES, and mainly uses interest-oriented economic instruments to adjust based on the grasp of macroeconomic operation laws and the conscious use of market mechanism.

Chapter 3
The Structure of National Economic System

NES consists of several interconnected and mutually influencing subsystems. The structure of NES includes numerous structures, and this chapter focuses on industrial structure, regional structure, and urban-rural structure. It mainly analyzes the laws of industrial structure evolution and the influence of industrial structure optimization on national economic growth. It also discusses the relationship between regional structure optimization and coordinated development of the national economy, outlines the changes in urban and rural structures, and the promotion of integrated and coordinated development of urban and rural areas.

3.1 Industrial Structure

Industrial structure and economic growth are closely linked and mutually reinforcing in economic growth. In other words, the evolution of industrial structure promotes the growth of economic aggregates, and vice versa. Therefore, the adjustment and optimization of the industrial structure play a vital role in the overall optimization of the structure of NES, and in turn, on the functioning of NES.

3.1.1 The Implications of Industrial Structure

Industries derived from and develop in line with the social division of labor. Specifically, industry refers to a group of socio-economic units with the same socio-economic functions. With the continuous improvement of social productivity, the connotation of the industry is constantly enriched and extended. The term structure refers to the matching and arranging of various parts of the whole.

M. Lin and T. Huang, *National Economics*,
https://doi.org/10.1007/978-981-96-9618-5_3

From the perspective of the systems theory, the industrial structure is dynamic. It refers to the composition among the industrial sectors of the national economy and within each industrial sector, as well as mutually reinforcing and constraining economic linkages and quantitative relationships between the sectors.

From the perspective of National Economics, it mainly involves the laws of industrial structure evolution, the path of industrial structure adjustment and optimization as well as its impact on the functioning of NES.

3.1.2 Division of Industrial Structure

According to the Industrial Classification for National Economic Activities (GB/T 4754-2017) promulgated by the General Administration of Quality Supervision, Inspection and Quarantine the People's Republic of China and the National Standardization Administration of the People's Republic of China, China's entire national economy is divided into 20 major categories:

A Agriculture, forestry, animal husbandry, and fishery
B Mining
C Manufacturing
D Production and supply of electricity, heat, gas and water
E Construction
F Wholesale and retail trades
G Transportation, storage, and post
H Hotels and catering services
I Information transmission, software, and information technology
J Financial intermediation
K Real estate
L Leasing and business services
M Scientific research and technical services
N Management of water conservancy, environment and public facilities
O Household service, repair, and other services
P Education
Q Health and social services
R Culture, sports and entertainment
S Public management, social security and social organization
T International organization

According to the descriptions of main statistical indicators provided in the *China Statistical Yearbook 2016*, the primary industry refers to agriculture, forestry, animal husbandry and fishery industries (not including services in support of agriculture, forestry, animal husbandry and fishery industries); the secondary industry refers to mining and quarrying(not including support activities for mining), manufacturing(not including repair service of metal products, machinery and equipment), production and supply of electricity, heat, gas and water, and construction; the tertiary industry refers to all other economic activities not included in the primary or secondary industries.

3.1.3 Industrial Structure Evolution

3.1.3.1 The Implication of Industrial Structure Evolution

Industrial structure evolution refers to the continuous growth or upgrading to an advanced industrial structure from a lower to a higher level. The level of industries are judged by the degree of their dependence on resources and science & technology. The industrial structure can be roughly divided into three levels.

(1) Low-level. Mainly determined by resource endowment. Industrial settings depend on the type and quantity of natural resources owned by or at the disposal of the country. The speed and scale of industrial growth depend on the reserves and quality of resources, as well as their development costs.
(2) Medium-level. Both resources and technology are major determinants, but the proportion of technology-led industries is gradually higher than that of resource-led industries.
(3) High-level. The level of technology mainly determines it. Improving production efficiency has led to the shortening of the production process. End products with high technical content tend to be the mainstay of social production.

3.1.3.2 Factors Affecting and Determining Industrial Structure Evolution

The process of industrial structure evolution is influenced by various factors, for example, domestic and overseas factors, its natural evolution, and external industrial transfer.

(1) *Changes in demand structure*

Demand structure differs due to different per capita income of countries, and fluctuates temporally for the same country. In general, the evolution of demand structure can be divided into three stages as per capita income rises, i.e., from the demand structure based on survival materials, to development materials, and then to enjoyment materials. Demand structure contributes to the upgrading the industrial structure. Relatively speaking, the higher the per capita income is, the faster the demand structure is upgraded and the faster the industrial structure evolves.

(2) *The technological innovation level*

Technological innovation is a complete process from the conception of new products or manufacturing processes to their application in the market, including activities from generating new ideas, research, development, and commercial production to diffusion of products. In essence, it involves the integration of science & technology with economy, mainly composed of two major links: technology development and utilization. Technological innovation is always a decisive factor in the industrial structure evolution. However, the degree of reliance on technology varies in different stages. In the development stage featuring a quantity-based economy, economic growth is mainly achieved by the widespread application of lower-level homogeneous technologies, homogeneous products dominating the market, as a result. Such a mode features slow product replacement, and long industrial life cycles. In the development stage for the all-around improvement in the quality of life, heterogeneous products dominate the market with an acceleration product replacement and a shortened industry life cycles; the industrial structure is upgraded mainly by accelerating technological innovations.

(3) *The ccale and speed of capital accumulation*

At different stages of economic development, scales of capital accumulation differ for unit productivity. In a certain sense, the scale and speed of capital accumulation determine the process of industrialization and the upgrading of industrial structure. Industries in the early stages of industrialization, were mainly labor-intensive, while in mid-industrialization stage capital-intensive, and finally in the post-industrialization stage knowledge and technology-intensive. At the final stage, human capital is decisive in the evolution of industrial structure, but capital accumulation remains a solid basis for human capital accumulation.

(4) *The depth and breadth of participating in the international division of labor*

As economic globalization accelerates, the international economic ties are posing greater influence on a country's economic development and industrial structure evolution. Therefore, the breadth and depth of participation in the international division of labor is an essential indicator of a country's economic development potential and the basis for a country to formulate and implement long-term development strategies, affecting the evolution of industrial structure mainly in the following three aspects. First, due to each country's different resource endowments, it is difficult to form a complete industrial system to support its long-term sustainable economic development. Second, there are differences in each country's economic development phases. Therefore, participating in the international division of labor can capitalize on the spillover effects of developed countries' technology, management, and capital to promote domestic economic development and industrial structure evolution. Third, it can give full play to comparative advantages, seek more development opportunities, and promote faster growth of young and emerging domestic industries.

3.1.3.3 Main Features of Industrial Structure Evolution

The advanced and rationalized industrial structure has continuously pushed the economy forward, as is experienced by many developed and newly industrializing countries. The evolution of industrial structure generally has the following main characteristics.

(1) *Changes in predominant industries*

In the process of industrial structure evolution, many industries have occupied a dominant position and have gone through the following stages.

The first stage was dominated by agriculture, which accounted for the vast majority, and the development of both secondary and tertiary industries was minimal.

The light textile industry dominated the second stage. The separation of handicrafts and agriculture, as well as the cheap workforce, enabled it to develop faster and finally replace agriculture as the predominant industry.

The third stage is heavy-chemical industrialization, which focuses on basic industries such as raw materials and fuel power. The light textile industry continues to develop but decelerates. In contrast, the heavy-chemical industry, focusing on raw materials, fuel, power, infrastructure, and other basic industries, gradually takes over the light textile industry's predominant role.

The fourth is the high-processing stage, with the processing and assembling industries as the lead. The accelerated rate of technological innovation has led to the rapid development of assembling industries with high-tech requirements and higher added value, such as precision machinery, fine chemicals, electronic computers, aircraft manufacturing, spacecraft, automobiles, and machine tools, which enables it to become the primary impetus for national economic growth.

The tertiary industry dominates the fifth stage. The proportion of the secondary industry in the national economy declines. However, the development of the new tertiary industry, especially the high-tech, finance, insurance, logistics, information, and other productive modern services, accelerate significantly and gradually become the predominant industry of the national economy.

(2) *The development of industrialization*

In 1978, China's secondary industry (industry and construction) accounted for the lion's share (47.7%) of the three-tier industrial structures. In contrast, the shares of the primary and tertiary industries were 27.7% and 24.6%, respectively. In a certain sense, the industrial structure evolution equals the development of industrialization. Industrialization has gone through the following stages:

In pre-industrialization, when the primary industry dominated, the secondary industry emerged, and the tertiary industry was minimal.

In early industrialization, when the primary industry kept declining, the secondary industry gradually rose, and the tertiary industry began to develop.

In mid-industrialization, the tertiary industry gradually rose when industry focuses changed from basic to high-processing industries. As a result, in 2013, the value added of the tertiary sector accounted for 46.7% of GDP, exceeding the share of the secondary sector (44%) for the first time. After 2014, the share of the secondary sector continued to decline, and the tertiary sector developed rapidly, assuming a dominant position in the national economy.

Post-industrialization is mainly characterized by informatization and intellectualization.

(3) *Changes in the internal structure of the three industries*

While the structure among the three industries keeps changing, their internal structure is also changing accordingly. (i) Primary industry evolves from extensive agriculture characterized by backward technology to intensive agriculture characterized by high technical requirements, then to green and ecological agriculture characterized by biological, environmental, biochemical, and ecological technologies, it also shifts from plantation agriculture to livestock agriculture, and from field agriculture to factory agriculture. (ii) Within the secondary industry, the industrial structure evolves in the path of light textile industry → heavy-chemical industry → processing industry, the element structure evolves along the direction of resource-intensive → labor-intensive → capital-intensive → knowledge (technology) intensive industries and the market evolves from closed → import substitution → export-oriented → market globalization. (iii) Finally, within the tertiary industry, the industrial structure evolves in the direction of traditional services → diversified services → modern services → information industry → knowledge industry.

3.1.4 Industrial Structure Optimization

Industrial structure plays a dominant role in the overall economic structure, whose changes have a decisive impact on economic growth. However, if capital, labor, and technology are held constant, the contribution of different industrial structures to economic growth varies.

3.1.4.1 The Impact of Industrial Structure on Economic Growth

The industrial structure is the foremost component of the economic structure and can be explored two perspectives. One is from the "quality" perspective to reveal the dynamic trend of continuous development and changes of technical and economic relations among industries, as well as the law of continuous substitution of dominant or mainstay industrial sectors and their corresponding "structural" benefits. The other is from the "quantity" perspective to analyze the static proportional relationship between inputs and outputs of each industry in a certain period. Through the qualitative and quantitative relations between industries, the distribution structure of economic resources and output distribution structure take their shapes and make up the organic connections between industries.

Industrial structure has the following crucial effects on economic growth.

(1) Economic growth depends on industrial structure up to a point. Economic growth mainly depends on mobilizing such resources as labor, capital, and technology, as well as their effective allocation, the efficiency of which is determined largely by industrial structure. Therefore, only when allocation of resources is so balanced that it suitable for domestic and foreign demand conditions and compatible with technological development, can it promote and ensure economic growth. Otherwise, economic growth is bound to be slow or unsustainable.
(2) Economic growth depends on industrial structure optimization, which is mainly reflected in the fact that economic growth depends increasingly on technological progress and innovation. Economic growth as a result of the structural effect derived from industrial structure optimization equate to the economic growth derived from technological progress. The optimization of industrial structure sparked by technological innovation in today's world has showcased its tremendous impact on economic growth, mainly due to the following reasons.

Firstly, industrial structure optimization allows resources to be more reasonably and effectively allocated. When the demand structure changes so that the supply structure is no longer compatible with it, if the industrial structure can be adjusted in time, and scarce resources can be allocated efficiently in various sectors of social production, the output efficiency per unit of resources will be improved, thereby stimulating economic growth, and conversely, the opposite holds for untimely adjustment of structure and inefficient allocation. From the perspectives of supply and demand of resources, the supply status of resources differs among various industrial sectors, resulting in different degrees of dependence on resources and different demands of resources for production growth. if the industrial structure can be adjusted in time to either establish new industrial sectors to replace the ones short of production resources, or to improve the efficiency of resource utilization, or to expand the scale of production in sectors with abundant in resources, it can promote economic growth; conversely, the opposite holds true if the structure is not adjusted accordingly. Although the input of large amounts of resources is a necessary for economic growth, the efficiency often depends mainly on the industrial structure.

Secondly, changing predominant industries is essential to promoting economic growth. Modern economic growth is the growth of sectors, starting from a specific industrial sector that takes the lead in adopting advanced technology, and finally driving the growth of the entire national economy in many ways. The predominant industrial sector is the driver of economic growth, and finally is replaced by a new leading sector after it emerges and develops, the whole process closely linked to economic growth. When the new predominant industry replaces the original one, it will promote faster growth of the national economy with newer technology and higher labor productivity.

Thirdly, the transformation of the industrial structure caused by the social division of labor and scientific and technological development drives economic growth. As the economy grows, the social division of labor becomes increasingly refined, and industries become increasingly interconnected. science and technology optimizes industrial structure and economic growth in two main paths: the development and application of innovative technology lead to the emergence and rapid growth of new industries, continuously diffusing to other industries resulting in the growth of economic aggregates; applying the improved technology leads to the transformation, renewal, and development of existing industries, thus promoting efficient allocation of resources and increasing labor productivity. The combined force of these two paths drives changes in the industrial structure and the rapid growth of the entire economy.

3.1.4.2 Optimizing China's Industrial Structure

According to China's 13th Five-year Plan (2016–2020), industrial structure optimization lies mainly in transforming and upgrading traditional industries, cultivating and growing new industries, revitalizing the real economy sectors, promoting supply-side structural reform, and making profound adjustments to the industrial structure. Building a modern industrial system is also the top priority, featuring solid innovation capability, excellent service, close collaboration, and environmental friendliness. The following strategies are proposed.

(1) *To strive for a manufacturing power*

The main focus is to enhance the innovation and basic capabilities of the manufacturing industry, help it shift towards high-end, intelligent, green, and service-oriented mode, and develop its new competitive advantages.

The first is to improving the fundamental industrial capacity. The basic industrial capabilities determine the properties and quality of products, core to building a strong manufacturing country. Therefore, to reinforce the industrial foundation is to break through various bottlenecks including critical materials, core parts, advanced processes, basic industrial technology and to facilitate collaborative innovation and research across all sectors.

The second is to transforming and upgrading traditional industries. Traditional industries mainly refer to those that enter into matured industrial life cycles. upgrading traditional industries with advanced technology is a crucial for transforming of economic development mode and optimizing of industrial structure, including measures like major technological upgrading projects in manufacture, improving policy system, achieving a mass breakthrough in focal areas to the middle- and high-end. Mergers and acquisitions are encouraged to form industrial organizations that are concentrated around large enterprise groups, characterized by refined division of labor, collaborative and efficient.

The third is to reducing enterprises' costs in the real economy. The government should further streamline administration and delegate power, clean up unreasonable fees, improve relevant mechanisms, reducing taxation, institutional transaction costs, financial costs, costs of labor, energy, and logistics that are imposed on real economy.

The fourth is to boosting new manufacturing industries. It mainly cloes the following: (i) implementing high-end equipment innovation and improving independent design and systematic integration capabilities, (ii) strengthening industrial *Internet* facilities, technological verification, demonstration, and popularization to make breakthroughs in the "Made in China + Internet" model, (iii) implementing green manufacturing projects to promote product entire life-cycle green management and manufacturing system, and (iv) transforming the manufacturing industry from production-oriented to production & services-oriented and encouraging enterprises to extend their service chain and provide value-added services.

(2) *To support the of emerging strategic industries*

Emerging strategic industries, sprung from technological breakthroughs and development needs, represent the trend of future science & technology and industrial development and steer the direction of the economy and long-term economic and social development. Such industries include those that are knowledge and technology-intensive, cost-effective, consume less material resources, and possess enormous growth potential.

The following were the priorities for 13th Five-year Plan period:

- developing new-generation information technology, new energy vehicles, biotechnology, low-carbon green technology, high-end equipment and materials, digital creativity industry, etc.;
- forward-looking industrial planning, nurturing a batch of strategic industries in outer space, ocean, information networks, life sciences, nuclear technology, etc.;
- supporting industrial innovation centers and new technology popularization and application centers; developing cities with high-intensity innovation resources into the source of innovation and birth of emerging industries;
- implementing industrial policies to guide industrial development and facilitate competition; designing entry criteria, regulatory rules, and standards conducive to new technologies, new products, and new business forms and modes.

(3) *To accelerate service industries*

- accelerating service industries;
- opening up the service industry to the outside world;
- optimizing the environment for service industries;
- broadening market access for social capital;
- opening competitive businesses in electricity, civil aviation, railroads, postal services, municipal utilities, and other industries;
- increase openness of fields of Internet, finance, education, medical care, trade, logistics, etc.;
- carrying out pilot projects to open more service industries.

Specific measures fall into two categories. The first categories of measures aim for the services for production to further specialize and extend to the high end of the value chain, by (i) upgrading industry and increasing efficiency, developing industrial design and originality, engineering consulting, legal accounting, credit rating, after-sales service, testing, detection, and certification, modern insurance, human resources services, etc. and implementing high-tech services innovation projects; (ii) deepening circulation system reform, promoting circulation informatization, standardization, and intensification, developing third-party logistics and green logistics, and promoting traditional commerce so as to accelerate the transformation and upgrading of circulation; (iii) guiding manufacturers to accelerate the division and outsourcing of service links; and (iv) establishing standardization system for production services in line with international standards and promoting its globalized development.

The second category of measures aim to provide better and finer services for people's lives by (i) accelerating the development of education and training, health and elderly care, culture and entertainment, physical fitness, etc.; (ii) improving the quality and efficiency of tourism, and developing various types of tourism such as ecology, culture, leisure, mountain, etc.; (iii) helping household services to specialize, scale up, and form networks; (iv) promoting the integration of living services, encouraging customized services for individual needs, implementing life services reassurance action plans, popularizing the excellent service commitment identification and management system, and cultivating famous brands for services.

3.2 Regional Structure

The national economy is a three-dimensional system of sector, space, and time. From the spatial dimension, it is an organic coupling of heterogeneous regional economies. The regional structure can be regarded as a subsystem of the national economy.

3.2.1 Classification and Nature of Regional Structure

3.2.1.1 Classification

A region is a specific spatial area where human beings engage in social and economic activities. The regional economy has a relatively complete structure and independent functions. It is an organic part of NES.

Regions can be classified from different angles:

(1) *Natural factors*

For example, China can be divided into eastern, central, western, and northeastern regions by geographical location; coastal and inland regions by distance from the ocean; and the Yellow River and Yangtze River basins by water resources;

(2) *Administrative division*

It includes four levels: provinces (including municipalities directly under the Central Government and autonomous regions), cities, counties, and townships. Under the current conditions in China, governments at various levels play an essential role in organizing, guiding, and regulating economic activities. Therefore, economic performance appraisal and evaluation are also mainly conducted based on the division of administrative regions.

(3) *Economic functions*

It can be roughly divided into four categories. First, economic and technical coordination zone. It mainly refers to the integration and collaboration of regional economy, following the principle of equality and mutual benefit on the premise of close industrial connection and complementary advantages among neighboring regions. Such zones aim to promote coordinated development based on integrated programming and reasonable division of labor, such as the Pearl River Delta Economic Zone, Yangtze River Delta Economic Zone, Beijing-Tianjin-Hebei Economic Zone and a variety of different levels of economic consortia, economic and technical collaboration zones. Second, regions with different levels of economic development. It can be mainly divided into developed and less developed regions. Third, areas with different policies granted. It can be divided into special economic zones, coastal open cities, coastal economic development zones, and various development zones. Fourth, functional zoning. Based on the resource environmental carrying capacity, economic development density, and future potential, they can be divided into optimized, prioritized, restricted, and prohibited development zones.

3.2.1.2 The Nature and Characteristics of the Regional Structure

(1) *Differentiation*

Each region varies due to its natural conditions, resource endowment, geographical location, economic foundation, market size, cultural deposits, and personnel quality. Thus, they form regional strengths and weaknesses, directly affecting their economic development and industrial structure.

(2) *Openness*

The regional structure is a microcosm of NES structure. However, it is never an independent closed economic system but an organic part of NES. It requires an extensive exchange of materials, energy, and information with other regions, aiming at forming an organically integrated national economic regional structure system featuring interdependence, mutual constraints, and mutual promotion.

(3) *Hierarchy*

Whether economic zones or administrative regions, there are several hierarchies. Consequently, the coordination, division of labor, and collaboration relations are intricate in performing economic activities. It's necessary to deal well with the nexus between the giant system, subsystems, and branch systems in terms of regional structure.

(4) *Dynamic evolution*

Since the development and the interrelationship of regions are inevitably affected by various factors, the development stages of the regional economies and their positions in NES are subject to constant changes; i.e., advanced regions are not always ahead, and may be overtaken by latecomers quickly. These changes are chiefly driven by significant innovations in technology and management, discoveries of new resources, institutional reforms, and the construction of a development environment.

The above-mentioned characteristics are an essential starting point for studying the regional structure system of the national economy and basis for its continuously improvement.

3.2.2 Evolution of Regional Structure

3.2.2.1 Main Factors Affecting the Evolution of Regional Structure

(1) *Natural endowment*

It has an important influence on the evolution of regional structure. Due to the disproportionate distribution of natural resources, there exist differences in resource endowments between regions, thus affecting the formation and changes of regional economic structure. Although factors such as capital, labor, technology, and raw materials can flow between regions as reform deepens, there are still some other factors such as land, mines, water, and geographical location that cannot be changed, which are factors that cannot be ignored in forming regional division of labor and regional structure.

(2) *Institutional mechanisms*

The difference in economic growth between regions is closely related to the degree of economic system reform and market mechanism refinement. In general, less developed regions are mostly likely those where economic system reform lags, whose people are expectant of reform. Therefore, accelerating institutional reform, stimulating the vitality of people and enterprises, and fully releasing the suppressed potential productive forces will significantly accelerate the development of these regions.

(3) *Technological progress*

In the modern era, science and technology are changing rapidly and have become critical in driving economic and social development. Various actions are taken to speed up the process for backward regions to catch up with the advanced, such as the proliferation of technology, the introduction and application of advanced technology. Efforts are also made to improve innovativeness the competitiveness of the regional economy. Furthermore, from a macro perspective, the accelerated technological renewal and continuous industrial upgrading will also enhance regional economic development and promote the continuous optimization of regional economic structure.

(4) *Social culture*

Culture is a general term gradually formed in human socio-economic activities, including the ideology, values, spiritual pursuits, moral norms, and social customs. Economic activities are governed by spiritual culture and ideology. Therefore, culture is the soul of economic activities and a vital driving force behind regional economic development.

(5) *Government support*

The impact of the government's strategic intention, policy orientation, nurturing measures, and fiscal capital investment on the development of different regions varies. From the overall perspective, the government should differentiate regional policies, priorities and preferential policies to the regions, according to their economic and social development stages, national strategic tasks, as well as prominent problems of regional economic structures of each period. Currently, the government's policy orientation and support are among the most important factors in promoting regional economic development and the evolution and optimization of regional economic structures.

3.2.2.2 The Evolution of China's Regional Structure and its Trends

Since the reform and opening up, China's regional economic development has undergone a strategic shift from imbalanced toward coordinated development. It is roughly divided into three stages.

(1) *The imbalanced development favoring the Eastern region (1979–1990)*

In 1978, China established a significant strategic policy of opening up to the outside world and revitalizing the domestic economy. Five special economic zones, including Shenzhen, 14 open coastal cities, were established as well as 14 coastal economic and technological development zones, to speed up the pace of opening up to the outside world. At the same time, regional economic development and capital investment were also tilted toward the coastal areas, utilizing the existing foundation of the coastal areas to capitalize on their specialties and boost inland economy. Consequently, national infrastructure investment was increasingly directed towards the coastal areas from 1985 to 1988, resulting in a shift in the distribution of investment, with the ratio between the coast and the inland regions increasing from 1.07:1 to 1.36:1 and 1.29:1 in 1990. Two economic growth poles, the Pearl River Delta and the Yangtze River Delta, were formed as major economic regions. Moving further north, a third economic growth engine, the Circum-Bohai Sea Economic Zone, emerged.

(2) *The formation of the regional coordinated development strategy (1991–1998)*

Since the 1990s, China has established guidelines for coordinated regional development to bridge the widening gap between the Eastern and Western regions. In March 1991, the government first proposed "the rational division of labor and coordinated development of regional economies." In 1995, it was explicitly stated that "adhering to the coordinated development of regional economies and gradually reducing the regional development gap" is one of the essential guidelines that must be implemented in the future. Simultaneously, a new regional economic development strategy was implemented in order to (i) open up the country to the outside world in all dimensions, (ii) adjust the national investment and industrial distribution policies and raise the proportion of investment in the central and western regions, and (iii) improve the policies for national poverty alleviation and ethnic minority areas.

(3) *The comprehensive implementation of the regional coordinated development strategy (after 1999)*

Since 1999, China has formulated and implemented strategies of developing the Western region, revitalizing old industrial bases such as the Northeastern region, the rise of the Central region, and the trailblazing development of the Eastern region, in order to promote coordinated regional economic development. As a result, it has formed a new horizon of development: opening up along the coast, rivers, and borderlines; interactive development of the old industrial bases in the East, West, Central, and Northeast. Since 2012, based on the above four regions, China has implemented the Belt and Road Initiative, the Yangtze River Economic Belt, and the Beijing-Tianjin-Hebei cooperative development strategy.

Thus, gradually reducing the regional economic gap and achieving coordinated regional development is an inevitable trend in the evolution of regional structure, a long-term task that can only be accomplished through continuous efforts.

3.2.3 Regional Structure Optimization

The structure of NES is closely related not only to the industrial structure and its optimization, but also to the regional structure and its optimization. The distribution and allocation of production factors among regions largely determine the level and quality of economic growth, thus affecting the operation of the national economy and even the function of the NES structure.

3.2.3.1 The Goal of Regional Structure Optimization

In the context of opening up to the outside world, each region that constitutes NES is not isolated but interconnected. Therefore, it is necessary to give full play to the enthusiasm of each region in developing its economy and adapt it to the requirements of the overall development of the system. However, in real economic life, instances of discord occur, such as blockade between regions, blind competition, duplication of construction, structural convergence, competitive price cutting in export, rivalry investment incentives, overlooking safety and ecological environment to pursue GDP, all of which bring negative effects. Thus, optimizing regional structure is an important issue, in an aim to promote the free flow of inter-regional resources and factors, optimal allocation, and coordinated regional development by fully exploiting regional strengths and potentials. Ultimately, a regional structure system of the national economy characterized by interdependence, mutual promotion, mutual collaboration, and benign interaction should be formed to realize the best economic, social, and ecological benefits.

Such measures include: (i) a reasonable division of labor, with distinct characteristics and giving full play to its advantages; (ii) mutual benefit, extensive cooperation, complementary and coordinated progress, joint development, and balanced development by narrowing the regional gap; and (iii) coordination of human and nature, economy and society, and equity and efficiency to achieve comprehensive, coordinated, and sustainable development.

3.2.3.2 Regional Structure Optimization Strategy for the 13th Five-Year Plan

The Outline of the 13th Five-Year Plan adopted in March 2016 specifies a new pattern of coordinated development of China's regional economic structure: Based on the overall regional development strategy and guided by the Belt and Road Initiative, the coordinated development of the Beijing-Tianjin-Hebei Region, and the Yangtze River Economic Belt, vertical and horizontal economic bands have taken shape, with economic belts along the coast, rivers, and traffic lines taking the lead.

(1) *A new stage of development in the Western China*

Priority should be given to implement the Strategy for Large-scale Development of Western China to leverage the Belt and Road Initiative's leading role in promoting the development of the Western China. Since the implementation of the Western Development Policy in 2000, infrastructure in the western region has been significantly reinforced, the investment environment has been gradually improved, and the poverty-stricken population has been reduced. On top of that, the following measures are to be taken.

- develop green agricultural products processing industry, cultural tourism, and other industries that are advantageous in the western region;

- set up several national industrial transfer demonstration zones and develop industrial clusters;
- rely on areas of high carrying capacity of resources and the environment to increase the proportion of locally processed and transformed resources;
- improve long-term stable funding channels, continue to increase transfer payments and government investment, and equalize basic public services;
- strengthen eco-environmental protection, with stronger defense for ecological security.

(2) *Promoting the revitalization of the old industrial bases, including the Northeast China*

The key is to raise the vitality of old industrial bases, their endogenous power, and overall competitiveness. Specific approaches are as follows: first, to build more robust market-oriented institutional mechanisms and service-oriented governments, promote structural adjustment, improve the business environment, and increase the proportion of the private economy; second, to make innovation a major driving force for developing the northeast region, encourage entrepreneurship and innovation, build more technology and industrial innovation centers to attract resources favorable for innovations such as talents; third, to raise the quality and efficiency of traditionally advantageous industries, build industrial transformation and upgradation demonstration areas, enhance advanced equipment manufacturing bases and strategic bases for major technical equipment and fourth, to support resource-based cities for their transformation and development; implement major livelihood projects, such as transforming old urban areas and subsidence areas.

(3) *Supporting the rise of the Central China*

In the new era, the objectives for central region are to refine the policy support system, encourage the organic combination of urbanization with industrialization and population concentration, and turn the central region into a crucial strategic support area. The focuses will be as follows: (i) accelerate the construction of modern transportation and logistics systems which connect the north with the south, and the west with the east, taking advantage of its central location; fostering and strengthening city clusters and metropolitan areas along the rivers and traffic lines as growth poles; (ii) based on its industries, the central region should undertake industry transfer, accelerate the development of modern agriculture and advanced manufacturing industry, support the transformation of the energy industry, build a batch of strategic emerging industries and high-tech industrial bases, and cultivate a batch of industrial clusters; and (iii) based on its rich water resources, it should strengthen water environmental protection and governance, and promote the construction of eco-economic zones around Poyang Lake and Dongting Lake, and eco-economic belts along Hanjiang River and Huaihe River.

(4) *Supporting the Eastern China to take the lead*

To further enhance the eastern region to support, lead, radiate, and drive national economic development, the following work needs (i) accelerating the transformation of innovation-driven development in the eastern region and creating an innovation highland with international influence; (ii) speeding up the industrial upgrading to steer the development of emerging industries and modern services for a global advanced manufacturing base; and (iii) expediting the establishment of a comprehensive open economic system to participate in international cooperation and competition at a higher level.

The regional prioritized development includes (i) supporting the Pearl River Delta region to build a new transformation and upgrading highland in open and innovation, and accelerating the construction of the Shenzhen Sci-Tech and Industrial Innovation Center; and (ii) deepening the Pan-Pearl River Delta regional cooperation, accelerating the development of the Pearl River - Xijiang River Economic Belt to become a significant growth pole to drive China's economic growth.

(5) *Promoting the coordinated development of Beijing, Tianjin, and Hebei*

Its main objective is to build a spatial pattern of "one core, two cities, three axes, four districts, and multiple nodes." One core refers to Beijing, building a world-class city cluster with the capital as the core. Two cities, Beijing and Tianjin, are the main engines driving Beijing-Tianjin-Hebei cooperative development. Three axes refer to the three industrial development belts and axial areas where many towns are clustered, i.e., Beijing-Tianjin, Beijing-Baoding-Shijiazhuang, and Beijing-Tangshan-Qinhuangdao. They are the main framework supporting the coordinated development of Beijing- Tianjin-Hebei Regions. Four districts include the central core function zone, the eastern coastal development zone, the southern function expansion zone, and the northwestern ecological conservation zone, each with a clear spatial scope and development priority. Multiple nodes include regional Central cities such as Shijiazhuang, Tangshan, Baoding, and Handan and node cities such as Zhangjiakou, Chengde, Langfang, Qinhuangdao, Cangzhou, Xingtai, and Hengshui. The work focuses on improving their synthetical urban carrying capacities and service capabilities to promote the orderly gathering of industries and populations. Beijing, Tianjin, and Hebei should determine the direction of synergistic development according to their respective characteristics. Beijing focuses on developing a knowledge economy, a service economy, and a green economy and accelerates the construction of a high-grade, sophisticated, and cutting-edge industrial structure. Tianjin prioritizes developing advanced manufacturing, strategic emerging, and modern service industries. It builds a national advanced manufacturing research and development base and a demonstration zone for financial innovation and operation. Hebei actively undertakes transferring non-capital functions from Beijing and transforming scientific and technological achievements from Beijing and Tianjin. Moreover, it should focuses on building an important base for modern trade and logistics, a new industrialization base, and a pilot zone for industrial transformation and upgrading.

(6) *Promoting the development of the Yangtze River Economic Belt*

The Yangtze River Economic Belt straddles the East China, Central China, and West China, which is essential for steady economic growth. The goal is to promote the synergistic development of the upper, middle, and lower reaches of the Yangtze River, promote interactive cooperation among the eastern, central, and western regions, and then build the Yangtze River Economic Belt into a pioneering demonstration, innovation-driven, and coordinated development belt for building an ecological civilization in China. The main approaches are as follows:

The first is to build a green ecological corridor along the river. The main objective is to protect water resources and control the water pollution in the whole river basin. As a result, the water quality of the Yangtze River mainstream will reach or exceed the Class III level.

The second is to build a high-quality, comprehensive, three-dimensional transportation corridor. It should develop multiple transportation modes with a holistic view relying on the Yangtze River Golden Waterway.

The third is to optimize the layout of towns and industries along the river. It mainly refers to upgrading the functions of the three major city clusters, namely the Yangtze River Delta, the middle reaches of the Yangtze River, and Chengdu-Chongqing. Its objective is to guide industries' reasonable distribution and orderly transfer, cultivate strategic emerging industries, and build modern industrial corridors featuring high concentration, strong competitiveness, and low-carbon according to the resource environmental bear capacity.

3.3 Urban-Rural Structure

In the process of economic development, both industrial and regional structures involve urban and rural distribution. The urban-rural structure is a concrete manifestation of the industrial and regional structures. It also impacts them and even the structure of NES. In a certain sense, the urban-rural structure is a microcosm of a country's or region's industrialization, urbanization, and modernization.

3.3.1 The Basic Characteristics of Urban and Rural Areas and the Main Elements of Urban-Rural Structure

The structure of a country's national economic system can be divided into two aspects: industrial and regional. It can also be subdivided. The urban-rural structure belongs to the regional structure. However, since urban and rural areas are two regions with specific implications, they differ from the general regional structure in terms of industrial composition, development level, influencing factors, and development trends, as well as the resulting relationships, and thus should be analyzed specifically.

In brief, cities are areas of concentrated but predominantly non-agricultural population and thriving business and industry. Regarding spatial carriers, cities reflect the high organization of the environment and the centralization of material facilities. The former refers to the artificial transformation of the natural environment, aiming to make the environment suitable for human needs; the latter manifests itself in the high-density distribution of various work and living places and transportation facilities in the urban area. Regarding population, its population concentration is much higher than that of the countryside, and the majority of them are engaged in non-agricultural industries. Its industrial structure is economically dominated by secondary and tertiary industries, with a relatively complete range of economic sectors.

The countryside is a category relative to the city and primarily refers to the gathering place of the population mainly engaged in agricultural production and the area for agricultural production. Compared with the cities, the countryside is mainly characterized as follows: in terms of the spatial carrier, it presents the low organization of the environment and the decentralization of material facilities; in terms of population, it is less concentrated, and most people are engaged in agricultural production; and in terms of economy, the industrial structure is relatively simple and usually dominated by the primary industry.

The urban-rural structure is divided by the characteristics and the natural geographical regions in urban and rural areas, combined with the administrative districts. Therefore, the urban-rural structure is different from the general regional structure: from the perspective of the industrial layout of urban and rural areas, it mainly involves the relationship between agriculture and non-agriculture; from the perspective of the agent of economic activities in urban and rural areas, it mainly involves the relationship between farmers and urban residents; and from the analysis of the development trend of urban-rural structure, it mainly involves the distribution of urban and rural population.

Therefore, the main contents of urban-rural structure research include three aspects mainly: (i) the urban-rural industrial structure reflecting the industrial layout, mainly the structure of agricultural and non-agricultural industries; (ii) the urban-rural income distribution structure reflecting the relationship between farmers and urban residents; mainly the disposable income of urban residents and the per capita net income of farmers; and (iii) the urban-rural population structure reflecting the development trend of urban-rural structure, mainly the population distribution in urban and rural areas.

The development history of human civilization is the history of urban evolution. Today, the world's developed countries are those with high urbanization rates whose development has gone through the process from agriculture to industry and from rural to urban. Urbanization is the historical transformation of human production and lifestyle, as it ranges from rural to urban. It is mainly manifested by transforming the rural population into cities and towns, as well as the continuous development and refinement of cities and towns. So far, most developed countries have completed the historical tasks of industrialization and urbanization. With the advancement of science, technology and economy, the gap between urban and rural areas regarding economic development and social civilization has been largely eliminated. However, the urban-rural dual economic structure still exists in developing countries' industrialization, and thus, breaking it is their core issue to be solved urgently from theory to practice in developing countries.

3.3.2 The Evolution of Urban-Rural Structure

In the light of the international experience, the urban-rural structure evolves through the following three stages.

First, the stage in which agriculture supports industry, and the countryside supports cities. This stage features the rapid development of industry and cities. Many countries, especially the independent developing countries after World War II, generally adopted the urban-biased development strategy prioritizing industrial development, particularly heavy industry. Therefore, this stage is roughly equivalent to the initial stage of industrialization.

Second, the stage in which industry nurtures agriculture, and cities nurture the countryside. With the development of industrialization and urbanization, the economic strength of industry and cities is increasing, the proportion of industrial value added to GDP is expanding, and the urbanization rate is gradually increasing. Therefore, the strength and conditions for the two nurtures are available. At this time, national governments generally adopted fiscal transfers to agriculture and rural areas, as well as expanding investment in rural public infrastructure. In addition, they took adequate measures to control and close the development gap between urban and rural areas and between industry and agriculture. In other words, equitable urban and rural development becomes one of the priorities. This stage roughly equates to the middle stage of industrialization.

Third, the stage in which agriculture and industry, rural and urban areas develop in parallel. During this period, the imbalance between urban and rural areas and the widening gap between industry and agriculture began to be reversed and effectively controlled. Therefore, the gap between urban and rural areas gradually narrowed, allowing agriculture and rural areas to gain more development opportunities. In turn, the development of rural areas and agriculture effectively promoted that of cities and industries. At the same time, the development of urban and rural areas took into account equity and efficiency to a certain extent. As a result, economic and social development gradually embarked on the track of coordinated development of urban and rural areas. This stage roughly equates to the late industrialization period or post-industrialization period.

3.3.3 *The Status Quo of China's Urban-Rural Structure and Its Trends*

3.3.3.1 The Status Quo of Urban-Rural Structure in China

Specifically, the urban-rural structure and its changes can be examined from three aspects: urban-rural industrial structure, urban-rural income distribution structure, and urban-rural population.

(1) *The urban and rural industrial structure*

The urban and rural industrial structure mainly refers to the ratio or structure of agricultural and non-agricultural industries. It is usually examined by the ratio of primary industry to secondary and tertiary industry in value-added structure to employment structure. In terms of the structure of agricultural and non-agricultural output, in 2024, the proportion of value added by a primary industry to GDP in China was 6.8%, and 93.2% by the secondary and tertiary industries; in terms of the employment structure of agriculture and non-agriculture, the proportion of employed persons in the primary industry to the total employment of society was 22.8%, but 77.2% in the secondary and tertiary industries to the total employment of society. Therefore, the secondary and tertiary industries dominate in Chinese cities, whether analyzed in terms of output value structure or employment structure.

In the urban-rural industrial structure, the share of agricultural value added to GDP is much lower than that of agricultural employment in total employment, with a difference of 32 percentage points. It indicates that the transformation of agricultural employment structure lags far more behind that of value-added structure in urban-rural structure change. The theoretical community usually uses the dual contrast coefficient to measure the intensity of the binary economic structure in developing countries. The dual contrast coefficient is a ratio of agricultural and non-agricultural comparative labor productivity, i.e., the ratio of agricultural to non-agricultural output to their share of employment. The dual contrast coefficient varies in the opposite direction with the intensity of the binary economic structure: the larger the dual contrast coefficient, the smaller the intensity of the binary economic structure, and vice versa. Theoretically, the maximum value of the dual contrast coefficient is 1, usually always lower than 1. China's dual contrast coefficient is not only far below that of developed countries but also far below the average level of developing countries. It indicates that the characteristics of China's urban-rural binary economic structure are still very prominent when analyzed from the perspective of urban-rural industrial structure.

(2) *The urban and rural areas' income distribution structure*

Since the reform and opening up, China's income distribution gap between urban and rural residents has changed from narrowing to widening, then to narrowing again. In 1978, China's urban-rural residents' income ratio was 2.5704, while the rural-urban residents' income ratio was 0.3891, and the difference of urban-rural

Gini index was 0.1802. By the mid-1980s, the urban-rural residents' income ratio had reduced to 1.8184, and the rural-urban residents' income ratio rose to 0.5502. Thus, the urban-rural Gini index difference decreased to 0.1213 (the average value of 1983, 1984, and 1985, respectively). After that, the urban-rural residents' income gap tended to widen again. Since the late 1990s, the urban-rural residents' income gap has increased significantly, reaching its highest value in 2007. It was indicated through the urban-rural residents' income ratio rose to 3.3296, and the rural-urban residents' income ratio falling to 0.3003, with the Gini index difference rising to 0.3196. From 2008 onward, the urban-rural residents' income gap showed a trend of gradual reduction.

(3) *The urban and rural population structure*

The results of the Seventh National Census show that the population of China at the standard time point of November 1, 2020, is 1,411.78 million, of which the urban population is 901.99 million, accounting for 63.89%, and the rural population is 506.79 million, accounting for 36.11%. According to *China Statistical Yearbook 2024*, China's total population at the end of 2023 was 1,409.7 million, of which 932.67 million were urban, accounting for 66.16%, and 477 million were rural population, accounting for 33.84%.

3.3.3.2 Trends of Urban-Rural Structure Changes in China

In the world development experience, the urban-rural structure evolution mainly depends on economic development and industrialization. For more than 70 years of development since 1949, China has entered the middle stage of industrialization and transformed from a country with high agricultural output to a major industrial power. As a result, its comprehensive national power and the state's macro-adjustment ability over the economy have been significantly enhanced. After more than 40 years of the reform and opening up, a rural economic system suitable for China's national conditions and the development of social productivity have been initially formed. Moreover, the supply of major agricultural products has changed from a long-term shortage to a primary balance of the total amount and a surplus in the year. Furthermore, the increasingly robust and diversified market demand for agricultural products has brought broad development prospects for agriculture, and the new agricultural science and technology revolution has also provided solid technical backing for agricultural development.

However, the deep-rooted contradictions still exist, caused by the urban-rural dual economic structure. The issues related agriculture, rural area and rural people are still the critical links that restrict the healthy development of China's economy. It shows that China has generally entered the development stage of promoting agriculture with industry and leading rural areas with urban areas. It also indicates that China is in the critical moment of accelerating the transformation of traditional agriculture and taking the road of agricultural modernization with Chinese characteristics, so as to the crucial period of striving to break the urban-rural binary economic structure to form a new pattern of integrated development of urban and rural economy and society, i.e., the second stage of urban and rural structure evolution. It is foreseeable that, with the deepening of China's economic development and institutional transformation, the intensity of China's urban-rural binary economic structure will gradually weaken and transform into the direction of urban-rural integration.

In order to promote the transformation of the urban-rural binary economic structure, the following points must be achieved:

- adhere to the scientific outlook on development, make overall programs for the industrialization, urbanization, and agricultural modernization in urban and rural areas, and then establish and improve the long-term mechanism of promoting agriculture with industry and leading rural areas with cities;
- promote the reform of the rural land-use proper transfer system, social security system, and urban-rural household registration system, accelerate the construction of institutional mechanisms for integrating urban and rural economic and social development, and then promote the reasonable flow and optimal allocation of production factors between urban and rural areas;
- adjust the pattern of the national income distribution, put the focus of national infrastructure construction and social undertakings development on rural areas, and promote equitable access to primary public services in urban and rural areas, these efforts will enable the majority of farmers to participate equally in the modernization process and share the fruits of reform and development.

3.3.4 Integration of Urban and Rural Development in the Process of New Urbanization

The goal of promoting the integration of urban and rural development is to accelerate the pace of new urbanization, vigorously improve the construction of new socialist countryside, and strive to close the gap between urban and rural development. It can be achieved by adhering to the urbanization with people as its core, urban clusters as the main pattern, comprehensive urban carrying capacity as the backbone, and institutional mechanism innovation as the guarantee.

3.3.4.1 Refine the Institutional Mechanism of Urban-Rural Development Integration

Unsound and inadequate institutional mechanisms have hindered the healthy development of urbanization. Therefore, China currently needs to accelerate the elimination of institutional mechanisms hindering the urban-rural dual economic structure. Moreover, China should also promote the equal exchange of urban and rural factors, and the balanced allocation of public resources. These efforts will allow the majority of farmers to participate equally in the modernization process and share the fruits of economic development.

(1) *Promoting the construction of unified urban-rural factor markets*

It mainly does the following: (i) accelerating the establishment of a unified urban-rural human resources market to implement the system of equal employment and "equal pay for equal work" for urban and rural workers; (ii) establishing and perfecting the incentive and benefit-sharing mechanism beneficial for agricultural technicians to work and research in the countryside, transforming agricultural science and technology achievements, and popularizing advanced agricultural technology; (iii) coordinating the role of policy-based, commercial, and cooperative finance to ensure that financial institutions' rural deposits are mainly used for agriculture and in rural areas, then encouraging social capital to invest in rural construction, and guiding more talents, technology, capital, and other factors to invest in agriculture and rural areas; and (iv) accelerating innovation in agricultural insurance products and operating organization forms and then refining the agricultural insurance system to provide farmers with safer protection.

(2) *Promoting the integration of urban-rural planning, infrastructure, and public services*

There are two main tasks: (i) coordinate the planning of urban and rural infrastructure networks, improve the long-term mechanism for investment in rural infrastructure, and scientifically program the spatial layout of village construction, farmland protection, village distribution, and ecological conservation. Additionally, we should promote urban and rural networking of infrastructure such as water, electricity, roads, gas and telecommunications, as well as the uniform layout and construction of ecological and environmental protection facilities in urban and rural areas; and (ii) accelerate the coverage of public services to rural areas, extend the public employment service network to below the county level, comprehensively build social security system covering urban and rural residents, articulate the urban and rural social security systems, expand the scope of public finance coverage in rural areas, accelerate the formation of a government-led, urban and rural, sustainable basic public service system, and integrate the primary public services in urban and rural areas.

3.3.4.2 Accelerate the Agricultural Modernization

It should adhere to the path of new agricultural modernization with Chinese characteristics, accelerate agricultural development transformation. The agriculture's comprehensive production capacity, risk resistance, market competitiveness, and sustainable development should also be enhanced.

(1) *Developing a specific county economy*

The main tasks are (i) to nurture and develop a vibrant, characteristic, and specialized county economy, enhance the ability to undertake the transfer of urban functions, drive rural development through radiation, and expand the autonomy of county development based on adjusting measures to local conditions; (ii) rely on superior resources to develop the deep processing of agricultural products, rural services, and labor-intensive industries, increase the added value of products, and actively explore new modes of undertaking industrial transfer to integrate into regional industrial chains and production networks; and (iii) formulate preferential policies to actively guide rural secondary and tertiary industries to concentrate in county towns, key townships, and industrial parks.

(2) *Enhancing the modern agricultural development level*

The main work includes (i) accelerating the refinement of modern agricultural industry system and actively developing agriculture featuring high-output, high-quality, high-efficiency, ecology, safety, and so forth; (ii) playing the role of science and technology in enhancing the agricultural modernization, such as improving the capacity of agricultural scientific and technological innovation, perfecting the comprehensive service system of agricultural technology, boosting the modern seed industry, and encouraging agricultural technicians to reach out to rural areas aiming at popularizing modern agricultural technologies; (iii) innovating agricultural business patterns while keeping the foundational status of the household operation in agriculture, actively promoting the diversified development of household operation, collective business, cooperative business, and enterprise business, then encouraging and guiding industrial and commercial capital to develop modern seed and breeding industries suitable for running as enterprises in rural areas, and importing modern production factors and business models into agriculture; and (iv) speeding up the new agricultural socialization service system featuring integrated public welfare and commercial services and coordinated special and comprehensive services.

3.3.4.3 Building a New Socialist Countryside

Adhering to the principles of following the natural laws as well as differentiated development of urban-rural space, it should scientifically program the county's village and township system and make overall arrangements for rural infrastructure construction and social undertakings development to build beautiful homes for farmers to live happily.

(1) *Speeding up constructing beautiful and livable villages*

It mainly involves (i) accelerating the rehabilitation of broadband, highways, dangerous houses, drinking water, lighting, sanitation, firefighting, and other facilities in rural areas to improve comprehensive rural production and living conditions; (ii) scientifically guiding the construction of rural residences and housing estates to facilitate farmers' production and living in line with the requirements of developing central villages, protecting characteristic villages and renovating hollow villages, and respecting farmers' wishes; and (iii) constructing eco-progress villages and towns for demonstration and intensifying comprehensive governance of the rural living environment. Furthermore, while enhancing the function of naturally formed villages, we should also intensify the protection of traditional villages with historical, artistic, and scientific value and villages and towns with ethnic characteristics. The purposes are to inherit rural civilization and build livable villages nestled among idyllic pastoral scenes, picturesque mountains, and invitingly clear water where villagers live together in harmony and happiness.

(2) *Accelerating the development of rural social undertakings*

It mainly involves (i) allocating reasonably educational resources, standardizing compulsory schools, strengthening the construction of rural teaching forces, and improving rural school conditions, the quality and balanced development of compulsory education in rural areas, as well as teachers' working and living conditions; (ii) strengthening the construction of grassroots medical and health institutions and rural doctors, prioritizing the construction and development of county-level hospitals, and improving the three-tier medical and health service network in rural areas featuring the county-level hospitals as the leading role based on township health centers and village clinics. This will provide farmers with safe and affordable primary medical and health services; and (iii) strengthening the construction of rural public cultural and sports facilities such as township comprehensive cultural stations, improving the adequate supply of cultural products and services, and enriching farmers' spiritual and cultural life.

The structure of NES is analyzed from three above-mentioned aspects: industrial structure, regional structure, and urban-rural structure. Analyzing the constraints, evolution laws, and trends of the above structures show their different roles and impacts on functioning NES structure. However, in the meantime, optimizing the structure of NES and fully performing its functions and roles require the interaction, mutual promotion, coordination, and interconnection of the sub-structures to jointly achieve greater overall effectiveness and comprehensive benefits.

Chapter 4
National Economic System Environment

Various external factors influencing and restricting the NES movement are called the system environment. Therefore, the healthy operation of NES can only be achieved with the harmonious state of the system environment. This chapter proceeds with the harmonious relationship among the economy, society, population, and resource environment and examines the composition of NES environment, discusses the ways to coordinate NES and its operating environment from the perspective of sustainable development and expounds the nexus between NES and economic globalization in the view of an open pattern.

4.1 The Coordination Between Economic, Social, Population, and Resource Environment

4.1.1 Economic System and Population System—Coordination of Two Productions

4.1.1.1 The Need for Coordinating the Two Productions

As early as 1884, Engels pointed out that "this itself is again of a twofold character. On the one hand, the production of the means of subsistence, of food, clothing and shelter and the implements required for this; on the other hand, the production of human being themselves, the propagation of the species."[1]

In 1789, Malthus, in his book *An Essay on the Principle of Population*, started his discussion from the law of diminishing fertility of the land and asserted that population, when unchecked, would increase in a geometrical ratio during subsistence for

[1] Engels, Frederick, *Karl Marx, Frederick Engels: Collected Works*, Vol. 26, Engels: 1882–1889, Intl Pub, 1990, pp. 131–132.

M. Lin and T. Huang, *National Economics*,
https://doi.org/10.1007/978-981-96-9618-5_4

humans such as food in an arithmetical ratio. Thus, the power of the population was infinitely superior to the increase in the means of subsistence. On this basis, he made three propositions: (i) "population cannot increase without the means of subsistence," (ii) "population does invariably increase where there are the means of subsistence increase," and (iii) "the superior power of the population cannot be checked without producing misery and vice." He also pointed out that there are two sorts of checks on the population in any country: (i) positive check, i.e., the constant and natural reduction of the population due to objective reasons, such as disease, extreme poverty, pestilence, and famine; and (ii) preventive check, i.e., limiting reproduction through primarily moral restraints.[2]

In 1817, David Ricardo, the English classical economist, also suggested that "under the most favorable circumstances, the power of production is still greater than that of population, it will not last long. For the land being limited in quantity, and differing in quality, with every increased portion of capital employed on it, there will be a decreased rate of production, whilst the power of population remains constant."[3] Generally, the population exceeds the workforce demand, i.e., beyond the number of people it can regularly employ in its agriculture and manufacturing industries. Under such conditions, considerable demographic pressure results as productivity cannot keep pace with population growth.

According to Malthus and Ricardo, population and economic growth follow different laws, resulting in an imbalance. Modern development economics uses the "low-level equilibrium trap" model to illustrate the impedimental role of rapid population growth in developing countries to economic growth. There is a correlation between population growth and per capita national income growth: when a country's per capita income rises above the minimum subsistence level, it may cause population growth faster than national income growth. It will cause per capita income to fall, forcing it down to a certain minimum level, moreover, the fall in per capita income will force the population growth rate to slow down, followed by per capita income growth due to the slowdown in population growth, and then causing population growth and a decline in per capita income. Eventually, this circulating results in a low-level equilibrium trap.

4.1.1.2 Two Ways of Production Coordination

According to classical and modern theories, there are two ways to solve the imbalance between the production of material goods and population production and then to escape from the trap of low-level equilibrium: one is to give a strong impetus to economic growth with the help of increased investment and technological progress,

[2] Malthus, Thomas Robert, *An Essay on the Principle of Population and A Summary View of the Principle of Population*, Penguin Books, 1988, pp. 27, 28, 71, 73, 79, 86, 93, 103, 104, 119.

[3] Ricardo, David, and J. R. McCulloch, *The Works of David Ricardo with A Notice of the Life and Writing of the Author*, John Murry, London, 1888, p. 53.

the other is to take robust measures to control population growth. The optimal population size is dynamic in the model created by the demographer Ansley Coale and the economist Edgar Hoover. Taking India as an example, they show that "a reduction in the birthrate would help raise per capita income in two important ways. First, slower population growth would lower the dependency ratio, reduce consumption and increase saving at any given level of income. Second, as labor force growth slowed about 15 years later, the amount of investment needed to provide a constant amount of capital per worker for a growing number of workers would go down, permitting more investment used to increase capital per worker. These two benefits from slower population growth would be felt both at the household and national levels."[4]

Based on the above theories, there is a real problem of optimal population size, i.e., the state at which the population is more reasonable and better able to meet sustainable development needs. The optimal population size is the one that maximizes per capita income over a certain period when a country's resources other than its workforce are constant.

It is important to note that developing countries with low per capita income often have inadequate capacity for capital accumulation. As a result, technological progress and improvement of natural resource supply conditions are unlikely to be rapid. Therefore, in developing countries, when there are inadequate conditions and impetus to increase the optimal population size, only through taking effective measures to reduce the population growth rate can it be adapted to the optimal population size. There is a lag in adjusting the population size to the optimal one because the current population size is too large. Moreover, because of the inertia in population growth and the rejuvenation of the age structure caused by high fertility in the past, it will now take decades to stabilize population size even with a birth control policy. This timeline is essential for developing countries striving for takeoff. However, the critical question is how long the lag between the decline in mortality rate and the shift from a rising to a falling birth rate. The length of the time lag determines the near-term future of countries moving from the transition phase and striving for takeoff into self-sustaining growth.

4.1.2 The Economic System, Population, and Resource Environmental Systems—Coordinating the Three Sorts of Production

4.1.2.1 The Need for Their Coordination

Constructing the "two production theories" objectively basically assumes that the natural environment can supply unlimited environmental resources and dissipate

[4] Perkins, Dwight H., Steven Radelet, Donald R. Snodgrass, Malcolm Gillis, and Michael Roemer, *Economics of Development*, 5e, W. W. Norton, 1983, pp. 267–268.

unlimited waste. Suppose the impact of human beings on the environment does not exceed the carrying capacity of the natural environment, i.e., environmental production can meet the needs of human and material production indefinitely. Guided by the two production theories, the nexus between human and material production can be well coordinated to ensure society's sustainable development. In fact, since the middle of the twentieth century, social production, especially large-scale industrialization and urbanization, has been unrestrainedly consuming resources and emitting waste, making this assumption no longer exist. Faced with the gradual emergence of environmental pollution and ecological damage and the transformation of environmental resources from "unlimited" to "limited", just emphasizing coordinating two sorts of production is no longer adequate to ensure smooth socio-economic development.

Since there is a limit to the ability of environmental production to support the other two in practice, especially with the growing population and the increasing exploitation of nature, this limit is nearly being breached. Thus, reducing the number of materials consumed and emitted by human activities has become a fundamental prerequisite for smoothly implementing the entire production. Therefore, meeting the requirement of harmonizing the relationship between humans and the environment, which is endogenous in both production processes. In other words, harmonizing population- material-environmental production nexus, is the fundamental guarantee for the sustainable development of today's society.

Environmental production is the most fundamental of the three sorts of production. The production capacity of the environmental production system expresses the essential functions of the natural environmental system. It emanates mainly from the movement of energy and materials within that system and is also the basis for generating and developing the other two sorts of production. Moreover, it is the intrinsic mechanism for the forward development of the ecosystem. It ensures the generation and continuation of life on Earth and creates good conditions for further development of various biological systems. Since humans must maintain their survival and reproduction through material connections with the surrounding environment, human society must ensure that its economic and social activities are a benign link in the material cycle of the natural system, and maintain the material cycle of nature. These endeavors will ensure the reproduction of natural resources in the environmental system and the dissipative capacity of environmental pollution.

4.1.2.2 The Path to Harmonizing the Three Sorts of Production

Coordinating the three sorts of production depends on humankind's production and consumption patterns. Humans' primary mode of production throughout the history can be summarized as a linear one from resource through product to waste, circulated by taking material resources from nature, processing them into products, distributing them to consumers through circulation, consuming these products, and finally disposing of the waste generated by every link mentioned above into the environment. This mode of production is the root cause of the unsustainable development of human society, because it increasingly imbalanced the material exchange between human society and the natural environment. Since the Industrial Revolution, there has been a dramatic increase in the need to improve their material living standards with the expanding population. Moreover, with the continuous improvement of technology, the volume and speed of material movement in human society have been increasing. As a result, the material movement in the environment, its decomposition and transformation speed, as well as its total volume are decreasing. Eventually such actions make the environment's ability to supply natural resources and dissipate pollutants under unbearable pressure.

In the social division of labor corresponding to this mode of production, human productive activities are divided into three main categories: primary industries obtaining resources from nature, secondary industries processing natural resources into products, and tertiary industries serving both primary and secondary industries and aim to improve their efficiency and effectiveness. Evidently, this industrial sector division excludes from the economic activities of human society the transformation of critically important waste into resources or their safe return of waste to the environment. However, the rapid deteriorating environment shows that under the present-day mode of production, the decomposers in nature cannot promptly decompose all the waste produced by human society. Suppose humans cannot realize this soon enough or do not act accordingly to adjust their behavior, the imbalanced material exchange between human society and nature will bring severe catastrophic ramifications to the survival and development of human society soon.

As human being's most basic behavioral activity, consumption includes finding, buying, using, evaluating, and disposing of the products and services used to satisfy their needs. Moreover, these consumption activities imply resource consumption and waste emission. Therefore, consumers' consumption behaviors at each stage significantly impact the natural ecosystem directly and indirectly.

The traditional consumption pattern is linear. With people's living standards improving, the higher the consumer needs, the larger the number of products produced, moreover, the more resources consumed, and the more waste discharged. Then a linear model is formed: consumer needs—resource consumption—environmental pollution. The current consumption pattern was formed gradually with the rapid development of industrial technology. The cumulative development of technology has accelerated the demand for products and services, thus intensely worsening resource consumption and environmental pollution. The development of technology has created the illusion that the era of material scarcity is gone. People can consume as many products as possible within their income as if technology can solve the scarcity of any resource. To put it another way, under the illusion that technology is omnipotent, traditional consumption pattern has become accelerated consumption. With the superposition of population growth and increasing consumption levels, people's resources consumption rate dramatically exceeds that of population growth. In satisfying the ever-growing human demand, wastes from production and life also increase in large quantities, thus heavily increasing the pressure on the environment. Therefore, the additive and cumulative nature of consumers' consumption behavior is the leading cause of enormous resource environmental problems, thus seriously affects the economy's and society's sustainable development.

Agenda 21, adopted by the United Nations Conference on Environment and Development (UNCED), states that "the major cause of the continued deterioration of the global environment is the unsustainable consumption and production patterns, particularly in industrialized countries."[5] It is thus clear that two traditional patterns are an essential cause of environmental degradation. Thus, the fundamental way to reconcile the three types of production is by changing them.

First, the traditional linear production pattern of resource—product—waste should be converted into a circular economy production pattern featuring resource—product—resource. A circular economy is essentially an ecological one, which follows the law of ecology and organizes the economic and social system into a net and chain structure with multiple utilization and recycling of substances, forming a feedback process of resource— product— recycled resources. Through the laddering and closed-loop use of material and energy, it maximizes the use of material and energy entering the system and minimizes the emission of pollutants, in this way, the demand for natural resources is kept within the production capacity of nature. At the same time, it also controls the natural emissions of garbage and waste within the natural environment's capacity to dissipate them. These efforts will thus maintain the harmony between economy, society, and nature, and the ecological balance, and realize the sustainable development of human society as well.

Second, traditional unsustainable consumption pattern should be transformed into green and sustainable. Regarding the relationship between humans and nature, the sustainability of consumption mainly refers to the fact that current consumption should be conducive to environmental protection and ecological balance rather than exceed the ecological environment's bear capacity to meet the needs of consumption development. Regarding the relationship among people, sustainability of consumption means fair and equitable consumption, i.e., the right to pursue a quality of life should be equally enjoyed by all people of the present and future generations. No one should endanger the survival and consumption of others because of its own consumption, i.e., intragenerational equity. At the same time, the present generation should not endanger the survival and consumption of future generations because of the consumption of the present generation, i.e., intergenerational equity.

In reality, sustainable consumption does not mean to suppress routine human needs but only to change consumption concepts, methods, and structures that are not conducive to sustainable development and the establishment of civilized consumption concepts, which mainly include: (i) The concept of moderate consumption. For countries and individuals, we should oppose both excessive consumption and excessive saving. For instance, we should insist on taking human needs as the starting point and healthy survival as the goal, and gradually reduce meaningless and foolish consumption that is not beneficial or even harmful to human health. (ii) The concept of fair consumption. In consumption selection and the process of consumption, it

---

[5] Agenda 21, United Nations Conference on Environment & Development, Rio de Janeiro, Brazil, June 3 to 14, 1992, p. 18.

should not only consider consumers' interests but also avoid bringing negative utility to others, society as a whole, and the ecological environment. Under certain conditions, it should also be considered to bring positive utility to others, society, and the ecological environment. (iii) The concept of reasonable consumption. Quantity-oriented consumption should be shifted to quality-oriented. Diversified consumer needs should be pursued, and the proportion of spiritual values and enjoyment in total consumption should be continuously increased to improve the quality of life.

4.1.3 Economic System and Social, Population, Resource Environmental Systems—Coordinating the Four Sorts of Production

4.1.3.1 Theoretical Basis of the Four Sorts of Production

In addition to the production of population, economy, and nature, there's also the production of social relations and spiritual production in human society, the latter two of which can be called the fourth sort of production. In Volume III, *Capital*, Marx pointed out that the social production process "is both a process of the material conditions of existence for human life, and also a process proceeding in specific economic and historical relations of production. It produces and reproduces these relations of production themselves, and with which the bearers of this process, their material conditions of existence, and their mutual relationships, i.e., the specific economic form of their society."[6] When Marx studied the problem of social reproduction, he not only studied the reproduction of material means and that of human beings themselves, but also placed the reproduction of production relations in a critical position. In addition, Marx did not study the reproduction of material, human beings, or the relations of production separately as isolated aspects but studied them as an organic whole, distinct and interrelated. In this way, it is conducive to revealing a series of regularities of social reproduction in a complete, comprehensive, and profound way.

According to Marx's theory of reproduction, the process of social reproduction is the perfect combination and unification of the reproductions of material, human beings, and production relations. It then constitutes the entirety of social reproduction. The production and reproduction of material are fundamental for human society to exist and develop; the production and reproduction of human beings themselves create new members of society and players of social activities; and the reproduction of socio-productive relations constantly regulates the interrelationship formed by people in the process of material production, i.e., a particular form of social economy. The three are interdependent and indispensable. Social reproduction can be carried out smoothly only when they organically combine to form a unified whole.

Regarding intellectual production as a category was also originally articulated by Marx. In revealing the role of primitive accumulation of capital in disintegrating

[6] Marx, Karl, *Capital*, Vol. III, Penguin Books, 1991, p. 957.

slavery and serfdom, he pointed out, "[c]loser examination will also reveal that all the relations dissolved were possible only at a certain level in developing the material (and therefore also of the mental) production forces."[7] Here, Marx saw that changes in production relations depended not only on the development of the material production forces but also on the role of the mental production forces. Both factors are interdependent and complementary to each other and drive human society forward. Furthermore, it includes the significant role of natural science and technology in securing the development of social productivity. Thus, he asserted that science and technology are productive forces. While discussing the development of capitalist industrial civilization after the *Industrial Revolution*, he pointed out that "[t]he bourgeoisie, during its rule of scarce one hundred years, has created more massive and more colossal productive forces than have all preceding generations together."[8] In this regard, Engels commented that "[s]cience was for Marx a historically dynamic, revolutionary force."[9] Marx also noted that "however, the development of the production power of labour in one branch of production, e.g. of iron, coal, machines, construction, etc., which may in turn be partly connected with advances in the areas of intellectual production, i.e. the natural sciences and their application."[10] The "advances in the areas of intellectual production" mentioned by Marx here includes the natural and social sciences. However, in many places, he also mentioned the role of the division of labor, education and training, operational decision-making, business management, and other social sciences in transforming intellectual productivity into material productivity in reality.

Based on above Marx's statement, the productions of social relations and ideology and culture are the refinement of the social institution's structure and cultural and ideological progress. It's regarded as another kind of production different from the population and material ones.

Not coincidentally, social capital emerged in Western sociology in the 1970s. Social capital can be divided into micro- and macro-ones according to different levels. Micro-level social capital mainly exists in geographical, blood, and kinship relationships. At this level, social capital also emphasizes the patterns and characteristics of the relational networks between individuals. They are mainly displayed in formal and informal institutions, organizational practices, customs, and rules. Macro-level social capital focuses on how social networks and organizations are embedded in politics, economy, or cultural and normative systems. In this way it enables the environments of society, institution, culture, politics, policy, law, and others constitute the macro-level social capital.

According to functional differences, social capital can also be divided into structural and cognitive. Structural social capital involves social relationships, networks,

---

[7] Marx, Karl, *Karl Marx and Frederick Engels Collected Works*, Vol. 28, Marx: 1857–1861, International Publishers, 1986, p. 426.

[8] Tucker, Robert C. Ed. *The Marx-Engels Reader*, 2nd edition, W. W. Norton, 1978, p. 477.

[9] Engels, Frederick, *Karl Marx, and Frederick Engels Collected Works*, Vol. 24, Marx and Engels: 1874–83, International Publishers, 1989, p. 468.

[10] Marx, Karl, *Capital*, Vol. III, Penguin Books, 1991, p. 174.

and interactive behaviors, whereas cognitive social capital involves social relationships, specific norms, values, and attitudes reflecting solidarity and mutual trust. Therefore, social capital is an ability existed in social organizations and networks and also benefits its subjects. All relationships, norms, customs, rules, institutions, and environments in social networks and organizations with this ability should be considered one element of social capital. As an intangible one, social capital is consistent with the above- mentioned social relations and spiritual and cultural categories.

Economists mainly study social capital in terms of innovation, institutional economics, economic development, and national policies. They highly affirm its economic significance. For example, the economic system is defined as a set of constraints to regulate people's behavior as well as coordinate mutual relations and incentive structure for economic and social development. Its primary functions include: (i) Reducing transaction costs. Effective institutions can reduce the market's uncertainty, inhibit people's opportunistic behavior, and, therefore, reduce transaction costs. (ii) Serving the economy. The relevant institutions in the market economy serve economic activities. For instance, the institutional provisions in insurance, education, trading, and others provide the conditions and convenience for conducting economic activities. (iii) Creating conditions for cooperation. The relevant institutions in the market economy provide the basic framework and action norms for people to compete and cooperate and then guarantee the smooth implementation of cooperation. (iv) Providing incentives. Institutionalized facilities can offer people incentives to align individual efforts to pursue economic interests with group interests, achieve the goals of economic organizations, and improve the operational efficiency of market economy organizations. (v) Internalizing externalities. For example, through establishing an exclusive property rights system.

4.1.3.2 The Necessity for Coordinating the Four Sorts of Production

The production relations must conform to the production forces, and the superstructure must conform to the economic basis. This is a universal law of human social development, and is integral to all stages and periods of social development. In a certain sense, the law that the relations of production must be coordinated with the nature and requirements of developing productive forces is one of the most basic implications of coordinately developing the four sorts of production.

According to Marx, social development should be a comprehensive and coordinated overall development of the organic system. It should consist of forces and relations of production, economic basis, and superstructure, namely a comprehensive development of all aspects of politics, economy, culture, and humans. Therefore, while emphasizing the central position of the productive forces in social development, as well as the fundamental and decisive role of the production of material goods and economic factors in developing the society as a whole, we shouldn't neglect the development of other non-economic factors of society, mainly for the following reasons.

Firstly, the facts show that among the factors affecting economic development in modern society, the role that politics, culture, science and technology, education, law, civilization, and other social undertakings play in economic development is becoming increasingly prominent. If economic development is the foundation, then the purpose is to refine the society's institutional structure and develop science and culture. The way to achieve real development is to and only to unite both. Specifically, the economic function of social development is mainly reflected in the following aspects: (i) To create a good social environment for economic development. All areas of social development are closely related to people's immediate interests. Through promoting social development, adjusting human conflicts and interest relations, then eventually improves social equity and civilization. Concurrently, the construction of a democracy and legal system and cultural and ideological progress provide solid political and legal guarantees, spiritual motivation, intellectual support, and a cultural atmosphere for developing economy and maintain social stability. (ii) To provide a lasting impetus and solid foundation for economic development. The primary path of modern economic development is summarized as *six improvements*: improving labor productivity, speeding up the transfer rate of scientific and technological achievements, increasing management benefits, perfecting industrial structure, raising the quality of the national economy, and enhancing the quality of human capital. All of these six aspects of improvement rely on improving the overall quality and development of society on science and technology, culture, education, health service, and other undertakings. (iii) To be the starting point and destination of economic development. If economic development does not transform into social development, it has lost its purpose. No matter how fast the growth rate is, economic development deviating from the purpose is labor in vain. On the other hand, if the economy achieves hyper-speed growth but deviates from social development, some dysfunctional factors must be at work, either fishing out by pumping off the water or at the expense of social development and, otherwise, the opposite. Therefore, ensuring the coordinated development of the economy and society is not only necessary for economic development, but also for the survival and development of the entire human society.

Secondly, a sound social system and cultural factors are basic guarantees for establishing a sustainable population reproduction model, effectively controlling the population size and improving its quality. The sustainable population reproduction model is characterized by three low rates: birth, death, and growth. The shift from a high birth rate, low death rate, and high growth rate model to a three-low model has occurred over a long period in developed countries. For instance, the process has lasted 150 years in Europe and North America. The motivation for this shift was the refining structure of social institutions based on economic development as well as cultural and ideological progress, such as the fair social income distribution system, the refining social security system, the improving culture and education, the advancing health care technology, the population's enhancing scientific and cultural literacy, and their changing outlook on marriage and procreation. These developments and transformations have enabled families to self-regulate their marriage and childbearing behavior, resulting in a lower fertility rate and a much lower mortality rate. Thus, the population growth rate is kept within the range compatible with environmental and economic production. As a result, the population growth rate is kept within the range compatible with environmental and economic production, thus advancing the sustainable development of the natural—economic—social system.

Finally, the improving ecological civilization is reflected in the institutions and concepts related to resources, environment, and ecology in the process of social development, including laws, regulations, culture, ethics, social customs, and others. It offers a necessity for protecting the ecological environment, improving ecological production efficiency, and sustaining natural production.

So far, human civilization has emerged in four primary forms: primitive, agricultural, industrial, and emerging knowledge-based civilizations. As a new civilization, knowledge-based civilization includes the knowledge revolution of civilization and the rise of ecological civilization. At different stages of civilization, humans have different production and consumption patterns. They use and consume different natural resources, and generate environmental problems with different natures, scales, and ramifications. The rise of ecological civilization refers to enhanced people's ecological awareness, established ecological ethics, and developed ecological culture, improved technical and institutional structures for maintaining ecological health. It also means established environment-friendly and resource-efficient production and consumption methods. All these advances mean that the nexus between humans and nature is more harmonious than in previous periods.

To sum up, the production of social relations and spirit, or the refinement of the social institution's structure as well as cultural and ideological progress, are necessary for the sustainable production of a country's population, material production, and natural production. It's also the soft power in the comprehensive national power on which a country depends for its survival and development. Improving this soft power can improve hard power, such as population, economy, and natural productivity. In this regard, coordinately developing population, resource environment, economy, and society, or jointly developing the four kinds of production, are the fundamental guarantee of a country's sustainable development.

4.1.3.3 The Paths of Coordinating the Four Sorts of Production

The first is providing an institutional guarantee for constructing a harmonious society. The primary approach is to adjust timely productive relations. This can be achieved in line with people's material and cultural demands, and the need for their comprehensive development, as well as the social and economic development, and constantly improve the superstructure. In this way can it adapt to economic development and better meet people's material and spiritual needs, including refining the management system, improving the legal system and carrying out institutional innovation.

In modern society, as a public authority, the government is not only the creator and maintainer of the major systems but also needs to establish a sound system to restrain itself aiming at serving society more effectively and preventing the abuse of public power. Therefore, institutional innovation should firstly focus on improving the government's public management system to ensure that governments at various levels can better perform their social management and public service functions, improve management, enhance effectiveness, and shift from a political man to a social man and an economic man to a public man.

From the experience of developed countries, the development process of market economy, industrialization, and post-industrialization will generate a series of social risks, mainly in the form of social polarization between rich and poor, class antagonism, and social unrest. However, after a long period of groping, especially after experiencing serious class struggles, western countries have gradually developed social systems and policies to solve the above social problems. The solutions mainly include income distribution adjustment, social security, education, health care, employment, public finance, and other systems.

In addition, to harmoniously develop the society, there must be institutional guarantees that can realize the primary conditions of fairness and justice so that the rights and interests of members of society in political, economic, cultural, and social aspects are safeguarded. Furthermore, it can provide formal channels and normative bases for them to express their interests and demands, fulfill their obligations, and deal with interrelations to build people's essential trust in the government and society. This include constructing a system for protecting democratic rights and legal and judicial systems.

The second is vigorously developing education, science, and other cultural undertakings to accelerate society's cultural and ideological progress. Cultural life is a phenomenon unique to humans, and they will instinctively pursue it. It not only reflects the human's essence but also manifests their pursuit and realization of happiness. The affluence in material life is only one aspect of the happy life that people pursue. The pursuit and desire for cultural life not only does not decrease with the enrichment of material life but becomes more intense and demanding. For this fundamental reason, human development includes abundant material life and considerable cultural and ideological progress.

Socialism is a society pursuing the overall development of human beings. Cultural and ideological progress is one of its due meanings. The practice of human social development shows that when social and economic development reaches a particular stage, people's life needs will develop in high quality, from focusing on meeting material needs to high-quality cultural life. In today's era, culture is becoming an essential source of national cohesion and creativity, so as to an important factor in competing for comprehensive national power. Moreover, naturally enriching human cultural life is their increasingly ardent desire.

The third is vigorously developing social undertakings and comprehensively improving people's lives. Social undertakings refer to various public service industries organized by government agencies, institutions, and other organizations at various levels with state-owned assets for social welfare. Narrow social undertakings include education, health, science and technology, culture, sports, birth control, radio, and television. Besides, broad social undertakings include income distribution, employment, social security, public safety, social relief, environmental protection, disaster prevention and relief, habitation services, as well as energy and water supply.

Social undertakings are important carriers and manifestations of a sound social system structure and cultural and ideological progress. Therefore, their development degree affects and restricts overall social development.

The fourth is promoting reform and innovation in social undertakings. Building a harmoniously developing society must do the following:

- deepening education reform and striving to improve the modern national education system and lifelong education system aiming at raising the level of education for all and cultivate innovative talents;
- improving the institutional mechanism for promoting employment and entrepreneurship and actively expanding employment to achieve full employment;
- establishing a more equitable and sustainable social security system so that everyone can enjoy a minimum standard of living;
- creating a reasonable and orderly income distribution structure, raising the middle-income class proportion, and largely eliminating absolute poverty;
- deepening the reform of the medical and health care system so that everyone can enjoy basic medical services.

4.2 National Economic System and International Economic Environment

Suppose it is bounded by a country's national territory. In that case, the country's national economy is an independent system, and the international economic system outside NES is its environment. According to whether there is a connection between NES and the international economic environment, NES can be divided into a closed and an open system. It is impossible for a system not to connect with the outside world, or rather, economic systems, in general, are open systems. In an open economy, the economic activities of a country often break the national boundaries and extend abroad, such as international trade, global production, and transnational investment. Opening to the outside world and developing international economic interactions are the objective requirements of developing social productivity and an important symbol of social development and human progress.

4.2.1 The Evolution of International Economic Development

As is seen from the history of international economic development, economic ties between countries can be divided into two major development stages: (i) the international division of labor of production, mainly in the form of international trade, and (ii) the international cooperation of production factors, mainly in the form of international investment.

4.2.1.1 The Stage Where the International Division of Labor of Production with International Trade as Its Main Form

International trade is exchanging goods, labor services, and others between various countries or regions. The economic ties between countries in the main form of international trade are primarily in commodity circulation. The countries involved in international trade benefit from trade. Initially, the economic ties between countries were mainly international trade, and the international division of labor in production tailored to meet the trade needs. The development of international trade at this stage has undergone the process from country-specific markets to regional markets, then to the early world markets, and finally, to a unified world market.

Country-specific markets, i.e., trade exchanges between neighboring countries, existed mainly in the medieval period. However, due to the low productivity levels, the self-sufficient natural economy was dominant, and the transportation of goods relied mainly on human or animal-powered transportation. Therefore, only a few spices, tea, silk, and precious stones could be exchanged between countries. Thus, due to the narrow trade scope, international trade was mainly a means for nobles to satisfy their consumption demands.

Regional markets existed before the sixteenth century. It was achieved mainly through the Silk Road running through Eurasia. A wide variety of goods were traded along the route, such as silk from China, fur, woolen knitwear, jade, livestock from Central Asia, amber from the Baltic, glass, coral, pearls, linen, gold from Rome, and spices and gems from India. In the Middle Ages, cities sprang up over Western Europe and promoted crafts and commerce, driving local commodity and monetary relations. The trade among European countries grew so that fixed international bazaars gradually formed, attracting other countries and regions, which further expanded the scope of regional markets. As a result, international trade has developed even more, but trade was mainly the mutual exchange of needed products.

By the sixteenth and eighteenth centuries, an early world market emerged. At that time, capitalism began to sprout, colonial policies were introduced, and advancing means of transportation brought about great geographical discoveries. Together with other factors, it prompted regional markets to knit together into a relatively unified world market, forming two major trading circles, the Pacific and the Atlantic. The former mainly conducted trade between European and Asian countries, whereas the latter covered trade between Europe, America, and Africa. The scale and scope of commodities traded thus expanded. The smaller trade scale in the early days made commodities such as tea, a luxury item. By this time, tea had become a mass commodity due to trade expansion. The slave trade from Africa to the Americas also occurred during this period. At this time, international trade ceased to be a tool for the aristocracy to satisfy their consumption but became a means of capital accumulation for the emerging bourgeoisie. European governments also began using international trade to develop their economies and adopting mercantilist policies to promote trade and domestic industries. Western European colonialists plundered Asian, African, and Latin American countries with advanced weapons, so international trade at that time was predatory. The initial division of labor between the suzerain states and the colonies also emerged during this period. This was shown as the products involved in international trade were mainly based on different natural conditions of each country, exporting their specialties in exchange for products that were not produced or produced in small quantities in their countries.

The unified world market was formed in the mid-nineteenth century. The Industrial Revolution in Europe and the United States broke out in the late 18th and early nineteenth centuries. The initial establishment of the large machine production mode played a decisive role in its formation, thus changing the market's commodity structure and price mechanism. Previously, the artisanal production mode had resulted in a small and costly production capacity for goods, whereas the development of the large-scale machine industry, has created a large number of low-cost manufactured goods such as textiles, metal products, machinery, and equipment, which dismantled the self-sufficient natural economy. Moreover, as developed countries in Europe built ports and railroads and mined mineral resources in the colonies, the relevant machinery and equipment became important European exports. In contrast, the commodities exported from the colonies to the European suzerains were raw materials and fuel needed by these countries for industrial manufactures. Establishing this trade structure marked the formation of a unified world market. Moreover, in the early days, international trade was mainly a matter of plundering the colonies by their suzerains, and the prices of commodities were not determined by their value and the nexus between supply and demand, but by the will and military forces of the suzerains.

With the formation of the unified world market, the mechanism of equivalence exchange with international value at its core was gradually established. However, unequal transactions in the unified world market were also abundant due to unreasonable prices of industrially manufactured goods and raw materials, as well as unequal terms of trade. Nevertheless, after the world market emerged, the trade has expanded unprecedentedly in the wake of forming a trade network among involved countries. From the Industrial Revolution to the twentieth century, the big machine industry considerably expanded the world market, and international trade gained rapid development, except during the two World Wars.

4.2.1.2 The Stage Where Production Factors Cooperate Internationally with International Investment as the Main Form

International investment is the economic behavior of transnational corporations and other investors to realize value-added through cross-border flow and operation of their owned monetary or industrial capital. This stage began with the second technological revolution emerging in the last 30 years of the nineteenth century. The results of this technological revolution included railroads, automobiles, shipping, telegraph, telephone, and wireless communication technologies. These new transportation and communication means significantly reduced the distance between countries worldwide in terms of time and space. Therefore, they have laid the technological foundation for connecting global capital markets and the international movement of capital.

The technological revolution and the developing heavy chemical industry increased the enterprises' demand for capital, thereby concentrating the capital and production, leading to the emergence of monopolistic organizations such as cartels and trusts, which became the dominant force in the economies of developed countries. However, while monopolies rapidly amassed their colossal capital, they also severely inhibited domestic investment opportunities. In this way they create a relative surplus capital in major developed countries. The surplus capital inevitably went abroad to find a way out. Therefore, capital export became the main phenomenon in international economic relations during this period. At that time, major capitalist countries were sharing the global market, establishing their colonies, and controlling the political and economic lifelines of the colonial countries. They also treated such countries as their sources of raw materials, investment sites, and outlets for goods. During this period, capital export and market segmentation was the primary means of competition among the world's major capitalist countries. Also, they expanded the market economy production mode of capitalist countries from Europe and America to almost the whole world.

Although international investment has gradually became the majority of international economic activity in developed countries since the 1870s, until the Second World War, it was mainly featured by international indirect investment, i.e., investment activities in international capital markets, including international credit and portfolio investments. Such investments were mainly carried out by a government, a bank, or an international financial organization to provide credit funds to a third country's government, bank, natural or legal person or by purchasing foreign stocks and other marketable securities to achieve currency appreciation. International direct investment accounts for only 10%, and the capital import does not cause transnational mobility of production factors.

International direct investment refers to the outward capital export by investors through controlling part of the enterprise's property rights and participating directly in its management, primarily aiming at obtaining profits. It can be divided into two forms: establishing new enterprises and controlling the equity of foreign enterprises, and are also known as greenfield investment, and cross-border mergers and acquisitions (M&A). The former refers to the investor's direct investment abroad to establish new factories, mines, subsidiaries, and branches and acquire existing foreign enterprises or companies to engage in production and business activities. The latter refers to purchasing shares of foreign enterprises to a certain percentage for a controlling stake in the foreign enterprise. International direct investment in developed countries began in the 1880s but only developed rapidly after the Second World War. In the 1970s, the growth rate of international direct investment outpaced that of international trade.

Multinational corporations are generally the principal part of international direct investments, with greenfield investment as the primary way, especially for developing countries. Because there are gaps in some modern industrial sectors in these countries with sound growth prospects in their markets, unlike the limited developed countries' market capacity and difficulty in earning a profit. Therefore, foreign investors have poured into the market in developing countries to establish new enterprises. Cross-border mergers and acquisitions are the main forms of international direct investment between developed countries, whose capital markets are more developed and liberalized. However, as emerging economies and multinational corporations arising rapidly, cross-border mergers have also appeared between emerging economies and developed countries. The rapid development of international direct investment has profoundly changed the way of international trade, expanded international trade, and formed the transnationalization and integration of production. International investment is the movement of production factors between countries in the form of capital, which has changed how countries are linked economically. It shifts from a globalized economy based on internationally dividing production and commodity trade to the one based on internationally combining production factors.

Since the 1970s, the international direct investment has been expanding. The primary reason is the impetus of the Third Scientific and Technological Revolution marked by atomic energy, electronic computers, and space technology. It has revolutionized the means of production, thus promoting the economic development and structural upgrading in developed countries. Moreover, it transited the international division of labor from a traditional one to a modern one. This transmission included four main shifts, namely from the vertical division of labor between industrial manufactures and primary products to the horizontal one between industrial manufactures, then from the labor division between different economic sectors to the intra-sector specialized one in products, components, processes, and procedures, moreover, the indirect labor division in the field of commodity circulation to one in various countries' field of production, and eventually from the labor division imposed on backward countries by a few developed countries to the active participation of developing countries in the international labor division.

Improvements in the international labor division have linked countries at different levels of economic development on multiple levels and in multiple forms, giving them access to their development opportunities. Among them, the growing number of multinational companies plays a vital role in developing a modern international labor division. Multinational corporations organize production and sales worldwide, deepening the international labor division from the macro level between countries to the micro level between enterprises. As a result, the internationalization of production has entered a new development stage, and international direct investment has entered a new epoch, thus reinforcing the trend of world economic integration.

After the Second World War, the international financial market expanded rapidly and has formed many large trading centers where multinational banks, stock exchanges, as well as investment institutions congregated and financial transaction networks connected through modern communication equipment. All above have facilitated international trade, investment, and financing. Thus, global capital flows and cross-border investment have accelerated significantly.

Since the 1970s, governments of developed countries have deregulated international trade, investment, and finance to encourage international trade and investment. They implemented liberalization policies to encourage the development of internationalization. In addition, developing countries have chosen to follow the path of the reform and opening up, aiming at establishing the market economy system and allowing the market to determine the resource allocation. These endeavors adapted to the requirements of international investment and provided the social conditions that international direct investment needs.

4.2.1.3 Economic Globalization and Its Characteristics

The shift from the international circulation of commodities to the international movement of production factors has changed the basis of economic development and the links of economic ties worldwide. It endows economic globalization nowadays with new characteristics.

(1) Reduce or eliminate barriers to international trade, resulting in a significant increase in the volume and scale of trade and significantly expanding the trade structure. The reason is twofold. On the one hand, international direct investment makes full use of the excess capital and idle resources of the investing country and the host country, promoting the economic growth of both countries and thus expanding the trade scale. On the other hand, by integrating the host country into the investing country's production and distribution system, international direct investment constructs an international labor division in the value chain, thus creating intra-product trade and expanding the total trade scale. Moreover, the movement of production factors has given developing countries access to capital, technology, and other advanced factors of production. They instead become exporters of capital- and technology-intensive products, which, together with the emerging a new trade mode—processing trade, which have changed the traditional structure of international trade.
(2) The determinant of return distribution of the international labor division is changed from the difference in industrial structure to the law of earnings of factors, i.e., the factors' scarcity determines their prices and, then the returns of factors. In economic globalization, it is not the product market but the factors market that determines the returns of the international labor division. Whoever has more scarce production factors will get higher returns. Today's scarcest production factors are original core technologies and self-created brands, which can increase productivity and output levels. Since such production factors are mainly held by developed countries, these countries occupy a favorable position in the return distribution of the international labor division.
(3) National competitiveness is no longer marked by the traditional export scale and structure, international market share, and trade surplus size, but by the possession status of core technologies and brands. As today's countries at different development levels have become a link in the international chain of the value

division, developing countries attract a large amount of capital, technologies, and brands from developed countries with the advantages of cheap workforce, land, and natural resources. As a result, the production factors from both sides are pooled in developing countries for production. Therefore, possessing advanced production factors, such as technology and brands, has becoming a sign of a country's competitiveness.

(4) National core capacity has evolved into the ability to cluster factors and create and grow advanced production factors. For developing countries, implementing the opening-up strategy is capitalizing on international resources to compensate for the shortage of domestic capital, technology, management, and other advanced production factors. Therefore, the ability to attract and cluster foreign resources becomes the country's core competency. It mainly depends on the domestic system's perfectness, the market system's soundness, the service efficiency of government departments, and the supporting ability of industries and the workforce. For developed countries, under the condition of economic globalization, the core competence of a country is reflected in the growth and development mechanism of advanced production factors, such as a vibrant market, mature enterprise system, solid technology base, and immense talent pool. Only with them can advanced production factors, such as technology, patents, and brands, be continuously self-renewal and keep flowing the earnings of production factors in a steady stream for the country.

(5) The leading cause of recent economic growth is the international factor movements, thus increasing the total input of production factors in the world economy. It is because developing countries scarcely have advanced production factors, such as technology and management. However, they are abundant with such factors as labor, land, and natural resources, and a vast market development potential. On the contrary, developed countries are abundant in advanced production factors, such as technology and management, while short for some other factors, such as labor, land, and natural resources, and their domestic markets are close to saturation. International direct investment contributes to the international factors flow so that advanced production factors from developed countries flow to developing countries to combine with primary factors there. As a result, both sides' idle or underutilized production factors can be effectively allocated to achieve a win–win situation in economic development, thus extensively promoting world economic growth. In addition, the flow of production factors and large-scale agglomeration will influence enterprises' and industries' economies of scale so that factor productivity has been improved and contributes to the rapid growth of the world economy. At the same time, the technology spillover and learning effect generated by international direct investment will greatly promote technological and management innovation in developing countries, thus increasing their productivity.

(6) The changing pattern of world economic growth has brought about an imbalance in world trade, i.e., an international trade surplus in emerging economies

and a trade deficit in developed economies. The reason for this is that developed economies use international direct investment to transfer the capital, technology, brands, and other advanced production factors, or even industries, to the emerging economies. As a result, emerging economies become the producers of the world's major products. They export their products to the developed economies, and the developed economy countries become consumers. This economic pattern leads to trade imbalances between developing and developed countries. However, it should also be noted that there is also a problem with the trade structure here. Developed countries imported low-cost products from developing countries but maintained embargoes on high-technology products, especially those with core technologies, thus resulting in trade imbalances. Obviously, it is not the problem of developing countries, but developed countries' protection of high technology. In this regard, China's trade with the United States, European Union, and Japan is a typical example.

4.2.2 China's Position in the Global Economy and the Belt and Road Initiative

4.2.2.1 China's Position in the Global Economy[11]

(1) *Economic contribution and impact*

In 1979, China's share in the world economic aggregates was less than 1%, only 0.92%. However, in 2014, China's GDP exceeded US$10.4 trillion, accounting for 13.82% of the world's GDP, making it the second-largest economy after the U.S. In terms of its economic growth, China maintained an average annual growth rate of 9.8% over 32 years from 1980 to 2011, creating a miracle of world economic growth. Moreover, in terms of its contribution to and impact on the world economy, China's economy significantly influences the world economy, showing strong resilience against the backdrop of the world economy's slow recovery and becoming an essential engine of world economic growth. In 2014, China's economy contributed 29.7% to world economic growth, making it the largest contributor to world economic growth (19.6% for the U.S.).

(2) *The scale of trade in goods and services*

In 1978, China's goods trade exports and imports were US$9.95 billion and $11.13 billion, respectively, accounting for 0.76% and 0.82% of the world's share. From 1978 to 2014, the average annual growth rates of China's exports and imports reached 17.04% and 16.49%, respectively, much higher than the world's 8.19% and 8.07% in the same period. In 2013, China's total goods trade exceeded US$4 trillion for the first time, reaching US$4.16 trillion, surpassing the United States (US$3.91 trillion) to become the world's largest goods trading country. In 2014, China's total goods

[11] Data from the UNCTAD database.

imports and exports reached US$4.30 trillion, with exports accounting for 12.37% of the world's total, further consolidating its position as the world's largest goods trader.

Although there is still a gap in the scale of China's services trade compared with trade in goods, the standing of China's service trade in the world continues to rise. For example, in 1982, China's service trade exports and imports were US$2.51 billion and US$2.02 billion, accounting for only 0.63% and 0.45% of the global share. However, by 2014, China's service trade exports and imports were US$22.22 billion and US$382.13 billion, respectively, with its world share up to 4.50% and 7.86%, respectively. Therefore, China has become the world's fifth-largest exporter and second-largest services importer.

(3) *Foreign direct investment (FDI) and overseas direct investment (ODI)*

In 1980, China's FDI was only US$57 million, accounting for only 0.11% of the world's share. In 2014, China's FDI reached US$128 billion, accounting for 9.49% of the world's share, making it the world's top destination for foreign investment. It is also the first time since 2003, when China became the leading developing country in attracting foreign investment, that it surpassed the United States, jumping to the top globally. As of 2014, China's stock of FDI reached US$1,084.79 billion, accounting for 3.89% of the world's share, ranking sixth in the world.

While the size of China's FDI continues to climb, the rapid growth of China's ODI is even more remarkable. In 1982, China's ODI was only US$44 million, however, it reached US$2.85 billion in 2003, accounting for only 0.49% of the global share. In 2014, China's ODI reached US$140 billion, with its global share up to 11.1%, surpassing Japan to become the largest overseas investor in Asia and the second largest globally. From 2003 to 2014, China's ODI average annual growth rate was as high as 45.02%. As of 2014, China's ODI stock reached US$753.585 billion, accounting for 2.6% of the world, ranking 11th globally. Moreover, China's foreign currency reserve was US$3,843 billion, ranking the first globally.

(4) *Manufacturing and finance*

According to the World Bank, in 1990, the added-value of China's manufacturing industry was only US$117 billion, accounting for 2.6% of the global. In 2010, it reached US$1,924.96 billion, accounting for 18.6% of the world's manufacturing industry, surpassing the United States to become the world's top manufacturing country. In 2013, China accounted for the world's 23.2% manufacturing value-added and 18.4% manufacturing exports, with the output of more than 220 manufacturing products ranking the first globally.

4.2.2.2 New Changes in Domestic and International Economy

(1) *The new pattern of the world economy*

Since the 2008 global financial crisis, the world economic situation has undergone new changes.

Firstly, the two major economies have shifted positions. The position of developed economies has shifted downward. Their share of the world economy has fallen from 83.6% in 1992 to 61.9% in 2012, and the position of emerging economies has risen, with their share rising from 16.4% to 38.1%.

Secondly, a new pattern of world industrial production has emerged. Industrial production in developed economies has decelerated, some of which have hollowed out while emerging and developing countries have performed well in industrial growth. However, as the engine of industrial growth, it still has a long way to go before the manufacturing industry can highlight its leadership in the pattern of global industrial production.

Thirdly, the situation of world capital movement has reversed. Although developed capital-exporting countries significantly reduce overseas investment and accelerate the contraflow of global capital, emerging economies' momentum to expand outbound investment is unabated, and some areas have begun to challenge the developed economies.

Fourthly, the world trade pattern is further differentiated. Merchandise exports from the United States, European Union, and Asian developing countries grew faster under stimulus policies, whereas Japan's export deteriorated. Asian developing countries grew strongly in commodity imports and maintained a leading position. For a long time, the target of China's opening up to the outside world has mainly been the developed Western economies. In this regard, this pattern needs to be adjusted. Meanwhile, along with the pace of globalization and the accelerated regional economic integration, it is necessary to strengthen cooperation with developing countries and regions such as the Association of Southeast Asian Nations (ASEAN), Central Asia, and South Asia.

(2) *China's economy entering a new normal*

Concurrently, China's economy has entered a new normal, whereas the reform has entered a deep-water zone. As a result, economic development is in a new phase of three overlapping periods: shift gears of the economic growth rate, undergo restructuring throes, and address the impact of previous stimulus policies. On the one hand, the demographic dividend lasting for more than 30 years is gradually disappearing, and workforce cost is rising rapidly, which cause traditional industries to lose their competitiveness. On the other hand, due to over-optimistic capacity expansion in more than the last decade, overcapacity has emerged in some Chinese industries with the slowdown in economic growth. In addition, China's huge consumer market has spawned many large companies to become multinational corporations with multinational investment and global operations capabilities. These factors jointly drive China to a going global phase aiming at achieving a soft landing of the national economy from high to average and stable growth, thus maintaining sustainable and moderate growth.

4.2.2.3 China's Belt and Road Initiative

(1) *Implication of the Belt and Road Initiative*

The Belt and Road is short for the Silk Road Economic Belt and the 21st-Century Maritime Silk Road. On March 28, 2015, China's National Development and Reform Commission, the Ministry of Foreign Affairs, and the Ministry of Commerce jointly released the Vision and Action on Jointly Building Silk Road Economic Belt and the 21st Century Maritime Silk Road. In this document, the Chinese government issued an initiative to related countries along the road and route to actively develop economic partnerships with them, and work together to foster a community of shared interests, shared future, and shared responsibility featuring mutual political trust, economic integration, and cultural inclusiveness. All these endeavors result in the orderly and free economic element flow, the efficient resources allocation, and the deep market integration, and promote a broader, higher and deeper level of regional cooperation to jointly build an open, inclusive, balanced, and beneficial-to-all regional economic cooperation structure. Eventually, it will shape a new pattern of China's opening up to the outside world in the new era.

Historically, the Belt and Road has been a major pathway for trade cooperation and cultural exchanges between China and Central Asia, Southeast Asia, South Asia, West Asia, East Africa, and Europe. It runs through the Asian, European, and African continents, with the robust East Asian economic circle at one end and the developed European economic circle at the other. The vast in-between hinterland countries have great potential for economic development. The Silk Road Economic Belt focuses on the unimpeded passage from China to Europe (the Baltic Sea) via Central Asia and Russia, from China to the Persian Gulf and the Mediterranean Sea via Central Asia and West Asia, and from China to Southeast Asia, South Asia, and the Indian Ocean. The key direction of the 21st Century Maritime Silk Road is from China's coastal ports to the Indian Ocean, extending to Europe and the South Pacific across the South China Sea. Relying on the international major land transport routes and supported by the central cities along, the Silk Road by land aims at jointly building the international economic cooperation corridors: the New Eurasian Continental Bridge, China—Mongolia—Russia, China—Central Asia—West Asia, China—Indo-China Peninsula, with key economic and trade industrial parks as a platform for cooperation. Silk Road by Sea aims at jointly building an unimpeded, safe, and efficient transport route, with key ports as nodes. Whether it is to develop the economy, improve people's livelihood or respond to difficulties and accelerate adjustment, many countries along the route have common interests with China. As an inheritance and enhancement of the ancient Silk Road, the Belt and Road Initiative has gained wide recognition from countries along the route and related countries.

In May 2017, China hosted the Belt and Road Forum for International Cooperation in Beijing, attended by state leaders and heads of government from 29 countries and international organizations such as the UN Secretary-General and about 1,500 honored guests from all walks of life from more than 130 countries. They charted future cooperation schemes, built cooperation platforms, and shared cooperation outcomes to find solutions to the current problems facing the world and regional economies and inject fresh energy for pursuing interconnected development. In this way the Belt and Road Initiative delivers greater benefits to people of countries involved. The Initiative's introduction indicates that China looks forward to integrating more deeply into the global economic system and playing a more active role in leading world economic development in line with current world development mechanisms and trends.

(2) *Global economic and trade patterns under the Belt and Road Initiative*

Firstly, the Belt and Road Initiative and global trade and investment patterns. The Belt and Road Initiative (BRI) involves 65 countries, covering more than 60% of the world's population and about 1/3 of the world's total GDP. According to the United Nations Conference on Trade and Development (UNCTAD) statistics, during the period 1990–2013, especially the financial crisis period, these countries' average annual growth rate of foreign trade and cross-border investment was higher than the global average. The BRI partner countries have high economic complementarities, but the current trade situation is far from reflecting their true strength. The BRI will improve regional infrastructure, liberalize and facilitate trade and investment, and deeply integrate supply and value chains. Notably, it will fundamentally change the regional trade situation and ensure that the regional economic and trade cooperation along the route reaches new heights.

Western China and the Pan-Central Asian economic circle on the Belt and Road is a sagging economic area between East Asia and Europe. However, Central Asia is the heart of the Eurasian continent and the pivotal region affecting the international landscape. With the Belt and Road Initiative, Central Asian countries will not only open up access to the sea but also deeply integrate into the world economic and trade cooperation system, which stimulates the economic and trade cooperation between Asia and Europe as a whole. On the one hand, it can promote the development of China's central and western regions and the Pan-Central Asian economic circle and flatten the sagging area on the Silk Road Economic Belt. On the other hand, it can form a regional emerging growth pole.

The economic and trade cooperation between China and Europe mainly relies on the sea route. However, constructing The Belt and Road will expand the land route for China-EU cooperation and further expand the economic and trade exchanges between the two sides. As this strategy advances, the world will form a third-largest global trade axis with Asia and Europe as the core, thus restructuring the global trade. Moreover, China will play a more significant role in the future global trade pattern in the middle of the two major trade axes: the Pacific and Eurasian.

Secondly, the Belt and Road Initiative and the Asian industrial division of labor system. From the 1950s to the 1980s, the world underwent three industrial shifts:

the United States to Japan, Japan to the "Four Asian Tigers", and then the "Four Asian Tigers" to ASEAN and China, the famous flying-geese industrial transfer. Through the gradient transfer of industries and the vigorous development of an export-oriented economy, the East Asian region has created the East Asian miracle of economic development. However, since the 1990s, although Japan still acts as a leading goose in East Asia, its domestic economic growth has stagnated, and the pace of industrial upgrading transfer to East Asia has slowed down significantly. This setback is due to industrial hollowing, thereby significantly weakening East Asia's ability to adjust industrial structure. Moreover, by 2010, China took over Japan's position as the world's second-largest economy, and the flying-geese model in East Asia and the Asian region is gradually broken.

The BRI partner countries have apparent differences in their comparative advantages. In this regard, they can mutually complement in terms of industrial, commodity, and trade structures. As per the theory of labor division, they have the location conditions and industrial foundation that initially formed the flying-geese labor division in East Asia, as well as the policy advantages that were not available in East Asia initially. Therefore, the Belt and Road Initiative will change the pattern and layout of the industrial labor division in East Asia and Asia. China's labor-intensive industries and dominant capital-intensive industries will be transferred to the BRI partner countries successively based on the flying-geese labor division, thus driving their industrial restructuring and upgrading and optimizing their industrialization level. The above efforts will change the situation that the BRI partner countries have been relegated to sagging economic area, because they have only served as a passageway for developing world trade and restructuring the industrial division in the Asian region.

Thirdly, the Belt and Road Initiative and global governance model. After the Second World War, the major developed countries, with their influence and dominant position in the world economy, utilized the World Trade Organization (WTO) to promote and formulate various global governance and economic and trade rules beneficial to their interests. All along, emerging markets and developing economies have yet to have a proper and identity-appropriate say and the right to formulate international rules. One of the critical points of the Belt and Road Initiative is to accelerate implementing the free-trade zone (FTA) strategy, which will be conducive to forming multilateral economic and trade rules, deeply integrating and participating the majority of developing countries into globalization, and creating a favorable institutional environment for the peaceful development of developing countries.

Part II
National Economic Operation

Chapter 5
Impetus and Management of Demand in National Economic Operation

National economic operation is a process in which total social supply and demand strive for dynamic balance within the context of economic growth. From the perspective of total social demand, economic growth, as measured by GDP, is driven by three primary forces—the so-called troika of economic growth: investment, consumption, and net exports. This chapter examines the impact of these three demand components on national economic operation and explores the state management of national economic demand.

5.1 Investment Demand and National Economic Operation

Among the three primary drivers of economic growth, investment demand (or capital accumulation) plays a crucial role. Classical economists, such as Adam Smith, considered capital accumulation the most significant source of economic growth. For East Asian countries and many developing nations, investment demand is particularly vital. In a narrower sense, total social demand refers to the demand for society's final goods, with investment demand being a key component. Investment demand, also known as investment spending, represents the demand for investment goods generated by monetary societal expenditure over a specific period, such as one year. This demand can be analyzed in terms of its size (aggregate investment) and structure, as well as the mutually reinforcing relationship between these aspects.

M. Lin and T. Huang, *National Economics*,
https://doi.org/10.1007/978-981-96-9618-5_5

5.1.1 Investment Size and Its Decision

5.1.1.1 Implication of Investment Size

Investment size is an aggregate measure representing the social demand for investment goods, expressed through the expenditure of monetary funds during a specific period. Investment size can be classified mainly from the following aspects:

(1) *Composition*

The demand for gross social investment includes the demand for both fixed and liquid assets. The demand for investment in fixed assets further includes replacement demand and newly increased investments. Therefore, gross social investment can be divided into total investment in fixed assets and liquid assets. Investment in fixed assets can be further classified into replacement investments and newly increased investments.

(2) *Sources of funds*

The funds for investment demand come from various sources, including depreciation funds, accumulated funds, and temporarily unused consumption funds. These sources can be explicitly categorized into fiscal grants, bank loans, self-financing funds from regions, departments, or enterprises, personal investments, and other channels. Accordingly, aggregate investment can be divided into budgetary and extra-budgetary investment sizes.

Budgetary Investment. This refers to investments arranged using state budgetary funds, which can take the form of budget allocations or bank loans. Budgetary investments are managed at both the central and local levels, including provinces, municipalities directly led the Central Government, and autonomous regions.

Extra-Budgetary Investment. This refers to investments not included in the state budget. These investments are arranged by regions, departments, enterprises, and individuals through various other forms of investment.

(3) *Investment subjects*

With the transition from a centralized to a decentralized decision-making system, the range of investment actors has diversified. The main investors now include the state (both central and local governments), enterprises, and individuals (inclusive of those investing in housing in rural areas). Consequently, investment size can be categorized into the investment sizes of state-owned units and the broader society.

(4) *Time span*

Total Investment can be divided into annual investment size of the country and total investment in projects under construction. Narrowly, annual investment size refers to the amount of investment in fixed assets within a year, while, broadly, it refers to the total investment in fixed assets and liquid assets within a year. The total investment in projects under construction refers to the total investment required for completing all ongoing construction projects in the current year.

5.1.1.2 The Decision on Investment Size

The decision on the investment size depends on various factors, mainly as follows:

(1) *The growth of total social production*

The society's economic growth rate in a given period is an important factor restricting the changes in the investment scale. It is also a key determinant for economic growth. If GDP is taken as a comprehensive indicator of economic growth, the social investment size in a given period (e.g., within a year) depends, first of all, on the amount of funds allocated for depreciation of fixed assets in this period and the amount of net national income and its growth rate, i.e., the amount and growth rate of GDP.

Fixed asset depreciation funds are a component of GDP. Fixed assets, through wear and tear, transfer their value to new products, which is realized through product sales and accumulated into depreciation funds in monetary forms. These funds are withdrawn yearly over a set number of depreciable years. The length of depreciation depends on the country's technical policy and the resulting depreciation policy during a specific period.

When considering the replacement of production capacity, the depreciation period is primarily based on the natural service life of technical equipment, using the straight-line depreciation method. However, if focusing on technological advancement and renewal, the depreciation period is based on the economic service life of the technical equipment, adopting the accelerated depreciation method. The annual depreciation is generally calculated by multiplying the original value of fixed assets by the depreciation rate.

Depreciation funds can be used for both renovation and reformation investments, as well as capital construction investments, thereby forming a component of the annual investment size.

Net domestic product (NDP)[1] refers to the value newly created by labor within a specific period, representing the balance of GDP after deducting fixed asset depreciation. When the ratio of accumulated funds to consumption funds of NNI is fixed, the scale of new investments depends on the quantity of NNI and its growth rate. A higher amount of NNI leads to more funds available for investment, resulting in a larger investment scale. Similarly, a higher growth rate of NNI translates to a higher growth rate of investment. Conversely, lower NNI and its growth rate result in reduced investment capacity. Therefore, factors that influence NNI growth also impact and restrict changes in the investment size.

(2) *The consumption and accumulation rates*

The consumption rate refers to the portion of GDP spent on actual consumption, while the accumulation rate represents the portion of GDP allocated for accumulation, which serves as the source of funds available for investment. For a given GDP, these

[1] Net national income (NNI), previously referred to as National Income in China, is a macroeconomic indicator representing the total newly created value within a nation during a specific period. This total newly created value is expressed as $v + m$, where v is the value of variable capital advanced and m is the surplus value.

two rates are inversely related. Under normal circumstances, it is essential to ensure that per capita income and consumption for the existing population increase yearly. Therefore, the necessary consumption rate should be determined first, after which the accumulation rate can be established.

This approach means that the investment size over a given period is constrained by both the consumption rate and the corresponding accumulation rate. Consequently, the investment size increases as the accumulation rate increases and decreases as the accumulation rate decreases.

It is important to distinguish between the accumulation rate and the investment rate, as they are not equivalent concepts. The accumulation rate is the percentage of GDP not used for actual consumption, representing the sources of funds available for investment. In contrast, the investment rate is the ratio of gross social investment spending to GDP, representing the total investment demand.

In the absence of foreign capital or other domestic sources of funds, such as accumulated depreciation funds from the previous period, balanced financial, corporate, or personal funds from the previous period, fiscal deficit grants, or credit over-expansion, the funds for investment in the current period can only come from this period's accumulation (the part of GDP not used for actual consumption). Therefore, under prevailing circumstances, the investment rate cannot exceed the accumulation rate.

If the investment rate exceeds the accumulation rate, it indicates that the demand for investment goods surpasses their supply, suggesting that the investment size is too large. When existing equipment capacity is fully utilized, this imbalance will undoubtedly lead to demand expansion, thus affecting stable economic development. Conversely, if the investment rate is less than the accumulation rate, indicating insufficient investment size and demand, it is also not conducive to economic growth.

Only when the investment rate equals the accumulation rate can steady growth of the national economy be secured, ensuring that the investment size is reasonable and moderate.

(3) *The material and human resources that society can provide in a given period (short or long-term)*

Investment spending must ultimately be transformed into practical production factors, including investment goods and the means of production and workforce needed for them, to be effective. Therefore, the GDP ratio allocated to consumption and accumulation must correspond to the material and human resources available in society and their composition.

In terms of material resources, it's essential to consider not only investment goods, such as materials for infrastructure construction, energy, transportation, machinery, and equipment, but also the supply capacity of intermediate goods and corresponding consumer goods. Regarding human resources, although China currently has a large surplus of labor, the general level of education and technical skills is relatively low. Thus, there should be a special emphasis on the general education and training of the workforce to improve its quality. Without such improvements, it will be challenging to achieve the desired economic growth from investments.

(4) *The level of investment efficiency*

There is a close relationship between the size of investment and its efficiency. An important indicator of investment efficiency is the investment efficiency coefficient, which is the ratio of the increase in GDP to the amount of social fixed asset investment over a certain period. This coefficient is positive; the larger the investment efficiency coefficient, the greater the investment efficiency, and vice versa.

When the investment efficiency coefficient is low, GDP growth must rely on expanding the investment size or increasing the investment rate. If the investment efficiency coefficient is high, GDP growth mainly relies on investment efficiency. This means higher efficiency can be obtained with the same investment amount, or the same efficiency can be achieved with less investment. Consequently, the investment size can be appropriately controlled or the investment rate reduced.

(5) *The economic system's influence on investment subjects' behavior*

The previous analysis focused on the objective factors restricting investment size. However, in actual economic life, subjective factors, mainly the investment behavior of economic agents under a specific economic system, also affect the investment size. In a market economy, through the establishment of modern enterprise systems and corporate governance structures, enterprises have independent rights to make investment decisions. Therefore, the investment size largely depends on the decisions of diversified investors and their expectations of economic growth prospects and future investment returns.

Thus, the investment size will be greatly influenced by rational decision-making, but sometimes it might be motivated more by partial gains. Therefore, while fully utilizing the market mechanism's adjustment role, the state must use indirect means to macro-adjust the social investment size. This ensures a fundamental balance between total social demand and supply during the growth process, serving overall national interests.

5.1.2 *Investment Structure and Its Determination*

Developing the national economy requires the input of production factors such as capital. Given a particular investment size, there is an objective need to allocate and use investment reasonably, commonly known as the investment orientation or investment structure. The investment structure significantly influences the formation of industrial and regional structures, and its rationalization is crucial for the coordinated development of the national economy.

5.1.2.1 Investment Structure

Investment structure refers to the quantitative proportional relationship between investments used in various systems. It is a vital aspect of the economic structure. Broadly, it mainly includes: (i) the industrial structure of the investment. This reflects the ultimate direction of investment, i.e., investment among the three primary industries or the distribution ratio between various sectors of the national economy, including the proportion of capital construction investment and renewal investment; (ii) the regional structure of the investment. It mainly reflects the spatial distribution of investment, i.e., the proportional relationship between investment distribution in various regions; (iii) the structure of the investment subjects. It mainly reflects the behavior of the investment subjects, including the relationship between government (central government, local governments) investment, foreign investment, and private (enterprise) investment, and personal investment; (iv) the financing structure of the investment. It mainly reflects the source of funding channels for investment, including the proportional relationship between budgetary and extrabudgetary investment, replacement and new investment, direct and indirect financing, and foreign investment; (v) the scale structure of the investment. It mainly reflects the relationship or proportion between large, medium, and small project investments; (vi) the process structure of the investment. It mainly reflects the relationship or proportion between construction and installation investment, equipment, tools and appliances investment, and other investments; (vii) the reproduction structure of the investment. It mainly reflects the proportional relationships or interconnections of fixed or liquid assets investments, newly-increased or greenfield investments, replacement investments or reconstruction, expansion, and technical upgrading.

5.1.2.2 The Decision of Investment Structure

Investment structure and investment size are closely related. A reasonable investment structure must be based on a reasonable investment size; without expanding the investment size, optimizing the investment structure is impossible. However, a rational investment size does not necessarily mean a rational investment structure. Without rationalizing the investment structure, it is impossible to achieve proper coordination between various industrial sectors and the optimal allocation of production resources. This can cause a structural imbalance between total social supply and demand, hindering stable economic growth and, in turn, restricting the reasonable growth of investment size. Therefore, rationalizing the investment structure is essential for determining the appropriate investment size and promoting coordinated national economic development.

However, there is a distinction between optimizing the investment structure and controlling the investment size. Generally speaking, controlling the investment size mainly addresses whether total social demand and supply are balanced in terms of quantity, while optimizing the investment structure aims to solve the issue of aligning demand and supply structures. The arrangement of the investment structure primarily affects the supply structure (such as industrial, regional, technological, and product structures), and by adjusting the supply structure, it ultimately achieves balance with the demand structure, i.e., the structural balance of total social supply and demand.

Among various investment structures, the industrial and regional structures of investment are essential.

(1) *The industrial structure is the foremost investment structure*

Firstly, viewed from the interrelationship between industrial structure and demand structure, the social demand structure and its changes over a certain period will undoubtedly affect the supply structure. However, satisfying people's productive and living consumption demands directly depends on the condition of a country's supply structure or industrial structure and their changes, as well as the production capacity and product quantity of each industrial sector. A specific industrial structure is formed by the proportion of investment allocated to each industrial sector. Therefore, changes in the sectoral investment structure are linked to changes in the overall demand structure, ultimately determining whether the structure of total social supply and demand is mutually compatible.

Secondly, viewed from the industrial structure itself, a reasonable industrial structure requires articulation and close coordination between various sectors in production, maintaining a reasonable proportion between the production of investment goods, consumer goods, and intermediate goods. For this reason, investment must be reasonably allocated among various industrial sectors in specific proportions.

Thirdly, viewed form rational resources allocation, a country's production resources are always limited in a given period. The degree of development and utilization of production resources is constrained by domestic export exchange capacity and changes in international market conditions. Rationally allocating limited resources to achieve high efficiency in resource allocation depends on rationalizing the sectoral investment institutions.

(2) *Regional structure is also one of the essential investment structures*

Optimizing the regional investment structure is crucial for achieving the reasonable allocation of various production resources among regions and attaining better resource allocation efficiency. It also helps leverage each region's natural strengths, economic advantages, and scientific and technological edges, narrowing the gap between regions' economic development levels, promoting largely coordinated development among regions, and ensuring the balance of total social supply and demand.

China is a vast country with a large population. At the same time, it is a developing country with a lack of capital, a low per capita resource availability, and significant regional disparities. Given China's national conditions, it is crucial to strengthen macro-adjustment and rationalize the regional investment structure while fully utilizing the market mechanism's adjustment role.

5.2 Consumption Demand and National Economic Operation

Another component of total social demand is consumption demand. Its role in the national economic operation can also be analyzed from both aggregate and structural aspects.

5.2.1 The Level of Consumption and Its Determination

5.2.1.1 Implication of the Consumption Level

The consumption level, i.e., the level of consumption demand, refers to the sum of the quantity and quality of consumption materials and services consumed by people in a certain period. It indicates the degree to which social consumption demand is satisfied. There are two ways to express the consumption level: one is the total social consumption, i.e., the sum of the actual consumption of consumer goods by residents and social collectives; the other is the per capita consumption, namely the average consumption by population, calculated based on the previous indicator by adding the factor of population change.

5.2.1.2 Determination of the Level of Residents' Individual Consumption

The social consumption level formed in a certain period is influenced and conditioned by several factors. Fundamentally, it depends on the development level of social productivity, thereby governed by the GDP or national income level and a range of social, historical, and cultural factors. Therefore, analyzing the mechanism determining the social consumption level is crucial to achieving a balance between total social supply and demand. Since individual residents' consumption is the essential component of total social consumption, the following analysis focuses on the consumption level of individual residents.

In a market economy, residents first obtain money income through various means and then generate the demand for various consumer goods through money expenditure. This constitutes the majority of individual residents' consumption demand. Therefore, the consumption level of individual residents in a certain period depends primarily on their income level, which, in turn, depends on the GDP of that period. A higher proportion of GDP is transformed into the income of individual residents through primary distribution and redistribution, creating their affordable consumption demand. Individual residents' income includes labor income and various non-labor incomes, such as interest income, dividends and bonuses from purchasing stocks and bonds, as well as operating revenues and rent from rental housing.

After receiving money income, residents pay various individual income taxes according to the taxation system and rates, and deduct various non-tax payments. The remaining amount is their disposable personal income (DPI), which forms the basis for their consumption demand. However, the consumption funds formed by DPI are not equal to actual consumption. In real economic life, DPI is generally divided into two parts: expenditure for purchasing consumer goods and savings not used for current consumption. Therefore, the real consumption level depends on the actual consumer spending, i.e., DPI minus the residents' savings.

Regarding expenditure intention, DPI can be divided roughly into three levels: (i) daily expenditure: spending that meets basic needs; (ii) spending expenditure: spending beyond basic needs, which depends on specific circumstances to occur; (iii) preventive expenditure: savings for future needs, such as old age, living security, children's education, and life improvement. Among these components, basic consumer spending for the present and savings for future preventive needs are relatively stable. Only pending expenditure has substantial variability, transforming between consumption and savings according to different conditions, thus determining the actual consumption level.

Factors influencing the conversion of DPI into consumption or savings.

(1) *Income level of the residents*

Income and consumption are closely linked; income level determines consumption level and is the most critical factor affecting consumption and savings. Different income levels dictate different consumption and saving levels. Generally, as income levels rise, consumption and savings increase, and vice versa. Initially, as residents' income increases, they may save most of their new income due to long-established consumption habits, resulting in consumer spending lagging behind income growth (the hysteretic nature of consumption). However, continued income growth will gradually lead to proportionate increases in consumption and savings, forming new consumption habits.

However, if residents' income expectations are uncertain and their expenditure expectations, such as pensions, health care, housing, and children's education, are "rigid," their consumption demand (expenditure) will not increase significantly in the short term. For example, in previous years, China's lack of effective demand was related to unstable income and increased expenditure expectations caused by various reform measures enacted in a short time. Nowadays, the general increase in Chinese residents' income has led to increased consumption levels. However, the widening gap in income distribution will, in turn, lead to a decreasing propensity to consume and insufficient effective demand, thus inhibiting economic growth. Therefore, while raising the residents' income, it is also necessary to effectively adjust the widening income distribution gap.

(2) *Changes in the price level of consumer goods' and the price expectation*

If the price level is stable, consumer spending will increase steadily with income levels, and savings will also rise steadily. If prices rise in the short term, more money must be spent to maintain the original consumption level. If income remains unchanged or does not increase proportionally with prices, consumer spending can only increase by reducing savings. If residents expect prices to continue rising, they may withdraw savings to buy goods, leading to a decrease in savings, a sudden increase in consumption, and a tight market supply.

(3) *Consumer goods supply adapted to the residents' consumption structure*

If the supply of scarce marketable goods grows faster, the part of DPI spent on consumption will increase significantly, with savings decreasing accordingly. If the supply of such goods grows slowly, DPI will be partially forced to convert into savings because of the inability to spend on things, and the savings thus formed will have the form of "forced substitution". Especially in the case of rapid changes in the consumption structure caused by a significant increase in residents' income, if the supply structure of consumer goods cannot adapt to such changes in the short term, and if the supply of goods that can meet residents' consumption demand in the market is inadequate, most residents' new income will inevitably be converted into savings.

(4) *Savings deposits interest rate or return on assets (ROA)*

The extent to which the interest rate of deposits affects the proportion of the DPI transformed into consumption or savings also depends on the changes in the factors mentioned above. Suppose the DPI in the market is established, prices rise faster, and residents expect prices to continue to rise, or the goods supply in the market adapted to residents' consumption structure has increased by a larger margin, the higher deposit interest rates may not necessarily reduce consumption or increase savings. On the contrary, if the price increase is not significant, and the residents expect that the price level will be stable in the future, or the goods supply adapted to the residents' consumption structure in the market grows slowly, then raising the interest rate on deposits will play a significant role in attracting more savings. Since ROA moves inversely to the interest rate on savings deposits, they play different roles in converting income into savings, investment, or consumption.

(5) *Money illusion*

Under the condition that money income changes in proportion to prices while the real income remains unchanged, those who only see an increase in the price level but ignore the proportional increase in their money income will believe that their real income is decreasing and thus may save less and consume relatively more. On the contrary, those who only see an increase in money income but ignore the same proportional price level will believe that their real income has increased and thus may save more and consume less.

The various factors mentioned above have different effects on how the income is distributed between consumption or saving. The actual consumption level depends on the interaction of these factors.

5.2.2 *Consumption Structure and Its Determination*

Consumption structure is an essential part of the national economic structure. A reasonable consumption structure and its optimization and upgrading reflect the consumption rise and significantly contribute to establishing a reasonable industrial structure. Simultaneously, it's of great significance to the stable and coordinated development of the national economy.

5.2.2.1 Implication of Consumption Structure

The consumption structure can be interpreted from different perspectives. For instance, the proportional relationship between different types of consumption materials consumed in the consumption process, the respective shares of various types of consumer goods and labor services in the process of consumption behavior, as well as their mutual substitution and complementary relationships. Moreover, the proportion of various types of consumption materials (labor services) in the total consumer spending formed in the contradictory movement of demand and supply and their interrelationship, and the like can also be taken into consideration.

If starting from the definitive property of combining quality and quantity, consumption structure can be defined as the composition of various consumption objects consumed in the consumption process and the degree of their coordination. The quality of the consumption structure includes that of the consumer goods themselves, the mutual coordination of various consumer goods, the consumption environment, and the consumers' ability to enjoy various consumer goods, as well as the comfort and convenience of the consumption process, so as to the psychological and spiritual enjoyment and pleasure consumers get. The quantity of the consumption structure is the unity of various consumption objects' physical and value quantities.

5.2.2.2 Division of Consumption Structure

(1) *Physical value structures of consumption*

The material object's name and quantity of a series of consumption materials and services can express the physical consumption structure. In contrast, the value structure is expressed by the quantity and percentage of various money outlays in personal income. Farmers also have a certain amount of self-sufficient subsistence consumption in rural areas, which generally cannot be expressed through the value structure.

(2) *Household consumption structure and social consumption structure*

In actual life and economic statistics, the commonly used division criterion is dividing consumption materials into several categories, such as clothing, food, housing, and transportation, based on consumption behavior. They can be subdivided into clothing, food, supplies, and other compositions, among which food composition is at the fundamental level. The above division belongs to the residential household or micro consumption structure. Social consumption structure, or macro consumption structure, is not simply the sum of residents' household consumption structure but also includes elements beyond the summation, i.e., the ratio of residents' consumption to public consumption and the ratio of different social groups' consumption.

5.2.2.3 Changing Trend of Consumption Structure

Since the factors affecting the consumption structure are diverse and constantly changing, the consumption structure is also in a constant changing trend. With the development of the economy, the increase in income level, and the advancement of the society, the consumption structure will change as follows.

(1) *Changes in the hierarchy of needs*

Consumption means can be divided into subsistence, enjoyment, and development. With the development of production and the increase of income, the percentage of subsistence means is decreasing, and that enjoyment and development is increasing. A hierarchy of consumption demand exists objectively: subsistence means mainly meet the workers' most basic needs, belonging to lower-level needs. However, means of enjoyment and development enable workers to get healthier bodies, richer scientific and cultural knowledge, and more energy, belonging to higher-level needs. As time passes, these three kinds of materials will increase in an absolute amount. However, because of physiological factors, the demand for survival materials is limited, while the demand for enjoyment and development materials is endless. In the long run, the percentage of survival materials will gradually decrease. In contrast, the percentage of enjoyment and development materials will gradually increase.

(2) *Changes in consumption behavior*

Looking at the changes in consumption structure by distinguishing consumption behavior, i.e., the expenditures for food, clothing, housing, utility, transportation, and other spending categories, it is easy to find a trend: as the income level increases, the food percentage will keep decreasing, and that clothing, housing, and utility will increase in varying degrees. The above discovery can be illustrated by Engel's law. Ernst Engel, a famous German statistician in the nineteenth century, found that as a household's and individuals' income rises, the percentage of income spent on food decreases, and the coefficient reflecting this law is called Engel's Coefficient. Its commonly used formula is:

$$Engel's\ Coefficient = \frac{expenditure\ on\ food}{total\ living\ expenses} \tag{5.1}$$

Engel's Coefficient is widely applied by countries worldwide, and it depicts the quantitative relationship between residents' food expenditures and total living expenses. As a fundamental law measuring the change in consumption structure, Engel's law is applicable in China, mainly manifested in a marked increase in Chinese urban residents' income, the increase in yearly consumer spending, the significant improvement in living standards, and the general trend of Engel's Coefficient steadily decreasing. According to the standards proposed by the United Nations Food and Agriculture Organization (FAO), Engel's Coefficient can be used to distinguish between poor and wealthy consumers. The coefficient above 59% represents poverty, 50%–59% a state where daily needs are barely met (food and clothing), 40%–50% a moderately well-off standard of living, 30%–40% a wealthy life, and below 30% the most affluent.

Another American economist Paul Samuelson, in his book *Economics*, coauthored with William Nordhaus, further analyzed Engel's Law and proposed a Samuelson Engel's Coefficient that differs from Engel Engel's Coefficient as follows:

$$Samuelson\, Engel's\, coefficient = \frac{expenditure\, on food}{total\, spending} \tag{5.2}$$

where total spending = consumer spending + savings.

Samuelson Engel's Coefficient is somewhat different from Engel Engel's Coefficient: Samuelson Engel's Coefficient examines the relationship between food expenditure and total spending, reflecting the changing pattern of the proportion of total spending devoted to food, whereas Engel Engel's Coefficient examines only the relationship between food expenditures and all living expenses, without considering the factor of savings. Samuelson Engel's Coefficient includes savings because it can remind people to pay attention to the convertible relationship between savings and consumption when studying consumption.

The *China Statistical Yearbook* divides household consumption expenditures into eight items:

- food, including staple food, non-staple food, sugar, cigarettes, alcohol, and other food;
- clothing, including apparel, clothing materials, shoes, socks, hats, and others, and clothing processing costs;
- household facilities, articles, and services, including durable consumer goods, furniture, and household services;
- medicines and medical services, including medical apparatus, health care products, medical charges, and the like;
- transportation and communication, including traveling expenses, telephone bill, postage, and the like;
- cultural, educational, and recreational articles and services, including educational expenses, cultural and recreational fees, and the like;
- residence, including housing, water, electricity, and fuel costs;

- miscellaneous goods and services, including personal consumption, other commodities, and other service fees.

(3) *Changes in consumption forms*

With the transformation of agriculture from traditional subsistence and semi-subsistence economy to commercialization, specialization, and modernization, farmers' monetary income has increased significantly. Their production and life have becoming more integrated into a commodity-money relationship, which implies that traditional non-market consumption is gradually declining. As a result, the share of market consumption is increasing with that of non-market consumption is gradually decreasing. At the same time, labor service consumption has developed dramatically with the developing tertiary industry and its commercialization. With the growth of urban and rural residents' money income, the increasing socialization of domestic work, and the development of science, technology, culture, education, and other services, residents' labor expenditures will increase rapidly, leading to the increasing share of market consumption as a whole.

(4) *General changes in consumer groups*

From the long-term development trend, with the increase of residents' income level, the growth of residents' collective consumption accelerates, and its proportion increases day by day. The growth of individual consumption is slower than residents' collective consumption, and its proportion decreases relatively. Moreover, the absolute amount of social consumption is relatively stable or grows slowly, and its proportion in the overall consumption decreases gradually. In the individual consumption structure, residents' collective consumption, and social consumption, the collective consumption of residents grows the fastest. It's mainly because (i) culture, education, and scientific research are more important in economic and social development in modern times. However, their consumption is suitable to collective form, so their consumption amount is bound to become one staple of residents' collective consumption. The accelerated development of culture, education, and scientific research is bound to cause the whole populations' growth of collective consumption; and (ii) with the improving consumption level, people require more, better, and abundant literature and art, sports, medicines, and medical services, which also needs a faster growth of residents' collective consumption.

5.2.2.4 Determination from the Consumption Structure

In a certain period, people consume different kinds of consumer goods and services, thus constituting a certain consumption structure, which is an important symbol of the social consumption situation in a certain period. Since the consumption demand constantly changes, the associated consumption structure also changes constantly. In different countries or different periods of the same country, the consumption structure often shows considerable differences due to differences in economic conditions. The consumption structure in a given period results from a combination of factors. The main factors influencing its changes are as follows.

(1) *The income level of the residents*

It is the most fundamental factor affecting the consumption structure. Engel's Law points out an inherent regular connection between the residents' income level and consumption structure. Using this law, the trend of consumption structure changes can be examined and used as a criterion to measure the consumption level. From the long-term development trend, when people reach a certain level of improvement in food after a certain period, the proportion of food expenditure in the residents' consumption structure tends to decline as their income increases.

(2) *Income structure of residents*

Based on the income level of households, residents' income is divided into high, medium, and low levels. The structure of residents' income refers to the income groups of different levels and their composition shares. The social consumption structure depends on the proportion of income groups of different levels in the total residential households and their consumption structure. By and large, Engel's Coefficient is smaller for a larger share of households at higher income levels but larger for a larger share at lower income levels.

(3) *The price*

By price here, we mean both the absolute price of consumer goods and their relative prices. The latter refers to the proportionality of prices of various consumer goods, including price differences between similar products and price ratios between dissimilar products. The rise and fall and adjusting the price system will impact consumption demand and structure. For commodities of different natures, the sensitivity of the demand's response to price changes—i.e., the price elasticity of demand—is different. Generally speaking, those commodities and non-essential goods accounting for a larger share of consumer expenditures and having more substitutes have higher price elasticity. In this regard, price changes have a greater impact on the consumption structure. In comparison, those commodities and essential goods accounting for a smaller share of consumer expenditures and with fewer substitutes have lower price elasticity, and thus, price changes have a minor impact on the consumption structure. In addition to the price of the goods themselves, prices related to their utility, maintenance, and restoration also have ramifications for the residents' consumption behavior and, thus, the consumption structure.

(4) *The commodity*

It refers to the influence of the variety, quantity, quality, design and color, packaging, and merchandise available on consumption behavior. Products meeting the consumers' needs in all aspects can promote consumer purchases. While, on the contrary, those products failing to meet consumer satisfaction in all aspects may influence consumer purchases. In this way, the factors of the goods influence the change in consumption structure by affecting consumption behavior.

(5) *The individual consumers*

It is a wide range of factors, including consumer knowledge, consumer preferences, the content of knowing market information, the exemplary influence of the consumption level in the surrounding social environment, the consumer's evaluation of time, judgment or expectation caused by the uncertainty of the economic development process and future conditions, and the like, and even factors of purely psychological activities.

(6) *Society's guidance on consumption behavior*

It refers to the guiding ideology of consumption advocated by society, the consumption policies formulated by the government, and the propaganda of products by enterprises through advertising and publicity campaigns. All of these influence the residents' consumption behavior and thus affect the consumption structure.

(7) *The industrial and supply structures also directly affect the consumption structure*

Consumer goods' production and supply status ultimately govern the type and quantity of residents' consumption. In addition, the composition of the population (including regions, ethnic groups, age, gender, occupation, as well as cultural and educational levels), consumption traditions, and external consumption culture all influence the residents' consumption views, thereby affecting their consumption behavior and structure.

The development level of social productivity fundamentally governs the consumption structure of a particular period, which is determined by people's income level and the production industrial structure governed by a certain level of social productivity. With the production developing and people's income level increasing, the consumption structure will change accordingly, which, in turn, will have a meaningful impact on the status and development trend of industrial structure. The industrial structure must be adapted to and follow the changes in the consumption structure. If this is taken as the starting point when arranging social production, then social demand and social production will be closely dovetailed, thus achieving the balance of total social supply and demand.

5.2.3 The Function of Consumption Demand on Operating the National Economy

5.2.3.1 The Function of Consumption Demand in Driving Economic Growth

Consumption demand must be subject to the following two conditions. One is the desire to obtain a particular commodity, the other is possessing an equivalent good that can be offered in exchange. Specifically, demand implies the unity of the purchasing desire and the means. In a sense, consumption demand refers to the part of the demand paid in money, and only such a demand is regarded as an actual demand.

The pulling effect of expanding consumption demand on economic growth can be divided between direct and indirect pulls. The direct pull refers to the growing consumer goods production as a direct result of expansion in consumption demand within the boundaries of existing production capacity. By contrast, the indirect pull refers to consumption demand as the initial variable, driving economic growth by pulling other variables. Specifically, the process begins when the growing consumption demand enlarges the market and induces additional investment by manufacturers, which, in turn, drives economic growth more substantially. This process can be interpreted as the "acceleration principle," i.e., a little increase in consumption demand will lead to an enormous increase in investment demand. However, consumption demand must maintain sustained expansion to remain investment demand growth unchanged.

Marx's conditions of realizing social reproduction can illustrate this problem. Since the products of department II, i.e., II $(c + v + m)$, consist entirely of consumption means in physical form. Therefore, the conditions of realizing the value of department II products directly reflecting the constraining effect of consumption demand on economic growth. From the supply point of view, whether it is simple or expanded reproduction, as one of the conditions for realizing social reproduction, the total amount of department II products must meet the needs of the two major departments of physical compensation for consumption means. However, from the demand point of view, the value of all department II products must equal the consumption demand of the whole society. Without the growing consumption demand, the value of the products produced by department II cannot be fully realized in the market, the expansion of reproduction cannot be carried out, neither can the growth of variable capital be realized in the two major departments. As a result, the additional demand for production means will not be formed in department II, which will eventually restrict production growth in department I.

However, the pulling effect of consumption demand on economic growth is conditional on the absence of resource constraints in economic activity. If not, the demand increase will fail to lead to a corresponding supply increase, instead, it will lead to inflation or even to the coexistence of inflation and shortage. This was an important reason for the successive inflation experienced by China in the 1980s.

Even if investment demand is stimulated to boost economic growth, it ultimately depends on the residents' marginal propensity to consume, i.e., on the response of consumption demand to macro policies. Without consumption demand, the multiplier effect of investment demand is also difficult to generate or achieve the established multiplier effect of investment.

In China's economic development, the pull of consumption demand on the economy is especially significant. From the late 1970s to the early 1990s, consumption demand played an important role in pulling various demand factors on China's GDP growth. The rapidly expanding consumption demand posed great pressure on

China's economy. However, objectively, it also created a relaxed market environment for developing non-public enterprises and reforming state-owned enterprises (SOEs), thus laying the foundation for economic growth. Given the global financial crisis and the weakening role of net export demand in driving economic growth, expanding domestic demand, especially domestic consumption demand, has become increasingly important in driving China's economic growth. At present, consumption demand is playing an increasingly important role in driving economic growth.

5.2.3.2 The Stabilizing Effect of Consumption Demand on Economic Growth

Economic growth does not follow a continuous upward or downward trend; fluctuations are an inevitable part of every business cycle. Economic fluctuations can arise from either supply-side or demand-side factors, leading to demand-volatility or supply-volatility cycles. In a demand-driven cycle, the primary factor causing economic fluctuations may be investment or consumption demand. The relationship between the growth rates of consumption demand and investment demand determines whether consumption demand is the main factor driving economic fluctuations. Ultimately, whether these fluctuations are due to investment demand or consumption demand, they are constrained by consumption demand. Therefore, adjusting consumption demand is a crucial countercyclical tool.

The relatively stable fluctuations in consumption demand can be explained in different ways. Firstly, there is rigidity in consumer spending, based on the relative income hypothesis consumption function. According to this theory, a household's expenditure level depends not on its absolute income but on its relative income. For overall consumption behavior, since current consumer spending is determined by the highest income level previously attained, consumers strive to maintain a relatively constant consumption level, forming a non-proportional consumption-income relationship in the short term. As a result, the share of consumer spending in income inversely correlates with income level changes during economic fluctuations. Secondly, as long as economic fluctuations do not significantly impact consumer income in the short term to the extent that they alter consumers' expectations of future income, they are unlikely to change consumer behavior patterns. Consequently, these fluctuations cannot have a decisive impact on total consumption demand.

Both expenditure and income factors contribute to the stability of consumption demand, but determining which factor is more influential requires case-by-case analysis. The stability of consumption demand in the business cycle is evident as its fluctuations are smaller in magnitude compared to those of investment demand and GDP. Additionally, consumption demand tends to lag behind investment demand in terms of timing. This relatively stable consumer spending behavior is a crucial factor in maintaining economic cycle stability.

In addition, as the final demand in the national economy, consumption demand consistently restrains the fluctuations in investment demand. During periods of rapid decline in investment demand, consumption demand tends to decrease more slowly. Especially in the early stages of a decline in investment demand, consumption demand might continue to grow, thereby mitigating the decline in investment demand from a market demand perspective. Conversely, during periods of rapid increase in investment demand, the relatively slower rise in consumption demand limits the potential for further investment expansion, eventually causing investment demand to slow down and stabilize. In summary, when fluctuations in investment demand cause turbulence in the national economy, consumption demand can significantly prevent the economy from rising or falling too rapidly, thereby reducing overall economic volatility.

5.3 Net Export Demand and National Economic Operation

A market economy is inherently an open economy. Under open conditions, it is essential to analyze the performance of import and export trade and the balance of payments, examining their impact on the overall balance of supply and demand in society. A country's foreign economic ties encompass a wide range of elements, with the primary ones being the international flow of goods (export and import trade) and capital flows.

After export trade occurs, the domestically produced products supply domestic demand for consumer goods and investment goods and export a portion of them abroad to supply foreign demand. At this point, the total social demand comprises domestic and foreign demand. The growth of investment demand, a component of total social demand, can lead to total social demand growth and supply multiplied by expanding in investment demand itself under the condition that the existing production resources of the society are not fully utilized. This expansion process is realized through the mechanism of investment multipliers. After the export trade occurs, the exports growth caused by that foreign demand has the same effect on the growth of total social demand. In this way, total social supply as the aforementioned growth of investment demand. The exports growth must also cause a multiplied growth of aggregate demand and supply. The difference is that in an open economy, where there are exports, there are imports. When there is a specific initial increase in exports, part of the resulting equivalent income, in addition to consumption and savings, will be used for imports, increasing aggregate demand and supply to several times the initial increase in exports. The mechanism of this expansion process is the same as that of the above-mentioned investment multiplier, with the difference that $\frac{1}{s}$ in the multiplier formula is transformed into $\frac{1}{s+m}$, which is less than $\frac{1}{s}$.

The core of the foreign trade multiplier theory is that since the income increase caused by the exports increase cannot be fully used for savings and imports, a trade surplus is always beneficial for the growth of domestic employment and income.

The theory of foreign trade multiplier suggests that export growth causes a multiplication of aggregate demand and aggregate supply. However, its realization must have certain preconditions: (i) Productive resources (including workforce) are not fully utilized. For example, the equipment capacity of the relevant industrial sector is still partially unused, and the workforce is not yet fully employed. (ii) The demand for investment goods, intermediate goods, and consumer goods directly or indirectly caused by the growing export demand can be satisfied smoothly. In other words, the production of the relevant sectors to satisfy these demands can proceed smoothly without bottlenecks. (iii) The marginal consumption rate, or the marginal savings rate, as well as the marginal import rate are relatively stable, and the like.

Only under these conditions will the growth of exports cause a multiplication of aggregate demand, supply, and income growth. Suppose the growth of aggregate demand caused by that of exports, together with that of investment, directly and indirectly, exceeds the limits of the growth of total productive capacity constrained by domestic production resources. In that case, it leads to imbalances in the structure of aggregate domestic demand and the balance of payments, increasing the overall price level.

5.3.1 The Impact of Import Trade on Aggregate Supply and Demand

In an open economy, whether the total social demand grows due to the growth of investment, exports, or consumption, part of this demand will inevitably be directed towards foreign products, leading to an increase in imports. The marginal import rate is the ratio between income growth amount caused by the growth of total social demand, as mentioned earlier, and the amount of import growth caused by it. Assuming a constant exchange rate and import prices, the size of the marginal import rate depends on the income elasticity of a country's demand for imports (the ratio of the growth rate of imports to the growth rate of income). This income elasticity of demand for imports is, in turn, influenced by the country's demand patterns and industrial structure.

When domestic production capacity is fully utilized, expanding imports can reduce the pressure of demand expansion, because imports have shifted some demand to foreign products, thus easing the pressure on the demand for domestic products. However, excessive imports may cause a trade deficit. Thus, increasing imports can be detrimental to domestic economic growth when domestic production resources are underutilized. Imports are necessary only when they can, in turn, promote significant export growth.

5.3.2 Net Export Demand and Economic Growth

By examining the relationship between import and export trades and the total social supply and demand, it is evident that exports expand total social demand while imports expand total social supply. However, imports and exports do not operate in isolation, they affect both total social demand and supply. Therefore, it is necessary to consider imports and exports together to understand the impact of international trade on total social supply and demand, as well as the conditions required for their balance. In an open economy, total social demand consists of domestic consumption, investment, and foreign demands, while total social supply consists of domestically produced consumer and investment goods and imported products. Due to the influence of imports and exports, to maintain the balance of total social supply and demand, the following condition must be met: exports must equal imports.

However, typically, it is rarely the case that international trade achieves exact equality between exports and imports, because there is always a certain balance between them. When exports exceed imports, there is a trade surplus (net exports), while when imports exceed exports, there is a trade deficit (net imports). Focusing solely on import and export trades, two scenarios may emerge when there is a trade surplus or deficit: (i) There is an imbalance between domestic total social supply and demand. This imbalance can be compensated by the trade deficit or surplus, ensuring that aggregate demand, including foreign demand, and aggregate supply, including foreign supply, are balanced overall. (ii) The gross domestic supply and demand are balanced in the aggregate, but due to the emerging total import and export deficit or surplus, total social supply and demand become imbalanced. If the gross domestic supply exceeds the gross domestic demand, achieving a balance in total social supply and demand requires net exports, resulting in an international trade surplus. Conversely, suppose the gross domestic demand exceeds the gross domestic supply, this balance must be achieved through net imports, resulting in an international trade deficit. However, a chronic trade deficit must be addressed promptly to avoid negative impacts on economic growth.

5.3.3 Optimizing Import and Export Structure and National Economic Operation

The level of imports and exports not only influences the operation of the national economy under open conditions but is also closely related to the import and export structure. A country's or region's import and export structure reflects its comparative advantage, resource advantage, and scale advantage within the global division of labor. The import and export structure can be understood on two levels. In a narrow sense, it primarily refers to the proportional relationship between various import and export products of a country or region, which is the core aspect related to upgrading a country's or region's industrial structure and its position within the center-periphery model. In a broader sense, it's based on the structure of import and export products and includes various other aspects such as trade modes, patterns, subjects, and regional trade distribution.

5.3.3.1 Implication of the Broadly Defined Import and Export Structure

When analyzing the role of optimizing the import and export structure in promoting the national economy, we focus primarily on the broadly defined import and export structure. This broader structure encompasses several key aspects, including:

(1) *The structure of import and export commodities*

The structure of import and export commodities refers to the composition of major or specific commodities in a country's external trade during a specific period. Among them, the structure of import trade commodities is the ratio of the import volume of various major categories of commodities, or a certain commodity, to the total value of import trade, while the structure of export trade commodities is the ratio related to the same indicator of the export. These ratios are typically expressed as percentages.

According to the different factor intensities, export commodities can be divided into four categories: resource-intensive, labor-intensive, capital-intensive, and technology-intensive. The amount of various factor-intensive products that a country exports is closely related to its economic base and its comparative advantage within the global division of labor. The exports of different factor-intensive products reflect the level of economic and technological development, industrial structure status, and resource status of the country or region.

Regardless of transaction costs, a balanced international division of labor and trade structure would be as follows: Resource-rich countries would export resource-intensive products, countries with large populations and abundant workforces would develop labor-intensive industries, and developed countries would dominate the production and export of capital-intensive and technology-intensive products, positioning themselves as the "front-runners" of the world economy. However, due to transaction costs, market incompleteness, and other constraints, this balanced structural system is difficult to establish. The factor endowment advantages of each country tend to operate within a region below the equilibrium point, resulting in an imbalanced global trade commodity structure.

Several possible forms of an imbalanced foreign trade commodity structure can be formed in the Pareto improvement state of the general participating countries. Firstly, relatively backward countries with low-level factor endowments (natural resources or workforces) may be over-exploited, forcing them to continue exporting resource- intensive and labor-intensive products. This situation can trap them in a comparative advantage trap, relegating them to the "periphery" of the world economy due to their low-level foreign trade export structure. Meanwhile, any country has a strong national consciousness and a strong desire to establish an advanced industrial system, so the advanced factor advantages of developed countries (abundant capital and advanced technology) may be constrained to varying degrees. As a result, these advantages cannot be fully utilized in a perfectly competitive market, making it challenging to achieve Pareto efficiency. Additionally, some newly industrialized or post-industrialized countries undergoing rapid development and transition may sacrifice their temporary comparative advantages to achieve explosive upgrades in their overall economic structure. However, this approach can sometimes run counter to promoting global interests, leading to more complex non-equilibrium characteristics in their foreign trade structure.

Of course, in a two-country trade exchange model consisting of developed and lagging countries, the developed country may achieve a disequilibrium of super Pareto optimal. For example, in a center-periphery pattern, the advanced countries may subordinate the lagging countries while becoming more robust. In contrast, the late-developing countries may fully leverage their comparative advantages to leapfrog.

(2) *The structure of foreign trade patterns*

It mainly refers to the proportion of various trade patterns in a country's foreign trade pattern. The term "foreign trade mode" here refers not limited to the foreign commodity trade mode, i.e., the specific practices used by a country or region in trading with other countries or regions, such as general, processing, barter, and compensatory trades. It also includes trades in services, technology, and other areas.

The primary modes of trade adopted by different countries vary in foreign trade transactions. In periods of low economic development, general trade has been the primary method of conducting trade between countries. Hence, the implication of trade is the import and export of commodities. After the mid-twentieth century, the proportion of processing trade began to increase, especially in countries with abundant labor resources but extremely scarce capital and technology. These countries tended to put more effort into developing processing trade, and this structural policy choice and practice basically features the trade structure of most countries in the "take-off" stage. When a country's economy further develops, its share of trade in services, technology, and others areas is increasing.

In fact, the characteristics of a country's trade mode structure are often linked to that of its factor endowment structure and commodity structure. For example, in a country with a strong labor force but weaknesses in other factors, the processing trade relying on foreign resources and markets can tap into local strengths and accommodate other countries' interests. Therefore, it is a prudent policy choice.

(3) *The structure of the foreign trade mode*

It mainly refers to foreign trade activities based on a specific form of labor division. There are two basic models. One is the vertical labor division based on comparative advantage and factor endowment structure, and the corresponding inter-industry trade mode is formed between participating countries. The other is the horizontal labor division based on product differentiation and economies of scale, and the corresponding intra-industry trade model is formed between participating countries. Obviously, developed countries hope to realize inter-industry labor divisions and trade with developing countries, and the share of the intra-industry labor division and trade among developed countries has risen after the Second World War. Since all countries have the enthusiasm and urge to accelerate their economic development, a continuous mutual game emerges in the real world, characterized by imbalanced trade modes to build a more favorable imbalanced structure for their countries.

(4) *Market structure of foreign trade*

It mainly refers to the position where the trade volume of each country or region in the total import and export trades of a country or region in a certain period. In other words, it implicates the geographical structure of foreign trade. Specifically, there are two market structure types. One is the export market structure. It is mainly expressed by the share of a country's or region's exports to other countries or regions in total exports. The other is the import market structure. It is mainly expressed by the proportion of a country's or region's imports from other countries or regions relative to the total imports. Moreover, the geographical structure of foreign trade includes external and internal regional structures. The former is the geographical direction of foreign trade, which reflects the position of different countries or regions in their foreign trade process, mainly influenced by the economic boom, interconnectedness, geopolitics, and other factors. The latter refers to a country's regional structure, that is, the distribution of foreign trade within different regions of a country.

5.3.3.2 Optimization of Import and Export Structure and National Economic Operation

Due to market incompleteness, information asymmetry, or underemployment, any country's or region's import and export structure tends to be imbalanced. Two important reasons determining the imbalanced state of import and export structure are particularly pointed out here. (i) The factor supply market of any country or region is imbalanced due to resource scarcity. This imbalance in the factor market translates into an imbalanced product market structure. Foreign trade and its structure, a further extension of the domestic economy, will also exhibit imbalanced characteristics. Even large countries with abundant and diverse resources cannot establish a balanced economic structure due to their gradient differences in regional economic conditions. (ii) In an open economy, every country or region always participates in the international division of labor system and occupies the corresponding position on the premise of promoting the welfare of the world or participating countries. Therefore, almost any country or region must first recognize the comparative advantage of each participating country. In this regard, the initial imbalanced foreign trade structure exists. At the same time, an open economy brings not only changes in the domestic goods market. For example, influenced by international resource allocation, factor markets are constantly changing, while commodity markets have contributed to evolving foreign trade structure production capacity, influenced by international industrial transfers.

International trade theory and empirical studies have demonstrated that a country or region's foreign trade structure constantly changes with economic and trade growth. There is an important pattern to this change: economic and trade growth can increase the proportion of manufactured goods in exports. In other words, in a country's economic growth, the proportion of exports of primary products will continue to decrease while that of manufactured goods continues to rise.

This pattern can be examined in the context of developed countries. Prior to the First Industrial Revolution, all countries were in the stage of agricultural societies with relatively low productivity. The foreign trade structure of major exporting countries was mainly luxury goods, some agricultural products and foodstuffs demanded by enslavers, feudal lords, or other upper classes. With the advent of the First Industrial Revolution, the industrial structure of Britain, France, and other European countries began to industrialize, following a progression from "light industry — heavy industry — high-tech industry" toward the advanced level. This period also marked a new phase in human consumption, characterized by a hierarchical progression from "light industrial goods to heavy industrial goods to high-tech goods." When the domestic demand of these industrialized "leading countries" reaches a certain satisfaction degree, their exports of related products tend to reach an advanced foreign trade structure, showing a trend from "light industrial goods export-oriented" to "heavy industrial goods export-oriented" and ultimately to "high-tech goods export-oriented."

Two main facilitation approaches exist on this general foreign trade structure evolution path.

The first is the facilitation of comparative advantage. The upgrading of the foreign trade structure is achieved mainly through the continuous dynamic enhancement of a country's comparative advantage. According to the doctrine of comparative advantage, labor division under this principle can promote the comparative interests of participating countries as well as the upgrading of the domestic industrial structure while increasing interests. In particular, the pre-existing advantages of industrialization in developed countries will be strengthened and naturally take the lead in upgrading industrial structures. Over time, the late-developing countries will follow the same path to realize upgrading industrial structures.

It should be noted that under the arrangement of this labor division principle, it is an eternal affirmation and strengthening of static comparative advantage. The first-mover countries always stand at the forefront of innovation, i.e., "the strong get stronger, and the weak get weaker", showing the "strong non-equilibrium" structural characteristics. The early-developing countries are always at the forefront of innovation, i.e., "the strong are getting stronger while the weak are always weaker," showing the structural characteristics of strong disequilibrium. In contrast, the late-developing countries remain relatively behind, displaying the characteristics of "weak disequilibrium".

The second is the facilitation of late-developing advantages. It is mainly for the late-developing countries to catch up with the early-developing ones despite their relatively backward conditions. If the labor division is based solely on the principle of comparative advantage, late-developing countries can only follow the path taken by the early-developing ones, resulting in the imbalanced "natural evolution" of foreign trade structure. Consequently, they remain relatively inferior in the advanced structure, i.e., falling into the comparative advantage trap. For this reason, the late-developing countries must explore late-developing advantage, namely a unique advantage brought by backwardness, to promote the advanced foreign trade structure. By doing so, they can catch up with early-developing countries and realize the fundamental transformation of the entire economy from weak disequilibrium to strong.

5.3.3.3 The Panorama of China's Foreign Trade Structure

In 2009, although China replaced Germany as the world's largest trading country, it still does not qualify as a trading power, particularly due to its relatively backward trade structure. Regarding the commodity structure of import and export trade, the trade development in tangible goods like merchandise is rapid, whereas intangible goods like services and technology lags. Moreover, regarding the export goods structure, most of the industrially manufactured goods exported are labor-intensive and low-value-added. In contrast, China remains a typical small trading country concerning capital and technology-intensive goods export trade. Furthermore, if regarding the trade mode structure, more than half of China's commodities are realized through processing trade, and the proportion of service trade is relatively small. As China's participation in the breadth and depth of the international division of labor strengths, intra-industry trade is expected to develop more rapidly. Regarding the trade market structure, China's foreign trade is focused on a few countries and regions, which increases the riskiness of foreign trade and weakens its flexibility and competitiveness. The changes in foreign trade structure reflect the development level of China's economy and technology, which is the deep-seated reason why foreign trade affects economic development. In the future, if China aims to become a trading power, it must accelerate the optimization of its import and export structure to promote better and faster development of the national economy.

5.3.4 The Influence of the Balance Between Payments and Exchange Rate on Balancing Total Social Supply and Demand

In an open economy, the balance of a country's aggregate supply and demand also involves the balance-of-payments equilibrium problem, which is influenced by international trade. An imbalance between gross domestic supply and demand will lead to the balance-of-payments disequilibrium. If this disequilibrium persists over time, adjustments in domestic supply and demand are necessary to stabilize the balance of payments.

5.3.4.1 Balance of Payments and Its Disequilibrium Expressions

The balance of payments, i.e., the international foreign exchange receipts and payments, mainly reflects a country's total foreign exchange balance over a specific period (usually one year). The balance of payments is divided into two fundamental parts.

One component is the current account, which represents spending and receipts on import and export trade. This account has two branches: tangible and intangible trade items (or non-trade transactions). Tangible trade refers to the import and export of goods, while intangible trade refers to the import and export of services, such as freight transport, port supply and services, tourism income, investment income and expenditure, the revenue and expenditure of the government system, income and expenditure of contracted services, and others. Exports generate foreign exchange earnings, while imports generate foreign exchange expenditures. Access of receipts over expenditures results in a trade surplus (i.e., the aforementioned net exports) while otherwise, a trade deficit (i.e., the aforementioned net imports). In addition, the current balance items also include non-reimbursable transfers, such as aid, donations, and overseas remittances.

The other is the capital account, which represents the income and expenditure account of international capital flows. It's divided into two branches: long-term and short-term.

Long-term capital flows primarily include direct investment, portfolio investment, and international loans. International direct investment refers to the direct investment by a country's residents in another country's plant and mining enterprises. Portfolio investment refers to the funds transfer from investors to the recipient country in the form of bonds and stocks issued by the recipient country. International loans mainly include foreign government aid loans and loans from international organizations or foreign private commercial banks.

Short-term capital flows refer to the funds flow with a maturity of less than one year, generally through various credit instruments—bills, including short-term government bonds, negotiable certificates of deposit, mercantile paper, bank acceptance bills, and certificate of demand deposit.

Regarding the balance-of-payments equilibrium or disequilibrium, long-term flows are recognized as an item in the balance of payments. In contrast, short-term flows are treated differently. Generally, autonomous short-term flows are recognized as a balance-of-payments item, whereas official compensatory flows, i.e., short-term flows used by the government to adjust the balance-of-payments disequilibrium, are treated as the balance-of-payments equilibrium item. The capital account, commonly called the balance of payments, includes only the first two items, i.e., long-term financial flows and autonomous short-term financial flows. Official compensatory financial flows are included in the balance of payments as a borrowing or lending item in reserve assets. It corresponds to the overall balance of payments and equals in amount to it. A deficit is expressed as a decrease in reserve assets, while a surplus is shown as an increase in reserve assets.

Many factors usually influence the balance of payments performance. In summary, the main ones are: (i) International trade performance. As mentioned earlier, the current account in the balance of payments reflects the income and expenditure items of import and export trade, and the trade surplus and excess of export and import are expressed in the balance of payments as the trade surplus and deficit. Therefore, all the factors affecting import and export trade will impact the balance of payments performance. (ii) The amount of capital inflow and outflow. As a rule, if the utilization of foreign capital, international loans in particular, is high, then the income from capital transactions will increase in the short term, which is conducive to improving the balance of payments performance. However, limited gold and foreign currency reserves may cause a balance-of-payments disequilibrium in the long term. (iii) Changes in the monetary value. Increasing inflation and rising price in a country can make its production costs and price levels relatively higher than those of other countries. If the exchange rate remains unchanged, the country's export capacity will be suppressed, and imports will become relatively easy, resulting in a trade deficit. Conversely, due to deflation, production costs and price levels are relatively lower than those of other countries, which can boost exports but suppress imports, resulting in a trade surplus. (iv) Situation of gross domestic demand and supply. As mentioned above, if a country's aggregate demand and supply balance, the balance of payments may be in equilibrium or disequilibrium. However, if gross domestic demand and supply are imbalance, the balance-of-payments disequilibrium will be required to adjust it. If gross domestic demand exceeds gross domestic supply, the trade deficit will be used to offset it. Conversely, if gross domestic demand is less than gross domestic supply, the trade surplus will be used to adjust it.

In addition, factors such as a country's income level and changes in its domestic economic structure, including industrial and consumption structures, can affect the balance of payments performance.

There are two forms of balance-of-payments disequilibrium. One is surplus. Generally, it indicates that if a country's economy is growing rapidly, then its currency is strong, and its export goods are competitive. However, a large and persistent surplus in the balance of payments can significantly impact the foreign exchange and capital markets. This may lead to an increase in the domestic currency price of foreign exchange, negatively affecting the national economy. In addition, a country's long-term surplus is bound to lead to trade friction between countries, so appropriate measures should be taken to adjust. The other is the deficit. Generally, it indicates that if a country's economy is in the doldrums, then the currency value is weakening, and the export goods are not very competitive. When there is a deficit, the government's gold and foreign currency reserves can be used to offset it in the short term. However, these reserves are finite. If the balance of payments continues to be in deficit, the reserves will have the risk of depletion, which requires adopting other adjustment measures to correct.

5.3.4.2 Reconciliation of Balance-of-Payments Equilibrium and Balance Between Gross Domestic Supply and Demand

An open economy's imbalance between gross domestic demand and supply often leads to balance-of-payments disequilibrium. Suppose the impact of international capital flows is not taken into account for the time being, if gross domestic demand exceeds gross domestic supply, it must be offset by the trade balance where imports exceed exports (net imports), aiming at keeping the balance between aggregate demand and supply. Conversely, when gross domestic supply exceeds gross domestic demand, it must be offset by the trade balance where exports exceed imports (net exports), aiming at keeping the balance between aggregate demand and supply. It means an imbalance between gross domestic supply and demand will inevitably lead to an imbalance in foreign trade positions. A trade deficit (where imports exceeds exports) occurs when aggregate demand exceeds GDP. Conversely, a trade surplus (where exports exceeds imports) can only be formed when aggregate demand is less than GDP. During periods of reform and opening up and economic growth, developing countries are usually prone to investment expansion and excessive consumption growth, causing aggregate demand to exceed aggregate supply, and occurring a trade deficit. If this deficit persists, it's necessary to correct the situation through adjustment measures other than using government reserve assets.

The main ways to correct this deficit are as follows: (i) Creating conditions for introducing foreign capital to offset the deficit in the current account with a surplus in the capital account of the balance of payments, i.e., offsetting net imports with net capital inflows. (ii) Using macro-adjustment measures to reduce domestic investment demand and consumption demand (i.e., retrench gross domestic expenditures), thus cutting imports and freeing up some domestic production capacity to increase the export production. (iii) In the long run, several fundamental measures should be taken to correct the trade deficit, such as enhancing the international competitiveness of domestic products and import substitution ability through technological progress, adjusting the industrial structure, improving labor productivity and capital-output rate, and reducing product costs. Although imports will increase with expanding aggregate social production capacity and growing economy, exports will increase more in relative terms. Moreover, this approach will eliminate the trade deficit trend fundamentally.

In addition, if a country's trade deficit is not only caused by exceeding gross domestic demand over gross domestic supply but also due to the overvaluing exchange rate of the domestic currency (i.e., the relative value of the domestic currency expressed through exchange rate is higher than its relative value expressed through real purchasing power), thus discouraging exports and favoring imports and resulting in a trade deficit. In such case, it's effective to correct the deficit through adjusting the national currency's exchange rate to depreciate appropriately.

The above is about the ways to correct the trade deficit. In recent years, China has experienced a significant international trade surplus, which should be analyzed specifically. In relative terms, a surplus is better than a deficit, but a long-term surplus can also generate trade friction or even cause pressure on renminbi appreciation.

Therefore, it must be adjusted differently from correcting trade deficits to balance total social supply and demand.

In conclusion, the balance-of-payments disequilibrium and the balance between gross domestic supply and demand mutually influence and constrain. Under the conditions of an open economy, the long-term goal of China's macro-adjustment is to maintain both the balance-of-payments equilibrium and the balanced growth of the domestic economy.

5.3.4.3 Exchange Rates and the Balance of Gross Domestic Supply and Demand

Analyzing international trade and balance of payments involves exchange rates. The exchange rate is the exchange ratio between domestic and foreign currencies. Internationally, exchange rates are priced in two ways. One is direct quotation, also known as the "giving quotation", which refers to exchanging one unit of foreign currency for several domestic currencies. The other is indirect quotation, also called the "receiving quotation", which refers to exchanging one unit of domestic currency for several foreign currencies.

(1) *Factors affecting exchange rates*

Currently, direct quotation is commonly used in major countries. Therefore, it is used below to illustrate the change in exchange rates and their impact. Changes in a country's exchange rate are subject to the influence of fluctuations in its monetary value of both parties involved in a transaction. Regardless of the changes in the other party's monetary value, the leading domestic factors affecting a country's exchange rate are as follows:

Firstly, the inflation degree. Inflation caused domestic prices to rise. If other conditions remain unchanged, rising prices will weaken the competitiveness of exports in the international market, thus reducing exports and increasing imports. As a result, foreign exchange supply exceeds the demand, causing the exchange rate to rise.

Secondly, the balance of payments performance, especially the trade balance. A country's balance of payments performance centrally reflects its foreign exchange supply and demand situation. When the balance of payments is a surplus, indicating that the supply of foreign exchange exceeds its demand and a resulting decline in the foreign exchange rate. However, if the balance of payments is a deficit, indicating that the demand of the foreign exchange exceeds its supply and a resulting rise in the foreign exchange rate. In the balance of payments, the trade balance plays a decisive role in exchange rate changes.

Thirdly, monetary policy. The central policies of a country to intervene in the exchange rate are (i) its interest rate policy. It mainly refers to raising or lowering interest rates to attract foreign capital inflows or prevent domestic capital outflows, thereby affecting the exchange rate. Namely, raising interest rates can increase foreign capital inflows and decrease domestic capital outflows. In this way, foreign exchange oversupply, foreign exchange rates fall, and otherwise, the opposite; (ii) its exchange policy. It mainly refers to the policy that national financial institutions buy and sell foreign exchange on the foreign exchange market to influence the exchange rates; and (iii) its exchange control. It mainly refers to direct intervention in international inter-currency receipts and payments to increase foreign exchange revenue and save foreign exchange expenditure, which also plays a role in stabilizing the exchange rate.

(2) *The impact of exchange rates on international trade and balance of payments*

Firstly, exchange rate changes will impact international trade. Generally, a stable exchange rate is conducive to cost accounting, realizing expected import and export trade profits, as well as developing international trade. Conversely, an unstable exchange rate and frequent changes will increase the risk of international trade, the difficulty of import and export trade cost accounting, and failure of achieving the expected profit. Moreover, if the exchange rate changes drastically and the external quotation changes frequently, it will not only seriously hinder the smooth progress of international trade but also significantly weaken the competitiveness of domestic goods in the international market.

Secondly, exchange rate variations also impact the balance of payments, especially the foreign trade position. Since trade deficits greatly impact the balance of payments performance, we focus on achieving a balance by adjusting the exchange rate after a trade deficit. As mentioned earlier, a country with a trade deficit will generally experience an increase in the foreign exchange rate due to the shortage of foreign currency, which also means a decrease in the exchange rate of the domestic currency against the foreign currency. In this way, the country has to change the initial exchange rate and reset the par exchange rate at a lower level, i.e., implementing a devaluation of the currency.[2] If a country's currency is in devaluation, the price of its exports denominated in foreign currency will decline, thus increasing the exports volume. At the same time, the devaluation can lead to an increase in import prices denominated in domestic currency, thus contributing to a decrease in the imports volume. However, this does not mean the trade deficit necessarily improves, because the trade balance refers to the trade value rather than its volume. The increase in the trade value is subject to certain conditions. The relative changes in the prices of imported and exported goods caused by lowering the exchange rate, in general, require one condition, namely the sum of the price elasticity of demand for exported goods and that for imported goods exceeds one. Otherwise, it is impossible to change the trade balance effectively. Practice proves that supply and demand in the international market have different elasticities concerning price changes, and exchange rate devaluation can improve the balance of payments performance through this mechanism under certain conditions.

(3) *China's exchange rate regime reform and balance of payments*

The exchange rate regime and foreign exchange management system reform are integral to China's financial system. Only by gradually and orderly promoting exchange

[2] A devaluation of a country's currency is a reduction in the exchange rate of the domestic currency against the foreign currency.

rate reform can we make full use of the exchange rate as an economic lever to adjust international trade and balance of payments and develop the export-oriented economy, and ultimately the entire national economy.

At present, there are two international exchange rate regimes. One is a fixed exchange rate regime, that is, a country's currency with the exchange rate of other countries' currencies is basically fixed, and its fluctuations are only limited to a specific range. If the exchange rate rises or falls beyond the prescribed range, the financial authorities must use the country's gold and foreign currency reserves to stabilize the official exchange rate. The other is a floating exchange rate regime, where the exchange rate of a country's currency is no longer limited to a fixed narrow range. Instead, it is determined spontaneously by the supply and demand conditions in the foreign exchange market. Most countries use this exchange rate regime.

Choosing an exchange rate regime depends on various factors, the most important of which are a country's specific economic system, economic environment, and economic development goals at a particular stage. Since the reform and opening up, the changes of China's exchange rate regime have been based on the economic system's reform. It has gradually realized the transformation from a planned exchange rate to a market exchange rate and then a fixed exchange rate to a managed floating exchange rate. Main contents of the reform of China's exchange rate regime and foreign exchange management system are as follows:

① Since January 1, 1994, the exchange rate was uniform, and a single, managed floating exchange rate regime based on market supply and demand was implemented.

Unifying exchange rates is the inevitable result of China's reform and opening up, the deepening of its exchange rate regime reform, and the core of its foreign exchange management system reform. Under the new foreign exchange management system, the exchange rate of renminbi is characterized by the following four main aspects:

First, it is based on market supply and demand. The main factor determining renminbi exchange rate level is the supply and demand situation in the foreign exchange market.

Second, it is a single exchange rate. The renminbi exchange rate is no longer directly set and announced by official administrative authorities, but rather determined and adjusted by designated foreign exchange banks according to the People's Bank of China (PBC) announced central parity rate and the fluctuation range of the exchange rate.

Third, a managed exchange rate is implemented. The PBC implements macro-adjustment and supervises renminbi exchange rate through the State Administration of Foreign Exchange, i.e., when the market exchange rate fluctuates more significantly, the PBC intervenes in the foreign exchange market mainly by gobbling foreign exchange to basically stabilize renminbi exchange rate at a reasonable level;

Fourth, floating exchange rate. The market exchange rate announced daily by the PBC is floating, and the exchange rate of foreign exchange listed for sale or purchase by each bank can float within the market exchange rate announced by renminbi and the floating range stipulated.

Unifying the exchange rate positively impacted the development of China's economy at that time, which was mainly summarized as follows:

First, it eliminated the confusion under the dual exchange rate system. It created a level playing field for enterprises and accelerated the economy's marketization, standardization, and internationalization.

Second, it made the foreign exchange management system in line with international practices. It created favorable conditions for China's accession to the world Trade Organization (WTO), thus entering a big international market. After the exchange rate is uniform, China will mainly use economic methods to adjust the supply and demand of foreign exchange and primarily stabilize the exchange rate to ensure it meets the basic requirements of the International Monetary Fund (IMF) and WTO.

Third, it is conducive to facilitating foreign trade enterprises to expand exports. Under the condition that the sum of price elasticity of demand for exported and imported goods is greater than 1, it will help improve the trade deficit at that time.

Fourth, it can further promote foreign capital inflow. After the unification, the foreign capital inflow and outflow were converted at market exchange rates, which means that the purchasing power of foreign currency was enhanced, thus benefiting foreign merchants and stimulating their interest in reinvestment.

Fifth, it positively impacted the development of the then-emerging industries such as securities, futures, and real estate.

② The system of exchange settlement and sales conducted through the banks is conducive to the conditional free convertibility of renminbi under the current account.

The so-called exchange settlement system refers to abolishing the retention of foreign exchange and the surrender of foreign exchange holdings. Besides the foreign exchange of foreign-invested enterprises, foreign exchange for overseas loans and debt repayments, foreign exchange of individual residents, as well as some other special-purposes foreign exchange can be retained, other foreign exchange proceeds shall be sold to the designated foreign exchange banks at the bank's nominal exchange rate. Implementing such a strict foreign exchange settlement system is essential for banks to ensure supplying foreign exchange, but it is also the prerequisite for implementing the foreign exchange sales system. The so-called exchange sale system refers to the foreign exchange for the general trade of enterprises. As long as there is an import contract and a payment notice from an overseas financial institution, enterprises can purchase foreign exchange from an authorized bank with renminbi. Vetting or approving plans for regular foreign exchange payments under the current account were canceled, thus the conditions for enterprises to use foreign exchange were less stringent after implementing the exchange sales system.

③ To establish an inter-bank foreign exchange market and upgrade the forming mechanism of exchange rate.

Inevitably, implementing an exchange settlement and sales system requires a national unified inter-bank foreign exchange market. Its main function is to transfer the balance and clearing services for each designated foreign exchange bank. The PBC, through the State Administration of Foreign Exchange, supervises and manages the inter-bank foreign exchange market.

The above reforms concerning the exchange rate regime and foreign exchange management system are conducive to the PBC's adjustment of the payments balance and, thus, to the macro-adjustment. Moreover, it is beneficial to be in a primary balance of economic aggregates, optimizing the economic structure, and achieving the sustained, rapid, and healthy development of the national economy.

However, the exchange rate regime currently adopted by China also has defects. This mainly includes that its market formation mechanism is not sound enough, and the exchange rate margin is far from the requirements of the floating exchange rate regime, which is outstandingly shown in a fixed and single peg to the US dollar.

④ Since 2005, China has abandoned the peg to a single dollar and started implementing a managed floating exchange rate regime based on market supply and demand, adjusted by referring to a basket of currencies.

Since the beginning of the twenty-first century, with China's growing economic and trade strength, especially after China's accession to the WTO, China's economic ties with the outside world have become increasingly tight. However, China is mainly under pressure to appreciate renminbi exchange rate (revaluation). Responding to this challenge, on July 27, 2005, the PBC issued the Announcement on Improving the Renminbi Exchange Rate Formation Mechanism, announcing that renminbi exchange rate had changed to RMB8.11 per US$ 1, an appreciation of 2%.

China has started to reform and expand renminbi exchange rate regime in a focused and systematic manner, mainly including changing the peg from a single US dollar to a basket of currencies. The currency basket in the new formation mechanism for renminbi exchange rate considers countries or regions with a large share of China's foreign trade, foreign debt, foreign direct investment activities, and their currencies. Thus, the US dollar, euro, yen, and South Korean won have become the main basket currencies, while the currencies of Singapore, the UK, Malaysia, Russia, Australia, Thailand, and Canada are also important to renminbi exchange rate. At the same time, the renminbi fluctuation range was expanded appropriately, and the determination of the central parity and the daily floating range were stipulated to increase the flexibility of the exchange rate. After that, related policy measures were introduced, gradually forming a whole set of organically integrated supporting systems for this exchange rate reform.

⑤ Progress in exchange rate regime reform.

On August 11, 2015, the PBC announced a reform of the RMB/USD central parity quoting mechanism. This reform included several key elements. Market makers should submit central parity quotations to the China Foreign Exchange Trading System (CFETS) before the opening of the American and Japanese bank forex markets, with the inter-bank closing rate of the previous day taken into account, and in conjunction with market demand and supply and exchange rate movements of major currencies. Moreover, while promoting the exchange rate reform, the PBC proposed accelerating the development of the foreign exchange market, enriching foreign exchange products, opening the foreign exchange market to international participants, and extending the foreign exchange trading hours. Meanwhile, it should introduce qualified foreign subjects to promote forming domestic and foreign consistent renminbi exchange rate programs. Through optimizing market maker quotes, this reform corrects the spread between the central parity and the market exchange rate at one time, which is conducive to improving the marketability of the central parity formation, expanding the actual operating space of the market exchange rate, and better playing the exchange rate's role in adjusting the supply and demand of foreign exchange. However, these changes do not negate the primary system or principles of the exchange rate but only further explore and reform its formation basis, composition principles, and operation mechanism under the framework of continuing to adhere to the managed, single, floating exchange rate regime. Therefore, maintaining the relative stability of the renminbi exchange rate continues to be an essential feature of China's exchange rate regime.

5.4 Demand Management for the National Economy

5.4.1 Implication of Demand Management

Demand management is a macroeconomic policy instrument used to achieve certain policy objectives by adjusting aggregate demand. It is also one of the policy instruments valued by Keynesianism, which emerged during the Great Depression of the 1930s. During this period, economic resources were severely underutilized, and insufficient effective demand was identified as the key factor hindering the increase in national income. The Keynesian national income determination theory explains the role that aggregate demand plays in determining national income under the assumption of infinite aggregate supply. Therefore, this policy instrument elicited by this theory is demand management. Demand management is to achieve the goal of neither unemployment nor inflation by adjusting aggregate demand, so that aggregate demand equals aggregate supply. If aggregate demand is less than aggregate supply, then demand is insufficient and unemployment arises. Under such conditions, expansionary fiscal and monetary policies are needed to continuously stimulate aggregate demand and promote economic growth.

Insufficient effective demand has its specific meaning. It mainly refers to insufficient consumption demand with purchasing power, resulting in total social commodity consumption being smaller than total social commodity supply, thus causing a surplus of goods and capital, enterprises running below their production capacity, and a decline in economic growth rate. Specifically, it includes three aspects: (i) Insufficient purchasing power of social spot goods; (ii) Consumers' unsatisfied consumption demands; (iii) Dislocation of purchasing power and consumption demand. In other words, the same consumer cannot simultaneously have purchasing power and consumption demand, i.e., those with power do not have enough demand. However, those without purchasing power have excessive consumption demand. This results in inadequate effective demand in the masses, which is concentrated in inadequate investment, consumption, and export.

Keynesianism argues that now that insufficient effective demand is an inevitable product of the spontaneous action of the market mechanism, therefore, the objectives of expanding effective demand and approaching full employment cannot be achieved by the market mechanism itself but by governments' macro-intervention to compensate for the lacking private demand by expanding government demand, thus promoting the equilibrium of aggregate demand and supply at the full-employment level. Thus, Keynes put forward his policy measures to stimulate investment, consumption, and exports. It should be noted that *Keynesianism* not only played its due role in rescuing the Great Depression, but also had an important influence on managing the national economy in the future. Moreover, they have a particular reference to the reform and development of China.

5.4.2 Structure of Demand Management

5.4.2.1 Demand Management for Consumption

Consumption demand is an integral component of aggregate demand. It's not only the essential need for economic and social development, but also the ultimate goal of national economic operation. Consumption level and structure have an important impact on the speed and structural evolution of economic and social growth, so it is necessary to play the fundamental role of consumption on growth. Consumption demand management is an important link in managing the national economy, and it is imperative to improve and strengthen consumption demand management. In the new economic situation, an essential aspect of transforming the economic development mode is to make economic development rely more on the pull of domestic demand, especially that of consumption demand. In this respect, it is necessary to expedite the establishment of a long-term mechanism to expand consumption demand and unleash residents' consumption potential. In light of this requirement, it is necessary to study the path of shifting the economic development engine from foreign trade to domestic demand and the related conditions based on playing the fundamental role of consumption demand in economic growth according to the situation at the current stage. In particular, it is necessary to study the content of the long-term mechanism for expanding consumption demand under the current conditions. Various measures are needed to adjust the consumption scale and level to prevent the adverse effects of consumption deviations on national economic growth and stability. Such policy instruments include taxation, interest rate, income distribution, and social security policies. Relatively speaking, consumption demand management generally responds to excessive or low consumption demand. If severely expanding consumption demand, measures such as retrenching government spending or reducing residents' welfare spending are required. In addition, if severely shortening consumption, measures such as raising government spending or increasing wages and residents' welfare support are needed.

5.4.2.2 Demand Management for Investment

Investment demand is another important component of aggregate demand. Investment and the resulting production capacity generate new supply, while the aggregate and structure of investments directly affect optimizing industrial structure and stable economic growth. Therefore, the importance of investment demand should not be ignored at any time, and the investment's crucial role in growth must be put to good use. In response to the saturating fixed asset investment, rising investment costs, declining investment profits, and unbalancing supply and demand structure of goods on the market, it is necessary to reasonably control the investment scale and adjust the investment structure. At the same time, it is also necessary to refine the mechanism for the price formation of production factors to reflect their scarcity degree and the state of market demand. Moreover, it should promote procedure-based management and reduce the cost of corporate investment to avoid excessive investment caused by the lack of institutions or market mechanisms. In order to better promote investment, governments should introduce related industrial policies to encourage and support the development of some industries, leverage private investment with fiscal investment while deepening the reform of the investment and financing system, optimizing the investment structure, innovating financing measures, promoting the cooperation model between government and social capital (i.e., PPP model). These above efforts will eventually cultivate new dynamic energy to secure economic development.

5.4.2.3 Demand Management for Net Exports

In an open economy, net export demand is an essential component of aggregate demand. During the decade since China's accession to the WTO from 2001 to 2011, net exports became a massive driver of its economic growth, also known as the WTO accession dividend. However, since the global financial crisis in 2008, the contribution of net export demand to economic growth has shifted from positive to negative. In this context, we should enhance the combination of foreign investment and export expansion, and cultivate new advantages in the foreign economy centered on technology, standards, brands, quality, and services. We should also implement the strategy for optimizing exports, promote international cooperation in production capacity and manufacturing, improve the technological content and added value of labor-intensive products, create new advantages in capital and technology-intensive industries, and finally improve the position of Chinese industries in the global value chain.

5.4.3 Key Features of Demand Management

Demand management mainly relies on consumption, investment, and net exports to drive economic growth from the demand side. The main characteristics of demand management are as follows:

First, it emphasizes aggregate management. The primary approach is to harness changes in aggregate demand through the two main levers, namely the fiscal redistribution of NNI and banks' issuing bank notes. By controlling two valves of aggregate demand, fiscal and banking, it is much less complicated for a state to adjust total social demand and, thus, total social supply. Moreover, it is relatively easy to operate with relatively quick results. Therefore, demand management has the strength of being easier to operate than supply management.

Second, it particularly emphasizes short-term equilibrium. In relative terms, the overall balance of total social demand is mainly a value balance, i.e., fiscal and monetary balances. Whether it is fiscal or monetary policy, it is emphasized that the impact on aggregate demand should be achieved in the short term or within a year to facilitate the overall balance of total social demand and supply. Therefore, demand management has the apparent characteristics of short-term management.

Third, it adjusts counter cyclically. Keynesianism was born during the Great Depression, and its policy ideas are inherently anti-crisis and counter-cyclical. For example, to expand effective demand, fiscal expenditure is expanded to stimulate consumption and thus promote economic growth. Meanwhile, increase the money supply by expanding investment to boost economic growth. It shows that it is mainly an emergency response to a temporary need but can be helpful at a significant turning point.

Fourth, it focuses on macro-level issues. The principal targets of demand management are total social demand and overall price levels, interest rate, and employment. As such, it is macro-level management.

Fifth, it emphasizes the role of government. The background of Keynesian demand management is market failure. Market mechanisms alone can hardly solve the problems of insufficient effective demand, massive unemployment, or stagnant growth. However, if the government, especially the central government, plays a role, it can accelerate economic growth.

5.4.4 Limitations of Demand Management

In essence, demand management is a macro-adjustment instrument or policy, and the following limitations inevitably exist in the process of concrete implementation:

First, it is challenging to solve structural or long-term problems. Fiscal and monetary policies, in general, are mainly aggregate ones. It is challenging to solve structural problems such as consumption, investment, industrial, and regional structures. The aggregate problem may be alleviated in the short run, but structural problems will take more than a year or longer to reverse. Demand management seems to have no better countermeasures.

Second, it is easy to ignore the role of micro-economic activities. Fiscal or monetary policies can address expanding aggregate demand, but the aggregate supply is different because the independent activities of countless enterprises achieve its fulfilment. If the government wants to directly adjust the changes in aggregate supply, it must involve the production activities of thousands of enterprises, which is relatively much more difficult to adjust or operate in the short term.

Third, the impact of demand management on the economy is somewhat asymmetric. Specifically, in implementing expansionary fiscal policy, the increased government investment, its driven credit and other funds will be mainly invested in infrastructure. This brings about inadequate investment in other areas. Investing while implementing contractionary monetary policy, the impact of credit tightening, through the transmission of the banking system, on traditional industries, large enterprises, and SOEs is relatively small but more intense on emerging industries, small and medium-sized enterprises (SMEs), and private enterprises. In this way the effect of unfavourable innovation development ensues. Therefore, the structural contradictions are not alleviated but accentuated.

Fourth, demand management tends to accumulate debt risk. Implementing large-scale demand management policies in response to crisis requires the central government's guiding capital investment and the local government's supporting capital investment. For reasons of GDP or tax contribution, local governments actively strived for big projects. However, the required supporting funds had to be solved by debts of the financing platform, thus creating a faster expansion of government debt. The subsequent policy adjustment caused by the rising inflation can result in the tension of follow-up credit and other sources of funds for ongoing projects, which further aggravates the debt risk.

To sum up, adapting the purely aggregate short-term demand management to China's macroeconomic adjustment requirements is challenging. To achieve long-term stable economic development, China should coordinate demand management with supply management, combine aggregate policy with structural policy, and short-term adjustment with long-term adjustment.

Chapter 6
Supply Thrust of National Economic Operation and Supply-Side Structural Reform

Operating the national economy needs not only the pull force from demand but also the push force from supply. This chapter analyzes the pushing role of production factors such as labor force, capital, natural resources like land, technological progress, and institutional innovation or institutional provision in the movement of the national economic system (NES). Moreover, it digs deeply into the theoretical and practical issues related to China's supply-side structural reform in the context of the new normal in economic development.

6.1 Workforce Supply and National Economic Operation

Production factors are the prerequisites and basis of economic growth, which is only achieved with the inputs of production factors. A country's economic growth process converts inputs of production factors such as labor, capital, land, and technological progress into total social output. The quantity of various production factors' inputs and the quality and efficiency of their combination determine the total social output, i.e., economic growth.

6.1.1 Labor as a Production Factor

Labor is workers' working capacity as long as they meet their normal physiological needs in social life. It is a natural labor force mainly characterized by physical labor embedded in any non-disabled worker. As a production factor, the labor, combined with other factors such as capital, creates social wealth or promote economic growth, which growth models can explain.

M. Lin and T. Huang, *National Economics*,
https://doi.org/10.1007/978-981-96-9618-5_6

The Harrod-Domar Model of economic growth includes the following central assumptions: (i) Labor grows at an invariable constant determined by external factors. (ii) Social production process uses only two production factors, labor and capital, which are not interchangeable. (iii) No technological progress exists. These are the conditions for economic growth when the workforce is fully employed, implying that for the economy to achieve equilibrium growth with full employment, the growth rate of total output must equal that of the workforce. Harrod refers to this growth rate as the natural growth rate.

Neoclassical economic growth theory abandons the Harrod-Domar model's assumptions of the irreplaceability of capital and labor and the absence of technological progress. However, it assumes that the workforce grows at a constant rate, thus accounting for the effect of population growth on output growth.

6.1.2 Effect of Workforce Supply on Economic Growth

As a traditional production factor, an increase in the workforce supply catalyzes economic growth in several ways: (i) Increasing workforce supply can lead to economies of scale and improved resource allocation. An important aspect of improved resource allocation in a market economy is transferring the workforce from less productive to more productive enterprises and sectors, which is often conditioned by an increased workforce supply. The rapid development of the more productive sectors leads to a massive increase in workforce demand, particularly evident when economic development enters the industrialization stage. (ii) The increase in workforce supply dynamically contributes to the progress of knowledge. In the long run, technology keeps advancing along with the increasing workforce supply, which puts forward higher requirements for workers' quality, specifically in the form of increased demand for skilled workers and higher requirements for workers' knowledge and skills. (iii) The quantity of workforce supplied has a more direct impact on residents' income distribution patterns, which consequently has a more direct and significant determining effect on income expectations, marginal propensity to consume, aggregate demand, and demand structure. Then, there is a greater supply push for knowledge innovation and human capital.

6.1.3 Analysis of Workforce Supply Sources and Its Undersupply

The quantity of workforce supplied depends on a country's social possession of the workforce and the quantity of workforce people are willing to provide. The social possession of the workforce is the limit of workforce supply in a country, which is determined by three factors: the size of the population, the age-sex composition, and the population's quality. From the present situation, China's urban workforce supply mainly comes from three aspects: (i) the population transformation out of working age to a population of working age in the urban population, (ii) the transfer of the rural workforce to urban non-agricultural industries, and (iii) the transfer of inter-city workforce, which is wholly reflected in the transfer of Central and Western cities to Eastern Coastal cities, or small and medium-sized cities (towns) to big cities, especially central cities.

In the long run, China's workforce supply is determined by the total population and future growth trends. On the one hand, it is an input factor for economic growth. On the other hand, it has to be absorbed by economic growth. According to the *Report on China's National Strategy on Population Development*, China's total population was about 1.37 billion in 2015 and is expected to peak at approximately 1.5 billion around 2033, after which it will show negative growth. This population change will significantly impact China's total labor resources, social dependency coefficient, and the workforce's long-term supply. It was predicted that the period before 2020 would be China's most abundant labor resource with a minimal population dependency ratio. Looking at it from another angle, it is also the period when China faced maximum employment pressure. After 2020, China will experience an increasing percentage of the aging population, a decreasing proportion of the working-age population, and an imbalance in the gender ratio.

Meanwhile, the workforce supply issue also concerns whether China has passed the Lewis turning point, i.e., where the workforce is changing from surplus to shortage. However, this opinion is controversial in the Chinese research community. One view is that China has passed the Lewis turning point. Its central argument is that since 2004, there has been a shortage of migrant workers in the Coastal areas of Southeastern China, and the wages of rural migrant workers have been increasing. The opponents argue that China is still in the period when rural migrant workers moving to cities because 200 million surplus rural laborers are waiting to be transferred. The coexisted workforce shortage and large amounts of surplus workforce is mainly caused by the structural shortage in the workforce market and institutional barriers. Regardless of these differing opinions, it is a basic fact that rural migrant workers' wages have risen. As a result, China's demographic dividend has decreased or even ceased to exist, significantly impacting the competitiveness of labor-intensive industries in particular. In this regard, innovation is required to drive transformation and upgrading to achieve sustainable economic development.

In addition, the workforce supply depends not only on the workers' quantity but also on their quality or competency. Due to continuous technological progress, workers should master more knowledge and skills. Some high-tech companies, in particular, require workers to have superior skills. Moreover, the advanced industrial structure, urbanization, and modernization also put forward new requirements for workforce quality. Furthermore, the improving workforce quality can, in turn, secure better and faster economic growth.

6.2 Capital Accumulation and National Economic Operation

6.2.1 *Capital Accumulation as an Input Factor*

With many other factors, the amount of capital stock and the speed of capital formation are primary to accelerate and restrict economic growth. With a given capital-labor ratio, the economic growth rate depends on the level of capital input, which, as well as the speed of capital formation, depends mainly on the domestic capacity of capital accumulation and the degree of foreign capital inflow.

As the economy grows, the types of capital are expanding, but material capital remains an important form. It mainly refers to all kinds of production materials that can exist and function in the production process for a long time, including machines, equipment, plants, various raw materials, goods in the process, and inventories. Although an essential characteristic of material capital is its capacity for accumulation, what is vital in the production and economic growth is, first and foremost, its productiveness, i.e., the role played in production.

6.2.2 *The Static Effect of Capital Accumulation on Economic Growth*

The increase in capital input (capital accumulation) has dynamic and static effects on economic growth. The static effect is manifested in the following:

(1) *The increase in capital input directly leads to savings of scale*

Both infrastructure and fixed capital in some enterprises have the characteristics of scale economies, but in reality, they often diseconomies of scale due to the relatively small production scale. Hence, scale savings can be generated through increased material capital input, thus improving total factor productivity and then promoting economic growth.

(2) *Improving the resource allocation*

Even in a developed economy, the production efficiency and the products' demand and supply in various sectors always vary and change at different rates, and this variation is more pronounced in developing countries or countries in transition. Therefore, there is always room for improvement in resource allocation, but its size varies from economy to economy or at different stages of development in the same economy. There are two basic ways to improve resource allocation. One is stock adjustment, and the other is incremental transformation. The reality is that completing stock adjustments often must be paired with incremental transformation. Improving resources allocation often accompanies an increase in the amount of capital input. For example, since the reform and opening up, with the rapid development of township enterprises and other non-state economies, the resources allocation has been significantly improved, essentially contributing to productivity improvement and economic growth. The increase in capital input (investment) has led to a rational flow of the original capital stock, workforce, human capital, and other factors, thus playing an important, even pioneering role in improving resource allocation.

(3) *Impelling technological progress or knowledge advancement*

In the early stage of technological innovation, intellectual capital still exists only in the form of ideas. Only when these ideas are actually applied to production does technological progress or knowledge advancement occur. There are two primary states of intellectual capital when applied to production. One exists in the form of technology materialized in material capital equipment. The other exists in non-materialized technology, e.g., process, organizational, or infrastructural-specific technology. The materialized technologies are usually realized by imputing new investments and then increases the capital stock. Therefore, increasing material capital stock can increase materialized technology, contributing to knowledge advancement and total factor productivity growth.

6.2.3 The Dynamism of Capital Inputs on Economic Growth

The dynamism of capital input on economic growth mainly refers to the increase in capital stock in the current period on the total factor productivity growth afterwards. It mainly includes two ways. One is the increase of capital stock in the current period → economic growth → increase of savings and expansion of market size (demand) → increase of capital stock (investment) in the next period → savings of scale and improvement of resource allocation → growth of total factor productivity. The second is that the increase of capital stock in the current period essentially contributes to the subsequent knowledge advancement.

Analyzing and generalizing these theories conclude that the increase in capital stock (capital accumulation) has direct and indirect effects on total factor productivity and economic growth. The direct effect occurs through learning-by-doing. With capital accumulation, knowledge is accumulated in the learning-by-doing process. This accumulation is expressed in human capital increase. On the one hand, and the increase of technology level contained in the capital goods and the relevant production process. On the other hand, among which the human capital increase (accumulation of experience) has a more decisive effect. The indirect effect of the increase in capital stock on knowledge advancement is manifested in the human capital increase and the improvement of production technology through some intermediate links.

The mechanism of such a dynamic process is that capital accumulation leads to economic growth and an increase in per capita income, thus leading to the expansion of the market size and changes in the market demand structure (advanced). On the one hand, expanding market size promotes labor division, thus promoting the invention and use of new technologies and increasing labor productivity. On the other hand, the changes in the market demand structure require corresponding changes in the industry's structure, thus stimulating technological innovation. Meanwhile, there is a growing demand for human capital, and the increase in labor productivity and income provides conditions for increasing human capital through education in terms of leisure and financial resources.

6.3 The Supply of Natural Resources and National Economic Operation

Natural resources are the production factors discovered and used by humankind, including all the materials in nature that are usable for humans, and the carriers that can provide valuable materials. It is the natural basis of social production and an essential reason for forming the geographical labor division and the different levels of regional labor productivity. Domestic resource stockpiles and possessions are one of the most critical conditions for a country's economic growth. A country's abundant natural resources can give objective economic growth a comparative advantage in resources. (i) The production and acquirement of a resource are at a lower cost, whereas its output is at a higher level. (ii) The more a particular resource is owned or the higher the share of world reserves it represents, the more monopolized its supply, market, and pricing will be. (iii) A specific world resource with a higher concentration reserve ratio can be used to exchange and supplement the country's other scarce or unavailable resources, thus maintaining the normal functioning of the national economy. (iv) Mining and mineral processing industries can lead to the development of other related industries like transportation, architecture, and manufacturing and maintenance of machinery and equipment.

6.3.1 Natural Resources and Their Characteristics

In contrast to manufactured resources, natural resources are helpful material elements existing naturally in nature without relying on human beings. The main characteristics of natural resources are as follows: (i) Scarcity. It mainly refers to natural resources being limited in quantity and substitutes. (ii) Regionalism. It mainly refers to the uneven distribution of natural resources, i.e., significant geographical differences in quantity and quality. (iii) Integrity. It mainly refers to the fact that the natural resource elements in each area are ecologically linked to each other, forming an integral whole. If one of them is touched, it may cause a chain reaction, affecting changes in the entire natural resource system. (iv) Multi-usage. It mainly refers to the fact that each natural resource has multiple uses and can satisfy multiple inputs and consumption. (v) Difficult to substitute. It mainly refers to the difficulty of finding substitutes for natural resources that are the basis of modern economic development and human life.

6.3.2 *The Role of Natural Resources in the Development of the National Economy*

Natural resources are the material basis of socioeconomic growth. In the era of agricultural and industrial economies, they are crucial in economic development. In the era of a knowledge-based economy, they are the essential foundation for economic development and industrial labor division. Although knowledge and technology have become the intrinsic core factors of economic growth, their status and role in economic growth are still irreplaceable by others. The crucial role of natural resources in economic growth is mainly reflected in the following.

6.3.2.1 Natural Resource Abundance Affects the Economic Growth Rate

Natural resource abundance encompasses both quantitative and qualitative aspects. Abundant, high-quality resources ensure sustained and stable economic growth, thus providing a stable basis for developing the national economy. Conversely, if resources are scarce, difficult to exploit and utilize, or of poor quality, developing the national economy will be severely limited, and the entire socioeconomic system will be affected to a greater extent.

The exploitation and utilization of resources involve both breadth and depth. In the early stages of exploitation and development, i.e., during the long historical period before human societies entered industrialization, the agricultural economy has always been dominant. The agricultural production modes, such as hunting, fishing, farming, and herding, directly depended on natural resources, especially shared natural resources, such as water, land, light, and heat, whose geographic distribution characteristics directly determined the regional differences in the type of agricultural economy. Their quantity, quality, and structure in turn constrained the improvement of the agricultural production level.

In the early stages of industrial development, handicrafts, mainly smelting, firing, and textile, while promoting the development of the agricultural economy, were constrained by mineral resources or through agricultural by-products like cotton, silk, and wool. They were ultimately constrained by the quantity, quality, distribution, and characteristics of natural resources. The leading industrial sectors in this period were natural resource-intensive ones, and natural resources played the most significant role at that stage. The abundance and structure of resources strictly limit its economic growth rate. After the extensive development reaches a particular stage, the marginal cost gradually increases until it equals the marginal benefit when the economic development is very slow, even stagnant. Then, people are required to carry out in-depth development of natural resources.

In the middle and late stages of industrialization, the exploitation and utilization of underground resources significantly advanced economic development. In those regions with rich mineral resources and where key mineral species are essential, it is most conducive to realizing the evolution of industrial structure. The specific formation of the industrial structure and the priorities for its development are directly conditioned by the scale of exploitation of mineral resources and their share in the whole country, the utilization rate of the resources in situ, and the degree of their further processing. For those regions lacking mineral resources, the vigorous development of their industrial economy is often due to favorable conditions such as location advantages. Thus, the economic growth rate in this period was mainly subject to the in-depth exploitation of resources as well as other factors like location, socioeconomic, and technological level.

6.3.2.2 Natural Resources Influence the Economic Development Pattern

The economic development pattern includes the composition of industries within the economic system and their interrelationships, i.e., the spatial and temporal layout of industrial structure and productive forces. The constraints of natural resource structure on industrial structure are manifested in the temporal scale as constraints on evolving industrial structure, i.e., on the economic growth rate, and in the spatial scale as constraints on forming and distributing industrial structure.

6.3.2.3 Natural Resources Affect Labor Productivity and the Geographical Labor Division

Favorable conditions of natural resources are conducive to increasing labor productivity, and otherwise, the opposite. The imbalance in the regional distribution of natural resources is objective, and such regional differences in the distribution of natural resources naturally form the basis for the geographical labor division. The enormous impact of natural resources on regional labor productivity will inevitably impact the geographical labor division. As the market economy develops constantly, inter-regional economic ties are becoming increasingly close. Therefore, the ability to make full use of regional advantages in organizing commodity production becomes the key to determining the success or failure of regional development. Commodities produced in regions with excellent natural conditions and lower production costs will inevitably flow to regions with unfavorable natural conditions and resources or higher production costs. In this way, a specific scale of geographical labor division is gradually formed.

6.3.2.4 Natural Resources Influence the Regional Industrial Structure

Factors affecting regional industrial structure are multifaceted, and natural resources are one of the important factors and often become the material basis for the formation and development of regional industrial structure. Especially in the early stage of regional development, natural resources are decisive in affecting the formation and structure of regional industries. On the one hand, in regions rich in natural resources, especially industrial natural resources, and with a good combination of natural resources, the regional industrial structure is formed based on exploitable natural resources. With the continuing development of regional natural resources and the rising level of regional economic development, the influence and constraints of natural resources on evolving and upgrading the regional industrial structure would strengthen. On the other hand, in regions poor in natural resources, especially in mineral and energy resources, forming and developing the industrial structure tend to rely more on conditions like location, transportation, science and technology, information, and market.

6.4 Technological Progress and National Economic Operation

Technological progress serves as the impetus and source of economic growth and socioeconomic development. It is increasingly important in the national economy. Fundamentally, technological advances are indispensable to transforming the economic development modes, structural evolution, industrial upgrading, improving economic efficiency, and drivers and means of improving the quality of economic growth.

6.4.1 Implication and Types of Technological Progress

Broadly, technological progress refers to the process by which all factors work together to enable the combination of a certain number of production factors to create more output. The main contents include: (i) improving the technical level of equipment and products; (ii) reforming processes; (iii) reducing energy consumption and saving resources; (iv) improving the workers' quality; (v) knowledge advancement and technological innovation; (vi) optimizing resource allocation; and (vii) improving the management level.

In the actual production process, different types of technological progress are different in terms of the allocative efficiency of each production factor, the degree of savings, and the increase in comprehensive productivity. Technological progress can be broadly classified into three main categories: capital-saving, labor-saving, and neutral. The type of technological progress chosen varies according to the factor endowments of each country or region. If the country or region is capital-scarce and workforce-rich, capital-saving technological progress is typically preferred, whereas the developed countries with a relatively scarce workforce may generally choose labor-saving technological progress.

6.4.2 Mechanisms of Technological Progress for Economic Growth

Technological progress is essential in promoting economic growth. Apart from capital and labor, technological progress is the most important source and a major contributor of economic growth. The main ways in which technological progress promotes economic growth are as follows: (i) using new equipment, technology, and processes results in improving production efficiency and increasing output per unit of time and labor input; (ii) technological progress changes the industrial structure and makes it evolve in the direction of sophistication, thus improving the structural efficiency of the economic system; and (iii) it creates new demand, thereby creating a new impetus for economic growth.

From the perspective of the essential elements of economic growth, technological progress has been generally recognized as an important factor in economic growth, according to the neoclassical theory of economic growth and the new growth theory. Ways in which technological progress promotes economic growth like: One is relying on primary factors. It is mainly through vigorously developing education and exploiting human resources in enterprises to enhance the quality and level of labor inputs, thus driving economic growth. The other is relying on efficiency-enhancing factors. In particular, through the progress of soft science and technology, strengthening the scientific management of the whole economic growth process, and improving the quality of capital inputs (the materialized technological level), thus promoting economic growth.

From the perspective of the primary links in economic growth and their interconnections, technological progress is an intrinsic mechanism for promoting economic growth. Among them, social production comes first and determines distribution, exchange, and consumption and their interrelationships. Whether the relationship between distribution, exchange, and consumption is rational or not, in turn, affects and constrains the development of production. At the same time, production, distribution, exchange, and consumption, as well as their interrelationships and interactions, influence and constrain the mode, quality, speed, and level of economic growth. Relying on technological progress, vigorously promoting the development of social production, and improving the quantity and quality of social products is the fundamental link in accelerating economic growth. In order to secure a stable economic growth, we should rely on technological progress, particularly soft technological progress, rationally and moderately deal with the proportion of consumption and accumulation in the distribution of NNI (Net National Income) and the consistency between immediate and long-term interests, improve and perfect the market system of commodity trading and information communication, change and guide people's consumption concepts to rational consumption, and coordinate the dynamic relationship among production, distribution, exchange, and consumption to maintain the virtuous operation of cyclic mutual reinforcement.

From the perspective of social development stages, technological progress promotes economic growth mainly through innovations in knowledge, products, enterprises, and industries. Among them, knowledge, product, and enterprise innovations are the micro-basis and constituent factors for achieving innovation in industrial sectors. Industrial innovation is the prerequisite and necessary way to form leading industries, bring about changes and upgrading of industrial structure, and realize the advanced industrial structure. Technological progress is an intrinsic mechanism for promoting economic growth.

6.4.3 Contribution of Technological Progress to Economic Growth

6.4.3.1 Technological Progress Contributes the Transformation of the Economic Development Mode

First, technological progress is the precursor of transforming the economic development mode. The essential characteristic of extensive management is repetitive production at a low technological level, while the essential characteristic of intensive management is that it relies on technological progress to increase the comprehensive utilization rate of input factors so that output tends to be maximized. The shift from extensive to intensive management can only be realized by relying on technological progress. Technological progress has become the precursor of transforming the economic development mode from extensive to intensive. Its fundamental performance lying in the fact that technological progress optimizes economic resource allocation, improves the utilization rate, and maximizes the profit of the enterprise operation. Moreover, technological advancements not only enhance product functions to meet human desires but also increase the variety of ways products can satisfy these desires, making such satisfaction more convenient.

Second, technological progress serves as an engine for transforming the economic development mode. It is because (i) technological progress can lead to the rationalization and advanced development of the economic structure, improve macroeconomic efficiency, and promote overall economic development; (ii) it is more capable of enabling the economic activity agents to achieve economies of scale and lead enterprises onto the track of intensive management; (iii) it can improve the output rate of production factors, reduce the production cost, and achieve intensive growth.

Third, technological progress creates favorable conditions for transforming the economic development mode. Technological progress can provide a material foundation for transforming the economic development mode and creating better economic benefits with the same scale of resources. Moreover, it breaks through various resistances and difficulties in transforming the economic development mode.

Fourth, technological progress multiplies economic development and its transformation of the development mode. Since there is an interactive use of technological progress and economic growth, scientific and technological achievements are applied to realize the diffusion of the economy. This brings about economic growth, and in turn, economic growth will affect scientific and technological research and development. In this way technological progress can expand in the process of sci-tech and economy interaction, and bring about a several-fold impact on the economic development process and its development mode transformation, thus accelerating the transformation of the economic development and its mode, similar to the multiplier effect of other input factors.

6.4.3.2 Technological Progress Contributes Upgrading and Optimizing Industrial Structure

Among the various effects of technological progress on changes in industrial structure, it is essential for technological progress to promote the formation of new leading industries and change the industrial structure, thus leading to the coordinated and sustained growth of the entire economy. Technological progress primarily affects the sectors that directly apply scientific and technological innovations, some of which become leading industries. In addition, developing a series of related industries can be driven by forward and backward linkages, thus driving the sustained growth of the entire national economy. This change in the correlation of industrial structure is mainly manifested in structural changes within the original industries and the newly-emerged industrial sectors.

The essence of optimizing industrial structure is to optimize the allocation of production factors across industries. Technological progress can affect other production functions, increase the marginal productivity of production factors, and have a substitution effect on other factors, i.e., producing more and better products than before with the same factor inputs. As a permeable factor, technological progress (i) expands people's ability to understand and utilize natural resource factors and improves the effectiveness of the original natural resources; (ii) improves the labor's quality and raises the marginal productivity of the labor factors; (iii) raises the marginal productivity of capital and changes the structure and quantity of capital; and (iv) changes the pattern of inter-industry factor flows, thus promoting the rationalization of the industrial structure.

6.5 Institutional Provision and National Economic Operation

National economic activities always operate within a specific institutional environment and under certain institutional arrangements, and institutional factors permeate the entire process of national economic operation. Institutions provide primary endogenous incentives for economic growth by acting on the immediate drivers of economic growth, clarifying property rights, effective contracting, lowering transaction costs, forming rational expectations, prompting the rational factor allocation, changing the distorted economic structure, and promoting technological progress and expanding economic aggregates.

6.5.1 *Formal and Informal Institutions*

In the course of human history, institutions arise primarily through two processes: spontaneous evolution and humanly devised. The reason for the emergence of institutions can be attributed to resource scarcity. Due to the scarcity, people will inevitably compete with each other, thus provoking conflict and friction in the competition process. Therefore, it becomes necessary to find ways to regulate interrelationships and competitive behavior, which eventually evolve into institutions. Some of these institutions may be conventional, while others are formulated by specific organizations that must be enforced. More often than not, institutions result from a combination of these two formation processes.

In terms of the institutions' forms, it can be categorized into formal and informal ones. However, their effectiveness also depends on their effective implementation, so it is necessary to analyze the institutions' implementation.

6.5.1.1 Formal Institutions

It refers to rules consciously designed by people based on informal institutions, including political and economic regulations as well as contracts.

At the state level, laws represent formal institutions, however, at the social level, the statutes of various organizations also belong to the formal institutions. The highest level of law is the Constitution, which determines a country's political regime. Beneath the Constitution are a series of civil and criminal laws that determine the rules of behavior in society, which can be divided into political and economic rules depending on the objects to which the laws are applied.

Political rules serve as guidelines for organizing and structuring political life, as well as standardizing individuals' political behavior. These rules stipulate (i) who is eligible to participate in political life and the specific political rights and powers they hold; (ii) the fundamental principles that guide various political actors in their activities and behaviors; and (iii) how political resources are allocated, i.e., determining what kind of value will be given to whom. The function of political rules is to prescribe and shape the political order, which is primary for ensuring political stability.

Economic rules define property rights, i.e., confirming people's rights to use and receive income from their possessions and the renunciation or transfer those rights. In particular, the rules governing the right transfer generate a series of protections and constraints within contracts, allowing people to protect their contractual interests by resorting to national institutions. The statutes of various organizations also belong to formal institutions. They regulate the rights and obligations of the organization's members, structure, and decision-making process. The economic rules' function is to define and shape the economic order.

6.5.1.2 Informal Institutions

An informal institution is an unwritten restriction on human behavior formed unconsciously by people in their long-term interactions. It's mainly composed of value beliefs, ethical norms, moral ideas, customs, and ideologies, with ideology and custom at its core.

Informal institution is a concept that corresponds to formal institutions, such as laws. The existence of informal institutions is objectively inevitable since formal institutions cannot exhaust all human behavior and thus cannot effectively stipulate every possible human behavior. In addition, some informal institutions exclude formal ones from involving in a particular area, resulting in the formal institutions' failure to be ineffective in that area. Since some formal institutions are costly to implement, informal ones can be used to complement and strengthen the implementation of formal institutions.

Informal institutions are universal in modern society. Specifically, they can be split into three types: (i) socially accepted codes of conduct; (ii) extensions, enrichment, and modifications of formal institutions aiming at making up for occasions that cannot be described or are inapplicable to be described by the formal institutions; and (iii) self-implemented conduct standards, which are based on the maximization of self-efficacy, are an expression of collective rationality.

6.5.1.3 Implementation of the Institutions

A set of institutions, whether formal or informal, will inevitably encounter challenges in implementation after they are established. To assess the effectiveness of a country's institutions, it is not enough to merely consider the completeness of its formal and informal institutions; more importantly, one must evaluate whether the implementation mechanisms are robust. Without a sound implementation mechanism, all institutions are essentially empty shells.

The main methods of implementing institutions are self-implementation and third-party implementation. Self-implementation is valid only when the amount paid by both parties to the contract is equal to the amount payable, i.e., when there is no cost associated with measuring or enforcing the contract, the proceeds gained from the contract will outweigh the costs. The conditions for valid self-implementation are (i) whether the times of the game repetition are infinite, (ii) whether the players are stable, and (iii) whether the players share knowledge about individual rationality and actions among themselves. Third-party implementation refers to implementing an institution without the above conditions for self-implementation. In this regard, national implementation has enormous scale economies.

6.5.2 The Determining Role of Institutional Innovation in Functioning the National Economy

Neither formal nor informal institutions are ever static, thus requiring constant innovation. Institutional innovation refers to replacing inefficient old institutional rules or organizations with more efficient new ones in society. It includes changes in various major formal rules such as the property rights system, competition rules, science and technology policies, and the political system, and the emergence of various transactional organizations with a new nature. Here, the institutions' efficiency is understood primarily from the resource allocation perspective. An efficient institution leads to a rational and efficient resource allocation, improves factor and mix efficiency, and magnifies the role of technological progress in driving output growth, thereby promoting economic development and increasing the output growth rate.

6.5.2.1 Formal and Informal Institutional Innovation

Wholly, the society, will benefit from institutional innovations that seize profit opportunities arising from institutional disequilibrium. Whether such innovation occurs, however, depends on the expected benefits and costs of individual innovators. The calculation of the benefits and costs to the innovator is more complex than that to the society. Formal and informal institutions each generate their problems in this regard.

Changes or modifications to rules within formal institutions require the permission from the group or individual whose behavior is governed by the institution. In other words, "no objection" is a prerequisite for formal institutional innovation. Thus, formal institutional innovations require the innovator to spend time and effort to organize and negotiate with obtain group or individual unanimity. In contrast, changes or modifications in the rules of the informal institutions are done purely by individuals, but do not or cannot by collective actions. Initially, individual innovators will be perceived by others as violating existing rules. Institutional innovation occurs only when the majority in a society abandons the old institution and embraces the new one.

In general, formal institutional innovations generate externalities and free-rider problems. Externalities occur because institutional arrangements cannot be patented. When a new institutional arrangement is created, other groups or individuals can imitate the innovation and significantly reduce their costs of organizing or designing new institutional arrangements. As a result, the innovators' benefits will be less than those to the society. This problem implies that the density and frequency of formal institutional innovation will be less than the optimal amount for society. Thus, there may be persistent institutional disequilibrium.

The "free-rider problem" arises primarily from institutional arrangements being public goods. Once an institutional arrangement has been innovated or established, every individual subject to it receives the same service, regardless of whether they have borne the burden of the innovation and the initial difficulties. The magnitude of such a phenomenon also depends on the relationship between groups or individuals. The "free-rider problem" is more likely to occur if there is a high degree of mobility within the group, as individual behaviors are less likely to be detected.

The problems arising from the process of informal institutional innovation are quite different. Because innovations in informal institutional arrangements do not involve group action, there is no "free-rider problem", although there are externalities. Accepting new rules depends entirely on individual calculations of the benefits and costs of the innovation. These costs of innovation are independent of time, effort, and resources spent in the innovation process. Because implementing informal institutions depends on social interactions, the innovators' costs come primarily from the social pressures surrounding them. Costs are incredibly high if the opportunity to profit is unequally distributed among community members. As a result, informal institutions tend to be more challenging to innovate than formal institutions. Even with government support, facilitating innovation in informal institutions remains a considerable challenge.

Nevertheless, the criteria and characteristics of informal institutional innovation remain the same. Values, habits, and social morality, have evolved throughout human history, just as ideologies, and they continue to do so. Innovators face the same severe problems as other economic decision-makers. When the expected benefits from institutional disequilibrium are substantial enough to outweigh the potential costs, individuals will push to adopt new values, morals, and habits, regardless of how deeply entrenched the existing rules may be.

6.5.2.2 Types of Institutional Innovation

(1) *Induced institutional change*

Essentially, it refers to the modification or replacement of an existing institutional arrangement or the creation of a new one. It is spontaneously initiated, organized, and implemented by an individual or a group of individuals responding to a profit opportunity. Economic institution innovation occurs because individuals or groups in society find it profitable to bear the costs of a new institutional arrangement, with the goal that the innovator will be able to make some profit unavailable under the old institution. The initial requirement for a new institutional arrangement is that the expected future benefits exceed the expected costs.

According to the economic man behavior hypothesis in neoclassical economics, institutional change can be viewed as a process of institutional equilibrium to disequilibrium to equilibrium caused by economic agents' pursuit of profit maximization, in line with orthodox cost-benefit analysis. The institutional equilibrium means that, under the established institutional arrangement, (i) the total increment of all potential incomes generated by various factor resources has been captured, (ii) although potential profits may exist, the cost of changing the existing institutional arrangement exceeds the potential profit, and (iii) if specific changes are not made to the institutional environment, redistributing incomes is not possible, in this regard, the existing system is in an equilibrium state, i.e., institutional equilibrium. Institutional equilibrium is a state of Pareto optimization of the existing system. In this state, no changes to the existing institutional arrangements can generate additional income for any individual or economic group.

However, institutional equilibrium is not permanent, because several external events can generate pressures on existing institutional arrangements. (i) Changes in conditions due to applying new technologies, internalizing external economies, shifting of transaction costs, and the like, can all generate potential revenues. Such revenues can only be obtained by arranging for institutional innovations. (ii) Costs of new institutional arrangements are altered by, for example, the emergence of new technologies. (iii) Some legal or political changes may impact the institutional environment, allowing certain groups to realize a redistribution or access to existing external profits. For these reasons, the existing institutional structure can yield new revenues through improvements or innovations, implying that there are disequilibria in the existing institution and that Pareto improvements are possible.

(2) *Coercive institutional change*

Coercive institutional change refers to changes introduced and implemented through governmental orders and laws. The executor of coercive institutional change is the state or government. Implementing coercive institutional change was mainly due to (i) institution provision is one of the state's fundamental functions; (ii) institutional arrangements are a kind of public goods, generally "produced" by the state; and (iii) the government can reduce or stifle free riding by virtue of its coercive power, ideology, and other advantages by bridging the gap in institutional provision.

In practice, it is sometimes difficult to distinguish between induced and coercive institutional change. Both of them are interlinked and mutually constrained and jointly drive society's institutional evolution. These two kinds of institutional change have many similarities. For instance, both are responding to institutional disequilibrium, and both have to follow the principle of cost-benefit comparison. However, there are some differences, mainly in the executor and advantages of institutional change, as well as the problems faced in this process, and the influencing factors of the two. Therefore, countries, or one country, at different times and on different issues, will make different choices from a practical viewpoint. For developing countries, it is not enough to rely solely on the profit-seeking behavior of economic agents themselves to get rid of inefficient institutions, and even such behavior may continue to entrench the inefficient institutions. Therefore, the state or government must play an active role in breaking this vicious circle.

6.5.2.3 The Role of Institutional Innovation in National Economic Development

(1) *Shifting resources from unproductive or low-productivity to productive or high-productivity sectors*

Although countries caught in a poverty trap have the problem of resource scarcity, it is not the root cause of poverty, as there are examples of resource-poor countries becoming rich and resource-rich countries that are still poor. Resource scarcity is a common problem faced by human societies in general, and the key is whether resources can be applied to highly efficient production sectors. In a closed economy, institutional innovation's significance is channeling people's efforts and resources to productive wealth-creating sectors by establishing new rules. While such innovations cannot alter the state of a country's resource endowment, they can result in an outward shift in the production-possibility curve, thus increasing output and accumulation without changing the total amount of available resources.

(2) *Promoting economic growth by changing incentive mechanisms*

An incentive mechanism reflects the relationship between individual effort and reward on the one hand, and the relationship between individual and social goals on the other hand. Different institutional arrangements create different incentive mechanisms. Effective mechanisms tightly match individual effort with reward and individual goals with social goals to simultaneously enhance individual welfare and social welfare, which is known as incentive compatibility. In contrast, poor mechanisms mismatch either reward from effort or individual goals from social goals, i.e., incentive repugnancy. Differences in long-term growth performance across countries arise from the different incentives set by different institutions. Among other things, efficient economic organization is crucial to economic growth. Hence, it should entail "establishing institutional arrangements and property rights that create an incentive to channel individual economic effort into activities bringing the private rate of return close to the social return rate."[1]

(3) *Increasing output growth rate by reducing transaction costs, mitigating transaction risks, improving transaction efficiency, and optimizing transaction behaviour*

---

[1] Douglass C. North, Robert Paul Thomas, *The Rise of the Western World: A New Economic History*, Cambridge University Press, 1973, p. 1.

In order to illustrate this issue, the assumptions of neoclassical theory on rational economic man and zero transaction costs should be amended.

First, the assumption of a limited rational man should be adopted. The subjective pursuit of rationality characterizes the behavior of the limited rational man. However, objectively, it can only be limited to do so, indicating that economic individuals have incomplete information about trading activities, which leads to uncertainty. The uncertainty may be derived from random variations in natural or market demand, or opportunistic motives of trading actors, such as cheating or laziness. While the uncertainty external to trading activities is unavoidable, the uncertainty arising from opportunistic motives can be reduced through institutional arrangements to set penalties for non-compliance.

Second, the assumption of positive transaction costs is made. In real-world economic activity, the cost of obtaining information in trading activities is huge due to incomplete information, i.e., transaction costs cannot be zero. Transaction costs are mainly used to coordinate trading behaviors between traders in the trading process but not for the direct production process. In this regard, the size of transaction costs can reflect the efficiency of a country's economic activities if the output is given. Therefore, for lagging countries, reducing transaction risks and uncertainties, optimizing transaction behaviors, and lowering transaction costs through institutional innovations can effectively promote output and growth.

6.5.2.4 The Effect of China's Institutional Innovation in Operating the National Economy

With fixed inputs of production factors, such as capital and labor, but without a major technological revolution or significant technological progress, economic growth can still be promoted by relying on institutional innovation, which has existed since ancient times. Since China's reform and opening up, implementing institutional innovation has vigorously promoted rapid economic growth and created the "Chinese miracle." This achievement reinforces the importance of institutional innovation. It is manifested mainly in the following areas:

(1) *Institutional innovation has boosted agricultural production*

As a significant turning point in China's history of economic development, the year 1978 saw 18 household spontaneous and voluntary implementation of the contracting system in Xiaogang Village, Fengyang County, Anhui Province. This event gave impetus to a change in the collective management system of agricultural production in certain rural areas of China, which resulted in the widespread establishment of the household contract responsibility system throughout rural China. The household contract responsibility system represents an internal distribution of production factors within the collective in the form of "contracting land with remuneration linked to output." Pre-production distribution determines the entire production process, and household contract responsibility system is redistributing production factors with through production, such as land, in collective ownership. Therefore, its essence is pre-production distribution. Post-contractual production and distribution were integrated, and the principle of distribution based on labor was applied, which corrected the phenomenon of egalitarianism and gave farmers autonomy in production and management. Incentivized by the new distribution system of "paying enough taxes in grain to the state, leaving enough for the collective, and the rest retained by the household," the farmers' production enthusiasm was greatly stimulated. This institutional innovation accelerated the development of Chinese agriculture, leading to faster national economic growth. The rural tax and fee system reform is another institutional change that has significantly impacted agricultural production. It began with spontaneous piloting by grass-roots governments, deepened through nationwide piloting and replication, and led to the complete abolition of the agricultural tax in 2006. This deepening reform of rural taxes and fees has left more room for increasing farmers' incomes.

(2) *Institutional innovation has boosted enterprises' development*

China's institutional innovation has significantly boosted economic growth, and this impetus emanates mainly from the fact that institutional change brings vitality to the development of enterprises. From the institutional level, since the reform and opening up and with the deepening of the reform, SOEs have made various degrees of progress in expanding their autonomy, organizing their production market-oriented, and reforming their management system. Therefore, the enterprise system has been optimized. In particular, the pace of SOE reform and the restructuring of the state-owned economy has accelerated since 1998. SOEs have achieved remarkable results by strengthening their reform, restructuring, and reorganizing on the one hand and on the other hand, intensifying their internal management through separating the main and subsidiary businesses and reducing staff to increase efficiency. All these efforts reflected in the continuous optimization of the state-owned economy's structure and the substantial and sustained increase in economic efficiency. Institutional innovation has not only improved the efficiency of SOEs but also promoted the rapid development of the non-state economy. With the deepening of reforms, the non-state economy's ideological, political, and legal status has continued to rise. The flexibility of its mechanisms, ability to fully mobilize producers' enthusiasm, and natural rapport with the market have essentially contributed to prospering the urban and rural economies, increased fiscal revenues, expanded social employment, improved people's lives, optimized the economic structure, and facilitated economic development.

(3) *Institutional innovation has promoted the overall national economy*

Judging from the practical situation of China's reform and opening up, institutional innovation has strongly promoted the overall development of China's economy: (i) Diversification of ownership relations. Reform and opening up has made China's economic composition run from single to pluralistic, with public and non-public economies developing together. (ii) Significant progress has been made in opening up to the outside world. Accessing WTO has brought China's opening up to the outside world to a new level. China has become an essential part of the world economy, away from a closed country. (iii) The marketization process has been accelerating. Reform and opening up has led to a rapid and comprehensive advance in the marketization process. This led to the rapid development of factor markets for capital, land, labor, technology, property rights, and other factors.

Institutional innovation brought about by reform is instrumental in economic growth. Market-oriented reforms have been conducive to more efficient resource allocation, while expanding the non-state sector of the economy has been conducive to establishing an efficient economy with perspicuous property rights. Moreover, opening up to the outside world has been conducive to rationally allocating resources globally and to acquiring a wealth of technology, capital, institutions, knowledge and other resources from abroad. These reforms have directly increased comprehensive productivity and contributed to the national economy's long-term sustained and rapid growth.

Over the past 30 years of the reform and opening up, China's economy has maintained an impressive average annual growth rate of 9.7%, which is attributable to a large extent to the effect of rational resource allocation emanating from institutional innovation. The change of three closely linked macroscopic institutions—diversification of ownership relations, marketization, and opening up to the outside world—has not only provided reliable institutional support for growing China's macroeconomic aggregates and exerted significant influence but also played a vital role in transforming the economic development mode and improving the quality of national economic operation.

6.6 National Economy's Supply Management and Supply-Side Structural Reform

6.6.1 *Characteristics of Supply Management*

Along with demand management, the state or government has to carry out supply management. It is mainly the management of production factors such as labor, capital, natural resources like land, and technological progress. It also includes structural optimization, institutional innovation, and other broader aspects. They are collectively called supply push. Like demand management, supply management is also an essential part of national economic management. Their difference lies in the focus on the management implementation and the policy tools used. The main features of supply management are as follows:

First, it focuses on structural optimization. This includes various aspects such as industrial, regional, investment, consumption, import and export, market, and income distribution structures. In this regard, it is necessary to adopt a coordinated policy system of industrial, regional, investment, consumption, foreign trade, price, and other policies to achieve the goal of structural optimization.

Second, it emphasizes long-term equilibrium. In comparison, the structural optimization of total social supply is mainly a material equilibrium, which takes longer to achieve. For example, the industrial structure's adjustment, optimization, and upgrading cannot be accomplished quickly. It may even require over one or two Five-year Plan periods or even longer. China's overall regional development strategy, including Large-Scale Development of Western China, revitalization of old industrial bases in the Northeastern region and other areas, the Rise of Central China, and the Eastern region's pioneering development, has undergone several Five-year Plan periods. Therefore, supply management focuses on immediate needs and considers long-term development, particularly medium- and long-term policy effects.

Third, it makes pro-cyclical adjustments. Counter-cyclical adjustment or demand management responding to the global financial crisis can yield immediate results in the short term. However, it is also prone to causing economic fluctuations, brings forth overcapacity, and breeds financial crises. Supply management is mainly to enhance its targeting and effectiveness, aiming at effectively averting and resolving various economic risks by ironing out short-term economic fluctuations through pre- and fine-tuning and micro-stimulation to keep the economy within a reasonable range.

Fourth, it focuses on solving micro-level problems. Supply management is more conducive to guiding firms and markets in the broader context of macro-management, such as creating new supply through encouraging innovation and entrepreneurship, fostering new growth drivers, and promoting vigorous development of new technologies, new industries, and new business forms to accelerate the change of growth drivers. Meanwhile, appropriate measures have been taken to better adapt total social supply to changes in total social demand, base the innovation development, and adhere to innovative development to improve the quality and effectiveness of economic development.

Fifth, it emphasizes increasing institutional supply. Institutional and technological innovations are the twin engines or wheels of economic development. In a sense, increasing institutional supply and accelerating institutional innovation can provide new growth drivers for technological innovation: (i) developing capital market can provide a financial guarantee for technological innovation, (ii) accelerating the reform of the distribution system can bring a new motivational mechanism for technological innovation, (iii) strengthening the protection of intellectual property rights can provide legal protection for technological innovation, and (iv) streamlining administration, delegating powers, and transforming government can invigorate enterprises and exert market's decisive role properly in resource allocation. In order to improve and strengthen supply management, it is necessary to do an excellent job in terms of institutional mechanism innovation, i.e., to implement supply-side structural reform.

6.6.2 *Necessity and Essence of Supply-Side Structural Reform*

Supply-side structural reform is a significant adjustment of China's economic development ideas and work focus. It's also a major initiative to resolve economic development's difficulties and contradictions. As its name implies, supply-side structural reform mainly refers to the reforms starting from the supply side and targeting the economy's structural problems. It focuses on releasing and developing a society's productive forces, i.e., conducting reform to promote structural adjustment, reducing ineffective and low-end supply, expanding effective and medium- and high-end supply, enhancing the adaptability and flexibility of the supply structure to demand changes, and raise total factor productivity. Specifically, supply in the narrow sense refers to the number of goods or services that producers are willing and able to provide at a certain price level for a specific time. However, supply in the broad sense refers to all supply-side factors or forces that can affect economic development and the improvement of economic efficiency, including the players in economic activities, production factors and their upgrading, institutional changes, and the like.

China's economic operation has faced prominent contradictions and problems. Although cyclical and aggregate factors have played a part, the root cause is a significant structural imbalance leading to a poor economic cycle. It needs to think of ways from the supply-side structural reform and strive to achieve a new dynamic equilibrium of supply and demand relations. Herein lies the need for supply-side structural reform.

The essence of supply-side structural reform is centered on three key aspects: (i) The ultimate goal is satisfying demand. That is, emancipating and developing the society's productive forces to better meet the people's growing material and cultural needs. (ii) The main direction is improving the supply quality. It mainly includes reducing ineffective supply, expanding adequate supply, improving the quality of the supply system and adaptability of the supply structure to the demand structure. (iii) The fundamental way is deepening reform. Finally, the goal is to achieve four improvements in profitability, labor productivity, total factor productivity, and potential growth rate through reform and innovation.

6.6.3 *Strategic Priorities of China's Supply-Side Structural Reform*

6.6.3.1 Allowing the Market to Play a Decisive Role, But the Government Should Work More Effectively

The key to supply-side structural reform lies in addressing the rational allocation of production factors, and the central issue is dealing with the relationship between the government and the market. The aim is to allow the market to play a decisive role in allocating resources and make the government work more effectively. For this purpose, it should: (i) Improve the property rights protection system. Property rights perspicuity is the primary prerequisite for market transactions and the effective functioning of market mechanisms. It is necessary to clarify and protect all types of public and private property rights and endeavor to improve the efficiency of allocating all types of property and public resources. (ii) Further dismantle monopolies. The free flow and fair competition of production factors should be realized at the utmost. For a few natural monopoly industries, it is also necessary to increase their competitiveness through government scientific regulation, for example, adopting competitive bidding and inter-regional comparing competition at the price setting and entry stages to incentivize enterprises to improve their internal efficiency. (iii) Undertake market-oriented price reforms, especially marketizing factor prices. It should actively promote price reforms in such areas as transportation, petroleum, telecommunications, water, electricity, and gas. Furthermore, it should liberalize the prices of competitive segments so that market prices can genuinely guide the flow and allocation of factors of production and resources. (iv) Make efforts to avoid the government's improper, overstepping, and deficient governance existed in the past although the government should play a more effective role. The government's essential functions should be creating favorable institutional conditions for the market, solving problems where the market fails, exercising effective macro-adjustment, and preventing polarization through income distribution policies. (v) Promote SOE reform. The reform aims to facilitate the rational flow and market allocation of factors of production and resources, thereby propelling economic development.

6.6.3.2 Implementing an Innovation-Driven Strategy

The innovation-driven is crucial to advancing supply-side structural reform. Only through innovation-driven transformation and upgrading in traditional industries and supporting all kinds of market entities to accelerate the innovative development of new technology, new products, and new business forms and modes can we truly expand effective and medium- and high-end supply. Deeply implementing the innovation- driven development strategy includes: (i) Creating a level playing field to stimulate innovation. To this end, it is necessary to reform the industrial access system by breaking down industry monopolies and market segmentation constraining innovation through strict intellectual property protection. (ii) Constructing institutional mechanisms to promote innovation. A market-oriented mechanism for technological innovation has been established by improving the industrial technology innovation mechanism with the enterprise as the mainstay and a sound procurement policy that prioritizes using innovative products. (iii) Encouraging entrepreneurship, innovation, and venture capital. Strengthening the function of financial innovation through expanding the scale of venture capital and enhancing capital market support to drive technological and institutional innovation. (iv) Accelerating the reform of the science and technology system. Improving incentive policies for transforming scientific and technological achievements by accelerating the decentralization of the right to use, dispose of and derive profits from scientific and technological achievements and by increasing the proportion of scientific and technological researchers' income from transforming achievements. (v) Improving the innovation system. It is necessary to build a market-oriented technological innovation system that integrates the efforts of industry, universities, and research institutions but with enterprises as the mainstay. This can be achieved by deepening the reform of scientific research institutes that have transformed into enterprises, optimizing the way supporting fundamental research and establishing a synergistic mechanism for scientific and technological innovation. (vi) Implementing bidirectional flow. Technological innovation will be accelerated by promoting efficient allocation and comprehensive integration of innovative resources, establishing a sound mechanism for the two-way flow of scientific research talents, upgrading mechanisms for training and utilizing innovative talents. All these endeavors result in establishing a scientific mechanism for evaluating innovation.

6.6.3.3 Comprehensively Raising the Level of Factor Resource Supply

Increasing total factor productivity (TFP) is one of the essential goals of supply-side reform. Labor, capital, and land are the most basic supply-side factor resources. Reforms should be accelerated to comprehensively raise the supply level of factor resources and form a supply-side driving force:

(1) *To raise the level of workforce supply*

There are two main adjustments. (i) Adjusting the population policy, focusing on implementing a population strategy centered on overall eugenics for the whole society and improving the population's quality. A human capital strategy centered on education and enhancing innovation capabilities should also be conducted. (ii) Adjusting the labor contract law. The aim is to ensure a flexible workforce market. Meanwhile, the person-centered household registration system and vocational training will be strengthened to increase the workforce supply.

(2) *To give full play to the role of land system innovation in promoting supply-side reforms*

It involves (i) promoting the reform of the land system and capitalizing on the positive role of land system innovation in reforming household registration system, promoting transformation and upgrading, resolving excess production capacity, and reducing land costs; (ii) promoting the utilization of land resources by optimizing the land-use structure; (iii) reducing the industrial land-use cost by strengthening land delicacy and differentiation management, enhancing industrial land adjustment, and reasonably raising compensation standards for land acquisition and relocation; and (iv) while adhering to the system of land conservation and arable land protection, it should implement classification control, push forward the land vetting reform and approving regime, and gradually establish a unified urban–rural land circulation system. Moreover, it should stabilize the land supply and improve its efficiency by revitalizing the stock of construction land and encouraging the use of uncultivated land, among other ways.

(3) *To enhance the level of financial supply*

The key measures are as follows: (i) Giving full play to the function of financial innovation by refining the system of financial institutions, improving the macro-adjustment way, and innovating the adjustment idea and policy instruments. The aim is to comprehensively boost the efficiency of financial services for the real economy. (ii) Continuously increasing the proportion of direct financing, expanding private capital's participation in the banking sector, and standardizing the development of Internet finance. The aim is to build a structurally balanced and sustainable financial system. (iii) Guiding commercial banks to establish and improve green credit mechanisms, giving full play to the function of the financial market in supporting green financing, with an aim to build a green financial system. (iv) Expanding the two-way opening up of the financial sector and actively participating in global financial governance. (v) Strengthening financial services for small-, medium- and micro-enterprises, rural areas, and especially impoverished areas, improving the agricultural insurance system and financing mechanism, and vigorously developing inclusive finance. (vi) Strengthening the construction of a financial macro-prudential management system, improving regulatory rules, establishing a safe and efficient financial infrastructure, and setting up a national financial security mechanism aiming at preventing systemic financial risks.

6.6.3.4 Increasing Institutional Supply

Implementing institutional innovation and ensuring an adequate supply of institutions are fundamental to advancing supply-side structural reform, for which the following five points should be achieved:

(1) *Innovating the government's governance system*

The main approaches are: (i) Accelerating the transformation of government functions. It is necessary to build a law-based and service-oriented government to fully play in macro-adjustment, correcting market failures, providing public services, and adjusting income distribution. (ii) Accelerating the government's governance system and capacity modernization. It should give full play to the decisive role of the market in allocating resources, utilizing new governance types such as contracting out, the third sector, and public–private partnerships, realizing democratic, participatory, and interactive multi-subject governance, and enhancing the effectiveness of governance. (iii) Streamlining administration and instituting decentralization. It should promote a negative list management, vigorously reduce items requiring administrative approval through loosening government regulations to build a small government. (iv) Realizing the rule of law. Building e-government systems and promoting transparency in governance ("government in the sunshine") are necessary to cage government power by the system, thus making the exercise of power proceduralized, standardized, and legalized.

(2) *Accelerating enterprise system innovation*

The main measures are: (i) Innovating the enterprise property rights system. It should propel the legalization of property rights protection to protect an economy of various ownership forms in compliance with the law. This is done through reducing the proportion of state-owned shares, fostering corporate shareholders and institutional investors, improving the employee stock ownership system, and other methods. (ii) Improving the corporate governance structure. It should improve the operational efficiency of the corporate governance structure of state-owned and private enterprises by refining the internal and external corporate governance structure. (iii) Innovating the enterprise management system. It is necessary to enhance the enterprises' management level and stimulate their intrinsic efficiency. This can be achieved through innovating management organizations and modes, emphasizing on enterprise cultural construction and its integration with enterprise management systems, implementing people-oriented management, and the like. (iv) Innovating enterprise culture. It should, adhering to the core values of being people-oriented, fully explore the valuable aspects of traditional Chinese culture and deal with the relationship between corporate and social culture to promote corporates' healthy development by fostering cultures of integrity, distinction, social responsibility, innovation, and a commitment to continuous learning.

(3) *Boosting market system innovation*

Its main tasks are: (i) Improving the market system. It should be based on the further development and improvement of various market types, such as the commodity, financial, human resources, property rights trading, information, and real estate markets. (ii) Optimizing the market operation mechanism. Its core is to give full play to the role of the competition mechanism to promote fair competition. Through innovations in the administrative system like a negative list, it should improve the laws and regulations related to regularly operating the market economy, thus preventing power from replacing the market, interfering with the market, excluding competition, illegal monopoly, and unfair competition. (iii) Innovating market organizational forms. It requires innovating various institution arrangements of market organizations at different levels based on improving and changing the spot, futures, retail, wholesale, comprehensive, specialized, tangible, intangible, and other markets. (iv) Innovating market circulation methods. It includes firstly taking advantage of modern technology to transform the traditional circulation model to vigorously promote the development of e-commerce and accelerate the circulation industry's informatization process. Then follows by accelerating the rapid development of various new business forms centered on chain business and a variety of modern retail business forms as the mainstay, and optimizing the policy environment, strengthening the sense of credit and contract, speeding up constructing the social credit system, and improving the security system of the circulation market.

(4) *Innovating the macro-adjustment system*

It involves: (i) Deepening the reform of the fiscal and taxation systems, including establishing a modern budgetary system featuring comprehensive, standardized, open, and transparent. Moreover, it should establish a sound tax system that is conducive to scientific development, social equity, and market unification. In addition, adjusting the financial relationship between the central and local governments and establishing a system in which authority of office matches responsibility for expenditure are important. And eventually, we should establish a modern fiscal system to remodel a fiscal revenue system that is in line with the new normal and the new economy. (ii) Accelerating the reform of the financial system. Effectively supporting the real economy can be done by resolving the dual-track interest rate system with the slightest delay possible, broadening the financing channels for small and micro enterprises, promoting the development of inclusive finance and other measures, and actively lifting financial disincentives. (iii) Propelling the reform of the income distribution system. The main focus is to deepen the reform of the income distribution system and promote distributional equity through several avenues. This include appropriately lowering the corporate and individual income tax rates, raising the minimum wage standard, improving the enterprise wage guideline, collective wage negotiation system, and mechanism for sharing the state-owned capital gains. It can also be achieved through perfecting the mechanism for remunerating production factors, such as capital, technology, and management. Moreover, it's important to strengthen the construction of a system for punishing and preventing corruption and intensify tax collection and management.

(5) *Promoting innovation in informal institutions*

The dominant methodologies include: (i) Shaping a culture of rules. The core requirement is to abide by the rule of law and be honest in economic activities. (ii) Converting the administrative culture, such as weakening the ideas of bureaucratic prioritization and social estate system, as well as eradicating the breeding ground of bad administrative culture to create an excellent administrative atmosphere for economic and social development. (iii) Arousing a reasonable utilitarian culture. In this respect, it is necessary to eliminate abnormal cultural mentality like harboring hatred towards the rich, arousing people's reasonable utilitarianism thought of pursuing and creating wealth, becoming better off through diligent work, and others through re-examining and correctly interpreting the utilitarian culture. In this way can we promote economic development and finally make the people wealthy and the nation strong. (iv) Cultivating a culture of entrepreneurship and innovation. It must break through the cultural psychology of self-isolation, self-conceit, settling for less, indulging in complacency, and unwillingness to take risks. It should also cultivate a culture of innovation and entrepreneurship that respects creativity, emphasizes openness, dares to take risks, and tolerates failure and entrepreneurial spirit that is aggressive and innovative in society as a whole. (v) Strengthening a culture of credibility. It must create an ambiance of honesty and trustworthiness, improve legal regimes related to integrity, strengthen integrity supervision, and enhance integrity systems within industries and government. By doing so, government credibility will be strengthened, ensuring the healthy and sustainable development of the market economy.

Chapter 7
Cyclical Fluctuations in the National Economic Operation

In operating the national economy, changes in total social supply and demand cause changes in the economic growth rate. When the economic growth rate fluctuates drastically, it indicates a severe imbalance between total social supply and demand. If cyclical variation characterizes such national economic fluctuations, they are referred to as business cycle fluctuations. This chapter mainly discusses the patterns, causes, and transmission mechanisms of cyclical fluctuations in the national economy.

7.1 Reasons and Transmission Mechanism for the Formation of Cyclical Fluctuations in China's Economy

7.1.1 China's Economic Cycle Fluctuations Since Reform and Opening Up

Since the reform and opening up, China's economy has experienced 30 years of rapid growth, which the World Bank has termed the China Miracle. Since 2010, China has entered a medium- to high-speed development phase, often referred to as the "new economic normal." It can be categorized into the following six significant cyclical fluctuations.

7.1.1.1 Basic Situation of Business Cycles

Based on the fluctuations in China's annual GDP growth rate (in comparable prices) from 1977 to 2015, the fluctuations in economic growth during this period can be

M. Lin and T. Huang, *National Economics*,
https://doi.org/10.1007/978-981-96-9618-5_7

divided into five established high-growth business cycles and one ongoing medium-high growth business cycle. The five established high-growth business cycles are as follows:

Cycle 1: 1977–1981, lasting five years
Cycle 2: 1982–1986, lasting five years
Cycle 3: 1987–1990, lasting four years
Cycle 4: 1991–1999, lasting nine years
Cycle 5: 2000–2009, lasting ten years

An ongoing business cycle of medium-high growth: 2010 to present.

7.1.1.2 Characteristics of Business Cycle Fluctuations

(1) *Five established high-growth business cycles*

The first is that the fluctuation magnitudes generally show a medium-amplitude pattern. The amplitude of fluctuation refers to the difference between the upward and downward fluctuations of the economic growth rate in each cycle, i.e., the gap between the highest and lowest growth rates. It is an important indicator to evaluate the stability of economic growth. The larger the amplitude of fluctuations, the less stable the economic growth. However, the smaller the fluctuation ranges, the more stable the economic growth. Fluctuations are usually categorized into three types based on the size of the peak-to-valley spread: (i) strong amplitude, where the peak-to-valley spread is greater than or equal to 10 percentage points; (ii) medium amplitude, where the peak-to-valley spread is less than ten but greater than or equal to 5 percentage points; and (iii) low amplitude, where the peak-to-valley spread is less than 5 percentage points. The average fluctuation amplitude of China's five rounds of business cycles since 1977 has been 6.64 percentage points, with an overall medium amplitude pattern. Regarding development trends, the decline in the fluctuation amplitude has been more significant, suggesting that the stability of China's economic growth is gradually increasing.

The second is that the fluctuation peak level generally shows a medium-peak pattern. According to the height of the economic growth rate in the peak year of each cycle, the fluctuations are categorized into three patterns: (i) the peak pattern, where the economic growth rate in the peak year is greater than or equal to 15%; (ii) the medium-peak pattern, where the economic growth rate in the peak year is less than 15%, and greater than or equal to 10%; and (iii) the low-peak pattern, where the economic growth rate in the peak year is less than 10%. The average value of China's five rounds of business cycle peaks since 1977 is 13.4%. Overall, it shows a medium-peak pattern. Among the five rounds of cycles, the second cycle stands out as a peak pattern, while the remaining four are categorized as the medium-peak pattern. Regarding development trends, gradually declining peaks indicate that the stability of economic growth is increasing to some extent.

The third is that the fluctuation depth is all manifested in the growth pattern. According to the positive or negative economic growth rate in the trough year of each cycle, the fluctuations can be categorized into growth and classical patterns. China's business cycle fluctuations show different characteristics from the classical pattern, in which the economic aggregates decline. The average depth of China's five rounds of business cycle troughs since 1977 has been 6.76%, and the cycle fluctuations have all been of the growth pattern with the troughs rising extremely remarkable. This change suggests that China's economic growth has strengthened its resistance to recession, thus contributing to more excellent economic stability.

The fourth is that the average fluctuation potential generally presents a high-point pattern. According to the average rate of economic growth of each cycle, the fluctuations can be divided into three patterns: (i) the high point, where the average economic growth rate is greater than or equal to 8%; (ii) the median point, where the average economic growth rate is less than 8% but greater than or equal to 5%; and (iii) the low point, where the average economic growth rate is less than 5%. China's average economic growth rate of the five rounds of business cycles since 1977 is 9.64% annually, a high-point pattern overall. Among the five rounds of business cycles, except for the first and third rounds, which were of the median-point pattern, the remaining three rounds were of the high-point pattern. It implies that China's overall economic growth level has increased significantly since its reform and opening up.

The fifth is that the expansion length of fluctuations generally shows a short expansion pattern. Through comparing the expansion length with that of contraction, the fluctuations can be categorized into two patterns: short expansion, which means that the expansion period is shorter than the contraction period, or the ratio of the expansion length to the contraction length is less than 1. Long expansion, which means that the expansion period is longer than the contraction period or the ratio of the expansion length to the contraction length is greater than or equal to 1.

The average total length of the five rounds of Chinese economic cycles since the reform was 6.6 years, with an average expansion length of 3.2 years and an average contraction length of 3.4 years, and the ratio of the two was 0.94, generally showing a short expansion. Among the five cycles, the expansion periods of the second and fifth cycles were more extensive than the contraction periods. In comparison, the expansion periods of the remaining three cycles were shorter than the contraction periods. In summary, the continuity of China's economic expansion is weak and less stable. However, in terms of development trends, the lengthening of the expansion period has been highly significant, suggesting that China's economic expansion is gradually increasing in sustainability.

(2) *Characteristics of an ongoing business cycle of medium-high speed growth*

After 2010, China's economic growth rate declined and fell below 7% in 2015. It shows that China's economic development has entered a new normal, shifting from high-speed to medium–high growth. Inevitably, it is the result of significantly adjusting economic structure and changing the development environment. At this point, there is no way to determine when this business cycle will bottom out and rebound.

7.1.2 Causes and Transmission Mechanism of China's Business Cycle Fluctuations

7.1.2.1 Agricultural Fluctuations Are the Foundation for Forming Business Cycle Fluctuations

China is a typical dual economy. Although agriculture does not have the most direct and marked impact on economic fluctuations, it has the most fundamental impact on economic growth. The transmission mechanism of agricultural fluctuations on national economic cycle fluctuations is that agricultural fluctuations affect investment fluctuations, and investment fluctuations affect industrial fluctuations, thereby national economic fluctuations. The impact of agricultural fluctuations on investment and industry is transmitted mainly in the following ways: (i) Product pathway. Agricultural products are the main source of foodstuffs and raw materials for light industry. Once food production decreases, investment in the current year and the following year will be significantly reduced, and otherwise the opposite. (ii) Market pathway. The agricultural production boom or bust also affects the national economy through market inflation and contraction caused by increased or decreased farmers' monetary income. A good or bad agricultural harvest will inevitably change farmers' income and consumption levels, leading to changes in the entire national economy. (iii) The factor pathway. Inputting production factors into different industrial sectors will result in differences in returns. After the basic needs are met and a slight accumulation occurs, farmers will transfer capital and labor to other non-agricultural sectors, which undoubtedly contributes to economic prosperity. On the contrary, it will be one of the most critical factors leading to economic recession.

7.1.2.2 Investment Fluctuations is the Primary Impetus of Economic Fluctuations

China's investment fluctuations are significantly correlated with economic fluctuations. Investment's effect on economic fluctuations is mainly formed through the multiplier-accelerator mechanism and, meanwhile, constrained by the upper-lower limit buffer mechanism. Sharp expanding investment in the expansionary period leads to the continuous expansion of industrial production, which causes a sharp expansion of demand, thereby leading to a sharp expansion of the entire social production. However, economic expansion is ultimately limited by supply and demand constraints, and following the transmission chain during expansion leads to a contraction of direct or indirect demand and fluctuations in economic growth.

7.1.2.3 Imbalanced Industrial Structures Are an Essential Part of Exacerbating the Fluctuations of the Business Cycle

The reasons for this are: (i) The bottleneck industries are lagging, thus constraining economic growth. China's energy, transportation, and fundamental industries are chronically underpriced, resulting in sizeable social capital being invested in the high-margin processing industry and other hotspot industries. In this regard, the original bottleneck industry becomes more and more lagging, inevitably resulting in economic fluctuation uptrends' inability to last and soon entering a downward phase due to the bottleneck sector constraints. (ii) Asymmetry between industrial and demand structures. The transformation rate of China's industrial structure and product structure is relatively low, resulting in a sharp increase in remnant purchasing power on the one hand and a large number of commodities backlogged in the stockpile that cannot be sold on the other hand. The above all phenomenon inevitably restricting further effective economic growth.

7.1.2.4 Factors Resulting from Policies Are Catalysts for Business Cycle Fluctuations

It is mainly manifested in the following regards. Expansionary policies beyond a specific limitation tend to lead to the mutual push between large-scale investment and production, thus causing the economy to turn from expansion to overheating quickly. However, once a tightening policy is overdone, it will soon bring about a rapid investment and production decline, as well as an accelerated rate of economic downturn. Ultimately, it leads to excessive fluctuations in the business cycle. The two situations are, in fact, unconducive to the stable growth of the national economy.

7.1.2.5 Cyclical Fluctuations in the World Economy Are Essential to China's Economic Fluctuations

After the reform and opening up, China has become more and more closely connected to the world market. Therefore, its economic growth has been increasingly affected by the world economy. The impact of demand on the cyclical fluctuations of the Chinese economy has gradually deepened. For example, the 1997 Southeast Asian financial crisis and the 2007–2008 U.S. financial crisis contributed somewhat to the Chinese economy's fluctuation.

7.2 Inflation and Deflation

7.2.1 Inflation and Its Causes in China

7.2.1.1 The Basic Situation of Inflation

Since the reform and opening up in 1978, China has experienced six more pronounced inflation episodes respectively in 1980, 1985, 1988–1989, 1993–1995, 2007–2008, and 2011.

The first inflation occurred in 1980 when the consumer price index (CPI) rose by 7.5%, an increase of 5.6 percentage points over the previous year, but fell to 2.5% in 1981. The broad money supply (M2), with RMB38.48 billion of new money added in 1980 over 1979, compared with an average of just over RMB9 billion of new money added each year from 1970 to 1979.

The second inflation occurred in 1985 when the CPI rose to 9.3% from 2.7% the previous year, and its subsequent two years continued to be high at 6.5% and 7.3%. In 1985, the producer price index (PPI) rose 8.7% year-on-year. In terms of M2, more than RMB40 billion of new money was added each year from 1981 to 1983 on average, with a monetary growth rate of 22%. Newly added money reached up to RMB107.13 billion in 1984 over 1983.

The third inflation occurred in 1988–1989. In 1988, the CPI rose by 18.8%, an increase of 11.5 percentage points over the previous year, setting a record for the highest increase in nearly 40 years. In 1989, it rose by 18.0% over 1988. The PPI also rose by 15% year-on-year. On average, the M2 increased by more than RMB150 billion per year from 1984 to 1989, and by 1989, the money stock had reached RMB1,194.96 billion.

The fourth inflation occurred in 1993–1995. The CPI rose 14.7%, 24.1%, and 17.1% year-on-year, and the PPI rose 24%, 19.5%, and 14.9% year-on-year. The M2 increased by RMB940 billion in 1993 over 1992, increasing 39% compared with last year, while the money stock reached RMB3,487.9 billion in 1993. In 1994, the growth of the money supply exceeded RMB1 trillion, with an additional RMB1204.4 billion in 1994 over 1993, increasing 34.6% compared with last year, and an additional RMB1,382.7 billion in 1995 over 1994, reaching RMB6,075.05 billion.

The fifth inflation occurred in 2007–2008. The CPI rose to 3.28%, above the warning line of 3%, in March 2007, then rose another 3.23% in December over March, and rose another 2.23% in February 2008 to 8.74% on top of December 2007 before declining somewhat but remaining high. The PPI rose 5.43% year-on-year in December 2007, then reached 11.06% in August 2008 and fell to 9.13% in September. The M2 increased by RMB5,145,818 million in December 2007 compared with January and increased by RMB3,505,239 million in September 2008 compared with January 2008.

The sixth inflation occurred in 2010–2011. The CPI rose to 3.3%, above the warning line of 3%, in July 2010. The CPI rose to 5.1% in November of that year, then declined somewhat, but rose again to 5.4% in March 2011, and then remained high around 6% before declining in October 2011. The PPI rose by 7.1% year-on-year in May 2010, then declined somewhat, and rebounded to 7.3% in March 2011, after which it stayed at a high level of around 7% before it began to fall back in October 2011. The M2 added RMB10,024.25 billion in December 2010 compared with January and RMB11,770.607 billion in December 2011 compared with January. From January 2010 to December 2011, although the M_2 year-on-year growth rate declined in fluctuation, it remained high.

7.2.1.2 Causes of Inflation

The first inflation was primarily due to: (i) Structural price adjustments. From 1979 onwards, the government raised the purchasing prices of 18 major agricultural products, including grain and cotton. In addition, a mark-up policy was introduced for over-purchased major agricultural and sideline products, such as grain, cotton, and edible oil. The scope of bargain purchasing was expanded. However, while the purchase price of agricultural products was raised, their sales price remained unadjusted accordingly, resulting in severe losses in producing and selling non-staple foods related to agricultural products. In November 1979, the government raised the prices of eight subsidiary foodstuffs, including livestock, aquatic, and vegetables. In April of the same year, the government systematically raised the ex-factory prices of coal, iron ore, pig iron, steel ingots, billets, non-ferrous metals, cement, and other products. (ii) The rapid growth of infrastructure investment. At the end of 1978, China was conducted with too much haste in introducing foreign equipment, and proposed constructing 120 new and renewed large-scale projects, basically realizing agricultural mechanization by 1980 and other high indicators. As a result, the construction scale was too large, and the investment in fixed assets remained high for several years. (iii) Large fiscal deficits. In order to support price adjustments and investment growth, more money had to be issued. This resulted in large national fiscal deficits, which ultimately led to excessively expanding total social demand and an upward trend in price indices.

The second inflation was primarily due to: (i) The structural price adjustments. In 1985, China decided to liberalize the prices of agricultural products, abolish the state monopoly of purchasing and marketing, and partially liberalize the prices of essential production means and industrial consumer goods. (ii) Enormous investment scale in fixed assets and sharp expansion of money and credit supply caused excessive total social demand. (iii) Rising incomes from wages and salaries exceeded the increase in labor productivity, resulting in the rise of costs, thus leading to cost-push inflation.

The leading causes of the third inflation were: (i) The structural price adjustments. In 1988, 12 price adjustments and supporting reform measures were introduced with the approval of the State Council and relevant departments. This mainly aimed at raising grain prices, edible oil, foodstuffs, crude oil, and electricity for industrial use. Then China raised the grain's purchase price in 1989 and, at the same time, the price of the production means of industry and transportation. (ii) National macro-adjustment capacity was severely weakened. In 1985, the Central Government adopted an austerity package. However, because of a rush for quick results in the guiding ideology, insufficient experience in reform, and an over-optimistic estimation of the prospect, the policies began to be loosened across the board in 1986 before the effects were seen. As a result, China has seen a severe imbalance in the ratio of industry to agriculture, an excessive decentralization of distributing funds, foreign exchange, and materials, a severe weakening of macro-adjustment capabilities, fiscal deficits year after year, and out-of-control banknote issuance. The above in turn has triggered inflation.

The causes of the fourth inflation were mainly: (i) Structural price adjustments. China completely liberalized the purchase and sale prices of grain and those of coal, steel, cement, and communication exchange equipment under centralized distribution and raised the prices of electric power, railroad freight, and crude oil in 1992–1993. With the still considerable pace of price reforms in 1994, coupled with the over-concentration of significant reforms in fiscal, taxation, finance, and foreign exchange, the pressure to increase prices accumulated over the years was released in a concentrated manner, which resulted in an unprecedentedly high inflation rate. (ii) China's economy entered the fast lane of rapid growth after 1992. However, rapidly expanding the investment scale in fixed assets at that time and continuously disrupt in financial order led to inflation, which can be summarized as four crazes, four highs, four constraints and one chaos. Four crazes refer to for real estate, development zone, capital raising, and stock. Four highs stand for investment expansion, industrial growth, banknote issuance, credit supply, and price raises. Four constraints are transportation, energy, critical raw materials, and capital. One chaos lies in the economic order, especially financial order.

The fifth inflation is mainly due to the following reasons. (i) Cost-push inflation. On the one hand, the prices of food, pork, energy, and other commodities have risen sharply. Since these commodities are closely related to residents' lives and the upstream products of industrial production, they will inevitably be transmitted to downstream products when their price increases accumulate to a certain extent. On the other hand, wage costs are rising. With the structural tightening of supply and demand for the workforce, together with the Government's accelerated pace of raising workers' welfare, the pressure for rising wages has increased. For four consecutive years, total and average wages for all workers nationwide have grown at double-digit rates, exceeding the GDP growth rate for the same period. The growth rate of average labor compensation nationwide has exceeded that of GDP for seven consecutive quarters. (ii) Demand-pull inflation, mainly because fixed asset investment was growing too fast. Since 2003, the growth rate of social investment in fixed assets has been above 20% and, in turn, 26.7% in 2003, 26.6% in 2004, 26% in 2005, 24% in 2006, and 24.8% in 2007. (iii) Excess liquidity. On the one hand, there is excess liquidity in the banks. The sustained economic growth since 2003 has led to a marked increase in the incomes of the State, enterprises, and residents. In addition to being used for investment and consumption, such incomes have been transformed in considerable part into savings. Its direct result is that the commercial banks' differences between deposit and loan have continued to widen, adding the impulse of the commercial banks to seek loans. Although somewhat controlled under the tightening of monetary policy, the growth rate of the money supply has yet to be fully reflected in prices, i.e., it has not materialized in the purchase of investment or consumer goods. It is still increasing savings or money, resulting in excess liquidity. On the other hand, there is imbalanced payments. With foreign direct investment growing rapidly, a large amount of hot money pouring into the Chinese market anticipating the appreciation of the yuan. The continuous increase in net exports has led to China's payment balance clearly out of balance, resulting in a large amount of foreign exchange savings. At the end of 2007, China's foreign currency reserve exceeded US$1.53 trillion, an increase of 43.3% over the previous year. Therefore, more renminbi is needed to maintain foreign currency reserves. For example, maintaining more than US$1 trillion of foreign currency reserves needs more than RMB10 trillion. Too many funds outstanding for foreign exchange means that the M2 supply, in addition to the ordinary bank credit of regular supply of the base currency, increased foreign currency reserve also led to an increased renminbi supply. Hence, the money in circulation increased rapidly.

Following the laws of the market economy, a continuously high PPI index should be gradually transmitted to the CPI index. However, there is an economic phenomenon of severe PPI and CPI inversion in this inflation round, which was mainly attributable to: (i) The two indexes' composition being different. Regarding composition, most of the over 4,000 commodities selected for the PPI survey are raw materials and production means, such as machinery, electronics, chemicals, and textile products. However, the living means used for residents' final consumption account for only one-third of them, whose price change has less than a 30% overall impact on the PPI. Only about half of the CPI's basket of goods includes industrial consumer goods, the other half includes foods and services whose prices are vulnerable to climatic factors. (ii) The price transmission mechanism between commodities in different segments is more complex in a buyer's market. When products' prices in the upstream, i.e., production link, increase, they affect the price fluctuations of products in the downstream, i.e., distribution or consumption link, mainly in the form of cost-push.

The sixth inflation was mainly due to (i) the Four Trillion Investment Program in 2009. At the same time, the central bank threw out RMB20 trillion to hedge the vast funds outstanding for foreign exchange, leading to excess liquidity and (ii) the rising price of bulk commodities. China's higher dependence on imports of bulk commodities, like crude oil and iron ore, brought imported inflationary pressure to China.

7.2.2 China's Deflation and Its Causes

Since the reform and opening up in 1978, China has experienced two more pronounced deflationary episodes, in 1997–2002 and 2009, respectively.

7.2.2.1 Deflation in 1997–2002

(1) *The basic situation of deflation*

Since the economy successfully secured soft landing in 1996, China's macroeconomic situation has undergone a fundamental change, with deflation appearing for the first time in economic operations. The main manifestations were:

First, the price index has continued to fall. The rising margin of the society-wide retail price index (RPI) slid from 21.7% in 1994, with a year-on-year increase of only 0.6% in 1997, and continued to be negative growth for the next five years. From 1998 to 2002, the margin of price rise was –2.6%, –3.0%, –1.0%, –1.4%, and –1.3%, respectively. The CPI was negative for the first time from April 1998, with a rising margin of –0.8% and –1.4% in 1998 and 1999, and slight positive increases in 2000 and 2001, with a rising margin of +0.4% and +0.7%. In 2002, negative growth continued at –0.8%, a 1.9 percentage point drop in prices compared to 1997, the year before the CPI drop. The PPI for manufactured products began to show negative growth in 1997, with a rising margin of –0.3%, followed by negative growth for two consecutive years, with a rising margin of –4.1% and –2.4%, respectively. After an uptick in 2000, there was negative growth again in 2001 and 2002, with a rising margin of –1.3% and –2.23%, respectively.

Second, the money growth and the flow velocity have declined. From 1991 to 1997, the year-on-year average annual growth rates of M1 and M2 were 22.8% and 26.9%, respectively. Since 1998, however, the growth rate of China's money supply at all levels has slowed markedly, with M1 growing at an average annual rate of 16.02% year-on-year and M2 growing at an average annual rate of 14.9%t year-on-year from 1998 to 2002, a decline of 6.78 and 12 percentage points, or 29.74% and 44.61%, respectively, compared with the period from 1991 to 1997. At the same time, the money velocity also continued to fall.

(2) *The causes of this deflation*

They are fourfold:

First, the direct cost of tackling high inflation since the early 1990s. In order to combat the economic overheating occurring in the second half of 1992 and the worst inflation since the reform and opening up, the central government adopted intense austerity measures on both counts, namely monetary and fiscal policies. These actions began in the summer of 1993, which achieved noticeable results by the end of 1996 and resulted in roughly zero inflation in 1997. At the same time, there was a general decline in corporate profitability, an increase in the number of loss-making firms, a sharp increase in layoffs and unemployment, and a widening of the output gap, which led to a deflationary situation.

Second, intensive reform measures unveiled have reduced effective demand. Since 1994, China's economic system reforms have intensified, covering reforms of education, health care, pension, and housing systems, streamlining governmental institutions, reforming SOEs, and other significant initiatives. These reform measures are intended to provide institutional guarantees for healthy economic development in the long term. However, since the reform involves almost all urban and some rural households, its short-term austerity effect is noticeable. On the one hand, increasing unemployment and layoffs reduce residents' current and expected future income levels. On the other hand, the reforms of education, health care, and housing systems lead to increasing expected future expenditures, thereby pressurizing residents to cut back on current expenditures to save and accumulate for the future.

Third, the supply and demand imbalance. At present, China's economic development is facing two problems. From the demand perspective, it is how to realize progress in the consumption structure quality towards the direction of "use" and continue to upgrade in the direction of "housing" and "transportation." From the supply perspective, it is how to smoothly realize a continuous replacement of industrial sectors by adjusting the industrial structure to establish new economic growth points. However, there are specific problems in both perspectives: (i) The widening gap between residents' incomes since the reforms have led to a slow consumption structure upgrading, which is an essential reason for the faltering investment growth. (ii) The slow industrial structure upgrading. With poorer continuity in developing the industrial sector, and a delay in forming new points of economic growth. The result is that, on the one hand, the leading industries capable of driving economic growth in the new phase of economic growth have yet to develop a strong growth momentum. On the other hand, it has also resulted in a severe overcapacity of traditional processing capacity used to satisfy the previous consumption structure, thus leading to insufficient domestic demand.

Fourth, the Southeast Asian financial crisis erupted in the second half of 1997, and its contagion. It mainly displays in two aspects. (i) Changes in external markets or foreign demand have accentuated insufficient domestic demand. Since the reform and opening up, China's economy is much more closely related to the international economy. The rapidly growing net export demand has become essential in supporting the rapid growth of total social demand. Following the financial crisis in Southeast Asia, countries in crisis have significantly devalued their currencies and lowered their export prices. Such actions significantly impacted China's exports, resulting in the conflict between domestic supply and demand even more acute, and the price level was forced to decrease further. (ii) Since international market prices for many commodities are significantly lower than domestic market prices, the decline in the imported commodities' prices, especially raw materials, has triggered a significant reduction in the relative import costs, which, through the trade channel, has pulled down the PPI, thereby causing the CPI to fall, mainly the retail price of consumer goods.

7.2.2.2 Deflation in 2009

(1) *The primary conditions of deflation*

The society-wide RPI was negative for the first time since February 2009, with a rising margin of –1.6%, followed by eight consecutive months of negative growth, before starting to rebound in November 2009. The CPI also showed negative growth from February 2009, with a rising margin of −1.56%, and then also continued to show negative growth for eight months. The PPI has seen negative growth since December 2008, with a rising margin of −1.1%, followed by 11 consecutive months of negative growth.

(2) *The causes of this deflation*

They are mainly: (i) The influence of the global economic slump triggered by the American financial crisis. In the second half of 2007, the subprime mortgage crisis started in the United States evolved into a global financial crisis, causing China to suffer a significant impact. Suddenly, the growth rate of foreign trade dropped sharply, many SMEs were shut down, and many rural migrant workers returned to their hometowns. (ii) Lagged impact of tightening policies. To fight the inflation emerging in the second half of 2007, the central government adopted tightening monetary and fiscal policy measures. For example, monetary growth declined from January 2008 to January 2009, with M1 falling from 20.5% to 6.7% and M2 from 18.9% to 14.8%. The effects of the austerity policies were concentrated by 2009, as monetary policy has a time lag of between 6 and 18 months.

7.2.2.3 China's Exposure to Deflationary Risks

There are two main risks:

First, the PPI was a continuous declination. In 2012, China's PPI showed negative growth, down 1.7 percentage point year-on-year. It then fell consecutively, and the falling margin widened, dropping to 94.1 in the second half of 2015. Although there was an uptick in 2016, reversing the negative growth trend is still tricky. The overall price level fluctuations generally occur in the production field first, then spread through the industrial chain to the downstream industries, and finally to consumer goods. As a result, the society-wide RPI and CPI also slipped with it, staying at a lower level. The society-wide RPI was negative in January 2015 and has since hovered around 100 despite an uptick. The CPI has also fluctuated mainly around 102, although no negative growth exists.

Second, the quantity of money supplied and its growth rate remained high, while the velocity of money fell. The main manifestations of this situation are: (i) Money increment declined from 2010 to 2014, and so did the money velocity. From 2010 to 2014, the quantity of M1 and M2 supplied increased by RMB8,143.491 billion and RMB50,252.3 billion respectively, with an average annual growth rate of 6.89% and 14.06%. However, the year-on-year growth rate continued to decline, with M1 dropping from 21.2% to 3.2% and M2 dropping from 19.7% to 12.2%. Meanwhile, the M2 velocity continues to fall while the M1 velocity continues to rise. (ii) Money growth rose in volatility, and the money velocity declined from January 2015 to May 2016. Starting from March 2015, the year-on-year growth rate of M1 has been picking up and reached 23.7% in May 2016. Starting from January 2015, the year-on-year growth rate of M1 picked up in fluctuations, reaching 14% in 2016 before a downtick. However, the M2 velocity continued to fall in 2015, while the M1 velocity also began to fall back. During the 15 months, the quantity of M1 and M2 supplied increased by RMB7,614.12 billion and RMB21,898.49 billion, respectively, with an average monthly growth of 14.23% and 11.66%.

As seen above, China's quantity of money supplied and growth rate since 2010 remained higher than the GDP growth rate. Instead of being accompanied by the inflation risk, it is deflationary. The reasons are as follows:

First, the newly increased quantity of money supplied is enormous but has yet to be invested entirely in the real economy. In order to stimulate the economy, the Central Bank began to massively expanding money supply, with M1 and M2 in May 2016 being 2.01 and 1.59 times higher than in 2010 and 9.23 and 7.09 times higher than in 2001, respectively. The M2/GDP was 213% in 2015 and always less than 100% in America. However, this massive amount of new money is not invested entirely in the real economy. Since October 2015, the M1 supply has multiplied, lasting longer than expected, while the M2 supply has yet to keep up with this growth rate, meaning that part of the new money supply shows up on the corporate ledger as a sight deposit and is not invested in the real economy.

Second, overcapacity brings deflation. China is facing overcapacity in some major industries, including coal, iron and steel, cement, petrochemicals, flat glass, electrolytic aluminum, photovoltaic solar power, wind power, and shipbuilding. The overcapacity and the slowdown in demand growth have led to a marked decline in the general price level, creating intense deflationary pressures.

Third, external transmission mechanisms affect domestic price trends. There are two main types. One is the cross-border capital flow. According to statistics from the People's Bank of China, China's foreign currency reserve decreased by US$96.19 billion and US$44.682 billion in the third and fourth quarters of 2014, growing by only US$21.668 billion for the year, less than 1% of the US$509.726 billion growth in 2013. The decrease in foreign currency reserves made the growth rate of funds outstanding for foreign exchange in December 2014 fall below 3%. Since funds outstanding for foreign exchange account for 80% of the central bank's assets, the growth rate of the base currency has slowed sharply with a specifically required-reserve ratio, and banknote issuance net of reserves has only grown at a rate of less than 4%, well below the pre-2013 average of around 15%. The base currency suffered from anemic growth, coupled with the monetary derivation capacity decline caused by credit grudging of the banking sector and the stagnation of the real economy, creating downward pressure on prices at the monetary level. The second is the transmission of international bulk commodity prices. From July 2014 to January 2016, the price of Brent crude oil fell 77% from US$115/bbl to US$26/bbl; gold fell 44.6% from September 2011 to December 2015, and iron ore fell 80% from February 2011 to December 2015; LME copper fell 57.5% from February 2011 to January 2016, and LME aluminum fell 48.8% from 2011 May to November 2015; and international soybean and soybean meal fell 53% and 60% from September 2010 to March 2016, respectively. Declining international bulk commodity prices have driven down domestic PPIs, creating deflationary pressures.

The main measures to solve the above problems are as follows:

First, strengthen macro-adjustment. (i) Maintaining the forward-thinking of government policies. Since there is a lag in the policy effects, maintaining a forward-looking judgment of the economic situation can shorten the policies' lag length and enhance their adjustment effects. (ii) Maintaining the stability of government policies. The inflation in 2007–2008 and 2010–2011 and the deflation in 2009 lasted less than a year, and in particular, the rapid turnaround of the inflation in 2007–2008 and the deflation of 2009 were closely related to misjudging the economic situation and more arbitrary policies. The resulting policy instability has led to a shortage of predictability in the policy environment, thus discouraging businesses from investing and people from consuming. The reason for this lies in the uncertain economic reform. It requires the government to be firm in the direction of supply-side structural reform and maintain policy consistency and coherence. (iii) Diversify the policy instruments. On the one hand, it should implement proactive fiscal policy, such as moderately lowering tax rates on consumption and investment, while on the other hand, it should implement prudent monetary policy. Quantitative easing alone is not enough for China's monetary policy, and it also needs to establish price mechanisms, quantitative policy instruments, and other combined monetary policy methods to implement monetary policy. (iv) Establishing a monitoring and early warning system for economic cycle fluctuations and paying close attention to and monitoring fluctuating conditions in the financial and investment areas.

Second, resolve excess capacity. For this purpose, it should (i) continue to focus on the iron, steel, and coal industries and resolutely dispose of or shut down enterprises and production capacity failing to meet standards for environmental protection, energy consumption, and safety and that produce unqualified or obsolete products, under the law; (ii) revamp and upgrade traditional production capacity, and improve environmental protection, quality, and safety and other standards and process levels.

Third, implement effective income distribution and employment policies. In the long run, it also needs to address two main issues. The first is to close the gap between rich and poor. The rich's low consumption rate with the poor's limited consumption capacity leads to shrinking consumption and sequentially deflation. The second is to expand employment. Expanding employment is the most direct means of increasing income, while the rising unemployment leads directly to workers losing or reducing their earnings and also shrinking consumption and deflation. Therefore, implementing effective income distribution and employment policies, as well as enhancing effective demand are the ultimate solutions to curb deflation.

Part III
National Economic Development Strategy and Planning

Chapter 8
National Economic and Social Development Strategy

Formulating development strategies aligning with national conditions and adapt to the development needs of different periods is of great strategic significance. This chapter mainly analyzes development strategies, strategy systems and their selection and formulation, and the major development strategies identified by China.

8.1 Characteristics and Functions of National Economic and Social Development Strategies

8.1.1 Basic Features of the National Economic and Social Development Strategy

Economic and social development strategies belong to the national macro-strategic decision-making level in a broad spatial and temporal context. It is characterized by different features from other macro-policies, the implementation of which will have an overall systematic impact on society as a whole, and whose success or failure will bring about systemic benefits or systemic risks to the national economy. Specifically, economic and social development strategies have the following basic characteristics.

8.1.1.1 A Holistic Approach

Economic and social development strategy relates to the overall direction, mega-trends, and overall deployment of some significant aspects within national economic and social development. It mainly considers every possible angle of economic and social activities within a specific scope or field, emphasizes searching development ideas from a holistic perspective, and seize the key and fundamental issues that

M. Lin and T. Huang, *National Economics*,
https://doi.org/10.1007/978-981-96-9618-5_8

can affect the overall situation to promote the forward development of the entire economy and society. In the process of formulating the development strategy, it is mainly from the overall perspective, like playing a chess game, to coordinate the overall interests and safeguard the public and long-term interests as the starting point and objective. However, it is also necessary to consider local and personal interests and contradictions.

8.1.1.2 Long Duration

Economic and social development strategies, concerning overall direction, megatrends, and overall deployment of some significant aspects within national economic and social development. They need to take ten years or even longer to realize, and the objectives they set or the tasks they propose have a long-term guiding significance for the whole situation. They are also the guiding principle and the fundamental basis for formulating short- and medium-term programs and various economic policies.

8.1.1.3 Overarching

Economic and social development strategies are the highest level of national decision-making, formulated by the highest national decision-making body following legal procedures. As a result of public choice and a realistic manifestation of the common interests and striving goals of all society members, it has authority and legal effect. Specific national and regional development programs and policies must be subordinated to the economic and social development strategy.

8.1.2 Functions of the National Economic and Social Development Strategy

National development strategies, as a holistic design plan for the overall operation of the national economy, are the leading national policy with a bearing on the country's prospects and destiny. Its primary functions are as follows:

8.1.2.1 Goal Orientation

One function of economic and social development strategies is to establish the goals and paths for sustainably developing the national economy in the future. A country's economic and social development is about more than just expanding scale or space in the short term. More importantly, it is also about achieving sustainability in time so that the next generation can have the same development capacity as the previous generation. Concerning concrete implementation, the latter is often more complicated than the former. Therefore, unlike other decision-making objectives, the strategic development objectives should take a long view of the country and nation's prosperity. They should also formulate to find the direction, objectives, and ways for sustainable economic and social development rather than problem-oriented, like treating the head with headache and the foot with pain.

8.1.2.2 System Coordination

Economic and social development strategies respond to the constant changes in the external environment by building internal order through organizational coordination. The national economy is a highly complex system comprising many interdependent sectors and industries with multi-levels. Moreover, its development is influenced by various external environmental factors, such as social, political, scientific, technological, natural, socio-cultural, and psycho-social factors. The only means to cope with the complex external environment is to build internal orderliness, i.e., make the national economy have a high degree of internal coordination and the ability to maintain dynamic equilibrium. The development strategy guides and restrains the system's internal behavior through the blueprint planning such as goal orientation, revealing opportunities and challenges, development steps, and implementation plans. All these will make the system internally coordinated and orderly and achieve the resilience of adapting to the external changing environment flexibly, or meeting changes with constancy.

8.1.2.3 Unite as a Single Force

This function of the economic and social development strategy is mainly embodied in the following: (i) Reflecting public opinions. A successful economic and social development strategy must reflect the consensus of the whole society on the goals and ways of economic and social development for a certain period in the future, and depict people's shared vision with a broad base of public opinion. (ii) Bringing together people's wisdom. It must fully and effectively mobilize the enthusiasm and creativity of all sectors of society to concertedly overcome difficulties and promote the implementation of the economic and social development strategy. (iii) Gathering people's strength. A successful development strategy should be able to mobilize the whole society's resources to the utmost extent to implement the development strategy. "Where collective strength is employed, it is always victorious. Where collective wisdom is employed, it is always successful."[1]

[1] Liu An (179–122 BC), *The Huainanzi: A guide to the theory and practice of government in early Han China*, translated and edited by John S. Major et al., Columbia University Press, 2010, p. 305.

8.1.2.4 Overall Optimization

Programming and deploying economic and social development strategies emphasize optimizing objectives. Because in the view of system theory, the system is intrinsically a beneficial constraint on its development. It emphasizes the wholeness, comprehensiveness, and organic nature of the system's development, not just the "growth" of a particular subsystem or element. It much less allows the one-sided development of a particular subsystem to undermine the normal functioning of its rest and impede the benign development of the whole. The same applies to economic and social development systems. Of course, since the national economic and social system is dynamically changing, the relationship between elements within the system is also constantly adjusting. Therefore, the optimization is a relative concept of time and space.

8.2 System and Model of National Economic Development Strategy

8.2.1 National Economic and Social Development Strategy System

Economic and social development strategies are an organic system consisting of some essential elements:

8.2.1.1 The Strategic Guideline

It's also known as the guiding ideology. It is the fundamental principle that must be followed in choosing development strategy and the "soul" of the entire development strategy, reflecting the development concept and values of their maker. The strategic guideline is also the result of creative thinking, reflecting the basic strategic conception of the subject of development and guiding the formulation and implementation of the entire development strategy. Therefore, the strategic guideline is the development strategy's most principled, valuable, and creative element.

8.2.1.2 Strategic Objectives or Strategic Tasks

They are a materialization of the strategic guideline, mainly referring to the essential tasks and the economic and social development results achieved by the subject of development in a given period. The strategic objectives of economic and social development are often not a single but pluralistic. Therefore, there is also a quantitative system indicator over and above qualitative descriptions. Strategic objectives are the core of the entire development strategy, while the core issue of the development strategy is, to a large extent, how to determine appropriate strategic objectives.

8.2.1.3 Strategic Priorities

It mainly refers to critical links and factors decisively impacting on realistic strategic objectives. Choosing strategic priorities generally falls into two categories. The first is to select advantageous links or sectors significantly driving the realization of strategic objectives for a limited period to give full play to their pioneering and leading roles in developing the entire national economy. The second is to identify the weak links or sectors shown up as bottlenecks in realizing strategic objectives, aiming at removing the "short slab" or limitations in the development and promoting the overall coordinated development of the national economy. Breakthroughs in strategic priorities are decisively significant to realizing strategic objectives.

8.2.1.4 Strategic Steps

They mainly refer to the specific action and temporal planning to realize the strategic objectives. It consists of three aspects: (i) breaking down the general assignment under the strategic objectives into some actionable units; (ii) arranging the action sequence of the tasks of each unit following the law of the development of things; (iii) determining the time required for completing the tasks of each unit. On this basis, the strategic tasks of economic and social development, which can only be accomplished over a long time, will be realized step by step and in stages.

8.2.1.5 Strategic Countermeasures

They are mainly the basic strategies and action plans for putting the strategic guidelines into action, realizing the strategic objectives, and implementing the strategic priorities and steps. It is a strategic element of the overall development strategy featuring more flexible and targeted. Strategic countermeasures are also necessary to put forward ideas from an overall perspective. However, it should begin with the actual conditions, identify operable acting points in the light of the specific situation, and make a scientific demonstration and test of their effects.

8.2.2 Models of National Economic and Social Development Strategies

Since different countries have different concrete national conditions, facing different development tasks at different development stages, the formulated economic and social development strategies are also distinctive. The leading national development strategies are as follows.

8.2.2.1 Single vs. Integrated Development Strategies

(1) *Single development strategy*

The so-called single development strategy mainly refers to that of the post-war developing countries that aims at catching up with the developed countries, takes industrialization as the main component, and one-sidedly pursues the development strategy of economic growth. This development strategy was once mainstream in both developed and developing countries in the post-World War II era, because they were primarily influenced by the notion that "economic growth is economic development." International Development Strategy for the First United Nations Development Decade (1960–1970) emphasized economic growth and the pace of industrial development as the overarching development goals and indicators for measuring economic growth. Consequently, in choosing their development strategies, the late-developing countries have coincidentally targeted their pursuit of economic growth, intending to catch up economically with the developed countries. These countries concentrate on developing capital goods industries, usually under the direction of the government, impose high tariff barriers externally to protect domestic manufacturing, and use guiding plans and direct (indirect) subsidies to direct the manufacturing sector towards external exports.

Most developing countries followed a single development strategy from early stages of economic development until the 1970s and achieved rapid economic growth during the first decade of implementing economic development strategy. However, this approach has brought about a series of drawbacks. (i) Some countries have one-sidedly emphasized economic growth and over emphasized industrialization while neglecting or failing to take into account developing agriculture and other industries, thus resulting in a dislocated national economic proportion. (ii) When agriculture and other industries become "bottlenecks", they in turn, constrain industrial development. (iii) As a result of the stagnating agricultural development, a large number of peasants have flocked to the cities, leading to the cities' overpopulation and exacerbating urban–rural and regional conflicts. (iv) A single development strategy has ensured rapid economic growth while neglecting the rational income distribution, thereby people's lives experiencing poverty, who make up the majority of the population, have not improved, and the number of people living below the poverty line is even increasing, only deepening polarization. (v) When the disparity between rich and poor widens to a certain extent, it will become a factor of social and political instability. Therefore, under a single development strategy, excessively developing heavy industries has led to resources waste, severe environmental pollution, and ecological balance disruption. Especially as developed countries have transferred some heavy industries to developing countries, which has exacerbated environmental pollution in developing countries.

(2) *Integrated development strategies*

In contrast to a single development strategy, an integrated development strategy emphasizes implementing a development strategy maintaining a harmonious state of economy, society, and environment. The aim is to enhance the national welfare with promoting economic development, social progress, and environmental protection as its main components.

It was to amend a single development strategy and a revolution in the development paradigm, mainly resulting from a leap in understanding the development concept. Experience and lessons learned have led to the gradual realization that economic growth refers only to the growing output, including goods and services, of a country or region over a specific time, while economic development refers to the changes in economic, social, and political structures appearing with the growth of output, including harmonizing and optimizing various structures, such as the input structure, the output structure, the industrial proportions, the distribution mode, and the pattern of consumption, social welfare, and culture, education, and health. Compared with economic growth, the economic scope and social development is much broader, and its connotation is much more profound. Therefore, in formulating and implementing development strategies, the government should consider economic issues and value solving social and eco-environmental problems to achieve coordinated economic growth, social progress, and environmental protection.

There has also been an evolution of integrated development strategies. Initially, the principal objective was to keep social development in line with economic growth. It then focused on meeting the basic needs of the major population, including the material needs for food, housing, clothing, health care, culture, education, public transportation, social infrastructure, and also the residents' non-material needs for freedom, security, and others. Since the 1970s, some countries in Asia, Africa, and Latin America have been practicing this type of development strategy that balances with social development, aiming at continuously satisfying the nationals' basic needs based on economic growth. It also increased employment opportunities by focusing on developing agriculture, commerce, services, and other labor-intensive enterprises, and established a social security system to ensure not only quantitative but also qualitative improvements in the economies and nationals' living standards in developing countries. The strategy is a national development strategy of historical progress because it emphasizes human values and social progress.

Thus, development strategy goals have evolved from a single goal of economic growth to a multi-goal system. For example, the American Social Health Organization (ASHA) has proposed six indicators that can be used as development strategy goals for developing countries, namely, the ASHA index. It is mainly composed of six sub-indicators, i.e., the employment rate, the literacy rate, the average life expectancy, the per capita gross national product (GNP) growth rate, the birth rate, and the infant mortality rate.

In contrast to the ASHA indicators, a widely used indicator with the widest repercussion today is the Human Development Index (HDI) developed by the United Nations Development Programme (UNDP). HDI is the result of data processing and then synthesizing the actual values of human development markers. It is a value between 0 and l, and its magnitude is used to assess national welfare and social progress. In calculating the HDI, UNDP selected four representative indexes: average national life expectancy, adult literacy rate, combined enrollment rates, and per capita GNP in purchasing power parity (PPP) terms. HDI is widely recognized and used in the international community. However, the national development strategy HDI represents does not cover resources and environment. It cannot effectively forecast future development, which means that the indicator system for measuring a country's economic and social development needs further improvement.

With the rapid economic growth and industrialization of all countries, global environmental pollution and ecological damage are intensifying. The development of human society is facing a crisis of unsustainability. The crisis has triggered a rethinking of how humans live, produce, and consume, the spirit of science and technological development, mainstream economics, the relationship between human beings and nature, and the prevailing development view. It has been realized that human economic and social development can only be sustainable if it remains in harmony with the ecological environment. Therefore, it can be a development that "meets the present needs without compromising the ability of future generations to meet their own needs."[2] The 1992 United Nations Conference on Environment and Development held in Rio de Janeiro, Brazil, with the participation of 183 countries' heads and more than 70 international organizations. It adopted a series of documents relating to sustainable development, such as the Rio Declaration on Environment and Development and Agenda 21, which served as a concrete action plan. It also put forward a concept: "think globally, act locally," which fully embodied the fact that the new ideology of sustainable development had been acknowledged and accepted by the worlds' overwhelming majority of the countries and organizations. Also, it had become the guiding ideology in forming the economic and social development strategies of the world's major countries. So far, the sustainable development strategy, which embodies the trinity of economy, society, and environment, has become the mainstream development strategy model worldwide.

---

[2] World Commission on Environment and Development (WCED), *Our Common Future*, Oxford University Press, 1987, p. 8.

8.2.2.2 Strategies of Imbalanced and Balanced Development

(1) *Strategies of imbalanced development*

The strategy of imbalanced development refers to the strategy that, at a particular stage of economic development, a country focuses its efforts from reality on prioritizing the development of industries and sectors having a strong driving force for growing the national economy in the areas with favorable development conditions. Then it leveraged internal economic linkages to propel the growth of other industries and sectors and ultimately developing the entire national economy.

The strategy of imbalanced development is based on the theory of imbalanced development. According to the theory, regional spatial differences in economic development exist due to differences in natural resource endowments and non-uniformity in allocating social resources across countries or regions. Imbalance is a universal law of economic and social development. Therefore, economic development only occurs in some regions and industries of a country simultaneously. Economic progress may initially begin with technological innovation in only one industry or even one product in one region. And then, with technological innovation continuously improving and developing, innovative industries are formed. The emerging new industrial sectors spurs the development of its closely related upstream and downstream industries, and their technology spillover and learning effects also facilitate technological innovation in the supporting industries. New technologies and products may replace traditional ones due to their high efficiency and quality. Therefore, the industry gradually becomes the new predominant industry, causing the original one to either decline or undergo technological renewal. All this will be transmitted through the industrial chain to seep into the circulation, exchange, distribution, and consumption of society. In this regard, it improves the overall technological level and modernizes the economy, greatly enhances economic operation efficiency, and improves the output level of social material products and services. Of course, the changes described above have led, above all, to the emerging regions with innovative industries as poles of economic growth. The polarization effect makes the region the heartland of economic growth, but the development will not stop at this region only. Later on, the diffusion effect occurring in the pole of growth will again lead to the economic growth of the neighboring regions. This series of changes breaks the original equilibrium relationship of the national economy and forms a new equilibrium relationship on a new and higher basis. In this process, the original composition and structure of the national economy have changed to varying degrees, leading to the evolution of the economic structure. Transforming and upgrading the industrial structure, and continuously innovating the technological industrial structure have enabled the economy to develop based on a new material and technological foundation, thus promoting economic and social development goals.

As can be seen, an imbalanced development strategy applies the law of unevenness in regional economic development. For developing countries, implementing an imbalanced development strategy is more realistic particularly in the early stages of economic development and the context of resource scarcity.

(2) *Balanced development strategy*

The so-called balanced development strategy refers to simultaneous large-scale investment in the entire industrial system or in all sectors of the national economy and all regions to maintain a synchronized, comprehensive, and balanced development at the same rate.

Its theoretical basis can be traced back to Say's Law, which posits that "supply creates its own demand," so supply and demand are always balanced, and there can be no imbalance in the macro or regional economies. In addition, there are two major balance theories, represented by P. N. Rosenstein-Rodan's theory of big push and Ragnar Nurkse's theory of balanced growth.

P. N. Rosenstein-Rodan, in his 1943 article Problems of Industrialization of Eastern and South-Eastern Europe, argued that "industrializations of 'international depressed areas' like Eastern and South-Eastern Europe (or the Far East) are in the general interest not only of those countries, but of the world as a whole." Capital and markets can only realize scale economies if they are holistic and outward-looking. Therefore, capital and markets, supply and demand, must complement and support each other. Accordingly, Rosenstein-Rodan put forward the theory of big push, namely, countries should make large-scale investments in all industrial sectors so that all industrial sectors can be developed to be interdependent, serve as a market for each other, and overcome indivisibility. Its specific approaches are (i) to invest simultaneously in complementary industry sectors, thereby creating a market of mutual demand and addressing demand shortfalls that impede economic development, and (ii) to reduce costs, increase profits, and then overcome the impediments to economic development caused by insufficient supply through the labor division and mutual service provision.

In 1953, Nurkse put forward the Vicious Circle of Poverty theory in his book *Problems of Capital Formation in Underdeveloped Countries.* Nurkse argued that there are vicious circles of insufficient supply and insufficient demand in developing countries. The cycle of inadequate supply runs from (a) the low-income level to (b) low savings capacity, hence to (c) a lack of capital, leading to (d) low productivity and so back to a low-income level. In contrast, the cycle of inadequate demand runs from (a) the low-income level to (b) the low buying power of consumers, hence to (c) deficient investment inducement, leading to (d) low productivity and so back to a low-income level. Nurkse expressed that developing countries must adopt a balanced growth strategy to unknot the vicious circle and invest comprehensively in all sectors of the national economy on a large scale. He emphasized the constraints of small market capacity on economic growth and the decisive role of expanding market capacity in economic development, while also stressing that balanced growth included not only industry but also agriculture, foreign trade, and the like, particularly emphasizing the role of agriculture.

However, the balanced growth theory ignores the fact that: (i) Regions in general, particularly underdeveloped areas, lack the capital or other resources to promote the balanced growth of all industries and areas. Therefore, it is challenging to achieve balanced growth at the early stage of economic development. (ii) Market power usually tends to increase rather than decrease regional disparities. Developed regions, with better infrastructure, services, and larger markets, are bound to be more attractive to capital and labor, thus generating polarization effects and forming economies of scale. Although there is an expansion effect from developed regions to the surrounding areas, polarization tends to outweigh the expansion effect in a complete market, leading to wider regional gaps. Furthermore, different technological conditions can make the capital gains rate very different. At this point, capital factor mobility can cause capital factors to become scarcer in underdeveloped regions, making their economic development even harder.

Clearly, the theory of balanced regional development starts from a rational conception. It oversimplifies the problem by adopting a static analytical approach, which diverges too far from the objective reality of developing countries to explain the actual process of economic growth. Neither can it offer solutions to regional development challenges. Therefore, based on regional development practices in countries worldwide, empirical evidence or successful cases of a balanced development strategy has yet to exist. Nevertheless, after the theory of balanced regional development has been put forward, it has received a certain degree of attention in some underdeveloped countries and regions and has had an impact on the tendency of one-sidedly emphasizing industrialization and neglecting the balanced and coordinated development of regions and sectors in the process of industrialization. The theory emphasizes the importance of large-scale, balanced investment and the efficient allocation of scarce resources. It also highlights the limitations of market mechanisms and underscores the necessity of implementing macroeconomic planning. These aspects have had some positive impacts on less developed countries and regions.

8.2.2.3 Inward-Looking vs. Outward-Looking Development Strategy

(1) *Inward-looking development strategy*

The so-called inward-looking economy mainly refers to the economy only targeting the domestic market and relies primarily on expanding the domestic market to drive the growth of the national economy. The inward-looking development strategy refers to a closed and self-sufficient approach in which some developing countries advocate non-dependence on the international market, emphasizing, in particular, decoupling from developed countries. All production is oriented toward the domestic market, with exports serving only to facilitate imports. Simply put, it is an economic and social development strategy oriented toward developing an inward-looking economy. To date, there are two main types of inward-looking development strategy:

The first is a strategy that closes the door to international intercourse. It mainly refers to secluding the country from the outside world, emphasizing implementing an economic policy of complete self-sufficiency and strictly restricting foreign investment and trade. This inward-looking economy is often forced to be implemented under some particular domestic and international circumstances.

The second is the import substitution strategy, or import substitution industrialization (ISI) strategy. It is a development strategy whereby the state takes measures to restrict specific foreign industries in the light of the domestic market's needs. Then it gradually replaces imported products with domestically produced primary, semi-manufactured, and manufactured products, and accumulates the funds needed for economic development. This promotes the industrialization process and enhances the overall national economic self-improvement and development. Implementing this strategy generally progresses step-by-step, starting with the import substitution of general consumer goods, then the import substitution of durable consumer goods, and then the import substitution of capital and intermediate goods. The import substitution strategy is a historical choice.

In the 1950s and 1960s, developing countries were in the initial stages of industrialization. Resource scarcity, capital shortage, severe dearth of productive capacity and external demand made it difficult to sustain the growth of primary exporting, thereby discouraging imports of manufactured goods in general. Import substitution strategy is more suitable for those countries with backward industrial technology, distorted production or trade structure, but sufficient workforce. By developing labor-intensive industries with less significant scale economies and substituting imports of consumer goods, these countries aimed to accelerate domestic industrialization, reduce or eliminate economic dependence on developed nations, and foster national economic development. At that time, many countries in Asia, Africa, Europe, and Latin America practiced import substitution strategies to varying degrees. The strategies became dominant in developing countries from the 1930s and 1940s to the 1960s. By the 1970s, Brazil, Mexico, Argentina, India, and other countries practicing the import substitution strategy had established a relatively complete industrial system and national economic system and got rid of their previous status as primarily exporters of agricultural and mining products. In this regard, the whole national economy moved towards autonomy and independence. Some countries continued to pursue this strategy until the 1980s.

The main measures of the import substitution strategy include (i) resisting the entry of foreign manufacturing industries through using trade protection policies such as trade barriers, import licenses, import quotas, tariff protection, exchange control, and high or compound exchange rates to reduce the competitive pressure on the domestic manufacturing industry; (ii) providing financial and technical support to substitution industries, reducing and waiving taxes, and allowing accelerated depreciation, moreover, imposing low tariffs or reducing and exempting tariffs on imported capital goods and intermediate products necessary for domestic production is also beneficial, thus supporting and protecting domestic manufacturing industry with preferential policies; (iii) subsidizing or directly investing in establishing new industrial sectors by the government, thereby expanding employment, reducing external dependence, enhancing economic self-sufficiency, and promoting economic growth.

In the case of some newly industrialized countries and regions, such as Asia and Latin America, due to the protective market provided by the import substitution strategy, they rapidly developed manufacturing industries. Moreover, some modernized or semi-modernized domestic sectors have been established, thus contributing to the transformation of their economic structure, which has gradually shifted from the previously aberrant single economies to diversified ones. Due to the increased economic autonomy, the share of imported industrial goods, especially consumer goods, has declined considerably, and the self-sufficiency degree in machinery and equipment has increased. At the same time, a pool of specialized technicians and skilled laborers has been nurtured, and government departments have gained experience and knowledge in economic management through a large variety of industrial construction activities. These advancements enabled these countries to strengthen their economies and expand their exports of manufactured goods, creating miracles of rapid growth one after another.

However, over time, by the 1960s and 1970s, the positive role of import substitution strategies in many developing countries and regions gradually diminished. The negative impacts unceasingly emerged, mainly in the following ways. (i) Domestic substitution industries, developing and growing under conditions of little or no competition, had no pressure or motivation to improve their technologies and strengthen economic management, which resulted in their inefficiency, high production costs, and poor product quality, thus severely weakening their international competitiveness. (ii) Since it was mainly oriented to the relatively small domestic market, when the domestic market was almost near its maximum capacity, it became tough for the economy to further develop. (iii) Import substitution strategies actually changed the import structure, reducing imports of consumer goods but sharply increasing those of capital goods, intermediate goods, and raw materials. In this way, it worsened the balance-of-payments situation rather than eased the foreign trade and balance-of-payments deficits of these countries. (iv) The inefficient domestic substitution industries and the high product costs and prices limited backward linkages of import-substituting industries. (v) When implementing import substitution strategies, many countries have grossly neglected developing agriculture. Agricultural output is a massive source of capital for developing domestic industry, thereby obstructing agricultural progress and exacerbating urban–rural economic disparities. Therefore, many developing countries have gradually abandoned their inward-looking development strategy and shifted to an outward-looking one under pressure from a domestic market on the verge of saturation.

(2) *Outward-looking development strategy*

Quite the opposite of an inward-looking economy, an outward-looking economy is mainly oriented toward the international market, relying on developing foreign trade to drive the growth of the national economy. Simply put, the outward-looking development strategy is an economic and social development strategy oriented to developing an export-oriented economy, which mainly has two strategies:

First, Primary exporting development strategy. It mainly means that the state prioritizes the production and export of primary products such as agriculture and mining to develop the whole national economy and improve people's living standards. It's also known as the primary outward-looking development strategy. This strategy is marked by leveraging the country's natural resources to propel economic development. It is an economic development strategy adopted by almost all developing countries that have just gained independence in the post-war period. It is obvious that exchanging primary products from developing countries with industrial products from developed countries would not be an equitable transaction, and developing countries would have to bear substantial economic losses. However, since it was difficult in the short term to change the single economic structure that had developed during the colonial period, they could only take advantage of their natural resources and concentrate on producing and exporting one or more traditional primary products to increase their foreign exchange earnings, accumulate their capital, and expand their employment opportunities. At the same time, the economies of developed countries entered a period of rapid growth in the early post-war period until the 1950s and 1960s, and their demand for industrial raw materials and petroleum increased rapidly. This created a vast market for some countries exporting industrial raw materials and oil. For all these reasons, the industrialization of developing countries generally begins with a primary exporting development strategy. During this period, primary exporting constituted a significant part of the foreign trade of developing countries.

Support measures generally used by countries implementing this strategy to encourage the development of the primary exporting sector include (i) tax and credit concessions for producing and exporting primary products; (ii) tariff reductions and exemptions on imported machinery, equipment, and inputs required for producing primary exporting; (iii) providing services for the infrastructure, sci-tech popularization, and expansion of foreign markets needed to produce primary exporting.

Implementing the primary exporting development strategy has two different effects. (i) Enabling developing countries to break away from the closed state to access international markets. Not only does it increase their foreign exchange earnings and accumulate funds for economic development, but it also promotes the development of national economies and, to a certain extent, accelerates the urbanization process. (ii) Developing countries are disadvantaged in the international labor division. They are deeply affected by fluctuations in global market demand and prices, and are exploited by international monopoly capital. Because of the low demand elasticity for primary commodities, advances in science and technology have led to a decrease in the consumption of agricultural and mining raw materials per unit of product. Moreover, substitutes have sprung up successively in major importing countries. Prices of primary commodities had been continuously suppressed, even falling to the lowest post-war level, and many primary-exporting developing countries have become ailing. Developing countries must, therefore, seek new development strategies to pursue growth.

Second, Export substitution strategy. It mainly refers to the situation where one country has a particular industrialization foundation and relatively excess resources. It establishes considerable capital- and technology-intensive industrial sectors targeting the international market to give full play to its advantages in producing high-quality, low-priced and industrial labor-intensive products. Their aim is to replace exporting primary products in agriculture and the mining industry with exporting processed primary products, semi-manufactured products, and manufactured products. On this basis, the country, using the exported foreign exchange as the payment means for imports, purchases resources, products, and various advanced technologies and equipment urgently needed or cannot yet be produced domestically, so that the industrial structure can be gradually upgraded and optimized. In practice, export substitution generally undergoes three stages. In the first stage, the focus is on maximizing the advantages of a cheap workforce, promoting the growth of the light industry so that the proportion of light industrial products in the total export value is much higher than that of primary products. In the second stage, after the workforce advantage gradually diminishes, industrial adjustment policies are adopted to give full play to the capital-technology advantage and develop the heavy chemical industries. In this way, the proportion of heavy chemical products in the total export value is greater than that of light industrial products. In the third stage, a few developing countries and regions begin to establish high-tech industries, trying to gain a foothold in the world's export trade in high-tech industrial products. Each substitution brings a significant change in the country's industrial structure, thus jumping to a new level.

Before the 1970s, the economic structure of industrialized countries in Europe and the United States saw a marked adjustment. After more than 20 years of high economic growth in the post-war period, the workforce cost in these countries rose, and competition among enterprises intensified. Some large multinational corporations began to seek overseas processing bases. The Four Asian Tigers represent the newly industrialized Asian countries and regions with relatively scarce land resources, a plentiful workforce, and a considerable number of skilled and semi-skilled workers capable of meeting the requirements for processing production. They seized the opportunity to implement an export substitution strategy and began developing labor-intensive export industries. By the 1970s, these countries and regions began to build capital- and technology-intensive sectors, exporting products that replaced those of labor-intensive industries.

Main measures of the export substitution strategy include (i) providing export enterprises with preferential policies such as export tariff reductions and exemptions, export tax rebates, export subsidies, export credits, and export insurance, with an aim to reduce the export cost, enhance the competitiveness of exported products, and open up foreign markets; (ii) speeding up the construction of infrastructure adapted to exporting and setting up an export-centered industrial structure to strengthen the programming, supervision, and guidance of exported commodities. These above efforts are more conducive to the expansion of commodity exports.

In the 1980s, the export substitution strategy pursued by developing countries objectively coincided with the trend toward economic globalization, thus establishing its mainstream status in development policy choices. Until the second half of the 1990s, these emerging developing countries achieved rapid economic growth along the export substitution path. The main manifestations were: (i) Breaking through the limits of domestic market capacity and enhancing the competitiveness of domestic products. (ii) The international mobility of capital, knowledge, technology, and managerial skills contributes to higher labor productivity in developing countries, while the workforce export contributes to lower domestic unemployment and higher wage rates for domestic workers. (iii) The export substitution strategy can accelerate the process of industrial restructuring and upgrading, guide the advanced and internationalized industrial structure, encourage changes in the export structure, and also create the potential for sustained export growth. (iv) Where the growth of the domestic market mechanism has yet to be sound, it's also beneficial to enhance the quality and competitiveness of domestic enterprises with the help of standardized enterprises in the international market and the global market mechanism.

However, the export substitution development strategy also has its inevitable limitations. (i) The primary purpose of industry in those countries was to export, especially to the developed countries, while machinery and equipment also depended on imports from the developed countries, leading to a high level of dependency that made the national economy vulnerable to fluctuations in the global market. (ii) Shortage of domestic consumption due to the indiscriminate pursuit of export growth at the expense of domestic consumption. (iii) In pursuit of high investment, the state desperately issued more currency, which, together with the relaxed imports and currency devaluation, led to severe inflation. (iv) While foreign investment influx has brought in a certain amount of capital and technology, it has also resulted in varying degrees of control over some critical domestic industrial sectors, particularly machinery, chemicals, electronics, and pharmaceuticals, by foreign investors. Moreover, most countries implementing an export substitution strategy have been experiencing rising balance-of-payments deficits due to the sharp rise in prices of energy, equipment, and other commodities on the international market and the increase in the external debt service.

8.2.2.4 Comparison of Economic and Social Development Strategy Models

Based on the practice of countries in the post-war world, especially developing countries, the four strategies mentioned above basically meet the requirements of different developing countries at various development stages, each with its own applicability:

First, inward-looking development strategies are those of last resort for developing countries. It is crucial for developing countries to establish their independent industrial systems at the early development stages when their economic autonomy is very poor. They can utilize this strategy to build separate and self-reliant industrial systems oriented toward the domestic market. However, development under prolonged closure could not enable developing countries to escape poverty and backwardness. Therefore, with a specific industrial base, opening up to the outside world was objectively necessary.

Second, primary exporting strategies represent the most basic and simplest form of outward-looking development strategy. They are particularly suitable for developing countries that are not yet in a position to change their aberrant single economic structure. Due to the constraints from subjective and objective conditions, developing countries usually leverage their comparative advantages in natural resources and participate in the international economy, mainly through exporting primary products. However, it is easy to fall into a vicious circle of "production and export of primary products—low economic returns and technology—production and export of primary products," and eventually end up in the predicament of deteriorating trade terms.

Third, import substitution development strategies are more suitable for larger developing countries with richer natural resources but low levels of economy, technology, and education. It can develop national industries, improve foreign trade conditions, and provide the basis for economic self-sufficiency and global integration. However, after implementing import substitution strategies to a particular stage, the domestic market is gradually saturated, making the sale of products increasingly tricky. It becomes challenging for inward-looking single import substitution strategies to adapt to the requirements of world economic development. Therefore, many developing countries are forced to adjust and change their economic development strategy to participate actively in international economic activities, leverages external forces for economic growth.

Fourth, export substitution development strategies apply to small and medium-sized developing countries with insufficient natural resources but relatively abundant human resources and high economic, technological, and educational levels. The main feature is that it is export-oriented to shift the focus of economic activity from the national or regional market to the international market. In this way, it promotes the development of the entire national or regional economy.

Overall, the above four strategies have advantages and disadvantages in promoting economic development. They complement each other rather than exclude each other. Studying the types or modes of economic development strategies focuses on a realistic understanding of the historical background, applicability conditions, and pros and cons of various strategies. By leveraging their strengths and addressing their weaknesses, countries can make the right choices in the critical junctures of economic development.

8.3 Selection and Formulation of China's National Economic Development Strategy

8.3.1 The Essence of Strategy Formulation and Selection

A development strategy is planning weighty issues that have a bearing on the national future long-term development. Its formulation is the highest level of national decision-making by the state's highest authority based on a profound analysis of the national context and the external environment in which economic and social development occurs. The first step and core part of strategic management is strategy formulation. Strategic decision-making must address two fundamental questions: What are the development goals? How can the development goals be achieved?

The core of strategy development lies in determining the government's mission and objectives for promoting economic and social development over a given period.

The mission mainly describes the vision, shared beliefs, and values of the country's future strategic management. The new three-step strategy for China's modernization depicts the following vision: "The first step was to double the 2000 GNP by 2010, to ensure the people live a better-off life and form a relatively complete system of socialist market economy; the second step was to achieve greater economic growth and establish more complete systems and institutions by 2020; and the third step was to realize basic modernization and build China into a prosperous, strong, democratic and culturally advanced socialist country by the mid-twenty-first century, when the PRC would celebrate its centenary in 2049." This vision fully embodies the values of realizing shared prosperity and the people-centered governance philosophy, and it serves as a source of motivation and a conduct code for implementing the government's strategies and its management work.

Objectives refer to the results expected by the national strategic management departments in carrying out its mission. The national development strategy covers various areas, including harmonizing the regions and sectors of the national economy and economic, social, and natural relations. Therefore, the objectives of the development strategy are to integrate various aspects of development, reflected in a comprehensive system of objectives.

Formulating development strategies, in addition to determining objectives, also includes selecting strategies, which involves determining the path, steps, means, and measures for realizing the development goals. Strategies are a series of specific policies and action plans, including introducing a series of laws, statutes, administrative rules, and regulations concerning establishing institutions, allocating and utilizing resources, and functioning governing agencies. Their core issue is allocating and using economic and social resources, which relates to how to maximize the use of actual and potential domestic and international resources in line with the principles of equity and efficiency, aiming to achieve the goals of national economic and social development.

8.3.2 Mechanisms for Selecting and Formulating Strategies

Formulating a national economic development strategy involves the activities within a public decision-making system, carried out by various decision-makers following a specific strategic decision-making process under a particular decision-making framework. The public decision-making system mainly consists of three essential components: the strategic decision-maker, the strategic decision-making framework, and the strategic decision-making process.

8.3.2.1 The Strategic Decision-Makers

The strategic decision-makers refer to individuals, groups, or organizations directly or indirectly involved in formulating strategies. Due to different modes of political system, levels of economic and social development, and countries' cultural traditions, the composition and functioning patterns of the strategic decision-makers are different. Generally, the main strategic decision-makers are as follows:

(1) *Official policymakers*

Official policymakers mainly refer to the government in a broad sense, including the legislative, executive, and judicial branches. In China, the governing party plays a crucial role in formulating development strategies. Therefore, official decision-makers in China mainly include:

First, the legislature. In China, it means the National People's Congress (NPC) and the local people's congress at various levels and their standing committees. It is the organ of supreme power with legislative, decision-making, appointment and removal, and supervisory powers. One of the manifestations of the decision-making power is the formulation, promulgation, and implementation of resolutions, decisions, orders, and regulations that pertain to national or regional major economic and social issues, including formulating strategies for national economic and social development.

Second, the executive. It mainly refers to the State Council, its constituent parts, and local people's governments at various levels, which are the executive bodies of the state power. The State Council, as the central government, is the supreme administrative organ with the power to manage the whole country administratively, economically, socially, diplomatically, and so on, including the right of strategic management.

Third, the judiciary. It refers mainly to the people's courts and procuratorates, which are essential parts of the state's power structure. They are delegated by the people's congress, exercising approval and procuratorial authority independently of the administrative organs.

Fourch, the governing party. The Communist Party of China (CPC) is China's governing party and political leader. The CPC's political leadership of the country is reflected in the Party's leadership over political principles, political direction, and vital policies. The CPC is responsible for formulating and proposing all fundamental principles, basic lines, significant guidelines, and important decisions of various fields involving the development of the state and society. Therefore, the CPC not only serves as the leading center of the government system, dominating the process of operating government, but also dominates the formulation of strategies and policies for national economic and social development. The other political parties, as participating parties, take part in formulating significant decisions on national economic and social development, mainly through participating in the Chinese People's Political Consultative Conference (CPPCC), focusing on political consultation and democratic supervision.

(2) *Non-official policymakers*

Non-official policymakers are mainly social forces outside the official policymakers directly or indirectly involved in strategic decision-making process for national economic and social development. They generally include:

First, interest groups. It mainly refers to groups of people with specific common values, shared interests, and common attitudes. It also refers to specific groups of people with the same occupation or industry. In modern society, interest groups with different interest demands are widespread, numerous, and diverse. Their influence on strategic decision-making depends on their social status, number of members, economic strength, organization degree, and others. In Western countries, the channels through which interest groups influence public decision-making include lobbying, dissemination, donations, and protests. The influence of interest groups on strategic decision-making has a positive significance, and their existence can form a social constraint on decision-making power. Since the reform and opening up, China's social foundations have undergone profound changes. With the market economic system and a diversified pattern of interests established, interest groups have become a social force with an increasingly important influence on the country's major decisions.

Second, mass media. In an information society, its role in influencing national development strategy decision-making is manifested in the following: (i) Direct influence. Since the information it disseminates is often selected or processed for social issues and strategic decision-making information before it is made available, it directly affects the audience's perceptions and attitudes toward social issues and the content and nature of decision-making information, thus influencing strategic decisions. (ii) Indirect influence. The direct, rapid, and extensive nature of mass media's disseminating information can affect the public social environment of strategic decision-making. (iii) Intermediary influence. The mass media can be an intermediary between the decision-making authorities and the public, thus increasing the degree of public participation in strategic decision-making.

Third, think tanks. They are primarily official, semi-official, or privately organized policy research institutes composed of various professional researchers engaged in interdisciplinary and cross-field comprehensive decision-making research. In modern society, decision-making problems are increasingly complex, as are the difficulties in making decisions and controlling their impact. Moreover, the requirements for decision-making quality are increasing. Scientific decision-making is increasingly inseparable from the participation of decision-making research institutions.

Fourth, individuals in the general public. In modern society, the public is the most widespread unofficial decision-maker. In China, individuals participate in decision-making on development strategies mainly by expressing their opinions and proposing policy ideas through selection by vote, hearings, letters and visits, and the Internet. Many decisions, such as environmental protection, can only be implemented with the public's cooperation. To ensure that strategic decisions align with the public's interests and enjoy broad public support, it is necessary to ensure full public participation in strategic decision-making and attach great importance to the public interests' appeal.

8.3.2.2 Strategic Decision-Making System

The strategic decision-making system is the organizational basis for strategic decision-making. It is also the patterns of power allocation and responsibility sharing formed by distributing decision-making power and responsibilities among decision-makers, and the rules that guide the labor division and activities of multiple decision-makers in the decision-making process. The decision-making system is generally composed of the following subsystems:

(1) *Decision-making subsystem*

It consists mainly of decision-makers in the power organs and is the core part of the decision-making system. It has the highest decision-making power, the primary leadership responsibility for final approval, and makes the final decisions on goals and implementation programs.

(2) *Advisory subsystem*

It comprises experts and scholars from official and private think tanks in various fields. It is an intellectual support organization or "staff" assisting the decision-making subsystem. Its primary responsibility is to provide the decision-making subsystem with policy information, sci-tech and intellectual support, and formulation of various options required for decision-making.

(3) *Information subsystem*

It mainly consists of various intelligence information agencies serving as the decision-making system's eyes, ears, and nervous system. It is mainly responsible for collecting, organizing, storing, and transmitting information to provide the information needed for strategic decision-making.

(4) *Monitoring subsystem*

It mainly consists of internal monitoring units at various levels within political parties, legislature, executive, and judiciary, and public supervision by interest groups, mass media, and citizens. It is mainly responsible for checking and supervising the legality of decision-making power, content, and process. Their aim is to ensure the legitimacy of strategic decisions.

8.3.2.3 Strategic Decision Process

The strategic decision-making process is its relevant steps and links. A reasonable strategic decision-making process should align with the law of and reflect the logic of scientific decision-making. When the decision-making process is institutionalized and elevated to the status of law, it becomes the decision-making process. The general decision-making procedure is as follows:

(1) *Identifying problems*

Problems are difficulties and obstacles to overcome in developing objective things. Finding problems is a prerequisite for solving problems and the starting point for strategic decision-making.

(2) *Determining the objectives*

The so-called objectives are the expected results to be achieved by the decision. The first step is to determine the appropriate objectives based on the problems identified and then ultimately solve the existing problems by realizing the objectives.

(3) *Formulating programs*

A program is an action plan for achieving objectives and solving problems. Based on the finalized objectives, the primary purpose is to find and formulate methods, ways, means, and countermeasures.

(4) *Assessing programs*

Assessment is analyzing, arguing, and evaluating alternatives. It also involves process of weighing and comparing multiple options' feasibility, coordination, benefits, and risks.

(5) *Program selection*

Selecting one of the proposed options for eventual implementation is known as "merit-based selection." The selection is based on evaluating options, and "merit" is not an absolute concept of "perfection" but a relative concept of "satisfaction under defined conditions." The outcome of program selection might be choosing one of the identified alternatives or integrating their strengths to form a new program.

The decision-making process is theoretically complete when the program selection process is finished. The next step is the decision-making implementation phase However, since "practice is the sole criterion for testing the truth," implementing the program can also be regarded as the final practical test of the decision-making results. By closely tracking the program's implementation process and the feedback of information on the implementation, it is possible to determine whether there is a deviation in the implementation or whether the decision itself is imperfect to decide whether there are inherent flaws in the decision itself. This will inform whether the decision needs further revision. Only when the decision-making program is successfully implemented, a complete decision-making process is truly complete.

8.3.3 *Decision-Making Based on Scientization, Democratization, and Legalization*

Strategic development decision-making is the highest level of decision-making in the country. It has a profound and lasting impact on society's long-term, overall fundamental interests and the glory and disgrace, rise and decline of the country and the nation. Therefore, every effort must be made to ensure that strategic decision-making is scientific, democratic, and legalized.

8.3.3.1 Scientific Strategic Decision-Making

Scientific strategic decision-making means that strategic decisions should be formulated based on scientific evidence and in accordance with objective laws. It should not only from the country's actual circumstances and respective capabilities but also in line with the international development trend, with a certain degree of foresight. Scientific strategic decision-making requires the following primary conditions:

(1) *Sensitive and efficient information system*

Information is the basis and raw material for decision-making, and decision-making involves processing and utilizing information. Without information, there is no decision-making. The information needed for strategic decision-making is considerable in quantity, high in quality, and diverse in type. It should also be timely, accurate, comprehensive, and applicable. In order to enhance the scientific approach to strategic decision-making, the information system must continue to improve the operational quality and efficiency, including (i) reasonably controlling the quantity of information and ensuring its quality; (ii) keeping the information channels unimpeded and transmitting the information in a high-quality and efficient manner; (iii) gradually expanding the information network and exploring useful information promptly; (iv) adopting advanced technologies to improve information processing capability.

(2) *Scientific and reasonable prediction*

Under the guidance of scientific theories based on historical and current information, scientific prediction refers to effectively foreseeing and speculating on the future to reveal the direction of development, development trends, opportunities, risks, and the like. It draws on a range of scientific approaches, thus providing the basis and services for scientific decision-making. Scientific forecasting is the preliminary stage of scientific decision-making. In order to improve the precision and scientific rigor of forecasting, it is necessary to (i) carefully observe the principles of systematic, objective, and continuous forecasting, as well as the principle of combining qualitative and quantitative analyses; (ii) determine the target of forecasting reasonably and define its purpose; (iii) select appropriate subjects for forecasting based on the merit of the objective matter to be forecasted; (iv) ensure the forecasts are based on historical and current information; (v) select appropriate forecasting methods to comprehensively predict with multiple methods to verify accurate predictions repeatedly where conditions permit; (vi) objectively evaluate the forecasting conclusions and make necessary adjustments and corrections to the errors.

(3) *Sound decision-making system*

Strategic decisions are made by decision-makers within a specific institutional framework and systemic arrangements. A reasonable decision-making system must be first built to ensure that strategic decision-making is scientific, democratic, and legalized. This system mainly includes:

First, reasonably dividing decision-making authority. (i) It involves the complete and proper execution of government functions. To this end, it is necessary to clearly define the reasonable labor division between the government and the market. It's also important to further simplify and decentralize government, which has a bearing on a vital and efficient market economic system. (ii) It pertains to the reasonable labor division within the government departments. Government management departments are administrative management systems with a labor division and cooperation at various levels and functions. The practice has proved that a rational division of decision-making authority among government departments is necessary for improving management effectiveness.

Second, a decision-making system combining planning and decision-making. Modern social economy is becoming increasingly enormous and complex, with technological reforms coming out in one wave after another and new things emerging in an endless stream. This results in rapid changes in the economic and social structure and the accelerated development pace. Hence, factors affecting modern decision-making are increasingly complex. Given the limitations of individual knowledge structure, it is often difficult for decision-makers to perform all decision-making tasks. Thus, the modern decision-making system has evolved into one that combines two phases: decision-making research and decision-making action. They are interconnected but separate, divided but coordinated. The former refers to the process by which official and/or private think tanks provide decision-makers with alternatives and argument data, while the latter refers to the process by which decision-makers reach a conclusion based on decision research. Decision-making research serves as the foundation for decision making action, while the action itself is the purpose of decision-making research. Decision-makers must consider various opinions from all stakeholders before making decisions but think tanks cannot replace decision-makers in the decision-making process. Ultimately, decision-making is the decision-makers' responsibility, which depends on their quality, courage, and determination.

Third, a sound system of monitoring and accountability for decision-making. All work needs appropriate rules and regulations to standardize and constrain. Since strategic decision-making is critical, institutionalizing its operation is all the more important. Below are some key decision-making systems:

The first is the decision-making responsibility system. It aims to strengthen the responsibility consciousness and constraints of the decision-makers to inhibit blind and arbitrary decision-making. Dividing decision-making authority and clearly defining decision-making responsibility are complementary, meaning the authority and responsibility should be parity. If the decision-making mistakes provoke a significant loss, the decision-maker, especially the core leaders, must bear the corresponding responsibility, including administrative and legal responsibility, possibly political responsibility.

The second is the vetting and approving regime for decision-making. Significant decisions must be subject to strict vetting and approving process. The people's congress system is China's fundamental political system. The people's congress is the highest authority at each level of government, so their role in approving significant decisions must be fully realized. All significant decisions must be examined and approved by them, and only after they have been approved can the decisions be put into effect.

The third is the decision-making supervision system. In order to prevent abusing decision-making authority and to supervise the correct implementation of decision-making programs, it is necessary to build a broad and effective decision-making supervision and monitoring system. Decision-making supervision consists of two parts: internal supervision and external supervision. Internal supervision is also known as government supervision or administrative supervision. It refers to the supervision within the government administrative system, mainly including vertical supervision at the upper and lower levels, horizontal supervision of functional departments, supervision by the NPC and CPPCC, and supervision by the discipline of the Party. External supervision is also called social supervision. It refers to supervision outside the government administrative system, mainly including legal supervision by the judiciary, public opinion supervision by media organizations, and democratic supervision by the public.

(4) *Well-designed decision-making processes and methods*

A decision-making procedure is an institutionalized arrangement and stipulation for decision-making work, indicating that decision-making work must be carried out in a particular logical order. Whether the decision-making procedure conforms to the objective law of scientific decision-making will affect whether the decision-making result is scientifically sound. Additionally, whether the decision-making procedure can fully incorporate democracy will determine whether the decision-making result reflects the democracy spirit and conforms to the public opinion. Moreover, whether the decision-making procedure conforms to the provisions of the law will determine whether decisions are made under the law.

Decision-making methods are the means, pathways, and tools for people to achieve goals, solve problems, and complete decision-making work. Whether the decision-making method is scientific directly determines the quality of decision-making work. Strategic decision-making is a highly complex management work involving multifaceted issues, considering complex factors, and achieving diverse objectives. Such intricate and complex decision-making work requires comprehensive application of various decision-making methods. In this regard, it is possible to make decisions with more foresight and more confidence in success.

8.3.3.2 Democratization of Strategic Decision-Making

Democratization of strategic decision-making means that strategic decision-making should be broadly based on public opinion, i.e., listening to the voice of all walks of life. This not only means to safeguard the right of citizens to participate in discussing and managing state affairs but also accept citizens' supervision and inspection consciously. It should be scientifically verified by experts and scholars and ultimately make strategic decisions in line with the people's fundamental interests. The basic requirements for the democratization of strategic decision-making include the following:

(1) *Value proposition of people-centered decision-making*

The value proposition or strategic values of strategic decision-making are the government's preferences, aspirations, and goals in formulating strategies. Strategic values of decision makers are decisive in determining whether a strategic goal is worth pursuing, which strategic goals should be prioritized, for whom and why a certain strategic action is undertaken, what means are appropriate, and whether certain outcomes of strategy implementation are desirable. The government's strategic values are the basis of its strategic decision-making, which influence and constrain the government's decision-making activities and permeate every stage of the decision-making process. These values are the conduct codes constraining the government's decision-making and the guiding principles. They ensure that the government makes appropriate choices and puts this value proposition into practice through government policy-making activities.

People are the country's masters and enjoy the democratic rights to manage national affairs, economic and cultural undertakings, and public affairs of society. Ensuring people's extensive participation in public decision-making is an essential requirement for building a democratic political system. It's also an important guarantee that decisions on national development strategies align with people's interests. The people-centered philosophy require the government to take the people's interests as the starting point and ultimate goal of all its work in decision-making. The aim is to meet people's multifaceted needs continuously and promote comprehensive human development. These values also serve as the primary criteria for focusing on decision-making issues, selecting decision-making goals, implementing programs, and evaluating the results of decision-making. In other words, the problems identified for strategic decision-making should be generally concern to the people, the goals set should be those generally desired by the people, the programs formulated should be those generally accepted by the people, and the evaluation of the program should be based on extensive consultation with the people's wishes and scientific verification by experts and scholars. In this way, it will be possible to open up a wide range of opinions, draw on collective wisdom, and form correct decisions on a democratic basis, transforming strategic decisions into a consensus among the people and ultimately into collective action. Meanwhile, the decision-making bodies should respect people's initiative spirit in the implementation of strategic decision-making, anchor on the practice of the people, and provide feedback on the practice of information continuously back to the decision-making bodies. Therefore, the strategic decision-making program is constantly verified, supplemented, and refined, thus unifying the subject and object, as well as the subjective and the objective elements of decision-making. In the area of public affairs like strategic decision-making, it is vital to be highly vigilant and resolutely oppose replacing public interests with sectoral or local benefits, guarding against the misuse of public power for personal gains or the abuse of public power to the detriment of the public interest.

(2) *Fully perform the people's rights as masters of national affairs*

The general public should be enabled to participate in national strategic or public decision-making through a variety of forms and channels, and the main measures are as follows:

First, further improving the system of people's congress. The system of people's congress is china's fundamental political system for ensuring that the people are masters of national affairs. All major decision-making by the government must be submitted to the people's congress for review and approval. There is an urgent need to improve the system of people's congress by deepening the reform of the political system, focusing on the following areas: (i) The people's representatives must be elected by the citizens, choosing those who can represent the people's will and who can genuinely work on behalf of the people. (ii) The representatives must consult widely with the people's wishes and suggestions. (iii) After the meeting, representatives must communicate how they have fulfilled their duties to their constituents. (iv) Establishing a system to ensure liaison between the representatives and the constituents is of great importance.

Second, establishing a system whereby leaders at various levels regularly reach the grassroots to gain a broad understanding of public opinion. It should give full play to the fine tradition of maintaining close ties with the masses and reach out to the public, aiming at understanding ordinary people's real lives, aspirations, and difficulties. The state and local authorities at various levels strive to be open and transparent in their major measures and policies related to economic development, key construction projects, public infrastructure, welfare facilities, science, education and culture, environmental governance, and the like. In this way, they can better gauge public views, solicit popular opinions, and pool collective wisdom, thus better mobilizing the enthusiasm of the general public.

Third, establishing a citizen monitoring feedback, and evaluation system for strategic decision-making. Citizens' political enthusiasm, motivation, and satisfaction in participating in a series of public decisions, including strategic development decisions, are closely related to the participation results. The so-called public participation result is whether the appeals expressed by citizens in the public decision-making process are respected and reflected in public decisions.

8.3.3.3 Legalization of Strategic Decision-Making

The legalization of strategic decision-making refers to the legal form of the decision-making system, procedures, and results clearly and specifically stipulated to ensure that strategic decision-making is carried out by the law. Legal means and legal system are used to ensure that the scientific and democratic strategic decision-making is put into practice. Strategic decision-making in development is a public choice. To ensure that public choices are truly in the best interests of the broadest possible range of people and conform to the requirements of scientization and democratization, it is necessary to formulate the required rules for public decision-making or public choices, providing the pattern, standards, style, and direction for governmental actions. Such rules are not the subjective will of any individual but the Constitution and the law. In this way, public decision-making fairness and justice can be ensured, accepted, and supported by the public.

(1) *Legitimization of the strategic decision-makers and their decision-making authority*

The main content includes two aspects: first, the legalization of the decision-maker. In a particular field of social life, whether or not the government has the decision-making power in the affairs of this field or what kind of decision-making power it has should be clarified by the law. Being a decision-maker means having the legal eligibility for decision-making. Only then shall the result of its decision-making have legitimacy and legal effect. Second, the legalization of decision-making authority. The government's and its agencies' decision-making authority should also be stipulated by law so that they can only make decisions or perform their duties within their respective legal authority. Any decision-making and governance behavior exceeding their legal authority is unlawful and thus ineffective.

(2) *Legalization of strategic decision-making procedures*

In view of the democratization of decision-making, the process of decision-making should be a bottom-up collaboration between the government and the people, aiming at finding a strategy for governing the country that benefits the people, based on investigating mass conditions, respecting the people's will, and integrating collective wisdom. This process requires a series of technical links and an institutionalized regulation to ensure that democracy is substantive rather than merely formal.

China's strategic decision-making process generally consists of four stages: problem identification, goal definition, program formulation, and program evaluation. How to fully reflect the requirements of scientization and democratization in these stages is the focus that the legal norms of the public decision-making process to be resolved. It is essential to put important governmental decisions on an open, transparent, and standardized procedural track. In this way, the administrative power can be effectively constrained, thereby preventing the abuse of public power and protecting citizens' fundamental rights and freedoms.

(3) *Legalization of strategic decisions*

The legalization of strategic decisions refers to the process of transforming development strategies into laws. A development strategy is a blueprint for a country's economic and social development over a more extended period, thus guiding the country's economic development and social progress. Legalizing strategic decisions gives them legal status and guarantees their implementation through the state's coercive force, thus greatly enhancing their effectiveness.

8.4 China's National Economic Strategy System

China's national economic strategy system has gone through four major stages.

8.4.1 Industrialization Strategy Prioritizing Heavy Industry

The People's Republic of China was founded in 1949, marking a critical moment for determining the development path and strategy choice. Under the specific historical background, China chose a path of industrialization prioritizing the development of heavy industry. China's focus was shifted to industrial construction commencing in 1953. All kinds of resources began to be tilted to industrial construction. The goal was to establish a group of new heavy industrial sectors of colossal scale and advanced technology, and to transform the existing industrial sectors. We also aimed to improve the strength of China's industries, especially the national defense industry and the heavy industry, meanwhile improving the industrial layout in the country's central and western regions. Regarding the construction content, the focus was on the 156 construction units built assisted by the Soviet Union. As for the construction direction, the metallurgical and mechanical industries were prioritized, with investments mainly in Northeast, Central-South, and East and North China.

Because of the enormous investment required for heavy industry, the long construction period, and the slow investment recovery, the industrialization led by heavy industry necessitated a substantial increase in the investment ratio in national income, focusing on developing heavy and defense industries at the expense of agriculture. It supported the cities by sacrificing the countryside, even prioritizing developing production by temporarily scrimping and saving.

After about five years of uphill battle, the foundation for China's industrialization was initially laid. During the First Five-year Plan period, the proportion of modern industry in the total value of industrial and agricultural output rose from 26.7% in 1952 to 33.6% in 1955. Forty manufacturing systems were initially formed, with manufacturing capability of more than 1,900 relatively important products, which have been able to meet the general needs of domestic construction in terms of quantity. Trains, automobiles, large machine tools, and large equipment have been produced independently. National defense, machinery, electronics, chemical, and energy industries, which are vital to national security and the economy, were established.

At the same time, the path of heavy-industry-led industrialization also had some adverse effects. The main one was that developing agriculture lagged far behind that of industry. When agriculture failed due to natural disasters, it significantly impacted the industries using agricultural products as raw materials, making it more challenging to continue industrialization and affecting people's living standards to a certain extent. Overall, however, many of the projects constructed during the First Five-year Plan period became the foundation and backbone of China's industry in later years, playing a pivotal role in the national economy and people's livelihood.

8.4.2 A Strategy Centered on Economic Construction, Internal Reform, and Opening to the Outside World

In 1978, China began to strengthen the Four Modernizations and strove to develop the social productive forces as the overriding central task. The aim was to prompt the country to shift the country's focus towards large-scale socialist economic construction.

After identifying the pathway centered on economic construction, the first and foremost task was to reform the economic system. Whether centralized or decentralized, the previous system of planned economy was unable to promote economic growth sustainably and effectively. For this reason, the traditional system must be reformed.

Reform began in the rural areas, a weak link in the planned economy. Solving the problem of feeding the population was the immediate motivation for the rural reforms. In 1978, the system of fixing farm output quotas for each household was resumed in areas such as Anhui and Sichuan that had been devastated by disasters, resulting in a substantial increase in food production. This system-based rural reform gradually spread across the whole country. It was of excellent demonstration value because it significantly increased agricultural productivity through the systemic innovation of the household contract responsibility system alone, without considerable capital investments or significant improvements in production technologies.

Reforms in the countryside spurred urban reforms. Urban economy involves the core areas of the planned economic system. Urban reforms made breakthroughs in three main aspects: (i) Enterprise reform. It began with expanding enterprises' autonomy and enhancing their vitality. Enterprises were allowed to make additional production plans based on market demand, and profits became an important indicator for assessing enterprises. (ii) Fiscal reforms in conjunction with urban reforms. Local autonomy was expanded, and the development of the private economy was de facto allowed and encouraged. (iii) Price reform. It was proposed that "reform of the price system is the linchpin upon which the success or failure of the entire reform depends," Its intention was to make prices reflect both value and changes in supply and demand.

With little progress in reforms within the planned economy, the non-public economy outside the system became a critical outcome and driving force in urban reform. Under the ideological conditions of the time, a roundabout approach was taken to the development of the non-public economy, i.e., acquiescence was given before recognition. It was only after the successful fixing farm output quotas for each household in the countryside that the non-public economy was gradually recognized. In 1984, breaking the restriction on the number of workers employed by private enterprises was, in fact, to recognize the development of the non-public economy. The non-public economy gained legal status and developed rapidly. By the mid-1980s, the non-public economy had assumed a pivotal position in the national economy.

In terms of reform methods, China's reforms have taken a gradually advanced path. It started with the more manageable tasks before moving on to the more difficult ones and advanced from outside to inside the system. The reason is that there are no precedents to follow in China's reforms and that China is a country with a large population, vast territory, and significant regional differences, which necessitate careful selection of reform strategies and paths. Gradually advanced reform has made it possible to sustain the survival of industries that lacked comparative advantages in the previous national economic system. In this way, it's conducive to preserve their role in economic growth, promoting employment, and avoiding the social unrest that could result from the mass closure of enterprises during the transition. Moreover, it also enabled the establishment of competitive industries with comparative advantages. Despite their positive role in achieving stability and promoting national economic development, gradually-advanced reforms also have drawbacks. Within the market economy framework, there still exists a mechanism whereby power determines resource allocation, and the market mechanism is insufficient. Power-determined resource allocation hinders efficient resource use, and the authorities reaping rent-seeking benefits are likely to drag on continued reform. Therefore, China's reforms must continue to deepen, implementing a broader and more vigorous reform strategy.

Another vital way China revitalized its economy was through its open-door strategy. Because of the economic system and mechanism, it was tough to fully integrate with the international market at the beginning of the reform and opening-up period. In this regard, China took a gradually advanced approach to opening up to the outside world. Coastal provinces adjacent to Hong Kong, Macao, and Taiwan region were first chosen to establish special economic zones, and then progressively expanded to other regions. Four special economic zones were set up in 1980, and fourteen open coastal cities were established in 1985. Opening up to the outside world was gradually implemented throughout the country when conditions became favorable.

Opening up to the outside world has facilitated domestic reforms. In the process of integrating with the international market, the pressure of competition has prompted Chinese business managers to improve their products' quality and reduce costs.

Meanwhile, the government has drawn on the successful experiences of economically developed countries. Especially after accession to the WTO, China's laws, policies, and business practices needed to adapt to internationally accepted norms. All these factors have contributed enormously to domestic reforms. Opening up to the outside world also allows the government and enterprises to learn from more mature experiences, eventually reducing the costs and risks of the reform process and making their behavior more disciplined.

Opening up to the outside world has robustly contributed to improving the quality of China's economy. At the beginning of the reform and opening up, when labor-intensive industries represented by the textile industry were being transferred from developed to developing countries, China successfully absorbed the industrial transfer and contributed to reviving China's textile industry. This industrial upgrading enhanced China's economic strength and improved people's living standards. In the 1990s, China, for the second time, seized the opportunity of international industrial restructuring and transfer, thus realizing industry upgrading. Since the twenty-first century, through the all-around opening up, China has become the preferred production place for the manufacturing segment of the IT technology industry in the latest global industrial shift, facilitating China's upgrading of industrial technologies for the third time. China's industrial structure, quality, and efficiency have been substantially upgraded through the reform and opening up, and domestic residents' living standards have also risen considerably.

8.4.3 Three-Step Strategy for Building Socialist Modernization

8.4.3.1 Objectives and Procedures of the Three-Step Strategy

In the early stages of the reform and opening-up period, it became a crucial issue to formulate a strategy in line with China's national conditions to guide the national economy to develop healthily and rapidly. As early as 1979, Deng Xiaoping proposed that the main task at present and for a lengthy period was to carry out the modernization program. Chinese path to modernization must start from China's characteristics and keep a foothold in two fundamental national conditions: a weak economic base, and a large population without enough arable land. These factors determined that China's modernization started from a deficient level, thereby the time for modernization will be longer. China can only achieve modernization gradually based on this low starting point in a phased and step-by-step manner. In 1987, Deng Xiaoping expressed in China's medium- and long-term development strategy: The first step was to double the per capita GNP by 1990, from US$250 in 1980 to US$500. The second step was to double it again by the century's turn, reaching a per capita GNP of US$1,000. Realizing this goal means China has entered a moderately prosperous society, transitioning from poverty to comparative prosperity. The third step was more critical about this goal, namely quadrupling the US$1 trillion figure of 2000 within another 30 to 50 years, roughly a per capita GNP of US$4,000, equivalent to the level of medium-developed countries. China's three-step medium- and long-term development strategy has been graphically summarized.

Since the 1980s, the three-step strategy has successfully guided China's economic development and achieved great success. China's GDP was RMB451.7 billion in 1980, RMB1,854.7 billion in 1990, and RMB8,944.2 billion in 2000, with a per capita GDP of RMB460, RMB1,634, and RMB7,084, respectively. At 2000 exchange rates, the GDP exceeded US$1 trillion. China's development in the last two decades of the twentieth century was basically in line with the three-step strategic program.

8.4.3.2 The New Three-Step Development Strategy

By the century's turn, through the concerted efforts of the entire nation, China had achieved the first two strategic modernization steps, with comprehensive economic and social development and a population that had generally attained a well-off standard of living. The third step of the three-step strategy is the most crucial. Upon completing it, China will have escaped from its backwardness and entered the ranks of moderately developed countries. In 1997, the third step of the three-step strategy was refined into a new three-step strategy, aiming to fulfill the third step's objectives well. According to this new strategic arrangement, after entering a moderately prosperous society at the end of the twentieth century, China will largely achieve the modernization goals in three stages: 2010, 2020, and 2050. In 2002, it was explicitly proposed that in the first two decades of this century, efforts should be concentrated on building a higher level of moderately prosperous society benefiting more than a billion people, and in 2007, it was further emphasized to "strive for new victories in building a moderately prosperous society in all aspects."

8.4.4 Development Strategy for Building a Moderately Prosperous Society in All Aspects

In 2012, China changed the slogan of "comprehensively building a moderately prosperous society" to "fully complete building a moderately prosperous society" by 2020 as a new goal for modernization. To achieve this goal on schedule, it is essential to adhere to Six Adherences. They refer to adherence to the people's dominant status, scientific development, deepening reforms, the rule of law, coordinating the domestic and international situations, and the Party's leadership. Moreover, efforts will be made to achieve Five Principal Goals, namely, maintaining medium- to high-speed economic growth, generally improving people's living standard and quality, significantly increasing the national quality and societal civility, generally improving the ecological environment quality, and establishing a more mature and stable system in all aspects. At the same time, it is necessary to uphold the five development concepts: innovative, coordinated, green, open, and shared development.

First, adhering to innovative development and striving to improve the quality and effectiveness of development. For this purpose, it is necessary to implement the innovation-driven development strategy, seeking growth based on innovation, cultivating new development engines, expanding new spaces for development, building a new industrial system, and establishing a new development mechanism. It's also crucial to innovate and improve macro-adjustment methods.

Second, adhering to coordinated development and striving to form a balanced development structure. For this reason, it is necessary to continue to implement the overall strategy of regional development, aiming at carrying out the new three main strategies based on the four major regions. They are to coordinately develop the Beijing-Tianjin-Hebei region, to construct the Yangtze River Economic Belt, and to promote the Belt and Road Initiative. This approach aims to coordinate the development of different regions, urban and rural areas, material and spiritual civilization, and integrate economic and national defense construction.

Third, adhering to green development and striving to improve the ecological environment. This involves promoting the harmonious coexistence of human beings and nature, accelerating the construction of functional zones, and propelling low-carbon cyclic development, thus comprehensively conserving and efficiently utilizing resources. Simultaneously, environmental management has been intensified to fasten an ecological security barrier.

Fourth, adhering to open-up development and realizing win–win cooperation. With regards to this, it is important to improve the strategic layout of opening up to the outside world, form a new open-door system, push forward the construction of the Belt and Road, and deepen cooperation and development between the mainland, Hong Kong, Macao, and Taiwan region. It is also essential to actively participate in global economic governance and assume international responsibilities and obligations.

Fifth, adhering to shared development and putting forth efforts to advance well-being for all. This involves increasing the public service supply, carrying out poverty alleviation projects, improving education quality, promoting employment and entrepreneurship, and narrowing the income gap. Moreover, it requires establishing a fairer and more sustainable social security system to promote the construction of a Healthy China and achieve balanced population development. Thus, all people will move into a moderately prosperous society in all respects.

Chapter 9
National Economic Planning

Development planning and strategy are two sides of the same coin, which are interlinked yet distinct. Development strategy is the basis of the development planning, and the development planning is an extension and refinement of the development strategy. Based on the analysis in the previous chapter, this chapter further discusses the national economic planning and its system, the indicator system, and the preparation of the national economic planning.

9.1 Features and Functions of the National Economic Planning

9.1.1 National Economic Planning and Its Characteristics

A national economic planning is an action plan for future economic development. It is an important function of national economic management, encompassing the dynamic process of drawing up a program, organizing and directing economic activities based on it.

The following features characterize economic planning: (i) Predictive. Planning is future-oriented, a pre-arranged outline of where and how the economy will develop before action is taken. (ii) Coordinative. The essence of the planning lies in coordination. It is a systematic and organized arrangement of future economic activities. (iii) Guiding. The planning is about action. It directly guides and broadly influences the reality of economic life and directly relates to effective economic activities. (iv) Selective. The planning involves choosing activities or decision, i.e., a choice and decision on possible goals and multiple paths for future economic development. (v) Multilevel. The economic planning is also multilevel due to the multilevel nature

M. Lin and T. Huang, *National Economics*,
https://doi.org/10.1007/978-981-96-9618-5_9

of the economic activities, which requires identifying different levels of planning: macro, meso, and micro.

A national economic planning is the program concerning the overall development of the national economy prepared by the state. To be more precise, it is a plan for national economic and social development. The predecessors of China's national economic and social development planning were the national economic plans or national economic and social development plans.

The Five-year Plan has been essential to China's national economic plan. Its primary purpose was to plan major national construction projects, the productive forces distribution, and the critical proportional relationships in the national economy, aiming at setting goals and directions for national economic development. Except for the period from 1949 to the end of 1952, a period of national economic recovery, and the period from 1963 to 1965, a period of national economic restructuring, China has consistently prepared five-year plans since the First Five-year Plan in 1953.

In 1982, the term "national economic plan" was changed to "national economic and social development plan," which incorporated the science and technology and social development plan in addition to the national economic development plan, and was renamed from the Seventh Five-year Plan onwards. The basic connotation of the national economic and social development plan is that it is a programmatic document guiding the development of the national economy based on the objective requirements of the economic laws. It reflects all the major aspects and processes of the social expanded reproduction. It also stipulates the direction, scale, speed, relationship of proportionality, and efficiency of national economic development.

The 13th Five-year Plan states that the purpose of the national economic plan is to articulate national strategic intent, and clarify ambitious goals, primary mission, and critical economic and social development initiatives. It is a behavioral guide for market entities, an important basis for the government's duties, and a shared vision for Chinese people of all ethnic groups.

9.1.2 Functions of the National Economic Planning

Planning is an essential function of management. National economic planning has the following functions when analyzed from the perspective of national economic management.

9.1.2.1 Goal Decomposition

"In all things, success comes from prior preparation; otherwise, the effort will be wasted."[1] One of the primary roles of planning is foreseeing and consciously arranging for the future, clarifying development goals, reducing the blind pursuit

[1] The Book of Rites (*Li Ki*), the State of Equilibrium and Harmony.

of economic activities and potential risks, and enhancing adaptability to changes in the internal and external environment. In this era of rapid change in the economy, society, science and technology, and market demand, it is all the more necessary to have a far-sighted vision of the future, organize it, and guide people toward it. The national economic program is a master plan related to the overall operation of the national economy and a vital national blueprint concerning where to direct the entire economy. By defining the main objectives and major strategic tasks, the planning not only sets out clear directions and requirements for development in various fields, but also points out the bright prospects and goals for the entire nation. In this way, it generates a powerful, cohesive force that mobilizes and organizes all trades and industries and hundreds of millions of people to actively promote the process of socialist modernization.

9.1.2.2 Concrete Coordination

Another main effect of the planning is to ensure that economic and social activities can be harmonized and that all forces can work together through unified planning and multifaceted coordination. In this way, it promotes comprehensive, coordinated, and sustainable economic and social development. The national economic system is a complex giant with multiple factors, variables, and objectives. With the progress of economic globalization, intellectualization, and modernization, the economy, society, science and technology, and the environment increasingly intertwine and integrate. Operating national economic system is not only affected and governed by many variables within the economic system and its movement laws, but also by various external factors and the state of the world's economy, technology, and markets. To solve the major problems within this complex system, it is objectively necessary to comprehensively consider all factors and interlinkages within and outside the system. It's also crucial to specifically coordinate the relationship between the development of many fields and the interests of many parties, balancing urban–rural, regional, and economic and social development, and the harmonious development of man and nature, as well as the requirements of integrating domestic development and opening up to the outside world. Comprehensively considering and coordinating the requirements of all aspects is one of the most complex programming tasks and the essence of planning.

9.1.2.3 Resource Allocation

Both government planning and market adjustment have the function of resource allocation. Because of the shortcomings of the market mechanism, there is an objective need for government macro-adjustment and micro-regulation. The practices in various countries have proved that effectively combining the "invisible hand" and the "visible hand" is more conducive to promoting the healthy development of the market economy. As far as the economy is concerned, the market's role in allocating resources is decisive. However, the planning also has the function of resource allocation, mainly reflected in (i) guiding and influencing the market entities' behavior and (ii) directly allocating public resources. From the perspective of development trends, on the one hand, with the deepening of institutional reform, the socialist market economic system is becoming increasingly mature, the government functions have gradually changed. As a service-oriented government, its public service functions are more prominent. On the other hand, with the economy and society developing, the public sphere is ever-expanding, and the demand for public products and services is ever-growing. At the same time, the land, water resources, energy, and other resources are becoming increasingly scarce, and employment, social security, and other social issues are increasingly prominent. Therefore, enhancing public resource allocation in programming is even more critical.

9.1.2.4 Priority Orientation

Facing a situation in which many sectors are waiting to be revitalized, it is necessary to determine priorities and concentrate the necessary resources on first resolving the critical aspects of a particular development stage that have a decisive impact on the success or failure of the overall situation. Meanwhile, resolving the prominent contradictions in social and economic life and the major issues playing a leading role in promoting modernization are of great importance. From the overall situation of the national economy, a crucial function of programming is to conduct comprehensive analyses, prioritize, and pinpoint the main focus direction with an eye to current conflicts and future trends.

Since the beginning of the twenty-first century, to strengthen the functions and roles of programming, China has stressed the following three points in the planning process. (i) Articulating national or regional strategic intentions. Economic planning must declare the overall development strategy publicly, with development direction, goals, and priorities as its main elements. The aim is to strengthen national cohesion and inspire people's spirits, and guide efforts to strengthen international and regional cooperation. (ii) Guiding the market entities' behavior. By its nature, this involves fully leveraging the market's decisive role in allocating resources and steering the healthy development of industries and enterprises toward effective competition through programming. (iii) Clearly defining the focus of the government's work. The primary purpose is to give better play to the government's role and strengthen the central government's macro-adjustment responsibilities and capacity, as well as local government's responsibilities, such as public services, market supervision, social management, and environmental protection. Meanwhile, the government has committed to the people through its programming to seek support from all sectors of society and accept the masses' oversight.

In 2012, China further proposed that the government should strengthen the formulation and implementation of development strategies, programming, policies, and standards. It emphasized the importance of a sound macro-adjustment system guided by national development strategies and planning, with fiscal and monetary policies as the main instruments. Thus, the function and role of national economic planning have become even more important in modernizing the country's governance system and capacity.

9.1.3 Relationship Between Development Strategy and Planning

National economic planning and strategy are interrelated but distinct, each with different emphases and focuses, mainly including:

First, development strategy is the core and soul of development planning and annual plans. In the medium- and long-term planning, the development strategy is usually expressed as part of the planning's content. However, there is generally no independent or complete direct carrier to clarify development strategy in annual plans; instead, it is embedded in an annual plan's guiding ideology and key objectives. Medium- and long-term planning must follow the established development strategy, which determines the development direction, objectives, and major tasks for the planning period. The annual plan is based on the medium- and long-term planning, specifically breaking down and implementing its tasks and indicators. Therefore, the development strategy is the basis of a development planning, while the development planning is the basis of the annual plan. Strategy comes first, and the program follows. Therefore, it becomes a concrete action plan that can be laid out and checked. In this sense, development planning and annual plans continue and refine development strategies.

Second, regarding the implementation scope, the development strategy is overarching, i.e., a comprehensive and highly generalized overall scheme. Development planning and annual plans differ: their master programs and aggregative plans are comprehensive deployments, whereas specialized and regional planning and plans are often localized arrangements. Therefore, implementing and realizing development strategies are not always on the same level as development planning and annual plans. Regarding implementation time, the development strategy is medium- and long-term, whereas the development planning is generally medium-term. Even when a visionary goal is attached to a five-year planning, it is usually only fifteen to twenty years. As for annual plans, the time frame is even shorter. This dictates that a significant development strategy may be carried out through several medium- and long-term development planning or a dozen to several dozen annual plans.

Third, regarding the content of implementation, the development strategy is directional and principle-oriented; the medium- and long-term planning is a contoured or broad-brush description, while the annual plan is concrete and fine-lined. From the viewpoint of implementation methods, the development strategy is mainly qualitative; the medium- and long-term planning attach equal importance to qualitative and quantitative measures, but the annual plan is mainly quantitative. The differences in their implementation content and methods are determined by the inherent nature of development strategies, medium- and long-term planning, and annual plans.

In short, the relationship between development strategy and the development planning is analogous to the relationship between strategy and tactics. Generally speaking, it is mainly about the whole and the part. Strategy refers to the overall scheme to reach the goals, and tactic refers to the specific action plans taken to reach the strategic goals. Furthermore, strategy and tactic are mainly about the relationship between ends and means; strategy comes first, and tactics follow, subordinating to and serving the strategy. From this point of view, the development strategy is strategic in nature, while the medium- and long-term planning and annual plan are tactical.

9.2 China's National Economic Planning System

A national economic planning is the concrete implementation of the national economic development strategy and a critical link in the strategy's implementation. A national economic planning is essential for the state to strengthen and improve its macro-adjustment. It also provides an important basis for the government to perform its duties in economic adjustment, market supervision, social management, and public services. The establishment of a sound national economic planning system and the scientific preparation and organization of the implementation of national economic and social development planning are conducive to the rational and effective allocation of public resources, guiding the market to play its basic role in allocating resource and promoting the sustained, rapid, coordinated and healthy development of the national economy and the overall progress of society.

At present, China's national economic planning system is a three-level-and-three-category management system, in which the national economic and social development program is divided into state-level, province-level (including autonomous regions and municipalities, the same applies hereafter), as well as city- and county-level planning based on the administrative structure. These planning can be categorized into master planning, subject-specific planning, and regional planning according to the objectives and functions.

State-, province- (including autonomous regions and municipalities), and city- and county-level master planning are prepared by the respective governments at each level and drafted by their development and reform departments in conjunction with the relevant departments. Dedicated planning are prepared by the relevant departments of the governments at various levels. Inter-provincial regional planning are prepared by the development and reform department of the State Council, in conjunction with the relevant departments of the State Council and the relevant departments of the provincial governments within the region.

9.2.1 State-, Province-, and City- and County-Level Planning

The national economic and social development planning is divided into three levels according to the administrative levels:

9.2.1.1 State-Level Planning

A state-level planning is a national planning formulated by the national functional departments responsible for planning. It is the state's overall scheme for national economic and social development, influencing the overall situation and long-term interests of the country. It intends to define the main directions and tasks of the country's economic and social development within a specific period and determines the strategic objectives, strategic priorities, and policies of development. The state-level planing mainly articulates its strategic intentions, specifies the ambitious goals, main tasks, and significant initiatives for economic and social development, guiding the behavior of market entities. Moreover, it is an important basis for the government to perform its duties.

9.2.1.2 Province-Level Planning

A province-level planning is formulated for the national economic and social development of the provincial administrative regions or their specific industries and fields, following the guidelines and policies of the central government and considering their specific conditions. It is a planning system compiled under the purview of the provincial government, with a reasonable hierarchy and a clear division of responsibilities but articulated and coordinated to each other and practical for implementation. It is also an integral part of the national planning system. The following two points shall be taken into consideration when preparing province-level planning: (i) The national medium- and long-term development planning must be taken as the overarching principle. In terms of guiding thoughts, development principles, strategic guidelines, and major indicators, which should be effectively articulated and coordinated with the national planning to realize the objectives of the national planning well. (ii) They shall be integrated with specific provincial conditions. Full consideration should be given to the specific characteristics of each province and its position in the overall country economic and social development so that development at the provincial and regional levels can be planned from an overall perspective.

The main elements of a province-level planning are as follows: (i) The preparation of a master development planning. This is a comprehensive, strategic, and spatial long-term planning for national economic and social development to guide the long-term development of the province's national economy and society. (ii) The preparation of a spatial planning. It is a comprehensive planning concentrating on the spatialization of the master development planning from large to small in terms of geography. (iii) The preparation of a subject-specific planning. It refers to subordinate plans that derived from dividing the master plan by areas, sectors, or development elements. However, they are also guided and constrained by the spatial planning at the same administrative level.

The points of focus during the operation of the province-level planning system structure are as follows: (i) Establishing the province-level development master planning and keeping them essentially unchanged. At the same time, territorial, urban-town system, and long-term national economic and social development planning are integrated into a cohesive whole. (ii) Strengthening the operation of spatial planning. The preparation of the corresponding subject-specific planning is determined based on the requirements for preparing a comprehensive spatial planning; the dedicated planning must be subordinate to the comprehensive spatial planning, while also emphasizing a top-down approach to planning. As the geographic level decreases, the timespan of the planning tends to be smaller, while the spatial constraints tend to be stronger. (iii) Pay attention to the coordination in the planning process. Because some subject-specific planning have a certain degree of synthesis, they have linkages and mutual influence with spatial planning, such as comprehensive transportation network planning and water resources allocation planning, both of which function as spatial guidance.

9.2.1.3 City- and County-Level Planning

City- and county-level planning are prepared by local governments at the city and county levels for the national economic and social development of the administrative regions under their jurisdiction or for their specific industries and fields, following the guidelines and policies of the central government's program and in consideration of the specific conditions of their regions. They are also an essential part of the national planning system.

At present, China's city- and county-level planning have many problems, such as an excessive number of planning, intersecting and repetitive content, and inadequate articulation and coordination, even contradiction among them, which are the important reasons leading to prominent contradictions in the process of industrialization and urbanization, such as excessive resource consumption, disordered spatial development, eco-environment deterioration, etc. In this context, we should also actively promote the reform and innovation of city- and county-level planning and promote the "integration of multiple planning" and "multiple planning in one", involving economic and social development, urban and rural, land use, and eco-environment protection, thus forming one planning or blueprint for one city or county. Doing so will bring the following benefits: (i) it is conducive to solving prominent problems in the city- and county-level planning, such as self-contained systems, content conflict, and inadequate articulation and coordination, thus ensuring the effective implementation; (ii) it contributes to strengthening the government's capacity for spatial control and realizing the intensive, efficient, and sustainable utilization of the space of national land; and (iii) it promotes the reform process of the government's planning system and establishes a unified, articulated, functionally complementary, and coordinated spatial planning system. They are of great significance in accelerating the transformation of economic development, optimizing the mode of spatial development, firmly implementing the system of functional zoning, and promoting the coordinated development of the economy, society, and the ecological environment.

The main tasks of the planning reform at city and county levels are to explore the specific ideas of "multiple planning in one" involving economic and social development, urban and rural, land use, eco-environment protection, The aim is to study and put forward replicable and generalizable pilot schemes to ensure a unified planning or blueprint for each city or county. At the same time, it should explore ways to improve the city's and county's spatial planning systems to establish a mechanism for articulating and coordinating related planning. Specific tasks include: (i) Rationally defining the planning periods. This involves considering the requirements of laws and statutes and the characteristics of relevant programs to explore the establishment of unified and coordinated medium-term and target planning years, which will serve as time nodes for various planning to articulate objectives and tasks. (ii) Reasonably determining planning objectives. This requires considering the related planning objectives involving economic and social development, urban and rural, land use, eco-environment protection, and others, to study the core objectives of "multiple planning in one" and rationally determine the indicator system in line with different main functional positions of counties and cities and the requirements of the upper planning in the context of large regions where cities and counties are situated. (iii) Rationally defining planning tasks. This involves properly guiding the development direction and layout priorities of population, industry, urban-town planning, public services, infrastructure, ecological environment, social management, and the like based on the resource and environmental bear capacity. Moreover, it involves exploring the spatial control subdivisions of relevant planning, delineating the urban development boundary, the permanent basic farmland red line, and the ecological protection red line to form a reasonable spatial layout of cities, towns, agriculture, and ecology. It should also explore improving economic and social, resource environmental policies and spatial control measures. (iv) Building a mechanism for articulating and coordinating cities and counties' spatial planning. This requires making suggestions to improve the planning systems at city and county levels and exploring the working mechanism for integrating, articulating, and coordinating various planning to meet the needs of supporting the effective implementation of spatial planning in cities and counties.

9.2.2 *Master, Subject-Specific, and Regional Planning*

9.2.2.1 Master Planning

A master planning is a strategic, programmatic, and comprehensive planning for national economic and social development and is the foundation for preparing dedicated and regional planning at peer and lower levels, and for formulating relevant policies and annual plans. The approved master planning holds an overarching position among the various peer planning, and other planning should be consistent with it.

National and provincial master planning are medium- and long-term planning with a horizon of at least five years. The programming horizon for medium-term planning is generally five years, while the long-term needs ten years or more. The programming horizon for city- and county-level master planning is determined based on actual needs.

National, provincial, and city- and county-level master planning are prepared by peer governments and drafted by their competent programming authorities in conjunction with the relevant departments.

9.2.2.2 Subject-Specific Planning

A subject-specific planning is prepared for specific areas of national economic and social development and serves as a refinement of the master planning in specific areas. A subject-specific planning often contains clear objectives and specific tasks, and is highly actionable. As a further extension and refinement of the tasks of a comprehensive planning, it is also the basis for the government to guide that field's development, approve and authorize major projects, arrange government investment and financial expenditure budgets, and formulate relevant policies in specific fields.

The planning period of a subject-specific planning is determined on an as-needed basis. It generally coincides with the five-year national economic and social development plan but may extend over a longer horizon for some major issues.

In principle, the areas for preparing a national subject-specific planning are confined to major projects concerning the overall situation of the national economy and social development so that they must be approved and authorized by the State Council. Also, there are areas where the state would arrange a large amount of investment, mainly including (i) the infrastructure construction of agriculture, water conservancy, energy, transportation, communications, and other sectors; (ii) the development and protection of land, water, ocean, coal, oil, natural gas, and other important resources; (iii) the ecological construction, environmental protection, and prevention and mitigation of natural disasters; (iv) public utilities and services, such as science and technology, education, culture, health care, social security, and national defense construction; (v) industries requiring government support or regulation; (vi) critical strategic tasks and projects identified by the national master planning; and

(vii) other areas stipulated by laws and administrative regulations or required by the State Council.

Subject-specific planning is prepared by the competent departments of the governments at various levels, generally the governments at or above the county level or their relevant departments, within the scope of their responsibilities. If the content of the subject-specific planning is related to other departments, then it should be prepared in conjunction with the relevant departments. If the content of the Subject-specific planning involves the responsibilities of multiple departments, it should be prepared by the departments designated by the government at the same level.

9.2.2.3 Regional Planning

A regional planning is the overall deployment of national economic and social development within the scope of a specific region, aiming to promote the coordinated development of the region under the guidance of the overall regional development strategy, thus realizing the regional advancement and the coordinated development of the planning region's economy, society, ecology, population, resources, and environment. China's 13th Five-year Plan stipulated a clear vision for regional planning: "Based on the master strategy for regional development and guided by the Belt and Road Initiative, the coordinated development of Beijing, Tianjin, and Hebei, and the Yangtze Economic Belt as leading plans, we will promote the formation of north–south and east–west intersecting economic belts primarily along the coastline, the Yangtze River, and major transportation routes as well as a pattern of coordinated regional development that ensures the mobile and well-ordered flow of factors of production, effective functional zoning, equitable access to basic public services, and development that aligns with the carrying capacity of the environment and natural resources."[2]

A regional planning is prepared for the national economic and social development of specific inter-administrative regions. It refines and implements a master plan in a specific region. The inter-provincial regional planning is the basis for preparing provincial master and subject-specific planning of provinces, autonomous regions, and municipalities directly under the central government within the region, with a planning period of approximately five years in general, which can be extended to more than ten years.

The scope for preparing national-level regional planning involves regions where the state prepares regional planning across the province (autonomous regions, municipalities). These include areas closely linked to economic and social development, megacity-based urban agglomerations with strong radiating capacity and attendant effects on overall development, and key development or protection areas identified in the national master planning. The main contents include forecasting and analyzing

---

[2] *The 13th Five-Year Plan for Economic and Social Development of the People's Republic of China (2016–2020)*, Central Compilation and Translation Press, 2016, p. 145.

population, economic growth, and the bearing capacity of resource and environment; dividing the region into the various functional areas for economic and social development; and proposing measures to ensure the implementation of the planning.

Regional planning across provinces are prepared by the development and reform departments of the State Council, which organizes its relevant departments and the relevant departments of the provincial governments in the region to work together.

What calls for special attention is that considerable weight must be given to strengthening the articulation and coordination between planning so that various planning can be harmonized to create synergies among them. The articulation should follow the principle that subject-specific and regional planning should be subordinate to peer and superior master planning, lower-level government planning should be subordinate to higher-level government planning, and subject-specific planning should not contradict each other. The requirements of territorial, urban, functional zoning, and other related fields' planning should also be fully considered in preparing regional planning across provinces.

9.2.3 Main Planning in Related Fields

There are four main types of planning in related fields that have a close relationship, complement, and mutually reinforce each other with national economic and social development planning:

9.2.3.1 Planning of Functional Zoning

The planning of functional zoning is strategic, fundamental, and binding. It also serves as the fundamental basis for master planning in national economic and social development, regional planning, urban planning, and others. Specifically, it contrives in an integrated manner the distribution of population in the future, economic layout, land use, and urbanization pattern, based on the bearing capacity of resource and environment, current development density, and development potential of different regions, divides the space of national land into four categories of development zones optimized development, key development, restricted development, prohibited development. Then, it will determine the orientation of the main functions, specify the direction of development, control the intensity of development, standardize the development order, improve the development policy, and gradually form a spatial development pattern in which the population, economy, and resource environment are harmonized.

Among the four functional zonings, optimized development zones are those with a higher density of land development and diminishing resource and environmental bearing capacity; key development zones are those with a more substantial resource and environmental bearing capacity and better conditions for economic and population agglomeration; restricted development zones are those with weaker carrying capacity of resources, inadequate conditions for large-scale economic and population agglomeration, which might pose a threat to the ecological security of the whole country or a larger region; prohibited development zones are those where various types of nature reserves have been established by law.

According to the division criteria, the national planning of functional zoning consists of both national and provincial planning, and is compiled at two levels.

The four functional zones at the national level do not cover the whole country. Optimized, key, and restricted development zones are, in principle, based on county-level administrative regions as the basic unit. In contrast, prohibited development zones are based on the legal boundaries or natural borders. Besides the current national leading group developing government planning, province-level governments are also required to form their own leading groups to prepare planning for the functional zones in their regions for the implementation of the regional planning.

In preparing provincial functional zone planning, the national functional zone within the administrative regions shall be identified as the same by the national functional zone planning to ensure consistency in the number, location, and scope.

For areas of national land outside the national functional zones within administrative regions, provincial functional zones shall be determined in accordance with the principles established by the state and tailored to the local situation. With the county-level administrative region as the basic unit in principle, predominantly agricultural areas shall be determined as restricted development zones by principle; areas located at the borders of province-level administrative regions with strong homogeneity shall be determined as the same functional zones; the land-based and sea-based functional zones in coastal provinces should be well-articulated, and their positioning of the main functions should be coordinated with each other; the time sequence of the development of the key development zones should be categorized into the short term, medium term, and long term. Areas with rich mineral resources but weak ecological carrying capacity can be developed moderately in mineral resources, but in principle, they should be identified as restricted development zones; various provincial-level natural and cultural protection zones established by law should be identified as prohibited development zones.

Preparing a national planning for functional zones has the following important significance:

First, as noted earlier, it is conducive to the gradual formation of a spatial development pattern that harmonizes population, economy, and the resource environment.

Second, it is a significant initiative for building a harmonious socialist society. (i) It is conducive to adhering to a people-centered guiding principle, narrowing the gap in public services between regions, and promoting coordinated regional development. (ii) It is conducive to guiding the economic layout and distribution of the population to be compatible with the resource and environmental carrying capacity, thus promoting the spatial balance of population, economy, and resource environment. (iii) It is conducive to addressing the root causes of the ecological issue to reverse their deterioration trend, adapting to and mitigating climate change, thus realizing the conservation of resources and environmental protection, and finally achieving sustainable development.

Third, it is conducive to breaking through the restrictions of administrative divisions. By formulating and implementing targeted policy measures and performance appraisal systems based on functional zones, it will help strengthen and improve regional adjustment.

In terms of policies and following measures, fiscal, investment, industrial, population, land, environmental, and performance assessment policies will be adjusted, mainly including the following aspects: (i) emphasizing increasing fiscal transfers for public services and eco-environment compensation to regions where development is restricted or prohibited; (ii) focusing government investment on supporting the construction of public service facilities, ecological construction, and environmental protection in restricted and prohibited development zones, and the infrastructure construction in key development zones; (iii) guiding the relocation and distribution of industries in each zone and implementing differentiated land-use policies; and (iv) adjusting the total population, guiding the orderly movement of the population, and gradually forming a mechanism for the same-direction movement of factors of production, such as population and capital.

Concerning government performance appraisal, different performance evaluation indicators and performance appraisal methods should be implemented according to the different positioning of the functional zones. For optimized development zones, the evaluation should place more emphasis on economic structure, resource consumption, independent innovation, while downplaying the evaluation of economic growth. For key development zones, a comprehensive evaluation of economic growth, quality and efficiency, levels of industrialization and urbanization, and the level of independent innovation in related fields should be conducted. For restricted development zones, the focus should be the evaluation of ecological construction, environmental protection and the like, while weakening the evaluation of economic growth, industrialization, and urbanization. Prohibited development zones should mainly be evaluated based on ecological construction and environmental protection.

Fourth, the strategic, fundamental, and binding planning. They serve as the fundamental basis for the spatial development and layout of master planning for national economic and social development and other various planning, such as the population, regional, urban, land-use, environmental protection, ecological construction, integrated river basin management, comprehensive water resources, sea area use, marine functional zones, grain production, transportation, and disaster prevention and mitigation planning. At the same time, the preparation of the national functional zone planning should be supported by the planning mentioned above and other relevant ones. Policies, statutes, and their implementation and management should be well-dovetailed.

Guiding ideology and principles for the preparation of the national functional zone planning are as follows:

First, it is the strategic idea of building a harmonious socialist society. Based on adhering to the implementation of the overall strategy for regional development, the basic pattern of the future national population and economy should be contrived in a forward-looking and holistic manner. This will guide the formation of a pattern of coordinated regional development in which the main functions are clearly defined, population, economy, and resource environment are harmonized with each other, and the gap between public services and the people's living standards will continue to narrow.

Second, it should adhere to a people-centered approach to guide the reasonable and balanced distribution of the population and the economy across the national land and gradually enable people in different regions and both urban and rural areas to enjoy equal public services. In addition, China should remain committed to the following "adherences": (i) adherence to intensive development to guide the industries to adopt a relative concentrated development and encourage the population to seek a relative agglomeration of settlements to form an urbanization pattern with city clusters as the primary form and other towns and cities distributed in a dispersed pattern, thus improving the efficiency of the use of resources such as land, water, and climate, and enhancing the capacity for sustainable development; (ii) adherence to respect for nature, so the exploitation prioritizes the protection of natural ecology, and the development must be based on the environmental capacity, thus ensuring ecological security, continuously improving environmental quality, and realizing harmony between man and nature; (iii) adherence to integrated urban and rural development, preventing the excessive encroachment of urbanized areas into rural areas while providing the necessary space for the rural population to move into the cities; and (iv) adherence to integrated land and sea development. To this end, it is necessary to strengthen maritime awareness, and fully consider the marine resource environmental carrying capacity, to harmonize land development with marine development.

Accordingly, the preparation of the national functional zone planning is mainly to handle the following relationships properly:

The first is the relationship between exploitation and development. Development is crucial, but it must be based on scientific, rational, orderly, and moderate exploitation. China is at a stage of accelerated industrialization and urbanization. The preparation and implementation of the national functional zone planning are intended to identify optimized and key development zones in large-scale development while designating restricted and prohibited zones based on the resource environmental carrying capacity, thus achieving sound and rapid development.

The second is the relationship between the government and the market. The national functional zone planning is the strategic design and overall layout for the development of national land space, formulated by the government to reflect the national strategic intent. The government should give the market full play in its fundamental role in allocating resources while rationally allocate public resources by the positioning of the functional zones. Meanwhile, laws, regulations, and regional policies should be improved and various means shall be comprehensively utilized to guide market entities' behavior to align with the positioning of the functional zonings.

The third is the relationship between the part and the whole. The formation of the functional zones is based on the overall interests of the whole, seeking to maximize the overall and long-term interests of the country and the people. For this purpose, it is necessary to ensure that the part is subordinate to the whole and that the whole takes into account the needs of the part.

The fourth is the relationship between the main function and other functions. The functional zones should stress the main function and leading role without excluding other auxiliary or subsidiary functions. The optimized and key development zones' main function is to agglomerate the economy and population, but there should also be ecological, agricultural, tourism, and recreational areas, among others. The main function of restricted development zones is to protect the ecological environment. However, they can also develop characteristic industries and moderately exploit mineral resources within the carrying capacity of the ecological and resource environment.

The fifth is the relationship between administrative regions and functional zones. Preparing a functional zone planning requires overcoming the boundaries of administrative regions and changing the approaches to regional policy formulation and performance evaluation that are based exclusively on administrative regions. In the meantime, implementing functional zone planning must rely on administrative regions at a certain level.

The sixth is the relationship between various functional zones. Functional zones should collaborate while working in their respective areas, promoting each other. Optimized development zones should reduce the pressure on the ecological environment caused by the large-scale cross-regional flows of population and resources by transferring industries to key development zones. Key development zones should promote the development of industrial clusters and enhance the capacity to absorb overloaded populations from restricted and prohibited development zones. Restricted and prohibited development zones should improve the ecological environment carrying capacity through ecological construction and environmental protection to gradually become national or regional ecological protective barriers and natural culture protection areas.

The seventh is the relationship between maintaining stability and dynamic adjustment. Once functional zones is established, it cannot be changed at will. Prohibited development zones should be protected strictly in accordance with the law. Restricted development zones should adhere to the protection priority and gradually expand their scope. Key development zones can be adjusted timely to optimized ones, in response to economic and social development and changes in the resource environmental carrying capacity.

The eighth is the coordination with related plannings. As a comprehensive planning, the coordination between the functional zone planning and related planning is crucial. There are two main aspects. One is coordination with spatial plannings, mainly urban, territorial, and regional plannings. The other is coordination with structural plannings, mainly the national economic and social development planning by the National Development and Reform Commission, the water resources planning by the Ministry of Water Resources, the outline of environmental protection by the Ministry of Ecology and Environment, and the planning for combating desertification by the National Forestry and Grassland Administration. Specific articulation or coordination should be carried out by improving the legal system, the spatial planning system, the unified preparation and approval process, and the unified technical standards.

9.2.3.2 National Territorial Planning

The national territorial planning refers to the integrated strategic deployment and comprehensive plan for development, utilization, governance and protection of territorial resources, including land, mining, water, biological resources, and the layout and regional combination of industry, agriculture, and transportation. The scope of the national territorial planning are vast and complex, concerning wide-ranging issues. Furthermore, they vary widely from country to country, region to region, and from one stage of development to another.

The primary task of national territorial planning is to generally coordinate the development, utilization, governance, and protection of territorial resources and harmonize the relationship between population, resources, and the environment to promote the regional economy's comprehensive development based on the advantages and characteristics of planning regions. For this purpose, it should undertake the following specific tasks: (i) clarifying the conservation objectives and basic guidelines for the development, utilization, and remediation of territorial resources; (ii) defining strategies for regional economic development and spatial development and determining the reasonable layout of population, production, and cities and towns; (iii) identifying the nature and size of the major cities and towns and their interrelationships; (iv) rationally arranging major regional infrastructure such as transportation, communication, power, and water sources; (v) rationally planning significant territorial development, utilization, remediation, and protection projects and the spatial layout of construction activities; and (vi) formulating policies and measures for implementing the planning.

The national territorial planning is generally divided into comprehensive and subject-specific planning. A comprehensive national territorial planning is the overall strategic deployment and arrangement for developing, utilizing, improving, and protecting all territorial resources in planning regions, mainly to solve cross-sectoral and cross-industry territorial resource allocation problems. The subject-specific national territorial planning is a plan that focuses on accomplishing a specific task of territorial development, utilization, management, and protection under the control of the framework of the territorial master planning.

The national territorial planning emphasizes particularly the spatial allocation and layout of resources, emphasizing comprehensive coordination in geographical space. Therefore, it is strategic and comprehensive. The national territorial planning fully embodies the ideas, objectives, and tasks of national economic and social development strategies and provides the basis and foundation for national economic and social development planning. Due to the lagging nature of the change and movement in spatial structure, national territorial planning must take a longer-term view than medium- and long-term planning for national economic and social development. It should forecast at least 15–20 years and, in some foreign countries, 30–50 years.

9.2.3.3 Urban Planning

Urban planning is the comprehensive deployment, specific arrangement, and implementation management of urban and social development, land use, spatial layout, and various constructions over a given period. The comprehensive urban planning involves various fields, such as economy, society, and engineering technology.

The urban planning has the following main characteristics. (i) Comprehensive. The preparation of an urban planning must comprehensively, holistically, and integrally analyze and solve problems and make overall arrangements for all city elements so that each can have its place and develop in a coordinated manner. (ii) Policy-driven. Urban planning is both a strategic deployment of urban construction and a means of organizing a rational production and living environment, involving almost every relevant sector of the country's economy, society, and culture. The solution to some significant issues must be based on the relevant national guidelines and policies. (iii) Foresighted. The function of an urban planning is to deploy and arrange reasonably for future urban development by analyzing and predicting in advance. The preparation of urban planning requires forward-looking awareness and strategy foresight. planning makers must study and analyze beforehand, predict problems in urban development, and then propose solutions. (iv) Long-term. An urban planning is a dynamic plan for urban development. It should be adjusted and supplemented timely to meet the needs of urban development as realities evolve and external factors change. Hence, the urban planning is a long-term and regular work. (v) Scientific. The preparation of urban planning must be based on the intrinsic laws of urban development and follow the scientific rules of the urban planning system, hierarchy, and other aspects to ensure planning are scientifically sound.

Urban planning is divided into urban system, master, and detailed planning according to their preparation stage and level. An urban system planning is a plan to distribute and develop towns or cities with different population sizes and functional divisions within a specific geographical area. This is based on the rational distribution of regional productivity and the division of functions between towns and cities. The urban master planning includes the deployment and implementation measures for the designated function of a city and its development objectives and scale, land use, spatial layout, and various constructions within a certain period. Before preparing an urban master planning, its outline is generally prepared in advance. At the stage of urban master planning, a recent construction planning and all dedicated planning concerned shall be prepared ahead. If the city is designated as a famous historical and cultural city, a conservation planning for it must also be prepared. Large and medium-sized cities are also required to prepare zoning planning during the stage of urban master planning. A detailed urban planning is a specific arrangement of land use, spatial environment, and construction land for a fixed period in localized areas of the city based on the urban master zone planning.

Urban planning is closely related to national territorial and regional planning. Like national territorial planning, urban planning must take national economic and social development planning as their macro guidance, Based on a clear definition of the direction and objectives of long-term development, urban planning comprehensively deploy various constructions in a given geographical area. Urban planning should be prepared under the macro-adjustment of national territorial planning, which can provide an essential foundation for the direction of urban development and productivity distribution. The development of regional territorial resources and economic, social, and cultural development, especially changes in industrial layout and population distribution, often play a decisive role in developing existing cities and forming new cities in the region. Urban development also affects the socio-economic development and construction layout of the region as a whole. The relationship between urban and regional planning is one of the dots and surfaces, organically linked and inseparable. A city is always connected with corresponding regions, and the region must have a corresponding economic center. Urban planning must be based on regional planning. On the one hand, it is necessary to rationally program and layout the city-town system based on a larger region; on the other hand, it is necessary to rationally determine the scale and function of the cities, the composition of various parts, the land use of each district to promote the coordinated development of the city and the region.

9.2.3.4 Environmental Protection Planning

The environmental protection planning refers to the comprehensive strategic deployment and overall planning of various natural and human-altered factors affecting the survival and development of human beings, including the atmosphere, water, sea, land, mineral deposits, forests, grasslands, wetlands, wildlife, natural relics, humanistic relics, nature reserves, scenic spots, the urban–rural ecological protection, and pollution prevention. It is the spatial and temporal rationalization of human activities and the environment to harmonize the environment with economic and social development.

Governments at or above the county level shall incorporate environmental protection into national economic and social development planning. In conjunction with the relevant departments, the competent department for environmental protection under the State Council shall prepare a national environmental protection planning by the national economic and social development program, then submit it to the State Council for approval, followed by its promulgation and implementation. The competent department for environmental protection of the local government at or above the county level, in conjunction with the relevant departments, shall, following the requirements of the national environmental protection planning, and prepare an environmental protection planning for their administrative regions. This planning shall be submitted to the government at the same level for approval and promulgated for implementation.

The significance of preparing environmental protection planning is as follows: (i) implementing the scientific outlook on development by protecting and improving the environment, preventing and remedying pollution and other public hazards, improving environmental quality, preventing environmental risks, safeguarding public health, accelerating the ecological civilization construction and promoting sustainable economic and social development; (ii) actively exploring new paths for green ecological development, the economic structure will be further optimized as China's economic development enters a new normal, it is vital to coordinate environmental protection and ecological construction with the economic growth mode to coordinate and integrate economic development and environmental protection; (iii) addressing multiple contradictions. The main manifestations are as follows:

- The pressure on the resource environment due to rapid industrialization and urbanization is increasing, as China's economy proliferates.
- With the continuous growth of the total population and the rapid advancement of industrialization and urbanization, the total amount of energy consumption is rising, and the pollutants output will continue to increase, thereby tightening the environmental constraints on economic growth.
- The overall deterioration of China's environmental situation has not yet been fundamentally curbed. Instead, environmental conflicts are becoming prominent, with pressures increasing.

Environmental protection planning must be dovetailed with the functional zones, land use, and urban–rural planning to strengthen the articulation of objectives and tasks, the spatial layout, and policies. This aims to promote the "multiple planning in one" in areas like the national economic development, the functional zone, land use, urban and rural, environmental protection planning, thus boosting the coordinated development of the economy, society, and ecological environment.

The main objectives of the environmental protection planning are to improve the ecological environment, promote resource conservation and intensive utilization, enhance the efforts in comprehensive environmental management, strengthen the prevention and control of environmental risks in key areas, enhance ecological protection and restoration, and improve the basic public service system for environmental protection. Specific indicators include targets for reducing major pollutants emission, improving the quality of the water environment, comprehensive control of air pollutants, and the like.

9.3 National Economic Planning Indicator System

A scientific and complete planning system and its indicator system are the concrete embodiment of the tasks and contents of a national economic planning and an essential condition for their successful realization.

9.3.1 Functions and Role of the National Economic Planning Indicator System

The implementation of planning requires a scientific indicator system. Indicators reflect the concepts and specific values of quantitative characteristics of the macro phenomenon in a quantitative, comprehensive, and specific way. Indicators for national economic programs are concrete and quantitative manifestations of the planning content. They are quantitative definitions of the characteristics and status of the overall activities of the country's future economic and social development, such as goals, speed, structure, and efficiency.

9.3.1.1 Information Guidance

The development strategy and objectives define the overall direction of a country's development for a certain period in the future, and the planning indicator system quantifies and specifies the state of the economic and social system as a whole to be achieved in terms of growth, prices, employment, balance of payments, and other aspects. The planning indicator system is the primary carrier for providing macro information to the economic and social entities. The information guidance role of the planning indicators is to indirectly influence the micro behavior of these entities through the provision of macro information, thus ensuring that the direction of their micro-activities is consistent with the national economy and social development as a whole. The planning indicator system must implement the development theme of a planning period. Since the 11th Five-year Plan, the indicator system has emphasized education, science and technology, sustainable development, resource environment, and people's lives on the theme of scientific development. The 13th Five-year Plan is based on the development ideas of innovation, coordination, green, openness, and sharing, centering on improving the quality and efficiency of development and focusing on supply-side structural reform. The leading indicators of the 13th Five-year Plan are economic development, innovation-driven growth, people's well-being, and resource environment to ensure that the goal of building a moderately prosperous society in all aspects is realized by 2020.

9.3.1.2 Responsibility Constraints

Starting with the 11th Five-year Plan period, the attributes of indicators have been defined, and the quantitative indicators of development goals have been divided into two categories: anticipatory and binding. Anticipatory indicators are the development goals expected by the state, mainly relying on the autonomous behavior of the market entities. For this purpose, the government must create a sound macroeconomic, institutional and market environment, adjust the direction and strength of macro- adjustment as needed, and make comprehensive use of all kinds of policies to guide the allocation of social resources to realize them. Binding indicators are those that further clarify and strengthen the government's responsibilities based on the anticipatory indicators, and they are the requirements that the central government puts forward to the local governments and the relevant departments of the central government in the areas of public services and those related to the interests of the general public. Local governments at all levels should ensure their realization through the rational allocation of public resources and the effective use of administrative authority. This distinction can better reflect the planning's positioning under the conditions of a socialist market economy. It is not only conducive to clarifying the responsibilities of the government and the market, strengthening the responsibilities that the government must fulfill in the areas of public services and those involving the public interest, and highlighting the operability of the planning, but it is also conducive to the establishment of a planning performance and political achievement evaluation system that meets the requirements of the scientific outlook on development. For indicators where the government must fulfill its duties, such as decreasing energy consumption, reducing pollution emissions, ensuring the minimum amount of cultivated areas, and increasing social security coverage, they are mandatory indicators of the government's duties and must be assessed to avoid the blind pursuit of GDP and the simple pursuit of growth rates. Among the 25 indicators in the 13th Five-Year Plan period, there are 13 binding indicators for government functions and 12 anticipatory indicators for guiding market entities and enterprises, with the former concentrated in two major categories, namely, the resource environment and public services for people's livelihoods, highlighting the importance attached to environmental protection and people's well-being.

9.3.1.3 Evaluation Examination

The primary purpose is to systematically and comprehensively assess the gap between the state of economic and social operation and the ideal goals. The economic and social system is a vast and complex system containing many subsystems such as economy, resources, and population, which are interdependent and mutually constraining in operating various subsystems. By scientifically designing the indicator system from various aspects and angles, it is possible to fully address the critical dimensions of the national economy and social development, such as the economy, society, education, science and technology, resource environment, and people's lives, to guide not only the state of economy and society but also the effectiveness and quality of that operation. This allows for a comprehensive evaluation and examination of the complex economic and social operating conditions. Based on an examination of the state and the effects of the planning's implementation, it provides a reliable basis for macro-adjustment to realize the predetermined goals of national economic and social development.

9.3.1.4 Indicator Adjustment

The main purpose is to enhance the systematicity and effectiveness of macro-adjustment. In national economic and social development planning, the various economic policies formulated by the government, such as fiscal, monetary, foreign trade, and industrial policies, should be based on the planning indicator system and simultaneously be expressed in the form of the indicator system. Some key indicators adjustments can affect the entire economic and social development system and thus change the complex system's operation to achieve the system's desired target state.

9.3.2 *Principles of the National Economic Planning Indicator System*

National economic planning indicators should meet the needs of the entire process of national economic and social development planning, implementation, and evaluation. Their design should reflect the following basic principles.

9.3.2.1 Scientificity

The basic starting point for setting up a system of indicators is to suit the cognitive object's nature, characteristics, relations, and movement processes and adapt to its development and change. It should standardize the design of the number of indicators, core indicators, the caliber of the indicators, the unit of measurement, the time of calculation, and the like. The prerequisite for correctly implementing development planning and conducting scientific statistics and evaluating economic and social performance is an accurate comprehension of planning indicators. Planning indicators, with precise connotation and clear denotation, should base on qualitative understanding for quantitative evaluation, thus describing and illustrating the total amount of the relevant statistical objects and their development and change clearly. The scientificity of the planning indicators is also reflected in the fact that they should be relatively stable for a certain period while maintaining a certain degree of dynamism so that they are not only operational on a stable basis, but also able to be adjusted appropriately to the economic and social development changes during the planning period. In this way, they are closer to the reality and more practical.

9.3.2.2 Comprehensiveness

In order to reflect the requirements of development strategies and goals, the indicator system of national economic and social development planning should reflect the requirements of the overall and structural nature of the macroeconomic and social systems from a comprehensive and systematic perspective. It must comprehensively reflect the overall level of national economic and social development and the development in all aspects, including aggregate indicators of economy, resources, population, and society, indicators reflecting quality and effectiveness, and indicators reflecting their internal structural relationship. The selected indicators should be representative, oriented, complete, widely covered, and highly generalized. Each indicator in the system is a well-bedded entirety; they are organically linked, but peer indicators should maintain independence to avoid duplication, cross-cutting, and mutual inclusion.

9.3.2.3 Normativity

The system of indicators should be set up with a holistic and global consideration of the linkages between the indicators, ensuring that the indicators are unified, standardized, and interconnected in terms of their names, contents, calibers, units of measurement, calculation methods, and scope of use. The planning indicators should also be consistent with the economic accounting system, statistical indicators, accounting indicators, and the like to make them comparable, thus forming a unified standard for statistics, evaluation, and analysis.

9.3.2.4 Purposiveness

The setting of an indicator system must be based on management requirements or research purposes. At different stages of economic development, various factors such as different domestic and international environments, operating conditions and development trends of the national economy and major economic variables, degrees of openness to the outside world and dependence on foreign trade, macro-adjustment tasks, and ways to seek economic development will differ, which directly determine the different goals of economic and social development and the planning indicator system. The planning indicator system should consider the requirements of development strategies and goals, accurately describe the intrinsic links in socio-economic operations, facilitate the implementation and evaluation of planning, and meet the needs of economic and social analysis and management.

9.3.3 Content of the National Economic Planning Indicator System

Indicators that comprehensively reflect national economic and social development generally include (i) indicators of economic development reflecting the level and extent of economic development; (ii) major indicators reflecting the economy structure; (iii) major indicators reflecting the coordinated development of the economy and society; (iv) major indicators reflecting science, technology, education, and talents cultivation; (v) major indicators reflecting resources and the eco-environment; (vi) major indicators reflecting the population and people's lives; and (vii) major indicators reflecting public services.

According to the principle of purposefulness in the setting of the indicator system, the indicator system for different periods should be established based on the requirements of the development strategy and goals, the economic and social development situation, the stage of development, the surrounding environment, and the like. This ensures the indicator system accurately reflects and implements the development theme.

The Outline of the 13th Five-Year Plan for the National Economic and Social Development adheres to the innovative, coordinated, green, open, and shared development concepts, centers on improving the quality and effectiveness of development, and focuses on supply-side structural reform. Based on these, it has formulated 25 major economic and social development indicators in four categories. The indicator system of the 13th Five-year Plan mainly focuses on economic development, innovation-driven growth, people's well-being, and resource environment to ensure that the realization of building a moderately prosperous society in all aspects by 2020.

Part IV
National Economic Management

Chapter 10
Objectives of National Economic Management

Improving and strengthening national economic management must have clear objectives. Since the NES movement involves many aspects, there are many levels of objectives in national economic management, including economic objectives, master objectives, and ultimate objectives, thus constituting a system of objectives for national economic management. Among them, the goal of long-term stable functioning of the national economy is the basis of national economic management.

10.1 General Objectives for Long-Term Stable Functioning of the National Economy

The long-term stable functioning of the national economy is the primary objective of national economic management. Whether it is macro-management or micro-regulation of the national economy, its objectives are subordinate to the overarching goal of economic operation without losing its characteristics. The common ground is to give full play to the role of the government in compensating for market failure. Through the joint effort of the government and the market, the long-term stable development of the national economy is ensured. In terms of macro-management, the general objective of long-term stable operation of the national economy can be specified as economic growth, full employment, price stability, and balance of payments. In contrast, the primary objective of micro-regulation can be specified as maintaining the order of economic operation and shaping a level playing field.

M. Lin and T. Huang, *National Economics*,
https://doi.org/10.1007/978-981-96-9618-5_10

10.1.1 Economic Growth

Economic growth is the increase of social final goods (cargoes) and services from expanded social reproduction. It refers to the increase in social final goods in a country over a given period (e.g., one year) compared to the previous period. Economic growth can be understood, if the population is considered, as final output per capita, i.e., an increase in final goods (and services) per capita. Growth in social final goods focuses on the increase in the overall economic strength of a country; growth in per capita final goods highlights the increase in people's living standards and economic efficiency.

Almost every country pursues the goal of long-term stable economic growth. Ensuring sustained economic growth is vital for a country's economy to embark on modernization. If China is to build a moderately prosperous society in all respects and realize the great rejuvenation of the Chinese nation, the most fundamental and urgent task is to liberate and develop further social productivity. Development must proceed at a certain pace, but that pace must be of quality and efficiency. From the economic development standpoint, improving the national living standards and the progress of the economic structure, social patterns, and other aspects largely depend on economic growth. Suppose some countries have historically experienced periods of rapid economic growth while others have experienced stagnant or slow economic growth, in that case, there would be a large difference between these two groups of countries, both in terms of their economic strength and the people's living standards. Therefore, stagnant or slow economic growth is what every country wants to avoid. However, as various resource conditions will limit economic growth, economic over-growth will have to pay a corresponding price, such as worse environmental pollution and sharpened social conflicts. Therefore, the macroeconomic objective of economic growth is to achieve a rate of economic growth appropriate to the country's specific situation.

10.1.2 Full Employment

Economic growth is contingent upon workforce employment, and workers seek to achieve full employment during periods of economic expansion. Full employment refers to a state where all individuals willing to work at prevailing wage levels can secure employment, serving as a critical condition for the stable functioning of the economy. The unemployment rate is commonly used as an inverse indicator of full employment.

Unemployment refers to a situation where there is an imbalance between the supply and demand of labor, either in total or structurally, resulting in individuals who are capable of working and seeking employment being without jobs. Based on the causes of its occurrence, unemployment can be categorized into voluntary, frictional, technological, structural, seasonal, and cyclical types.

Relatively speaking, if there are no other types of unemployment in the economy except voluntary and frictional unemployment, it can be called full employment. Most economists believe that as long as the unemployment rate is controlled within a specific range, it can be considered full employment. However, it depends on each country's situation. For example, it is generally controlled at 4%-6% in developed Western countries; in the United States, less than 5%.

Unemployment is very costly. Unemployment leads to the idleness and waste of some of the labor resources, resulting in a reduction in the scale of production, a slowdown in economic growth, reduced government tax revenues, increased social welfare expenditures, and a heavier financial burden. Most importantly, unemployment reduces people's incomes, causing the unemployed person to suffer from poverty and mental anguish. Meanwhile, an unduly high unemployment rate also affects social stability and then gives rise to other social problems.

China is a large developing country with an enormous population, employment has always been a primary objective to which the government attaches great importance. It has always emphasized that employment is the foundation of people's livelihoods. The guidelines are as follows: We must implement the principle of promoting self-reliant employment, market-regulated employment and government-backed employment and entrepreneurship, the strategy of giving top priority to employment and a proactive employment policy. In addition, it should guide workers to change their concept of employment, encourage multiple channels and forms of employment, promote entrepreneurship-led employment, do an excellent job of employing young people with a focus on college graduates, and improve the employment policies for the rural–urban workforce migration and vulnerable urban residents who have difficulty finding jobs.

10.1.3 Price Stability

Even if the economy grows and employment and incomes increase, growth and employment will be significantly reduced if the overall price level is high. Therefore, an important economic objective of national economic management is to achieve price stability. The price stability refers to the basic stability of the overall price level, which is one of the important elements of the stable operation of the national economy, an important symbol of the healthy and coordinated development of the national economy, also an important prerequisite for individuals and enterprises to arrange consumption and production under the expectation of more stable prices. In order to achieve moderate economic growth and growing employment, it is necessary to maintain a rough balance between total social supply and demand in both aggregate and structural terms to avoid marked ups and downs in the overall price level. For this purpose, both inflation and deflation must be prevented.

At the same time, price stability should not be interpreted as maintaining a fixed overall price level. Instead, it should be understood as keeping price fluctuations within a range that allows for the smooth functioning of the economy and is bearable for residents. Since price stability and economic growth are both complementary and contradictory, the government's regulatory focus and the macroeconomic policies it adopts will differ depending on various stages of economic development or within different phases of the same period. Consequently, the effects of these policies will also vary.

Therefore, it is necessary to implement the overall requirements of safeguarding and improving people's livelihoods, enhancing economic development's internal vitality and momentum, maintaining the basic stability of the overall price level, and realizing sustained and healthy economic development and social harmony and stability. In entering the middle-income stage, stabilizing price levels is one of the important objectives of macroeconomic management.

10.1.4 Balance of Payments

In an open economy, a country's economy is linked closely to the international market, and a country's balance of total social supply and demand is also closely related to the balance of payments. As mentioned earlier, the balance of payments, i.e., the foreign exchange balance between countries, reflects a country's total foreign exchange balance (including current account and capital and financial account) over a certain period (usually one year). Since exports (foreign demand) are part of the total social demand and imports are part of the total social supply, the scale and structure of foreign trade are related to the total social supply and demand and external balance of payments. Capital outflows and inflows between countries also have different degrees of influence on the aggregate of total social supply and demand. Moreover, a two-way regulation and complementary relationship exists between net capital flows and the trade balance. Thus, the balance of payments has become an important objective of national macro- adjustment.

Generally speaking, the four macroeconomic management objectives mentioned above are not fully consistent and sometimes even conflict. For example, unemployment rates and inflation rates are substituted from time to time. In order to reduce the unemployment rate, expansionary economic policies are generally adopted, which tend to lead to inflation, while maintaining price stability comes at the cost of a certain level of unemployment rate; that is to say, it is hard to reconcile full employment with price stability. In addition, there are also contradictions between economic growth and price stability and between the external equilibrium of balance of payments and the internal equilibrium of domestic employment and price stability. Therefore, in determining the objectives of national economic management, a country's government should not seek to optimize all four economic objectives to the extreme for a certain period but rather make comprehensive considerations and integrated arrangements in the context of a long-term, overall macroeconomic development strategy.

10.1.5 Maintaining Order in Economic Operations and Shaping a Level Playing Field

National economic management includes not only the objectives of macroeconomic adjustment but also the content of micro-regulation. Since free competition in the market does not consistently achieve optimal allocation of resources, i.e., there is a "market failure", the government needs to solve and deal with natural monopoly, information asymmetry, and a variety of factors and problems that jeopardize social and public safety, micro-regulation has thus become an important part of national economic management. Maintaining the order of economic operation, shaping a level playing field, realizing a fair and reasonable income distribution, and giving all members of society a fair chance to compete in the market have become one of the goals of national economic management.

The "market failure", thus requiring government micro-regulation, was usually for the following reasons:

10.1.5.1 Externalities

It refers primarily to the impact of an economic actor's activities on the welfare of other economic actors, which does not occur in price-based exchanges among the parties involved and whose impact is, therefore, external. If an economic actor's activities can enhance social welfare, but they themselves cannot get the corresponding benefits, it can be called a positive externality. On the contrary, when an economic actor's activities to others bring harm but no need to pay the corresponding cost, it is called a negative externality. Due to transaction costs, the private subject often finds it difficult to solve the problems caused by externalities. Therefore, government regulation is needed to clarify property rights and introduce mechanisms to reduce transaction costs, in particular, to avoid distortions in the efficiency of resource allocation and the loss of total social welfare caused by negative externalities.

10.1.5.2 Market Power

It primarily refers to the power a firm has to control prices and defeat competitors. Economies of scale can lead to monopoly and market control. Some industries have strong economies of scale determined by their technology. Meanwhile, the fixed capital in these industries is, in turn, highly long-lived and sedentary, thus easily constituting barriers to entry and natural monopolies. Natural monopoly enterprises use their market power to control monopoly prices and distort the efficiency of resource allocation, thus resulting in the loss of total social welfare. Under such circumstances, the government, by adopting price and entry regulations for natural monopoly industries (e.g., public utilities), prevents private enterprises from taking advantage of the market power stemming from the natural monopoly to gain additional benefits to maintain the order of economic operation and achieve the optimal allocation of social resources.

10.1.5.3 Incomplete Market Information

In a market economy, the incompleteness or asymmetry of information between supply and demand will often lead to adverse selection and moral hazard. Adverse selection refers to the fact that due to information asymmetry, a contracting party with the advantage of business information conceals the relevant information beforehand, thus harming the principal's interests. A moral hazard is the agent with the advantage of information to conceal the relevant activities, damaging the principal's interests after the fact. Because parties do not have equal access to information and there are many more ways to limit competition, the government micro-regulation is conducive to reshaping a level playing field to something approaching a complete information market.

10.1.5.4 Public Goods

It refers primarily to goods that all members of society share. The distinctive features of public goods are non-exclusivity, non-competitiveness, and positive externalities, which private individuals or enterprises are often reluctant to provide. Therefore, the government must provide public goods to maximize their utility to be effective. However, financing in an appropriate form is often required to cover the cost of public goods. This particular supply mode determines that the government is the most appropriate provider of public goods. In turn, micro-regulation by the government contributes to the most efficient use of public goods and maximizes social welfare.

10.2 The Goals of Comprehensively Coordinated and Sustainable Development of the National Economy

Based on understanding the goal of realizing the stable operation of the national economy, it is also necessary to fully grasp the higher-level goal of national economic management, i.e., the coordinated and sustainable development of the national economy, then building a moderately prosperous society in all respects. To this end, achieving socio-economic development goals is promoted through macroeconomic adjustment and implementing the philosophy of innovative, coordinated, green, open, and shared development.

10.2.1 Innovative Development

Innovation is the soul of a nation's progress and the inexhaustible power of a country's prosperity. It has a rich connotation, including: (i) Theoretical innovation. It mainly refers to breakthroughs in the original theoretical system or framework, new amendments and progress in the original theories and methods, and new explorations of theoretically restricted areas and unknown fields. (ii) Institutional innovation. It is mainly the innovation of political, economic, and management systems in a society, which changes the rules governing people's behavior and mutual relations and promotes changes in the mutual relations between the organizations and their external environment, as a direct result of which, people's creativity and enthusiasm are stimulated, and the creation of new knowledge, the rational allocation of social resources, and the continuous emergence of social wealth are promoted. (iii) Technological innovation. It mainly refers to a complete process from the conception of generating new products or new technology to the market application, which includes a series of activities such as the generation, research, development, commercialization, and diffusion of the new conception, which is in nature a process of scientific and technological and economic integration. It is a product of the joint action of technological advancement and application of innovation, which includes two major links: technological development and application. It is thus evident that technological innovation is the foundation and premise, institutional innovation is the guarantee and key, and theoretical innovation is the core and soul.

Institutional innovation functions in the following ways: (i) It can form an institutional architecture that facilitates innovation, shaping a leading-edge development that relies more on innovation-driven and capitalizes more on first-mover advantages, thereby conducive to fostering a new impetus for development. (ii) It can optimize the allocation of factors such as labor, capital, land, technology, and management, stimulate the vitality of innovation and entrepreneurship, and promote mass entrepreneurship and innovation. (iii) It can unleash new demand, create new supply, promote the vigorous development of new technologies, industries, and business forms, and accelerate power transformation. (iv) It is possible to build a new system of development, deepen the reform of the administrative system, innovate and improve macro-adjustment methods, and accelerate the formation of a market environment, property rights system, investment and financing system, distribution system, and mechanism for the cultivating, introduction, and using talents that are conducive to innovative development.

Scientific and technological progress and technological innovation play an important driving role. Scientific and technological progress is an important impetus for economic development, and innovation-driven is a key factor in promoting the transformation of the economic development mode. However, not all science and technology are conducive to sustainable development, and the invention of some technologies has even exacerbated the destruction of ecological environment systems. Therefore, it should accord high priority to whether or not it promotes sustainable development in measuring the criteria for technological progress to encourage the invention and promotion of technologies conducive to sustainable development, thus fully performing its leading role for scientific and technological innovation in overall innovation.

10.2.2 Coordinated Development

Coordinated development is vital for comprehensive, coordinated, and sustainable development. China covers a vast area, with uneven productivity development, prominent dual economic and social structure, and apparent urban–rural and regional differences. They have become weighty issues plaguing China's economic development and social construction. Therefore, closing the urban–rural and regional gaps and solving the problems of incoherence in development are the inevitable requirements of China's modernization and an urgent necessity for economic and social development.

Adherence to coordinated development must properly address the major relationships in development, focusing on coordinated urban–rural and regional development, promoting economic and social coordination, and promoting the simultaneous development of new industrialization, informatization, urbanization, and agricultural modernization. Specifically, the following should be done:

10.2.2.1 Coordinated Urban–Rural Development

The gap between urban and rural areas in China is long-standing. The main reason for this is that agricultural production is exposed to natural and economic risks, resulting in a significant lower comparative benefit than those of other industries. Equal inputs do not yield equal profits and may even result in losses, putting agriculture at a disadvantage in the market economy. In addition, the strategy of "prioritizing the development of heavy industry" implemented in the early stage of industrialization has left agriculture in a relatively backward state. However, agriculture is the basic industry of the national economy and plays a vital role in promoting the optimal allocation of social resources and optimizing the ecological environment. Therefore, it is imperative to strengthen the protection of agriculture in industrialization, and it is all the more necessary and possible to protect agriculture, especially after industrialization has achieved some progress.

Currently, China's agricultural base is relatively fragile, rural people' incomes are relatively low, the development of social undertakings in rural areas is lagging, and the urban–rural gap is still widening. At the same time, China has generally entered a stage of development that promotes agriculture through industry and rural areas through cities and has the initial capacity and conditions to increase its efforts to support agriculture, rural areas, and rural people. Therefore, realizing coordinated development in urban and rural areas is vital to achieving coordinated economic and social development. In order to achieve this goal, it is necessary to improve the mechanism for integrating urban and rural development, the long-term mechanism for investing in rural infrastructure, the extension of urban public services to the countryside, and finally, raising the level of construction of the new socialist countryside.

10.2.2.2 Coordinated Regional Development

Owing to the differences in the geographical location, resource endowment, population quality, original foundation, and technical level of each region, the disparities in the level of economic development, the pace of development, and the comprehensive strength of the regions are unavoidable. The uneven development of the regional economy and regional disparities are common to all countries in economic development. In a sense, it is economically rational to maintain a moderate gap between regions for a certain period. However, the gap should be slightly wider; otherwise, it will negatively impact economic and social development and jeopardize socio-economic development. Only through coordinated regional development can each region's comparative advantages and special functions be scientifically and effectively brought into play to form a distinctive regional economy with site-specific solutions, rational division of labor, complementary advantages, and joint development. Only then will a pattern of coordinated development be realized in which factors of production flow in an orderly and accessible manner between regions, the main functional constraints are practical, essential public services are equal to access, and the resource environment can bear. It is also conducive to forming a unified national market based on a just, open, and fair order of competition, thus realizing all-round, wide-ranging, and new economic and technical cooperation levels.

10.2.2.3 Integrating Economic and Social Development

Since the reform and opening up, China's social productivity has developed rapidly, economic efficiency has improved significantly, and the comprehensive national strength and people's living standards have reached the next level. However, there are still some contradictions and problems in the current economic and social development, mainly manifested in several major relative imbalances, such as between economic growth and the development of social undertakings, the distribution of income, the expansion of employment, residents' comprehensive development, and institutional innovations, respectively, so that the coordinated development of the economy and society has become an inevitable choice, which is one of the overall goals of China's national economic management.

There are two kinds of social development: broad and narrow. Broad social development, including ecological and economic development, is the progress of the entire social organism, i.e., the movement of human society from lower to higher levels. Narrow social development is a concept corresponding to economic development. It refers to the progress in other social fields and the development of various social undertakings besides economic development. The society in the coordinated development of economy and society is the social development in the narrow sense.

Economic development and social development are interdependent and mutually reinforcing. On the one hand, economic development provides society with an ever-increasing supply of material goods, which is the prerequisite and material basis for social development and the fundamental guarantee of social development. On the other hand, social development is the purpose of economic development and also provides economic development with spiritual impetus, intellectual support, and other necessary conditions.

To achieve coordinated economic and social development, it is necessary to develop the economy and other aspects of the social system, such as politics and culture. Meanwhile, it requires coherence and coordination among the various important components of the overall social system, i.e., the stable and coordinated development of the economic, political, and cultural systems.

10.2.3 Green Development

Green development is a necessary condition for sustainable development and an important manifestation of the people's pursuit of a better life. The inclusion of green development as an important element of "comprehensively coordinated and sustainable development" not only adheres to the traditional Chinese cultural concept of "harmony between nature and humanity" and "conforming to nature," but also represents a significant development of productivity theory. It is specifically understood in the following three aspects:

The first is a profound reflection on the laws governing the development of human civilization. The dialectical relationship between humans and nature is the eternal theme of human development. After more than 30 years of rapid development, China's economic and social development has encountered significant challenges and constraints. In 2012, China's economic aggregates accounted for about 11.5% of the world's total while consuming 21.3%, 45%, 43%, and 54% of the world's energy, steel, copper, and cement, respectively, and emitting the world's most enormous amount of carbon dioxide and nitrogen oxides. Realizing green development means correctly handling the relationship between economic development and eco-environmental protection, and firmly establishing the concept of protecting the eco-environment equates to protecting productivity and developing productivity, which is necessary for achieving sustainable development.

The second is a broad and profound transformation. The national economy is a complex dynamic system, and green development is a systematic revolution in the economy, lifestyle, social development, culture, and scientific and technological paradigms under the guidance of a new view of civilization. The benign movement of national economic system must follow not only the laws of economic development but also the laws of society, nature, and the development of human civilization. Ideas such as "lucid waters and lush mountains are invaluable assets" and "mountains, waters, forests, farmlands, and lakes form a community of life" are the conceptual underpinnings for establishing the concept of ecological civilization and guiding China towards the path of green development. They are also widely recognized and supported by the international community. In 2016, the Green is Gold: The Strategy and Actions of China's Ecological Civilization, a report released by the UNEP intending to advocate China's ecological civilization concepts and experiences, provides an essential reference for sustainable development worldwide.

The third is a beautiful vision for the future. The quality of the ecological environment is the key to comprehensively building a well-off society. Establishing a new development philosophy and changing the concept of political performance must be accompanied by institutional safeguards. At present, under the guidance of the new development philosophy, it is becoming a broad consensus and a new impetus and growth point for economic development to resolutely abandon the development model that damages or even destroys the ecological environment and the practice of sacrificing the ecological environment in exchange for temporary economic growth in one place.

10.2.4 Open Development

Open development is the only road to national prosperity and development. It is necessary to enrich the connotation of opening up to the outside world and raise its level to create a new situation of opening up to the outside world. In order to carry this out, the following should be maintained:

First, mutually beneficial cooperation should be the guiding principle of open development. At a time of deepening economic globalization, the world is witnessing a growing degree of interdependence between countries and increasingly close interconnections. However, while economic globalization promotes the complementarity of advantages and joint development among countries, it also brings about the problem of imbalance of returns among countries. How to solve the economic imbalance brought about by globalization tests the wisdom of humanity. China's open development must conform to the trend of deep integration of China's economy into the world economy, following a mutually beneficial and win–win opening-up strategy, and develop a higher level of open economy. It must enrich the connotation of opening up to the outside world, raise its level, synergize the promotion of strategic mutual trust, business cooperation, and humanistic exchanges, and strive to form a mutually beneficial cooperation pattern of deep integration. In foreign economic relations, adhering to mutually beneficial cooperation and seeking joint development among all countries will create a better international environment for open development.

Second, the goal is to harmonize internal and external demand. China's opening up process over the past more than 40 years has injected robust vitality and vigor into its development while simultaneously accumulating some problems. It notably concerns some regions' over-reliance on export-led development, low-end exports in general, and insufficient introduction of technical intelligence and utilization of international resources. For this reason, developing a higher level of open economy is necessary by insisting on coordinating internal and external demand, balancing imports and exports, paying equal attention to "bringing in" and "going global", and attracting capital, technology, and intelligence concurrently.

Third, efforts should be made to address the problem of imbalanced regional economic development. Differences in geographical location, resource endowment, and policy factors have led to the problem of insufficient coordination among different regions. Therefore, it is necessary to create a new pattern of comprehensive opening up that links land and sea, joints with internal- and external-oriented and opens up two-way between the East and West. On the one hand, China should be more closely linked to a wide range of countries, expand its development space, provide new development opportunities for many countries, and offer an important platform for win–win cooperation among the countries along the Belt and Road. On the other hand, it should integrate the land and sea and east and west. Further upgrading the level of opening up of the coast and opening up to the east will accelerate the pace of opening up the inland and opening up to the west to push the inland and border areas from the edge of opening up to the frontier, thus helping to solve the problem of imbalance in the development of domestic regions. In order to realize joint opening both at home and abroad, it is necessary to strengthen infrastructure connectivity and the construction of international corridors, enhance cooperation with international financial institutions to give full play to the functions and roles of the Asian Infrastructure Investment Bank (AIIB), the BRICS Development Bank, and the Silk Road Fund (SRF), so that the functions and roles of the Belt and Road as a comprehensive transportation corridor, a platform for economic and trade cooperation, and a link for humanistic exchanges can be further realized. Through joint consultation, mutual effort, and sharing benefits, China will achieve a faster development in this new pattern of opening up, and the countries along the route will also gain more benefits.

10.2.5 Shared Development

Shared development is an essential requirement of socialism with Chinese characteristics. Since the 1990s, China's economic system has undergone profound changes (i) from a planned economic system to a socialist market economic system, (ii) from the pursuit of pure public ownership to a fundamental economic system with public ownership as the mainstay and joint development of multiple ownership economies, (iii) from a single distribution system according to labor to a basic distribution system in which distribution based on labor is the mainstay and a combination of distribution according to labor and other factors of production is combined, and (iv) from an agriculture-oriented economy and society to an industry- and services-oriented one. These changes have given rise to major adjustments in the pattern of interests, bringing about great changes in the relationship of interests in the new period, as mainly manifested in the following:

First, social differentiation is evident, with a trend toward diversification of interest groups. The gradual establishment of the socialist market economic system has, on the one hand, broken through the highly consistent pattern of interests in all aspects of the planned economy, and, on the premise of the consistency of the overall interests, the state, the collective, and the individual have formed their different interests; on the other hand, due to the differences in the economic foundation, political resources, cultural conditions, and social status of the workers, farmers and other social strata diverse interest groups are emerging. In addition, due to the low level of social services in old revolutionary district, border region, ethnic regions, and impoverished areas and the significant differences in social services between regions, diversified interest groups emerge as well.

Second, conflicts of interest have become prominent, and the interest relationship tends to become more complex, which has led to the increasing emergence of contradictions between various interest groups, such as business managers and ordinary workers within SOEs and employers and employees in non-public enterprises. In addition, some interest groups suffer from psychological imbalance and a sense of unfairness in social distribution in the face of interest adjustment.

Third, labor-capital relations have become a meaningful social relationship. Establishing stable and harmonious labor-capital relations is an intrinsic requirement for guiding enterprises to adhere to a people-centered approach and establish a modern enterprise system, and also a significant measure and a concrete embodiment of safeguarding the legitimate rights and interests of the vast number of workers and practitioners and realizing the all-round development of the economy, society, and the humankind.

Resolving these challenges and problems must insist on shared development, i.e., development is for and by the people, and thus its fruits are shared by them. Based on this principle, more effective institutional arrangements should be made so that all people can have a greater sense of gain in co-building and sharing development; it is the basic guideline for promoting economic and social development in the new situation and one of the ultimate goals of national economic management. In the process of building shared development, the government is at the center of the coordination of social interests. It must conduct a global review and adjustment of the systemic aspects of the interaction of interest configurations from the perspective of possessing the three resources of wealth, power, and culture.

10.3 Ultimate Goals for National Economic Management

A prosperous nation with robust and healthy people, or a stable country with peaceful people, is the highest pursuit of administrators of all countries. Robust and healthy people are the foundation and the purpose of a prosperous nation, so the ultimate goal of national economic management is the comprehensive development of people, i.e., everything is for the people.

10.3.1 The Ideology of People-Centered

People are the subjects of economic activity. In order to satisfy their own needs, people must engage in all kinds of economic activities. People are always the subject of economic activity while interacting with nature to obtain material resources. Any scientific invention or economic progress is accomplished under the auspices of man. The economic differences between countries and nations are ultimately due to people adopting very different institutional forms and management methods in their economic activities. Only the worker, the people, is the prime mover behind socio-economic development.

Improving the quality of life is essential for promoting comprehensive human development. Quality of life must be considered as a criterion for measuring social and economic development to realize comprehensive human development because it is a comprehensive reflection of the conditions of social life on which people depend for their survival and development and measures the degree to which people's material, cultural, spiritual, and social needs are met. Quality of life is a comprehensive and profound concept because (i) it is a systemic concept that systematically reflects the situation of all aspects of people's lives; (ii) it is a concept that combines quality and quantity, it is not limited to reflecting how much people consume in their lives but, more importantly, reflecting the rich specific connotations of all aspects of people's lives; and (iii) it is a dynamic concept. With the growth of people's income and the material affluence, people's life goals are becoming increasingly diversified, thus higher demands on quality of life. Human society's continuous evolution and development will also enrich the connotation of quality of life.

From the perspective of national economic management, the following four points should be achieved to improve the quality of life and promote comprehensive human development.

The first is adhering to people-centered management to coordinate economic, sci-tech, and social development goals. People are the subjects of socio-economic activities and the mainspring of socio-economic development, so comprehensive development should be management's starting point and result. In so doing, it captures the essence of social development while encompassing all aspects of its content.

The second is strengthening the development and utilization of human resources, continuously improving labor productivity, and creating a solid material foundation for the comprehensive development of humankind. Humans' material production activities are the prerequisites for engaging in various other social activities. The higher the labor productivity of material production, and the richer the material resources produced, the more people will be able to control nature in more aspects and to a greater extent and gain more and more independence from nature, so that humankind will have the conditions and possibilities for engaging in other social activities and developing their other potentials. Under modern socialized mass production conditions, people are the most important of all factors of production, and human resources are the foremost. Especially with the massive emergence of high-tech industries, the supply of high- quality labor has become a key issue in economic activities. Therefore, full attention must be paid to the development and utilization of human resources to promote technological progress, increase labor productivity, and lay a solid material foundation for the comprehensive development of humankind.

The third is establishing a new management system centered on people to form a market mechanism that promotes the rational mobility of workers and fair competition to provide equal social opportunities for the comprehensive development of workers and creates conditions for them to participate in political, economic, management, and other social affairs. Simultaneously, it is necessary to effectively adjust and control all kinds of social relations and behaviors to maintain normal social order and security, thus enabling all kinds of activities and behaviors among people to be carried out in an orderly manner. It also adapts complex social relations to the needs of people's survival and development, and creates good social conditions for people's comprehensive development.

The fourth is establishing a management concept that respects and understands people. For this reason, it is necessary to create conditions for developing human personality, including hobbies, interests, specialties, talents, and unique potentials, utilizing medical care, education, and cultural activities. The so-called personality development refers to developing individual human capacities and qualities manifested in the individual's qualitative characteristics and unique attributes. In order to give full play to human potential and promote the development of the human personality, it is necessary to expand the scope and improve the quality of medical care, thus raising the level of human health to provide a material basis for the development of personal qualities and abilities. It will also need to attach great importance to education development. The core meaning of education is to enable people to acquire knowledge and skills through specific forms of learning and training, and its primary function is to shape people, i.e., develop their abilities and improve their qualities. In addition, it is also necessary to carry out richly colorful cultural activities, including cultural, recreational, and sports activities, to cultivate sentiments, enhance quality, stimulate wisdom, and improve qualities and relationships, thus promoting the development of the human personality.

10.3.2 From an Economic Giant to an Economic Power

For this purpose, efforts should be made in the following three areas.

First, it should concentrate on promoting the transformation of the economic development mode and restructuring the economy, including: (i) Increasing the quality and effectiveness of development. Development is the foundation, and efforts to achieve a new level of development are a condition for crossing the middle-income trap, for which it is necessary to intensify efforts in supply-side structural reform centered on the quality and effectiveness of economic development to achieve higher quality and more effective, equitable, and sustainable development. Only with sustainable development can the foundation for economic growth be consolidated, and also ultimately from a giant to a power, and solve the problems of "weighting increment over stock" and "focusing on scale rather than quality" in the course of development. (ii) Comprehensively deepening institutional reform. It should accelerate the formation of a mechanism conducive to the transformation of the mode of economic development, in particular, accelerate the transformation of government functions, normalize government behavior, and give full play to the decisive role of the market in the allocation of resources under the state's macro-adjustment. (iii) Accelerating the new-type industrialization, informatization, urbanization, agricultural modernization, and government governance modernization with Chinese characteristics. (iv) Building a new industrial system. It should cultivate strategic industries, build a modern agricultural industry system, and accelerate the construction of advanced manufacturing and the development of modern service industries. (v) Improving the quality of urbanization. It should accelerate the construction of the Yangtze River Delta, Pearl River Delta, and Beijing-Tianjin-Hebei city clusters, and gradually form some city clusters with international influence. (vi) Improving energy utilization efficiency to strive to build a beautiful China and make new contributions to global ecological security.

Second, it should strive to make enterprises grow bigger and stronger. The key is to create a favorable environment for the development of enterprises and form a favorable atmosphere full of support for enterprises and respect for entrepreneurs in the whole society. The government should strengthen the functions of service and coordination, maintain market order, break down barriers between regions and departments, and strive to create an equal, fair, and open competitive environment for the development of enterprises. It also should promote the establishment of large multinational enterprise groups with international competitiveness through various means and actively encourage them to grow further in international competition.

Third, it should implement innovation-driven development strategies. It is necessary to give full play to the center role of the government in the construction of innovation mechanisms and environments to accelerate the construction of a market-oriented technological innovation system that combines universities, industries, and science partnerships with enterprise as subject, and implement tax, financial, and government procurement policies in support of independent innovation. Meanwhile, it is necessary to strengthen the dominant role of independent innovation of enterprises, encourage them to increase investment in research and development, promote the construction of their technology research and development centers, and focus on fostering some backbone enterprises that master core technologies. Furthermore, creating an institutional environment that encourages and protects independent innovation is necessary. It should vigorously safeguard the rights and interests of innovative enterprises and innovators, resolutely combat all kinds of monopolistic behaviors that harm market competition, and stimulate technological innovation through competition. Finally, it is necessary to adhere to the people-oriented approach, pay more attention to education development, emphasize investment in human capital, advocate an innovative culture that inspires people to strive for progress and excel in discovering, cultivating, and gathering all kinds of scientific and technological talents, thus comprehensively improving China's capacity for independent innovation.

Chapter 11
Macro-Adjustment of the National Economy

While operating under established development strategies, programs, and goals, the national economy inevitably experiences regular fluctuations with alternating expansion and contraction. When the market mechanism alone cannot fully adjust it, an intervention is necessary, i.e., macro-adjustment of the national economy. In this way, the economic aggregates have been balanced, the overall structure has been continuously optimized, and the national economy has developed sustainably, rapidly, and steadily. Therefore, macro-adjustment is a crucial component of national economic management. The current chapter analyzes the targets and reasonable range, principles and instruments, policies and their effects on macro-adjustment of the national economy, and innovations and improvements in macro-adjustment methods.

11.1 Macro-Adjustment Targets and Reasonable Ranges

11.1.1 Targets and Basic Tasks of Macro-Adjustment Under the New Economic Normal

At present, China's economic development has entered a new normal. In order to realize the goal of building a moderately prosperous society in all aspects, economic growth has to be maintained at a medium–high speed, and industries have to move toward the middle and high end, invigorating China as an innovative and talent-strong country. Under such circumstances, new changes have occurred in macro-adjustment targets and key tasks.

M. Lin and T. Huang, *National Economics*,
https://doi.org/10.1007/978-981-96-9618-5_11

11.1.1.1 Macro-Adjustment Targets Under the New Economic Normal

(1) *To redouble efforts to improve the quality and efficiency of economic growth*

After more than 30 years of rapid growth, China has achieved middle-income country status. At the stage of advancing to a high-income country, China not simply pursues quantitative expansion of the economy but promotes industrial upgrading, structural optimization, and innovation-driven, i.e., "raising quality while increasing quantity". Therefore, choosing macro-adjustment targets requires seeking a balance and synergism between quantitative and qualitative growth to achieve the synergy of both. The leading economic indicators should be balanced and coordinated, the spatial pattern of development should be optimized, the efficiency of investment and enterprises should rise markedly, the integration of industrialization and informatization should be further improved, industries should move towards the medium–high-end levels, ensuring China move toward an innovative and talent-strong country.

(2) *To improve people's living standards and quality*

Economic growth is a critical issue in the economic construction of socialist countries, but it is not the only target. Ultimately, economic growth aims to increase employment and improve living standards and quality of people. Insisting on shared development and improving efforts to advance people's welfare requires prioritizing employment and implementing a more proactive employment policy to create more jobs. Moreover, it should devote great energy to solving structural employment contradictions to achieve relatively full employment. Not only that, but also to achieve a more sound public service system in education, culture, social security, medical care, and housing, to create a steady increase in the level of equalization of essential public services, narrow the income gap, and manage to rise the proportion of middle-income people. In particular, winning the battle against poverty is necessary to reflect development results in people's welfare.

(3) *To significantly improve national quality and social civilization*

Realizing the Chinese Dream of national rejuvenation will require people's decades of united struggle, which will call for a combination of economic and social development and unification of economic development with the improvement of civilian quality and social civilization. It is necessary to give better play to innovation as the primary driving force of growth, actively advocate a culture of entrepreneurship and innovation, and promote mass entrepreneurship and innovation to realize the goal of building a moderately prosperous society in all respects. Efforts should be made to raise urban and rural residents' cultural, educational, health, moral, and civilization levels. For this purpose, it is necessary to take corresponding macro-adjustment measures to cultivate a new impetus for development and expand new space for development, such as supporting the optimization and upgrading of traditional industries, accelerating the development of strategic emerging industries, and making the cultural industry a pillar industry of the national economy.

(4) *To overall improve the quality of the ecological environment*

Heading for a new era of ecological civilization and building a beautiful China is a new challenge and mission for macroeconomic adjustment. The realization of sustainable development requires the integration of ecological civilization construction into all aspects and processes of economic and social development. At present, eliminating the bottlenecks, such as tightening resource constraints, severe environmental pollution, and the contradiction between development and population, resources, and the environment, must adhere to the fundamental policy of resource conservation and environmental protection, exercise double control over the total volume and intensity of energy, water resources and land for construction, and build a resource-saving and environment-friendly society, thus promoting the formation of a new pattern of modernization and construction in which human beings develop in harmony with nature.

11.1.1.2 Critical Tasks of Macro-Adjustment Under the New Normal of Economic Development

China's economic development has entered a new normal where the economy maintains a medium–high growth rate, and industries move towards the medium–high end of the value chain, marking a new change in the macro-adjustment tasks. Therefore, macro-adjustment must fit in with the three primary characteristics of economic development: changes in the rate of growth, optimization of economic structure, and shift of growth engines to adapt to, grasp, and steer the new normal. The main basic tasks that must be accomplished by macro-adjustment under the new normal include the following:

(1) *To carry out macro-adjustment based on the targets of the national medium- and long-term development planning and the total supply and demand pattern*

The medium- and long-term development planning prepared by the state is the concrete realization of the national economic development strategy, which is not only a critical link in the strategy's implementation, but also an important means for the state to strengthen and improve macro-adjustment. Innovating and improving macro-adjustment ways as the targets of the national medium- and long-term development planning should pay primary attention to the rational articulation and organic cooperation between the three levels and three types of planning (i) the inter-coordination of planning at the national, provincial, and city- and county-level; (ii) the close cooperation between master, subject-specific, and regional planning; and (iii) the mutual supplementation of planning in related fields, such as national territorial, urban, and functional zone planning. In the meantime, China should strengthen the guiding and restraining role of national medium- and long-term planning and fully play the pivotal role of annual planning in implementing planning.

The pattern of total supply and demand refers to maintaining a fundamental balance between total social supply and demand in both aggregate and structural terms. The aggregate balance of total social supply and demand is mainly a balance in value, i.e., in all fiscal, credit, trade, and capital aspects. To keep the aggregate balance of total social supply and demand, fiscal and monetary policies shall be put into efforts. In contrast, the structural balance of total social supply and demand mainly promotes the coordination of major economic structures and the optimization of the productivity distribution. From the perspective of the supply structure, there are mainly industrial, regional, and urban–rural structures; from the perspective of the demand structure, there are mainly the structures of investment, consumption, and imports and exports. Adjusting this structural balance is mainly concerned with the functions of industrial, regional, investment, consumption, and price policies.

(2) *To innovate the adjustment way of thinking and policy instruments*

Under the new economic normal, innovating adjustment thinking must give prominence to and firmly establish the new development concept: innovation, coordination, greenness, openness, and sharing to create new growth momentum and expand space for more balanced, inclusive, and sustainable development. Furthermore, it should respond to economic fluctuations with flexible and effective adjustment, speed up the transformation and smooth succession of old and new growth drivers, further release the vitality of effective demand in a bigger way, cultivate new advantages in international competition and cooperation to maintain a medium- to high-speed economic growth. At the same time, it should implement an innovation-driven strategy by improving the economic structure and shifting the growth model to promote industries to move towards the middle and high end from both the supply and demand sides. With keeping policy keynote largely stable as a prerequisite, it should increase the intensity of targeted adjustment based on range adjustment to discretionarily and precisely adjust by carrying out a package of measures regarding innovating adjustment policy tools. Regarding carrying forward policies, the timing should be correct. When the economy is running smoothly, it should speed up the introduction of some policy measures aimed at facilitating reform and restructuring. When the economy fluctuates, it should increase the intensity of pre- and fine-tuning. When the economy declines, it should take more vigorous measures to stabilize growth.

(3) *To further improve the macro-adjustment policy system*

It is based on the following two aspects. First, the principal instruments are fiscal and monetary policies. In relative terms, fiscal and monetary policies are aggregate macro-adjustment policies mainly aimed at realizing the balance of total social supply and demand. Based on traditional fiscal policy instruments, the toolbox of fiscal policy can be appropriately added with new tools, such as various investment guiding funds, the public–private partnership (PPP) model, tax reform, and measures safeguarding the people's livelihood. Based on three practical ways of traditional monetary policy tools (see the details below), monetary policy can adopt appropriately new tools for targeted adjustment. While controlling short-term interest rates, interest rate policy should develop from medium-term interest rate guidance to long-term interest rate conduction and forward-looking guidance. Second, industrial, regional, investment, consumption, and price policies are coordinated. Comparatively speaking, the policies mentioned above are the micro-miniaturization of macro-policies or mainly the structural policies of macro-adjustment. These policies have adjustment objectives and main directions and are the concrete embodiment of macro-adjustments in various fields. For this purpose, it is necessary to correctly handle the relationship between sub-field adjustment and holistic approaches to controls, and through the improvement of the macro-adjustment system, to strengthen the coordination and cooperation between policies, thus achieving a synergy to ensure the overall realization of macro-adjustment objectives.

(4) *To establish risk identification and early warning mechanisms*

It should utilize big data technology to improve the timeliness and accuracy of economic operation information. There are cyclical fluctuations in the NES movement. The drastic economic fluctuations are detrimental to the smooth operation of NES and cause higher economic risks and enormous damage to the national economy. Therefore, from the standpoint of macro-adjustment, it is necessary to obtain timely and accurate information on economic performance and to monitor and provide early warning on the national economy so that the state can take timely and strong intervention policies to reverse the situation quickly. National economic monitoring effectively supervises, analyzes, forecasts, and evaluates the management of the national economy's operating conditions. National economic early warning is the management process of making timely analyses, accurate forecasts, or warnings when high volatility or deviation in the operation of the national economy is about to occur. National economic monitoring and early warning are closely linked; the most crucial purpose of monitoring is early warning, while early warning is a response to national economic monitoring. Both directly relate to the establishment of the indicator system, data collection, and data-processing technology. The era of big data provides sufficient information for national economic monitoring and early warning and proposes higher requirements for improving national economic monitoring and early warning analysis level. To this end, it is necessary to establish a sound system for the government to collect big data, which requires speeding up the construction of a smart government, integrating cyber security to realize interconnectivity, and establishing a government think tank. The government will then be able to provide a sufficient basis for timely counter-cyclical adjustments, the formulation of anti-crisis measures, and the maintenance of sustainable development of the national economy.

(5) *To promote price mechanism reform*

The price mechanism is the core of the market mechanism, and the market determining prices is the key to the market's decisive role in allocating resources. Proactive adaption to and guidance of the new normal of economic development should closely center on making the market play a decisive role in resource allocation and better play the role of the government. Therefore, it is necessary to comprehensively deepen the price reform, improve the price formation mechanism in critical areas, improve the government pricing system, and strengthen the market price supervision and anti-trust enforcement, thus creating a favorable price environment for economic and social development. Under the new economic normal, promoting the reform of the price mechanism should do the following four perseverance: (i) Persevering in the idea of being determined by the market. Anything that can be price-formed by the market shall be left to the market without government intervention. (ii) Persevering in the combination of decentralization and adjustment. In terms of price management, the government should adhere to this principle: concentrating on managing what it should manage by itself and leaving what it should not to the market. (iii) Persevering in reform and innovation. It should explore innovation in the price formation mechanism, adjustment system, and supervising pattern to serve the transformation of macro-adjustment. (iv) Persevering in the prudent promotion. Price reforms should be coordinated with reforms in finance and taxation, income distribution, industry management mechanisms, and the like. In addition, it should grasp the timing, tempo, and intensity, and take strict precautions against all kinds of risks, and ensure a smooth and orderly process.

(6) *To avert and mitigate economic risks*

During economic cyclical or imbalanced fluctuations, there is often a tendency for some economic risks to arise or for further cyclical fluctuations to be brought about by economic risks. Economic risks are mainly regional and systemic risks. Generally speaking, regional or localized risk is not a risk that has a significant impact on a country but only one that has a local impact on a particular region and industry. China should mainly guard against overcapacity, real estate, local bonds, shadow banking, capital markets, and other risks. Systematic risk mainly refers to the risk that significantly impacts the whole country, the most obvious of which is inflation and deflation. Economic risks can also be categorized into visible and invisible risks. From the point of accumulation and dissolution of economic risks, along with the decline in economic growth, all kinds of hidden risks will gradually become visible. Although the risks are generally controllable, the resolution of the various risks, mainly characterized by high leverage and bubbles, will continue for some time. It is necessary to address the symptoms and the root causes before the risks materialize, issue corresponding resolutions, and establish and improve the institutional mechanism to resolve the various risks. Close attention should be paid to trends in the development of risks and to tackle them gradually and orderly in line with the principles of strictly controlling increment, different treatment, and adopting differentiated measures according to categories to gradual solution. Meanwhile, it should adopt policy measures combining diversion and blockage and laying equal stress on control and prevention to prevent individual and localized risks from evolving into regional or systemic risks.

11.1.2 *The Range, Targeted, and Discretionary Adjustment of the Macroeconomy*

11.1.2.1 The Range Adjustment

The range adjustment of the macroeconomy refers to the adjustment that keeps the economic development within a reasonable range consisting of a reasonable ceiling, floor, and bottom line. As long as the economic operation does not slip out of this range, it is normal for the economic growth rate to be slightly higher or lower, and the macro-policy will remain broadly stable. In the past, when choosing targets for macro-adjustment, China usually chose a specific economic growth rate as the adjustment target, i.e., point adjustment. It made sense at that stage of development. However, under the new normal of economic development, it is not quite objective to specify a specific economic growth rate as the adjustment target in the face of the complex and changing international and domestic environment. Innovating and improving macro-adjustment methods and making them more scientific is of necessity to shift the selection of macro-adjustment targets from point adjustment to range adjustment.

The reasonable macroeconomic range involves the correlation between the economic growth rate and such indicators as the inflation rate, new jobs created, unemployment, levels of residents' income, energy, water resources, and land for construction.

The first is a reasonable ceiling, floor, and bottomline range for economic growth. The key to range adjustment is to maintain the ceiling (inflation prevention) and the floor (stabilizing growth and preserving employment) while assuring the bottom line of the reasonable range of economic operation so that there is enough room for maneuvering up and down in macro-adjustment. Theoretically, the ceiling and floor relies on the Phillips curve, centering around the pivot of the potential growth rate. Choosing the floor depends on the actual capacity of the economy and the medium- and long-term planning objectives, such as the minimum requirement of doubling the GDP for the average annual growth rate.

In order to ensure that the GDP and per capita income of urban and rural residents would be doubled by 2020 compared with 2010, the ceiling of economic growth in the 13th Five-year Plan period would be 7%, and the floor would be 6%. Meanwhile, it is also possible to set a bottom line for an upward fluctuating range, which is set to be 6.5% or more based on the analysis of the situation. Specifically, GDP growth is capped at a level that would not cause inflation. According to empirical data, when China's economy is overheated, the inflation rate generally reaches about 5%, which people can hardly bear, so it is necessary to carry out macro-adjustment to cool down the overheated economy. For example, in 2015, the economic growth rate was determined to be about 7%, and the inflation rate was about 3%, which is the result of the initiative to reduce the economic growth rate under the inflationary pressure formed in the digestion of the previous period of loose monetary policy in response to the financial crisis.

The floor of the reasonable range, i.e., the floor of the economic growth rate, is determined by the ceiling of the unemployment rate. If the economy is too cold, the unemployment rate will rise, which is hard for the people to bear. The current published unemployment rate is the registered unemployment rate, but in reality, many unemployed persons do not register, so it is not reliable to look at the registered data alone; what actually matters is the actual unemployment rate. Furthermore, the floor of China's economic growth rate should also consider the reasonable growth of residents' income. Moreover, according to the requirement of two synchronization, i.e., the residents' income increases in step with the economy and accelerating the upward convergence in labor remuneration and productivity, the bottom line of the economic growth rate is also 6.5%.

The second is a reasonable range for upward fluctuation in new jobs created and downward fluctuation in the unemployment rate. Five-year and annual planning usually set a target for new jobs created and a target for the urban registered unemployment rate. In general, macro-adjustment is mainly aimed at guiding upward fluctuation in new jobs created and downward fluctuation in the urban registered unemployment rate, thus forming a reasonable range. For example, China's 2015 urban unemployment rate was set at 4.5% maximum, suggesting that movements not exceeding 4.5% are acceptable.

The third is a reasonable range for dual-controlling energy, water resources, and construction land in aggregate and intensity. In general requirements, the aggregate control cannot be an upward breakthrough (i.e., not allowed to increase). In contrast, the intensity control can be a downward breakthrough (i.e., allowed or encouraged to reduce). For example, China accounted for 12% of the world's economic aggregates in 2012. However, it consumes 54% of the world's cement, 45% of the world's steel, and more than 80% of the world's iron ore, so its environmental bear capacity is close to its ceiling. Therefore, it is necessary to take the initiative to adjust the economic growth rate downward, eliminate the backward production capacity of high consumption and pollution, set strict energy intensity reduction targets, and implement strict environmental protection regulations. In 2015, China's target of reducing energy consumption intensity decreased by more than 3.1%, which in effect set a bottom line that cannot be slipped out.

Range adjustment is a new theory and model of national economic management, which focuses not only on the ultimate goal of adjustment but also on the movement of the adjustment goal within a reasonable range. So long as the movement of the adjustment goal does not exceed the reasonable range, it will serve its purpose. The definition of a reasonable range for macroeconomic adjustment reflects the innovation of macro- adjustment methods. (i) It is a fundamental guarantee that the market is decisive in allocating resources. The government can only implement a tight macro-adjustment policy when the macroeconomic operation exceeds the reasonable range. Within the reasonable range, the government no longer adjusts the market occasionally, thus leaving more room for the market to allocate resources autonomously. (ii) It is a reliable guarantee for improving the quality and effectiveness of economic growth. Suppose the government keeps applying fiscal and monetary policies to adjust the market, in that case, it somewhat contributes to government-driven economic growth, resulting in enterprises' one eye gazing on the market and the other gazing on the government. Range adjustment, on the other hand, can better reflect that economic growth is mainly driven by the market, thus providing a reliable guarantee for improving the quality and effectiveness of economic growth. (iii) It is an objective requirement to improving the quality of livelihood development. Previously, macro-adjustment target management takes a specific GDP growth value as a boundary. Now, there is more need for the quality and security of livelihood development to set the range based on economic and social stability indicators. Ultimately, range adjustment is to adhere to the bottom line of harmony and stability of livelihood and society.

11.1.2.2 The Targeted Adjustment

The government's macro-adjustment is not passive or negative in practicing macroeconomic range adjustment. Sometimes, to respond to emergencies, extraordinary changes, and the specific objectives of macro-adjustment, it is necessary to emphasize the implementation of targeted adjustment based on range adjustment so that it can be used in conjunction with range adjustment.

Targeted adjustment is the innovation and deepening of macro-adjustment methods under the new normal. It is an essential aspect of range adjustment and an inevitable requirement for adapting to the new economic normal. It is characterized as follows: (i) The idea of adjustment. It should change from the original aggregate management to structural adjustment and keep the policies stable with a precise focus. (ii) The adjustment objectives. They both focus on short-term policies to stabilize economic growth but also pay attention to the release of long-term development of the economic potential. Not only is it a combination of long- and short-term, but it is also a multi-directional approach. (iii) The specific adjustment measures. It should innovate macro-adjustment ideas and methods and enrich policy instruments. Moreover, it should also pinpoint the "target spot" aiming at key problems in the economic field and critical driving force of economic development, striving to hit the target with one shot.

The process of targeted adjustment is essentially to create a suited economic and financial environment for economic restructuring, transformation, and upgrading. Its connotation needs to be further deepened on this basis: (i) Reshaping the role of the government. The government should be the owner, regulator, but also facilitator in constructing financial infrastructure, investor protection, and the like. (ii) Comprehensively developing the finance function. Toward this end, it should emphasize the capital financing function of finance and pay more attention to the risk and social management functions. (iii) Promoting effective competition. It should avoid the case that the non-banking and quasi-financial systems are merely dependent on the banking system and instead enable them to form effective competition with the banking system in the diversification process of the financial system.

11.1.2.3 The Discretionary Adjustment

Discretionary adjustment is an essential means of macro-adjustment, and it completes the government's macroeconomic adjustment system following range and targeted adjustments. Keynes first coined the word "discretionary" in economics". It refers to in the counter-cyclical demand management process, the government's flexibility in deciding and choosing fiscal and monetary policies based on market conditions and the characteristics of the various measures following specific rules. Therefore, China proposed the implementation of macroeconomic discretionary adjustment in 2015 to make the range and targeted adjustments more effective and accurate. It means that grasping the timing and intensity of the introduction of various measures in the context of doing an excellent job in the policy reserves, the development of response plans, and clear objectives, making opportune and precise adjustments, thus constantly improving the discretionary level, rather than complying with the old rules in a deregulatory free market.

Discretionary adjustment is a balance to implementing targeted adjustment, the core of which is timely and appropriate pre- and fine-tuning, thus controlling risks. Therefore, it is characterized by intervening flexibly, efficiently, and in a decisive and timely manner and is not bound by any fixed procedures or principles. The government would introduce different policies for different regions and industries. For example, given the differentiation in the real estate market, the government has formulated targeted policies on deed tax and housing mortgage according to the different characteristics of the real estate market in first-, second-, third-, and fourth-tier cities.

In the government's macro-adjustment ideas, range adjustment aims to stabilize growth, targeted adjustment emphasizes the restructuring direction, and the core of discretionary adjustment is pre- and fine-tuning in a timely and appropriate manner. From range adjustment to targeted adjustment to discretionary adjustment, the instruments and means of macroeconomic adjustment are utilized flexibly and complement each other, centrally reflecting the new exploration and practice of macroeconomic adjustment under the new normal of the Chinese economy, not only perfecting macroeconomic theory but also guiding the sustained and healthy development of the national economy, thus accumulating experience for further improving the level of macro-adjustment and laying a solid foundation for promoting China's long-term stable economic development.

11.2 Principles and Instruments of Macro-Adjustment

11.2.1 Principles of Macro-Adjustment

The macro-adjustment is widely used in government management, whose principles are mainly rooted in economic cybernetics. Economic cybernetics is a qualitative and quantitative study of the laws of balance and optimization between the various levels and elements of NES, covering many fields, such as information theory, countermeasure theory, operations research, and systems engineering. Its main principles are as follows:

11.2.1.1 Equilibrium Deviation Principle

The principle of equilibrium deviation is to adjust the input of the system based on the deviation of the target output of NES from the actual output. For any control system, inputs and outputs correspond. The principle of equilibrium deviation can also be used to analyze the aggregate supply–demand imbalance. The government should take measures such as adjusting the money supply and stimulating or suppressing investment and consumption. In the case of economic expansion, the focus of macro-adjustment is to stabilize prices, striving to stabilize prices while maintaining moderate economic growth. Tightening monetary policy should be adopted at this point to curb the momentum of rising prices. On the contrary, in the case of economic recession, macro-adjustment focuses on promoting stable economic growth. At this time, expansionary fiscal policy is adopted to curb the momentum of the economic downturn.

11.2.1.2 Interference Compensation Principle

The interference compensation principle is to adjust the input according to the change of the external interference and, thus, indirectly adjusting the output to compensate for the external interference. However, the condition is aware of both the input and output information and the interference information; especially when the interference factors are numerous and constantly changing, it is necessary to know more. For example, China has been affected by the global financial crisis of 2008, which has hit its export trade and reduced the sales and profits of export enterprises. In order to mitigate the impact of the crisis on China's macroeconomy, the government has adopted a series of policies to stimulate the economy, which have played a positive role in promoting economic growth and maintaining macroeconomic stability. From the viewpoint of compensating for disruption, the proactive fiscal policy and moderately loosened monetary policy adopted by China compensated for the adverse impacts of the crisis by increasing investment and other methods and ensured the realization of macroeconomic objectives.

The interference compensation principle can also explain the measures governments take when events like natural disasters hit them. At that time, the government compensates for the losses caused by natural disasters such as earthquakes, droughts, and floods in the region through public inputs, financial subsidies, transfer payments, and preferential tax to ensure the economic development of the disaster-affected regions.

11.2.1.3 Interference Elimination Principle

The interference elimination principle is to minimize the impact of the external environment by adopting policy measures and to achieve economic goals through changes in internal factors themselves. For example, when the government implements an import substitution strategy, it raises the price of imported products through tariff barriers and non-tariff barriers like import licenses, which helps to reduce the impact of the external economy on the domestic peer industries and protects the development of domestic industries. Another example of the interference elimination principle is the managed floating exchange rate system adopted by China in implementing its exchange rate reform in order to maintain the stability of the foreign exchange market, aiming to avoid the impact of external market shocks, thus creating conditions for the financial system reform and the stable development of the macroeconomy.

11.2.2 Macro-Adjustment Means

There are two main types of macroeconomic adjustment: direct and indirect. During the planned economy period, China's macro-adjustment was mainly carried out in a direct way. After the reform and opening up, it has shifted to indirect adjustment, with economic instruments as the primary means, supplemented by the necessary legal, administrative, and programming means. The primary macroeconomic adjustment means are as follows:

11.2.2.1 Economic Instruments and Their Adjustment Effects

Economic instruments are the most basic means for the regulator to realize the goal of adjustment, including the economic policy instruments and a series of economic leverages adopted by the state. Economic policy instruments generally adjust and control, with inducement by economic interests, the changes in various economic variables and the activities of economic agents through the changes in the relevant economic parameters, mainly including fiscal, monetary, industrial, foreign economic and other policies. Economic leverages mainly include taxes, credit, finance, prices, interest rates, and exchange rates, in addition to the government's allocation and use of financial and material resources at its direct disposal. These two aspects are complementary and closely coordinated. On the one hand, the effective use of economic leverage must be based on the financial and material resources directly controlled by the government. On the other hand, the government must be closely integrated with economic leverages while using financial and material resources directly at its disposal to adjust investment activities, thereby improving its economic and social benefits, promoting and guiding investment activities towards the intended goals through the market mechanism. Economic leverages are the most essential tools chosen to achieve specific economic policy objectives and are of the following five types:

(1) *Price leverage*

It is an economic tool for the state to use the law of value to adjust the redistribution of national income by adjusting a certain degree of deviation of commodity prices from their values, thus adjusting production and consumption and realizing macro-adjustment objectives. Price leverage is more sensitive compared with other adjustment leverages. It adjusts a wide range of areas, from the supply and demand of commodities and the production and operation activities of enterprises to promote the rationality of the industrial structure, and adjust the distribution and redistribution of national income and the level and the structure of consumption. However, it has limitations too: (i) the adjustment of demand and supply for commodities with a slight elasticity of demand is relatively weak; (ii) it is not easy to adjust the differences in profitability levels of different enterprises producing the same commodity, depending on their resources, technology, and other conditions; (iii) it is often difficult to adjust when it is necessary to expand the production scale of certain commodities while stimulating the consumption of such commodities.

The price leverage needs the following conditions to play an adjustment role: (i) The state control of prices. The state adjusts the fluctuation of price and value through direct pricing to realize the adjustment of the economic interests of economic agents. (ii) The dependency of other economic leverages. The state's use of the price leverage can sometimes only determine the level of profitability among different commodities but cannot fully adjust the level of prices and profitability in the production of the same commodity, and it must rely on the complementary use of other leverages like taxes. (iii) The driving force behind the price leverage comes from the differentiation of material interests formed by economic adjustment. The material interests should be controlled by the will of the state regulators through price leverage to reflect the differences in the interests of different economic agents and sectors, thus realizing the adjustment goal. With the improvement of the commodity market and the liberalization of the state's price management authority, the carrier to play the role of price leverage has gradually shifted from commodity prices to factor prices.

(2) *Tax leverage*

As an adjustment lever, taxation mainly reflects the adjusting national income distribution by macro tax rates, tax structure, and tax preferences and penalties. Due to the three intrinsic qualities of mandatory, gratuitous, and regular, tax has a wide range of adjustments and great intensity. The adjustment role of tax leverage is manifested in the following ways: (i) The built-in stabilizer. Adjusting the tax revenue and structure can adjust society's total supply and demand and influence the balance of society's total supply and demand. Especially income tax, is particularly sensitive to economic fluctuations. When the economy is booming, more income means more taxes, which exerts a somewhat disincentive effect on the economy's further expansion. However, when the economy is in recession, less income means fewer taxes, which plays a somewhat supporting role for expanding the economy. (ii) Promotion and restriction. The government can support or restrict the development of specific industries, in order to adjust the industrial structure through tax design according to the decision-making objectives based on different objects, times, and forms. For example, levying product taxes and setting different tax rates for different products can adjust production and optimize industrial structure. Different tax burdens on different regions can effectively guide resource allocation. For example, tax levers have been used to support the development of the Western region and the revitalization of the old industrial bases in the Northeast. (iii) Income distribution adjustment. Taxation can adjust the distribution relationship among the state, enterprises, and individuals, thus achieving a fair income distribution. For example, personal income tax adopts a progressive tax rate system. The higher the income, the more tax is paid, thus adjusting income. (iv) Supply and demand adjustment. Tax leverage can improve the supply and demand of commodities and accelerate the circulation of commodities by imposing different taxation rates on different distribution sectors and flow directions.

Tax leverage also has its limitations: (i) it is relatively stable and less flexible than other economic levers because the state collects taxes following the provisions of the law; (ii) it mainly adjusts the micro-agents and has a limited role in adjusting critical macroeconomic issues.

(3) *Credit leverage*

It is a means by which the state adjusts the economy through credit in response to changes in the economic situation. As the main credit leverage, bank loans have imperfect substitutability compared with other financial assets, such as bonds. Therefore, specific borrowers can only satisfy their financing needs through bank loans. Sometimes, because the demand for loans is greater than whose supply, under the condition of information asymmetry, banks will selectively ration credit to different borrowers, thus affecting the real economy through the increase or decrease of bank loans, finally realizing the goal of macro-adjustment.

In developed countries, the role of macro-adjustment through bank lending has been weakened because banks can circumvent the effects of monetary tightening by issuing financial derivatives. The balance sheet reflects the financial position of enterprises. Credit leverage works more through the balance sheet transmission mechanism of enterprises. There are significant differences in its transmission mechanism compared to bank credit: it explains the impact of credit from the perspective of the effect of different monetary policies on the financial situation (balance sheet) of a particular borrower, while bank credit explains the impact of credit on the economy from the perspective of bank loan supply.

The balance sheet transmission mechanism is manifested in the fact that the central bank's economic policy can be transmitted through the asset-liability pathway, directly or indirectly affecting the enterprises' financial position, cash flow, and net asset-liability value, and eventually impacting the real economy. Specifically, expansionary monetary policy leads to higher asset prices, improved financial conditions for firms, reduced risk of moral choices by firms, increased willingness of banks to lend to firms. Therefore, the loan volume that can be obtained has increased, which in turn leads to an expansion of investment demand and aggregate demand. Expansionary monetary policy will also lead to a decline in the nominal rate. Since the nominal rate is closely related to the firms' cash flows, a decline in the nominal rate will lead to a fall in interest payments on corporate liabilities, an increase in cash flows, and a tendency towards the moral hazard to be moderated. In this regard, banks will face less risk and will be willing to provide more loans to firms, which will lead to a rise in investment and an increase in output. In addition, expansionary monetary policy causes an increase in the inflation rate, corresponding to a reducing actual debt of firms. However, the real value of firms' assets does not fall. As a result, the firms' net asset-liabilities value rises, again reducing firms' moral hazard, so that increased access to firms' loans will lead to increased investment and output.

The functioning of bank lending leverage requires certain preconditions: (i) The non-neutrality of money. Monetary policy can impact the real economy. (ii) Imperfect substitutability. Relative to other financial assets, bank loans are non-substitutable for some demanders of funds. That is to say, they have no other source of financing than bank loans, and banks cannot change their limited fund sources through financing other than savings deposits. (iii) Broad applicability. Central banks can influence the supply of loans through reserve operations. The balance-sheet transmission mechanism is more widely applicable because it does not presuppose that the central bank can influence the supply of bank loans. However, it must also satisfy the prerequisites of monetary non-neutrality and imperfect substitutability between loans and bonds.

(4) *Interest rate leverage*

The natural interest rate is defined as the interest rate that would formulate if the demand for borrowed capital were perfectly aligned with the supply of savings. In contrast, the money rate of interest is the interest rate paid when money is used to borrow. Interest rate leverage can be expressed as follows. In a closed economy, when the central bank utilizes monetary policy instruments, such as purchasing bonds through the open market or increasing commercial banks' reserves, the quantity of money supplied increases. This leads to a decrease in the yield on monetary assets, at which point economic units buy bonds with money, the price of the bonds increases, the real interest rate decreases. As a result, investors invest more, which in turn increases output. Here, the real interest rate becomes the centerpiece of monetary policy. However, the policy fails if an increase or decrease in the quantity of money supplied fails to impact the real interest rate.

Considering commodity markets, when the central bank adopts an expansionary monetary policy that increases the quantity of money supplied, interest rates fall accordingly, with the demand for money remaining unchanged. In this regard, it stimulates investment and causes a corresponding increase in total expenditure and income. However, the decline in interest rates reduces the willingness of depositors to make deposits, while borrowed funds are reduced or unchanged. Simultaneously, the real economy generates more money demand due to increased income, causing the quantity demanded to exceed the quantity supplied. Thus, the falling interest rate reverts up, showing how the money market reacts to the commodity market. The rising interest rate, in turn, prompts a fall in the demand for money and the interest rate. And this cycle eventually reaches equilibrium.

It is generally recognized that the preconditions for interest rate leverage playing its role include the following aspects: (i) Perfection. A perfect financial market includes money and capital markets. Each market is an organic whole without division, and the economy has only two assets: money and bonds. The central bank's monetary policy is transmitted through the money market to the capital and commodity markets. That is, under the market equilibrium interest rate, the supply of money is equal to its demand, the supply of bonds is equal to their demand, and the marginal substitution rate of money and bonds is equal to the ratio of the marginal utility of the two assets to the holders. (ii) Exogeneity. The central bank directly affects the nominal money supply through issuing base currency and adjusting reserve ratio. Thus, market interest rates, thereby reflecting the exogeneity of the money supply. (iii) Complete substitutability. For the demander of funds, loans and other financing channels are fully substitutable. That's to say, the demander of funds can satisfy the demand for funds from other channels if they cannot obtain timely financing from a bank. In other words, direct and indirect financing channels can be fully substitutable. (iv) Adaptability. It means that the micro-market and enterprise bases for the functioning of economic policy are relatively well-developed, i.e., changes in market interest rates cause changes in both the demand and supply of funds.

(5) *Exchange rate leverage*

It is a means of payment and circulation for the international liquidation and transfer of purchasing power expressed in foreign currencies. The role of exchange rate leverage is mainly manifested in the fact that, through changes in the exchange rate, the state intervenes in the foreign exchange market through the market mechanism to directly impact import and export trade and non-trade foreign exchange earnings, further adjusting the balance of payments. The exchange rate leverage also affects the utilization of foreign capital and other areas.

The transmission mechanism of exchange rate leverage is manifested in the following two ways: (i) It affects aggregate demand through change in exchange rate. Suppose the exchange rate of a country's currency floats downward, in that case, it will drop the domestic products' foreign price, thus favoring exports, while raising the foreign products' domestic price, thus unfavorable to imports. Increased demand for exports and import substitutes ultimately boosts aggregate demand. If a country has idle resources in terms of workforce, capital, and other production factors, it contributes to an increase in total output and a higher level of employment. (ii) It affects total output by influencing the formation of capital and the total investment volume. A downward monetary exchange rate, on the one hand, is conducive to the country's attraction of foreign direct investment through declined relative production costs and the wealth effect so that the country's investment increases, while on the other hand, due to the relative rise in the import prices, resulting in the propensity to consume imported goods declined and save increased, which is in favor of the formation of capital and the increase in investment. An increase in gross investment, in turn, contributes to an increase in total output and employment, and vice versa.

The exchange rate leverage can also change the industrial structure by affecting the structure of aggregate demand and its weight at home and abroad, thus affecting the structure of total output. Its transmission mechanism is manifested in the following ways: (i) the downward exchange rate prioritizes developing the tradable goods sector; (ii) the allocation effect of the exchange rate on resources can be reflected not only between the tradable and non-tradable goods sectors but also within the tradable goods sector; and (iii) the downward exchange rate favors resources in traded goods sectors with relatively low returns.

The exchange rate leverage on balancing payments is demonstrated by the downward fluctuation of the exchange rate, which favors exports and discourages imports. However, its foreign currency reserve would increase as the trade surplus widened. Meanwhile, the downward fluctuation of the exchange rate favors the inflow of foreign direct investment to the detriment of outward direct investment. The inflow of foreign direct investment will cause an increase in foreign currency reserves, a decline in interest rates, and an increase in investment, eventually create inflationary pressure. Conversely, the appreciation of the exchange rate, on the one hand, narrows the trade surplus and, on the other hand, reduces the inflow of foreign direct investment and increases outflows, thus creating declining prices and even deflationary pressure.

11.2.2.2 Legal Means and Its Adjustment Effect

The modern market economy is distinctively marked by establishing a complete system of economic laws to ensure the legalization of economic operations. The more developed the market economy is, the more economic laws there are. By formulating corresponding laws and regulations, the government reflects and implements its macro policies from different angles, standardizes the economic behavior of enterprises and residents, ensures the realization of the government's objectives of adjustment policies, and makes the adjustment measures taken by the government authoritative and universal. Compared with economic instruments, legal means have distinctive features: the law's seriousness, authority, and mandatory nature.

11.2.2.3 Necessary Administrative Means and Its Adjustment Effect

Administrative means in macro-adjustment refers to the government's behavior of directly adjusting and controlling the economic activities of enterprises and residents by the power and authority of the regime. They are implemented through issuing orders, instructions, decisions, policies, and other binding means. It is characterized by timeliness and rapidity. At the critical moment of economic operation, it can play the role that other means, such as economic and legal means, cannot play. Under certain conditions, it has an immediate effect on maintaining the stability of the national economy.

However, it must be noted that applying administrative means must be premised on respect for the market economy's objective laws without undermining the functioning of the market mechanism. The government's investment adjustment should rely mainly on economic and legal means. However, administrative means are only auxiliary and should not be used unless necessary. The serviceable range of the administrative means must be strictly controlled without exceeding the objective needs and government's administrative capacity and functions. Otherwise, not only will it fail to achieve its objectives, but it may also exacerbate the contradictions in the economic operation.

11.2.2.4 Planning Tools and Their Adjustment Effects

As an essential means of government's intervention and adjustment of economic life, economic Planning has functions and roles in macro-adjustment that are irreplaceable by other adjustment means. (i) It is favorable to macro-adjustment management. Planning tools can help the government analyze and grasp the macroeconomic condition, identify the main contradictions and problems to be solved in economic operation, and take appropriate countermeasures. (ii) It is favorable to coordination. It can provide a form of consultation and a channel for listening to the opinions of the business community, the theoretical community, and the public. (iii) It is favorable to guidance. It enables enterprises to understand macroeconomic development trends and the government's economic policy orientation, guides their expectations, and enables them to make decisions in accordance with market and social needs.

It should be pointed out that although the government's use of planning to adjust is a correction and compensation for the market mechanism to a certain degree, it should likewise not violate the principles of the market economy, instead, it should make use of the market mechanism to realize them, mainly through a variety of economic instruments and market intermediaries to adjust the activities of enterprises indirectly. Planning is not the government's administrative instructions, nor a kind of administrative behavior, but a government's economic behavior based on playing the role of the market mechanism.

The state adjusting the balance between total social supply and demand must comprehensively use economic, legal, Planning, and necessary administrative means to achieve the best results. For example, relying solely on economic means may lead to disorderly acts or even law violations because market entities aim to maximize profits. Relying on legal means, through economic legislative and judicial bodies, can adjust the economic interests of all links and aspects of economic operation and maintain the regular order of the market. Especially in the period of economic transition, the operating environment and the adjustment means of the national economy have not yet been perfected, it's critical to adjust the behavior of the market entities through the formulation and effective enforcement of laws and regulations. For another example, although the government's management of the social economy has shifted from direct to indirect management and the scope and proportion of using administrative means have been gradually reduced, China's national conditions at the primary stage of socialism dictate that the state still needs to use the necessary administrative means to manage and adjust the production and operation of key enterprises and strategic products. However, it should consider the market economy's characteristics and interests of different economic agents and combine them with economic and legal means to optimize the pattern and effect of adjustment.

11.3 Macro-Adjustment Policies and Effects

In macro-adjustment economic policies, different adjustment policies have different lags, roles, and effects. This mainly includes fiscal, monetary, industrial, and foreign economic policies and policies to promote the coordinated development of the economy, society, population, resources, and environment.

11.3.1 Fiscal Policy and Its Adjustment Effect

Fiscal policy is an economic policy influencing the level of macroeconomic activities through changes in fiscal revenue and expenditure according to the intention and goal of the regulator. It's one of the most important policy instruments of macro-adjustment. The adjustment effect of fiscal policy is manifested in the following: (i) it can adjust the total social supply and demand through using and operating fiscal policy so that both tend to be balanced; (ii) it can adjust the structure of the total social supply and demand, thus promoting the rationalization of the economic structure; (iii) it can adjust financial markets and money circulation to curb inflation in conjunction with monetary policy; and (iv) it can also adjust income distribution to promote increased satisfaction of social public needs.

Fiscal policy is a relatively structural macro-adjustment policy, whose object is the distribution and redistribution of national income. Its focus is on adjusting the pattern of national income distribution and the major proportionality of national economic development. Fiscal policy also has the properties of administrative adjustment, manifested in the mandatory nature of taxation in fiscal revenue and the distributive nature of fiscal expenditure. Through fiscal revenues and expenditures, public finance changes the flow of social funds to a certain extent, thereby optimizing the economic structure.

The fiscal policy functions in two main ways. Firstly, it is a built-in stabilizer. It mainly refers to fiscal policy instruments and means, including income tax and transfer payments in fiscal expenditure. It has a specific automatic economic adjustment function due to its characteristics. Secondly, it is the discretionary. It means that the regulator takes different fiscal policies according to changes in the situation. It is characterized by the regulator consciously adjusting objectives based on judging the macroeconomic situation, selectively using and operating the relevant policy instruments and means.

As one of the most fundamental macro-adjustment policies, fiscal policy plays an important role manifested in the following aspects:

The first is based on the built-in stabilizer and the discretionary, the two basic modes of action, correctly using fiscal policy can obtain practical and positive adjustment effects. The built-in stabilizer acts in such a way as to adjust the macroeconomy in an automatic and timely manner. After the relevant fiscal systems are in place, when aggregate demand and income increase, as in times of economic prosperity, tax revenues automatically and promptly increase as a result of the increase in income. Moreover, transfer payment is automatically reduced as a result of the decrease in the number of unemployed and others in need of relief assistance. The above situations curb the increase in consumption and investment, thus mitigating the inflation caused by excessive demand. Conversely, it would dampen the reduction in consumption and investment, thereby mitigating the extent of the economic contraction. In this way, it produces the effect of stabilizing macroeconomic operations. The role of the discretionary has substantial flexibility. The regulator can flexibly use various fiscal policy instruments according to the macroeconomic situation and carry out discretionary adjustment of various macroeconomic variables according to its intention. In this way, the adjustment intensity is controlled, thus achieving the expected adjustment objectives.

The second is utilizing a wide range of policy instruments and means at their disposal. The regulator can select them in line with the requirements of specific macro-adjustment objectives and employ them for specific adjustment objectives to achieve the specialized target performance of macro-adjustment. Fiscal policy instruments can be roughly categorized into fiscal expenditure, revenue, and balance policies. Policy instruments of fiscal expenditure generally include government investment, fiscal subsidies, and transfer payments. Policy instruments of fiscal revenue generally include taxes, public debt, and state credit. Policy instruments for the aggregate balance of fiscal revenues and expenditures refer to fiscal surpluses and fiscal deficits. In this regard, the regulator adjusts changes in total social demand by increasing or decreasing fiscal deficits. Each policy tool corresponds to a certain policy objective and produces corresponding policy effects. For example, the policy effect of expanding fiscal expenditure and increasing fiscal deficit is to expand total social demand, as well as stimulating investment to expand employment. In contrast, the policy effect of retrenching fiscal expenditures and narrowing fiscal deficits is to stabilize prices through reducing total social demand and suppressing economic overheating. Fiscal policy has a variety of policy instruments, and their effects vary, which leaves a great deal of room for the regulator to choose and apply adjustment instruments and means for different adjustment objectives.

The third is that various fiscal policy instruments and means can be combined and paired to achieve comprehensive reform policy effects. The regulator can coordinate the different instruments and means of fiscal policy in terms of the action direction and the implementation intensity, thereby achieving a higher degree of adjustment performance. Different policy instruments and means can be used together in the same direction. For example, different policy instruments and means can be combined to promote employment and economic growth by expanding total social demand, such as combining the expanded fiscal expenditure, increased fiscal deficits and subsidies, and government buying treasury bonds. In contrast, different policy instruments and means can be combined to stabilize prices and curb inflation by compressing total social demand. These include fiscal expenditure compression, fiscal deficits and subsidies reduction, as well as government selling treasury bonds. Different policy instruments and means can also be used oppositely. For example, when total social demand exceeds total social supply, on the one hand, aggregate demand can be narrowed through compressing fiscal expenditure and reducing fiscal deficits. On the other hand, tax cuts can stimulate an increase in supply. On the contrary, when total social supply exceeds total social demand, expanding aggregate demand can be stimulated by expanding fiscal expenditure and increasing the fiscal deficit on the one hand, and increasing supply can be appropriately curbed by increasing taxes on the other.

The mechanism of fiscal policy features its directness. In this regard, fiscal investment instruments are exceptionally typical. The transmission of fiscal policy does not need to go through commercial banks as the central bank to affect total social demand indirectly, but instead directly expand total social demand without going through an intermediate process. The government increases profits and wages through fiscal investment to stimulate the investment and consumption of enterprises and residents and drive the development of related industries, thereby directly boosting the total social demand. The expansion of demand brought about by this adjustment is often several times more effective than the fiscal investment itself.

11.3.2 Monetary Policy and Its Adjustment Effect

Monetary policy is a guideline and corresponding policy measures adopted by the central bank or monetary authority, with an aim to adjust the quantity of money supplied, interest rate, and such to realize specific macroeconomic objectives. It is the action guideline and means for a government to control the money supply through the central bank to realize national economic objectives. Monetary policy is relatively an indirect macro-adjustment policy on the aggregate. It strikes a balance between the total social supply and demand by adjusting the monetary aggregate relationship, thus generally adjusting economic activity rather than directly targeting individual banks or enterprises. Meanwhile, the monetary policy adjustment of the economy is generally using monetary policy instruments to adjust indirectly the economic variables through the economic operation mechanism. Therefore, monetary policy is an indirectly adjusted economic policy. The tools or instruments of monetary policy are the following three practical ways:

The first is the required-reserve ratio. The required reserve is the cash commercial banks hold in response to depositors' withdrawals and the required deposits with the central bank. The required-reserve ratio, i.e., the ratio of minimum reserves to demand deposits, determines financial institutions' excess reserves, representing the liquidity situation in financial markets. This policy instrument adjusts market liquidity. When liquidity is tight, the central bank can inject liquidity into the market with reserve funds, while when liquidity is loose, the central bank absorbs reserve funds, causing a liquidity crunch. The advantages of the required-reserve ratio are that it has a quick, direct, and non-selective impact on the market. It is also better suited for use in emergencies. However, its disadvantages are that they are inflexible and have a disproportionate impact on the market.

The second is the rediscount rates. As another crucial monetary policy instrument for adjusting the money supply, it mainly refers to the interest rate paid by commercial banks when borrowing from the central bank. Rediscount rate adjustment is more flexible, focusing on the short term. In a mature market economy, the central bank can adjust the interest rate at any time according to the market demand and supply of funds. It can further adjusting the supply and demand of funds in the market by influencing the behavior of the commercial banks. In other words, the central bank needs to indirectly adjust the supply and demand of funds in the market through commercial banks. Since the rediscount rate is related to the market interest rate in varying degrees, adjusting the rediscount rate only symbolizes the will of the central bank and mainly plays an announcement effect.

The third is the open market operations (OMOs). It primarily refers to the central bank buying or selling government bonds and foreign exchange in the open market (bond market and foreign exchange market), aiming at changing the quantity of money supplied. In a mature market, it is the most important monetary policy instrument, because it is the primary determinant of changes in interest rates and base currency, the main fluctuation factor in the money supply. Purchasing securities in the open market would increase reserves, base currency, and the money supply but lower short-term interest rates. Conversely, selling in the open market does the opposite. The prerequisites for functioning OMOs are that, in addition to the fact that the financial market must be nationwide, fairly independent, and have a whole range and requisite size of securities available for operations, other policy instruments, such as the reserve system, must be in place.

The above three monetary policy instruments affect the macroeconomy mainly through adjusting monetary aggregates. However, different monetary policy instruments should be used selectively to adjust different areas, because of the uneven development of the national economy, including consumer loans, control of credit used in the security market, control of credit based on real property, preferential interest rates, and prepayment of import deposits.

The monetary policy functions mainly for the central bank to increase or decrease the quantity of money supplied through monetary policy instruments to cause interest rates to fall or rise. In this way, it's conducive to an increase or decrease in investment and ultimately affecting aggregate demand and national income.

The mechanism of monetary policy action consists of two key components. Firstly, changes in the actual balance of money are bound to lead to changes in interest rates through forming imbalances in asset portfolios. Secondly, changes in interest rates alter aggregate demand. This transmission process implies the following corollary: if there is no significant change in the actual money supply, if the imbalance in the asset portfolio fails to lead to a significant change in the interest rate, or if expenditures do not respond significantly to a change in the interest rate, then the link between money and output does not exist.

Two situations can lead to monetary policy failure. One is the existence of a liquidity trap. When interest rates are so low that the public expects them not to be any lower, their speculative demand for money becomes infinitely elastic concerning interest rates. At this time, the money supply increased by the monetary authority would be absorbed by the public's speculative demand for money. In this way, interest rates cannot be lowered and the investment demand cannot be increased, thus making monetary policy ineffective. The other is the lack of interest rate elasticity of investment. At this time, although interest rates can be reduced by increasing the money supply, the investment will not increase; thus, monetary policy also fails. It follows that the factors affecting monetary policy are mainly the interest rate elasticity of money demand and investment demand. The lower the interest rate elasticity of the demand for money, the more the interest rate will fall as a result of an increase in the money supply. Moreover, the higher the interest rate elasticity of investment demand, the more investment will increase as a result of a fall in interest rates, and the greater the impact on aggregate demand, thus the more pronounced the effect of monetary policy. Otherwise, the opposite.

11.3.3 Industrial Policy and Its Adjustment Effect

Industrial policy is a macro and medium to long-term economic policy that the state, in line with the requirements of the strategic objectives of national economic development, exerts influence on specific industrial activities through intervening and guiding, aiming at promoting the development of the market mechanism and correcting its defects, thereby promoting the rapid and coordinated development of the national economy. Industrial policy aims to accelerate industrial restructuring and promote optimizing and upgrading industrial structures to achieve sustainable and healthy economic growth. Regarding content, industrial policy comprises various specific policies and some necessary dedicated and safeguard policies. There are four main policies.

11.3.3.1 Industrial Structure Policy

It mainly refers to a country's government programming the goal of gradually evolving industrial structure based on its current situation and trend of industrial structure in a certain period. It also refers to identifying the key strategic industries to be prioritized in phases, restricting the long-line industries, eliminating the declining industries, and promoting the balanced development and optimal combination of the industries to obtain high economic efficiency. The essence of industrial structure policy lies in improving economic growth and resource allocation efficiency by promoting the rational evolution of industrial structure.

The main roles of industrial structure policy are as follows:

The first is actively developing leading industries. The leading industries mainly refer to industries that will occupy a strategic position in the future development of the national economy. Although they have a leading function, they may be small or underdeveloped. Promoting their development is the core of policies on industrial adjustment. From the viewpoint of the economic growth process, promoting economic growth by structural adjustment and industrial upgrading is mainly reflected in converting the leading industries into new pillar industries, thus bringing new impetus to economic growth as a whole.

The second is properly protecting vulnerable industries. The vulnerable industries mainly refer to industries that have lost their comparative advantages and must be withdrawn as per market economy principles. However, as these industries significantly impact national socio-economic stability, the state must either support and retain them or orderly transfer and withdraw them. The proper protection, as suggested here, does not mean taking measures to protect lagging industries but instead mainly to prevent their exit from triggering large social shocks.

The third is vigorously developing pillar industries. Pillar industries mainly refer to the industries supporting the operation of the whole national economy, whose development aims to rationalize the whole industrial structure. The pillar industries generally have a process of development and growth for which strong support is needed. Developing countries must determine what industries should be their backbones that can rationally utilize resource endowments with a technological base according to the actual economic development situation. However, they should be reasonably adjusted according to the economic development stage.

The fourth is timely adjusting declining industries. Any industry goes through a boom-bust cycle. After going through emergence, growth, and mature stage, an industry would experience a decline period. When an industry is in or approaches a decline period, the market demand is a continuous downtrend. Conversely, the market demand for its alternatives is a rapid uptrend. The focus of the declining industries policy is to reduce barriers to the flow of production factors from low growth rates to high growth rates. Specific measures include helping them to contract or exit in an orderly manner and guiding the transfer of their capital stock to high-growth rate sectors, reducing the cost of eliminating declining industries by the market mechanism and mitigating the resulting social unrest, and facilitating the flow of production factors to the leading, infant, or pillar industries.

11.3.3.2 Industrial Organization Policies

It mainly refers to the government's policy mix to intervene, adjust the industrial structure and market behavior, and adjust inter-firm relations to obtain ideal market performance. The essence is that the government coordinates the relationship between competition and scale economies to establish a normal market order and improve market performance. Historically, industrial organization policy was introduced earlier than industrial structure policy, and its initial form was anti-trust or anti-monopoly policy.

Industrial organization policies focus on the changes affecting industrial organization. They are usually divided into three categories: (i) Policies to promote competition. It is mainly used to encourage competition and restrict monopoly, including anti-monopoly or anti-trust policies, anti-unfair competition policies, SME policies, and such, geared towards maintaining a normal market order. (ii) Industrial rationalization policies. It mainly applies to natural monopoly industries to encourage specialization and scale economies. It focuses on restricting excessive competition, directly manifesting in government regulation policies. (iii) Policies supporting SMEs. It is mainly used to support SMEs in merging and cooperating, thereby promoting the formation of scale economies and achieving rationalization and efficiency in industrial organizations.

Industrial organization policy is indispensably complementary to industrial structure policy. In implementing the industrial organization policy, the government should mainly pay attention to the following aspects: (i) it should depend on different national conditions and development stages of the industrial organization to gradually increase the industrial concentration ratio in industries with significant economies of scale, and establish a market access and exit system meeting the requirements of a market economy; and (ii) it should step up anti-monopoly efforts, accelerate the pace of establishing a modern enterprise system in monopolized industries, speed up constructing an effective competition pattern in monopolized industries, and gradually establish and improve an open, transparent, and firmly adjusted supervisory system.

11.3.3.3 Industrial Technology Policy

It is mainly a pioneering policy for industrial restructuring and upgrading, focusing on guiding or influencing the technological progress of industries. Since industrial technology policy involves almost all industries of the national economy, it is usually viewed as the technology policy of the whole country. In practice, it mainly includes: (i) Research and development assistance policies. It mainly refers to a series of assistance policy measures taken by the government to support the scientific and technological strength of the national industry and to carry out research and development on new technologies, products, and processes. (ii) High-tech incentive policies. It is mainly a variety of policy measures based on research and development policies, including high-tech structural, organizational, and development zone policies, aiming at realizing the industrialization, commercialization, and internationalization of high-tech research and development results. (iii) Technology introduction policies. These policies mainly aim to bridge the gap between domestic and international advanced technology, optimize the industrial structure, and ultimately realize the goal of independent development, including policies on importing, digesting, and absorbing technology, domestic market protection, and talent introduction.

11.3.3.4 Industrial Regional Policy

It mainly refers to the policy of industrial spatial arrangement pattern, which is a series of policy measures taken by the government to realize the goal of optimizing the spatial distribution and combination of industries and adjusting the reasonable allocation of production factors in geographic space according to the requirements for developing national and regional economy. The United Kingdom firstly implemented this policy. Japan and the United States began using industrial regional policy in the 1950s and 1960s to adjust and promote the rational resource allocation and avoid industry overconcentration in industrially developed areas, achieving sound effects. China's implementation of policies such as developing the western region, revitalizing old industrial bases in the northeast region, rising the central region, and pioneeringly developing the eastern region, the Belt and Road Initiative, as well as policies such as the coordinated development of the Beijing-Tianjin-Hebei, and the construction of the Yangtze River Economic Belt, are all part of the industrial regional policy.

Implementing industrial regional policies mainly addresses the question of how to take advantage of the "agglomeration benefits" arising from the relative concentration of production. The aim is to minimize the disparities in the economic development level between regions as a result of the density of economic activities and the different industrial structures of the regions.

From an economic viewpoint, the main factors affecting industrial distribution are: (i) The size of market demand. With little transportation cost of raw materials, enterprises will generally site close to the market. Therefore, the regional market's structure and size directly affect their industries' structure and size. (ii) Population size and quality. A large population is conducive to lowering workforce costs and promoting the development of labor-intensive industries in the region, while a high-quality population can provide a sound basis for the transition from labor-intensive to technology-intensive industries in the region. (iii) Infrastructure conditions, including productive and unproductive infrastructure. The infrastructure conditions affect the site selection of enterprises, indirectly affecting regional economic development and industrial layout. (iv) Transportation conditions. Transportation costs affect the industrial layout, and convenient regional transportation conditions can significantly reduce the transportation cost and time between the market and provenance, attracting enterprises to locate in the region. (v) External economic conditions. Enterprises producing similar products or having upstream and downstream relationships in the industry can take advantage of external public benefits and labor division with other enterprises to reduce R&D and production costs. Otherwise, the opposite.

In the early stage of economic development, densely populated areas with better infrastructure can gather capital, technology, and talents, attracting a large inflow of production factors such as capital, technology, and labor. This phenomenon is the polarization effect. In the mid-stage of economic development, when an industrial cluster develops to a certain extent, it causes diminishing returns to scale, i.e., the land rent and the production cost rise, the competition among enterprises intensifies, and the profitability declines. In this case, the industrial distribution generally exhibits a diffusion effect. Adequate supply capacity can be provided through point-axis and network development patterns formed through implementing different industrial regional policies in the process of economic development aiming to utilize the above two effects to cultivate economic growth poles for phased and graded development and capitalizing on the diffusion effect of growth poles to promote the development of economically underdeveloped areas between growth poles. Meanwhile, using the polarization effect of growth poles to establish a regional labor division and collaboration between growth poles based on regional comparative advantages will help to form a benign linkage of production division of labor and collaboration across the country.

Thus, industrial policy, as a critical macroeconomic adjustment policy, is an important guarantee for realizing the national economic development strategy and an essential means of rationalizing and high-leveling the industrial structure. In this way, the society's aggregate supply and demand structure is constantly coordinated and optimized. Compared with other macroeconomic adjustment policies, the adjustment of industrial policies has the following characteristics: (i) It focuses on adjusting supply. Through adjusting industrial activities, industrial policy enables supply to satisfy structurally total social demand, realizes the structural adaptation of supply and demand, and adjusts the product structure by promoting or restricting the development of specific industries to promote the coordination and dynamic balance between supply and demand. (ii) It focuses on individual adjustment methods. According to the development trend of the national economy, different industries and enterprises are adjusted in different ways so that the industrial structure is more suitable for the requirements of demand. (iii) Industrial policy is intrinsically linked to the market mechanism. In choosing the pillar industries to be supported, industrial policy relies mainly on the market competition mechanism to screen out promising enterprises. Moreover, the help of various signals provided by the market mechanism makes it more scientific and flexible in adjusting the industrial structure. (iv) Medium- to long-term time horizon. Compared with fiscal and monetary policies, industrial policy is primarily medium- to long-term with an extensive period. It is primarily due to a certain degree of rigidity of industrial policy, because once the entire industrial structure is formed, it has a large amount of sunk costs that cannot be changed easily, and only through a more extended period can the inherent industrial structure be changed. Although industrial policy can affect the short-term equilibrium in functioning the national economy, it mainly aims to achieve the long-term equilibrium of aggregate supply and demand by optimizing the resource allocation and adjusting the future supply capacity and structure.

11.3.4 Foreign Economic Policy and Its Adjustment Effect

Foreign economic policy is a series of guidelines and policies formulated by the state. The aim is to ensure the realization of the overall macroeconomic objectives under the conditions of opening up to the outside world, mainly including the following:

11.3.4.1 Foreign Trade Policy

It mainly refers to the guidelines for import and export trade activities within a certain period formulated by a country's government in line with its national development objectives. It is centrally embodied in laws, rules, regulations, and measures a country imposes on import and export trade within a certain period. It is vital to a country's overall economic and foreign policies.

The adjustment effect of foreign trade policy is twofold: (i) Adjusting the balance between total social supply and demand by adjusting the balance between imports and exports. It is manifested in using foreign trade policy to adjust the balance of trade between imports and exports by adopting policies that encourage exports, restrict imports, or contrary policies, following changes in the situation of the payment balance. (ii) Adjusting the balance of payments. Judging from the composition of the payment balance, the payment side reflects domestic purchases of foreign goods, services, and technology and capital outflows. In contrast, the receipt side reflects the export of domestic goods, services, and technology and the capital inflows, representing the country's foreign exchange supply. In the equilibrium formula of total social supply and demand, the demand and supply of foreign exchange are components of total social supply and total demand. If the payment balance is not equated, it will directly affect the balance of the macroeconomic aggregates. When such a situation arises, the state adjusts it through its foreign economic policies, mainly its foreign capital utilization and exchange rate policies, to adjust the supply and demand of foreign exchange, thus promoting the balance of payments.

11.3.4.2 The Policies for Importing Foreign Investments

It mainly includes utilizing foreign direct investment (FDI) and introducing foreign loans. Introducing FDI will increase the domestic supply capacity, and foreign loans will increase the domestic supply capacity and total social demand. However, it will increase external debt in the long run, needing adjustment. External debt adjustment is a supervisory and adjustment activity carried out by a country's macroeconomic adjustment departments based on scientifically analyzing the scale, structure, and repayment of principal and interest of the country's foreign capital, focusing on adjusting the inflow volume of foreign capital, the optimal allocation and use of foreign capital, an optimum cost-risk portfolio of foreign capital, and the relationship between external debts. Adjusting external debt includes the total external debt and its structure. Adjusting external debt controls the scale of total foreign capital so that external debt repayment does not exceed the country's bearing capacity. The moderate scale of utilizing external debt can be realized through the behavior of economic entities to attract foreign capital and the adjustment of the market mechanism. The structural adjustment of external debt mainly aims to adjust and optimize the mode, currency, interest rate, and maturity structures of external debt, aiming at improving the macro-efficiency of using foreign capital and reducing the burden of foreign debt.

11.3.4.3 External Investment Policy

It is also known as overseas direct investment (ODI) policy, mainly including greenfield investment and cross-border M&A. Greenfield investment includes establishing international wholly-owned companies and joint ventures. Cross-border M&A can be divided into horizontal, vertical, and conglomerate M&As, which is proposed according to the industry relations between the parties. It can be also categorized as direct and indirect M&As according to whether the M&A is through an intermediary. The external investment policy mainly adjusts greenfield investment and cross-border M&As. At the beginning of the reform and opening up, China's external investment was greenfield investment-oriented, after which its proportion declined. Instead, the proportion of cross-border M&As has continued to rise. Regarding the comparison between the utilization of foreign capital and external investment, the latter has been on par with the former and has tended to exceed the former in recent years.

11.3.4.4 Exchange Rate Policy

It has crucial implications mainly for international trade and balance of payments, as evidenced by the fact that exchange rate stability is conducive to smoothly realizing import and export trade, thereby promoting the development of international trade. On the contrary, volatile exchange rate movements will increase the risk of international trade, thus hindering its smooth progress. The impact of exchange rate changes on payment balance is manifested in the fact that when a country has a trade deficit due to the foreign exchange demand exceeding the supply, it will generally result in a rising exchange rate, implying a reduction in the exchange rate of the local currency against the foreign currency. In this regard, the country will have to change the original foreign exchange rate to re-provide for the lower rate of exchange. However, when a country's exchange rate depreciates, it reduces the price of a country's foreign-currency- denominated exports, thus contributing to a reducing import volume and an improving balance of trade.

11.3.5 Investment Policy and Its Adjustment Effect

Investment policy refers to the guiding principles and measures the state or government formulated to address investment management and its adjustment to promote socio-economic well-being. It is the government's conscious intervention in investment activities to achieve specific investment objectives. Therefore, any investment policy is formulated based on specific investment management and adjustment objectives. The goal of investment management and adjustment is to balance investment supply and demand. It specifically includes aggregate and structural balance. The aim is to achieve an optimal allocation of investment resources throughout society and promote sustained and rapid economic development and continuously improve people's living standards.

The adjustment effect of investment policy is manifested in adjusting the total scale and structure of investment through fiscal, monetary, price, and industrial policies. Specifically, the following three policies are included:

The first is policy instruments and means to adjust the total investment scale and structure, mainly as follows: (i) Fiscal revenue policy. It mainly includes taxes and fiscal charges. Changes in the overall level of the tax burden can be used to adjust the total investment scale, and the setting of appropriate taxes can be used to adjust the investment structure. (ii) Depreciation policy. Depreciation funds are the primary source of funds for enterprise replacement investment. The state can influence the scale of enterprise investment from the source of capital by stipulating and adjusting the depreciation rate, while differential depreciation rates for different enterprises can adjust the structure of enterprise investment. (iii) Fiscal expenditure policies. Since a society's investment is categorized into budgetary and extra-budgetary investment, changes in budgetary investment will lead to changes in the investment scale and structure throughout society. (iv) Fiscal subsidies. They mainly adjust the formation and use of investment funds. (v) Fiscal credit. Mobilizing and supplying part of the country's investment funds through credit can, on the one hand, make up for the lack of investment funds, while on the other hand, can change the investment structure.

The second is monetary policy to adjust the investment scale and structure. Its main policy instruments are threefold: (i) Required-reserve ratio. In case total social demand is less than total supply, the central bank would reduce the required-reserve ratio so that commercial banks expand lending with the demand deposits remaining unchanged. It's conducive to increasing the quantity of money supplied in the market, lowering the interest rate, and finally increasing business investment; otherwise, the opposite. (ii) Rediscount rate. The level of the rediscount rate affects the amount that commercial banks borrow or discount from the central bank, which in turn affects the level of interest rates and ultimately encourages or restricts business investment.

(iii) Open market operations (OMO). The central bank adjusts the quantity of money supplied and interest rates by buying and selling government bonds in the market, thereby affecting the investment scale.

The third is price policy. The price policies adjusting investment are mainly to adjust (i) the price of a small minority of commodities closely linked to the development of the national economy and people's lives and that of crucial national reserve materials; (ii) the price of a few commodities with scarce resources, such as oil and natural gas; (iii) the price of commodities operated by natural monopolies, such as the electricity price, telecommunications basic service expense; (iv) the price of critical public utilities, such as the price of water; and (v) the price of important public welfare services, such as charges for medicine. The government takes the initiative to adjust their prices, guide the investors' investment behavior in related industries, and then adjust the investment scale, ultimately optimizes the investment structure.

11.3.6 Consumption Policy and Its Adjustment Effect

Consumption policy is a general term for all kinds of guidelines, systems, and regulations related to consumption issued and implemented by the national or local governments. Formulating a consumption policy aims to align the appropriate and regular improvement of planned consumption levels, the change of the consumption structure and pattern in a certain period of time with the overall social and economic development strategy, and ensure the country's economic development. Consumption policy is characterized by its phased and time-sensitive nature. Its formulation needs to consider the level of national development, including political, economic, and cultural development. A rational consumption policy can stabilize the economy and transform economic growth patterns, promoting socio-economic development. In a socialist market economy, consumption policy is usually used to adjust two equilibrium relationships: the relationship between individual consumption and investment and their mutual transformation, the relationship between current and forward consumption.

Consumption policy includes both general and specific ones. General consumption policy provides general and relatively stable guidance for consumption within a certain period. A specific consumption policy is a policy provision adjusting the aggregate and structure of consumption within a certain period, thereby guiding the structure, mode, and quality of residents' current consumption, comprising mainly (i) consumption policies to increase the consumption level, such as policies adjusting the relationship between residents' income and economic growth, income distribution policies, social welfare and security policies; and (ii) policies adjusting the consumption structure, such as policies to adjust the industrial structure of consumer goods and consumer goods market policies.

Main consumption policy instruments and means are as follows:

The first is taxation. Taxes can encourage and promote consumption by adjusting the industrial structure, promoting or suppressing imports and exports, and adjusting consumers' income. Tax adjustment generally includes two major measures: tax increases and tax reductions, which can be used simultaneously in some cases. However, there are always primary and secondary considerations when they are used in conjunction. Increasing tax levies on long-line businesses during periods of inflated consumption demand, in this way, it will reduce the excess revenue they receive. Moreover, reducing tax on some businesses that produce consumer goods in short supply stimulates them to increase the supply. Instead, tax reduction is the primary measure, and a tax increase is secondary in times of insufficient consumption demand.

The second is interest rates. Interest rate policy can effectively adjust the ratio of consumer savings to consumption and significantly impact corporate finance in the market, thereby increasing or decreasing liquidity and releasing or inhibiting consumption. Interest rates adjust consumption mainly by adjusting interest rates on savings deposits and loans. Raising the savings interest rate when consumption is inflated can encourage residents to shift current consumption to future consumption. By contrast, lowering the savings interest rate at times of low consumption demand can increase residents' spending. When consumption demand is inflated, the lending rate should be raised, and investment loans should be reduced to avoid the increase in consumer spending caused by expanding the investment scale. However, when consumption demand is insufficient, the lending rate can be lowered, and investment loans can be increased, thus increasing the consumers' spending that goes along with investment spending;

The third is income adjustment policy. It includes two main aspects: (i) limiting the rapid growth of residents' disposable incomes when consumption demand is inflated, such as raising the personal income tax or levying new taxes; Conversely, (ii) seeking to increase residents' disposable incomes when consumption demand is insufficient, such as reducing personal income tax rates, ceasing or suspending taxes on certain taxable income related to personal income and consumer spending, and lowering the tax rate appropriately;

The fourth is bonds, government purchases, and transfer payments. National or local government bonds can affect consumers' incomes and influence industries through financing, thus adjusting consumption structure. Government purchases directly affect industries while transfer payments redistribute income. Changes in both ultimately affect consumption.

11.3.7 Price Policy and Its Adjustment Effect

The price policy is a general term for a series of behavioral norms, guidelines, and provisions adopted by the state, aiming at carrying out the necessary intervention and management of commodity prices in the market to achieve specific socio-economic objectives. It mainly includes the means to determine the price policy objective and choose the price policy. Price policy has different divisions: (i) the macro and micro price policies according to the price policy level; (ii) the flexible price policy and stable price policies according to modalities of price policy implementation; (iii) the promotive, competing, and neutral price policies according to the interrelationship between various specific price policies. Promotive price policy has a favorable impact on other price policies while competing price policy has an unfavorable impact on other price policies. A neutral price policy does not affect implementing other price policies.

Specific objectives of price policy include: (i) Establishing a reasonable price management system. It aims to divide price decision-making authority and establish the price administration authorities, which is the agency of formulating price policies. (ii) Adjusting unreasonable price structure. It mainly adjusts the relationship between commodity prices and price differentials, the main content of the government's indirect intervention through price policy. (iii) Stabilizing the overall price level. Only in this way can a rational allocation of resources be achieved. (iv) Promoting the realization of primary macroeconomic objectives. Designing and applying price policy create favorable conditions for smoothly developing the national economy, thereby promoting steady and orderly economic growth.

Realizing the objectives of price policy requires using specific adjustment instruments, which are mainly:

(1) *Direct intervention*

It mainly refers to the government directly stipulating the price level, specifically including: (i) Government price. The government directly stipulates the price of some goods and services to achieve the optimal resource allocation. (ii) Government guidance price. The enterprise sets the final price under the government-established standard price and fluctuation range or ceiling and floor prices. (iii) Price subsidies. The government subsidizes the price level of essential commodities by controlling the price differential rate, profit margin, and others to eliminate the losses caused by price changes to producers, operators, and consumers. (iv) Price freezes. During extraordinary periods when there are sharp fluctuations in the overall level of market prices, the government may take emergency measures such as temporary centralization of pricing authority, as well as partial or total price freezes at the national level or within sectors.

(2) *Indirect adjustment*

It is mainly a price policy for some resource commodities, commodities with a more significant impact on the environment, and commodities closely connected to the people's basic life. This is achieved through influencing and intervening in their prices to maintain the essential stability of the overall price level. The primary means adopted include: (i) Fiscal policy. It consists mainly of fiscal expenditure policy, taxation policy, and automatic fiscal stabilization instruments. (ii) Monetary policy. The main instruments are OMOs, rediscount rate, and required-reserve ratio. (iii) Import and export policies. The primary purpose is to increase or decrease supply in the domestic market, thereby promoting a balance between supply and demand in the domestic market and maintaining essential stability in the overall price level. (iv) An important commodity reserve system. The primary purpose is to adjust market supply and demand, as well as influence market prices through policies such as reserve, allocation, and production limitation or promotion of essential commodities.

(3) *Formalizing supervision*

It mainly refers to the government's supervision and inspection of price activities, penalizing and correcting price violations to establish a sound market order and promote fair competition. Specific means include convening price hearings, stipulating that some commodities should fulfill the procedures for filing price increase declarations and price adjustments. Additionally, strengthening supervision and inspection of market prices, guiding and disciplining market competition, and curbing price violations are also beneficial.

(4) *Service guidance*

It mainly refers to using their resources and channels by the competent price authorities to track and analyze the price situation and the factors affecting price trends, as well as studying the impact of price changes on social production and life, aiming at properly providing price forecasting and early warning. Specific means include (i) issuing reports of cost research, price index analysis, and price information and trend on essential commodities and services to guide production and consumption activities in the market; and (ii) publicizing and popularizing laws and regulations, standardizing the behavior of market operators and consumers, and creating a good market environment.

11.3.8 Policies and Effects in Promoting the Coordinated Development of Economy, Society, Population, Resources, and the Environment

At present, China's main development tasks are building a harmonious society and realizing sustainable economic and social development. The government must consider both economic and social development in its macro-adjustment. It should also comprehensively resolve all contradictions in economic and social development while effectively addressing the problem of coordinated development of human society and natural environment. Consequently, increasing employment, eliminating poverty, raising incomes, and protecting the environment have become the starting point and main content of macro-adjustment.

11.3.8.1 Employment, Income Distribution, and Social Security Policies

(1) *Employment policy*

It is an essential institution in modern countries. It is broadly divided into two opposed categories based on differences in the objectives and instruments of their employment policies. (i) Positive or active. It is mainly based on constructing a public employment service system, with inputs mainly used to improve vocational counseling, employment training, and the efficiency of the workforce market. (ii) Negative or passive. It refers to public programs whose inputs are focused mainly on fiscal transfer payments, unemployment protection, pensions, and improving the income distribution system. Regardless of the type of employment policy, its adjustment effect is mainly manifested in the following ways:

- lessening the impact of the business cycle on employment;
- depleting the workforce market's structural imbalances;
- improving the functioning of the general workforce market;
- enhancing the skills of workers to increase labor productivity;
- supporting disadvantaged groups or job-seekers in a state of long-term unemployment.

Currently, China is adhering to the strategy of prioritizing employment, implementing a more proactive employment policy, and striving to create more jobs. The aim is to spare no effort to tackle structural employment. Improving preferential policies to support entrepreneurship can form a new mechanism featuring government incentives for entrepreneurship, social support for entrepreneurship, and diligent entrepreneurship among workers. In this way, entrepreneurship can lead to employment.

(2) *Income distribution policy*

It is the state's formulation of principles, guidelines, and policies on distribution in response to the residents' income level and their income gaps, aiming to realize the general objectives and tasks of macroeconomic adjustment. As income distribution is divided into primary, secondary, and tertiary distributions, income distribution policies are also divided accordingly. Primary distribution policy is mainly concerned with properly handling the relationship between the state, enterprises, and workers on the premise of emphasizing fairness and efficiency. The main focus is on process fairness, such as tax policies and policies on the proceeds of state-owned resources and the upward transferring of SOEs' profits. Given the reality of a wider disparity in disposable income among various social classes and groups, the secondary distribution policy is aimed mainly at closing the social income gap through policy measures such as taxation, social security, and transfer payments. The enhanced focus lies in fairness in outcomes. The tertiary distribution policy encourages social donations, mutual aid, and charity by granting donors preferential tax and other concessions to promote further social equity.

The government's effect in adjusting income distribution is mainly reflected in two aspects: (i) Restrictive policies. That is, although they cannot reduce and control the imbalanced income distribution, they can limit its side effects within a specific range or control the existing imbalance to a certain degree, such as by increasing the investment in education and adjusting the structure of educational inputs. (ii)

The controlling income distribution policy. The government mainly carries out the mandatory adjustment income distribution policy through taxation and fiscal transfer payments, such as perfecting the individual income tax and establishing the social security tax.

Currently, the government departments are highly concerned about the widening gap in income distribution in China at all levels. The essence of the state's adjustment policy of income distribution is to continuously increase the residents' income, especially those of low-income earners. Its main measures include: (i) Establishing and improving a scientific mechanism for determining the wage levels, for their normal growth, and for guaranteeing their payment, improving the mechanism for the growth of minimum wages, and improving the mechanism for market to evaluate the contributions of factors and allocating them according to those contributions. The aim is to gradually increase the proportion of residents' income in national income distribution and labor remuneration in the primary distribution. (ii) In terms of adjustment means, it should strengthen the adjustment effect of taxation on income distribution and enhance the adjustment and supervision of personal income distribution of in monopolized industries. (iii) In terms of institutional improvement, it is achieved through deepening the reform of the income distribution system, implementing a system in which distribution based on labor is the mainstay coexisting with a variety of distribution methods, encouraging the participation of capital, technology, and other production factors in income distribution, and adjusting the wages and compensation of top managers and technicians in SOEs, while exercising strict constraints and supervision. Through its income distribution policy, the state adjusts and prevents the income distribution from expanding excessively between urban and rural areas, regions, and industries.

(3) *Social security policy*

It is an institutional arrangement whereby the state and society, to safeguard the primary livelihood of society members, assist in redistributive means to society members if they experience difficulties in their living due to old age, illness, work injury, unemployment, and other reasons. Social security consists of the following: (i) Social insurance. It is the core of the social security system. When workers become temporarily or permanently incapacitated or lose their financial resources due to unemployment, the state compensates these workers through legislation to ensure that they maintain a basic living standard. It mainly includes old-age, medical, unemployment, and occupational injury insurance. (ii) Social assistance. It mainly refers to the system whereby the state, through redistributing national income, assists members of society who are unable to maintain a minimum standard living due to natural disasters or other economic or social reasons, including disaster relief, poverty relief, and other support measures for socially vulnerable groups. (iii) Social welfare. It is a general term for social policies that enable all members of society to improve their living standard based on primary living conditions, including education, health, residential premises, and the urban environment, among others, through various welfare services, enterprises, or subsidies.

Social security has three adjustment effects: (i) It promotes the development of the national economy by ensuring that workers enjoy the survival and development environment to which members of society are entitled. Workers often lose their ability to work temporarily or permanently or lose their livelihood security due to unemployment. The state provides these workers with life support through social security, which is conducive to restoring their ability to work, reintegration into production, and avoiding frustrating their motivation to work. From a macro perspective, social security maintains stable consumption demand for social security participants through redistribution, which is beneficial to maintaining the stability of total social demand and smoothly operating the macroeconomy. (ii) Social security is conducive to solving problems such as demographic structure through the intergenerational distribution of people. By establishing old-age insurance, the government has changed the traditional concept of relying solely on children to care for the parents and elderly relatives, which is of great significance in adjusting the population size. Medical insurance enables sick workers to receive medical treatment and regain their ability to work. Unemployment insurance helps safeguard the workers' rights and their offspring to development and education. It is also conducive to improving the population's quality. Social security contributes to solving economic and social problems such as population aging through intergenerational distribution. (iii) Social security is conducive to maintaining economic and social stability. The government ensures that workers enjoy primary living conditions by providing workers with old-age, sickness, and unemployment insurance. Although the government has thus reduced its investment in the national economy, it has stabilized the economic and social order by stabilizing the workers' mood, which also contributes to developing the national economy.

(4) *Population policy*

It can be broadly and narrowly defined. Broadly, population policy refers to those adopted by the government to comprehensively guide and adjust changes in the natural, economic, social, and regional structures of the population, including the following four main items: (i) policies on social population changes, such as occupation, industry, urban–rural demographic transition, and population urbanization; (ii) policies on natural population changes, such as marriage, family, births, and deaths; (iii) policies related to changes in population movements, such as regional distribution of the population, international migration, and emigration; (iv) policies on the social activities of the population, such as universal education, employment, household registration management, health care, retirement settlement, together with social security for elderly persons living alone and people with disabilities.

Narrowly, population policy refers exclusively to fertility policy, the sum of a series of plans, norms, and measures formulated by governments to adjust fertility to achieve a predetermined population size, growth rate, and derelopment. Different countries have different population policies, which are adjusted appropriately in line with their demographic development. In formulating fertility policies, it is necessary to consider the overall strategic social, economic, political, resource, and ecological interests and the acceptability of the major population.

Adjustment effect of population policy is reflected in its ability to adjust all factors in the process of population development comprehensively. It adjusts and influences not only the reproductive behavior of the population but also factors such as population size, health of newborn, sex, composition, and distribution. In other words, population policy is not limited to adjusting or influencing the reproductive behavior of the population but also adjusts factors related to population and society, population and economy, and population and the natural environment in the process of population development and the evolution of demographic factors.

11.3.8.2 Policies Oriented Towards Resource-Efficient and Environment-Friendly

A resource-efficient and environment-friendly society is one in which resources are efficiently utilized and effectively allocated, the macroeconomy maintains rapid and healthy development, and harmony between humanity and nature is achieved. Among other things, a resource-efficient society requires the whole society to be mobilized and stimulated to conserve and make efficient use of all kinds of resources. This can be achieved through sound mechanisms, structural adjustments, technological advances, strengthened management, and publicity and education in the production, circulation, and consumption stages of social reproduction, with an aim to support a sustainable model of social development with a higher level of welfare for the whole society with the least possible resource consumption. The term "efficient" has two meanings: one is to eliminate waste, i.e., it is required to reduce the waste of resource consumption in economic operation; the other is economizing, i.e., it is required to create the same or even more wealth with as few resources and energy as possible in the production and consumption process. An environment- friendly society has three requirements: (i) adequately protecting natural ecology focusing on controlling irrational resource development activities by sticking to the principle of conservation priority and ordered development; (ii) enhancing the level of environmental protection and strengthening ecological protection of natural resources such as water, land, forests, grasslands, and oceans; (iii) giving priority to prevention and comprehensive treatment as well as strengthen pollution control and ecosystem protection at source. It also includes resolutely changing the situation of pollution before treatment and pollution while treatment is being carried out. In substance, environment-friendly mainly includes (i) establishing environment-friendly production and consumption modes; (ii) adopting non-polluting or low-polluting technologies, processes, and products; (iii) constructing an ecologically compatible layout of productive forces; (iv) forming a less-pollution and low-loss industrial structure, and (v) vigorously developing sustainable green industries among other things.

Adjustment effect of resource-efficient and environment-friendly policies is manifested in the following ways. The state mobilizes, through economic policies, the enthusiasm of enterprises and other micro-entities to adopt production methods that conserve resources and protect the environment, with an aim to establish a resource- efficient and environment-friendly society. These include industrial, regional, taxation, and investment policies:

The first is industrial policy. It implements resource-efficient and environment-friendly concepts in formulating industrial structure and organization policies and makes them operational in all aspects. Regarding industrial structure policy, the goals of saving resources and protecting the environment are to be realized by determining the scale and priority of developing different industries, encouraging the development of resource-saving industries while strictly restricting or even prohibiting the development of high-energy-consuming and high-polluting industries. They can also be achieved through eliminating traditional protection and support measures for resource-intensive industries, and prioritizing the development of environmentally friendly industries. Regarding industrial organization policy, the goal of low-input, high-output, and low-pollution is achieved by restricting or prohibiting the construction of small polluting enterprises, while achieving economies of scale by encouraging enterprises to utilize resources most effectively.

The second is regional policy. The main elements are: (i) Defining the rational layout of regional productivity. Whether the regional industrial layout is reasonable depends on regional resource endowment, economic efficiency, environmental capacity, and ecological carrying capacity. A reasonable industrial layout requires that while giving full play to regional comparative advantages, environmental pollution and ecological degradation should be reduced or avoided. (ii) Coordinating regional resource development with regional industrial policy. Based on scientific analysis and correct evaluation of regional development conditions, the direction of industrial development is determined, and the region's industrial structure is optimized to achieve the sustainable use of resources. (iii) Promoting collaborative regional development. It should strengthen economic and technical cooperation between economically developed and less developed regions, encourage capital and talent flow to less developed regions, and promote regional joint development. (iv) Improving the comprehensive management of regional ecosystems. Following the guidelines and planning programs for the comprehensive management of the ecological environment, soil erosion, land desertification, pastureland degradation, and industrial pollution are comprehensively managed.

The third is taxation policy. The main elements are: (i) Improving the tax system and levying environmental taxes on wastewater and exhaust gas. Its essence is to internalize the social costs caused by external diseconomies and increase the enthusiasm of enterprises to combat pollution. Although China has partially practiced the tax policy on resource development and utilization, its revenue collection method is still not adapted to the needs of China's development, and resource compensation fees should be gradually incorporated into the scope of resource tax in the future. (ii) Encouraging enterprises to produce products conducive to realizing resource-efficient and environment-friendly products by formulating specific tax conditions or tax breaks policies. (iii) Implementing differential tax rates to support developing environmental protection industries and restrict developing industries that harm environmental resources.

The fourth is investment policy. The main elements are (i) increasing government investment in ecological projects and expanding investment in developing environmental protection technologies and industries, since most of these projects are public goods, which are challenging to adjust by relying on the market mechanism, the government should be their investor; and (ii) prioritizing the support of major areas or projects related to economic growth, people's lives, and the protection of environmental resources.

11.4 Innovating and Improving Macro-Adjustment Methods

11.4.1 Overall Requirements for Scientific Macro-Adjustment

11.4.1.1 Insisting on Carrying Aggregate Adjustment and Targeted Executing Policies in Tandem

Macroeconomic aggregate adjustment adjusts the balance between total social demand and supply. In this sense, aggregate adjustment must balance "stabilizing growth" and "adjusting the structure." It is necessary to prevent excessive economic growth from going beyond the ceiling and the resource environmental carrying capacity. It brings about inflation, and to prevent economic growth from slipping out of the floor, which causes enormous employment pressure. That is to say, it is necessary to maintain the bottom line of economic growth. Aggregate adjustment and targeted executing policies carried out in tandem are designed to address the imbalance, incoherence, and unsustainability between investment demand, consumption demand, net export demand, and economic growth. Eventually, it will achieve stable national economy development.

11.4.1.2 Insisting on the Short- and Long-Term Combination

For a large developing country like China, it's necessary to achieve both short-term stable development and the national economy's medium- and long-term sustainable development. In this context, macro-adjustment should not only make efforts from the demand side, but also focus on strengthening the supply-side structural reform and promote the industry toward the middle and high end by making efforts on both sides. As investment, consumption, and net export demands are inside the scope of total social demand, it is a short-term policy to solve the contradiction of the insufficient aggregate demand relying on the "troika of economic growth." Boosting economic growth by expanding aggregate demand belongs to demand-side aggregate management regarding macroeconomic adjustment, which mainly facilitates short-term counter-cyclical adjustments by macro-adjustment. Production factors that directly contribute to economic growth, such as labor, capital, land, technology, management, and enterprises and industries as an aggregate of various production factors, constitute the social total production or supply side. They fall within the ambit of supply-side management in terms of macro-adjustment. The formation of enterprise and industrial competitiveness, even national competitiveness, takes a long time without an immediate effect in the short run. Therefore, these elements belong to medium- and long-term management. Simultaneously, since adjusting enterprise and industrial structures is also a medium- to long-term process, it can be called supply-side structural management. In the new normal of economy, such structural management would not be possible in isolation from enterprise, the fiscal and monetary system, and other reforms. Therefore, while moderately expanding aggregate demand, it's necessary to reinforce efforts through innovating and improving macro-adjustment in the following fields. First is strengthening the supply-side structural reform and improving the quality and efficiency of the supply system, then enhancing the impetus for sustained economic growth, and finally pushing the production level in Chinese society to realize an overall leap. Specific measures are (i) to deepen enterprise reform and enhance enterprise vitality; (ii) to reduce the burden on enterprises so that enterprises can develop with their burdens discarded; (iii) to reduce the cost of enterprise financing and enhance the financial support for the real economy; (iv) to simplify government and decentralization and help entrepreneurship and innovation. At the same time, it should eliminate excess backward capacity and accelerate the pace of transformation and upgrading of industrial structure.

11.4.1.3 Insisting on Domestic and Foreign Integration

In order to achieve the goal of an essential balance between total social supply and demand, macroeconomic adjustment under open economic conditions must consider not only domestic factors but also international trade and capital flows. International trade has to consider the factors of goods (and services) and the changes in prices of international commodities, especially bulk commodities. Cross-border capital flows must also consider the impact of exchange rate changes on local and foreign currencies. Against China's profound economic integration into the world economy, it's necessary to enrich the connotation of opening up and macro-adjustment, open wider to the outside world, and realize the essential balance of total social supply and demand under open conditions.

11.4.1.4 Insisting on the Coordination of Reform and Development

The stable, coordinated, and sustainable development of the national economy is the prerequisite and foundation for comprehensively deepening reform, and the latter is the driving force and guarantee for the former. Innovating and improving macro-adjustment methods must be combined with deepening economic system reform. For this purpose, it should (i) deepen the fiscal and taxation system reform, which will be done by establishing a sound and modern financial system, setting up a normative debt financing system for local governments, and reducing taxes and fees to provide incentives for enterprise development; (ii) accelerate the reform of the financial system, which will be done by improving the efficiency of financial services for the real economy and solving the problems of complicated and expensive financing for SMEs; (iii) deepen the enterprise reform, which will be done by enhancing the vitality, control, influence, and risk-resistance of the state-owned economy, accelerating the development of the non-public economy, and effectively resolving overcapacity; and (iv) speed up transforming government functions, which will be done by simplifying and decentralizing government, enhancing government transparency, and creating a legalized, internationalized and convenient business environment thereby providing good services for enterprise and market improvement.

11.4.2 Effectively Combining Macro-Adjustment Instruments

National economy is a complex system with interconnected, mutually constrained, and constantly changing components. Because of the different stages of economic development, the tasks needed to be accomplished at each stage are different, and different macro-adjustment instruments have different effects. Therefore, it is necessary to combine the instruments effectively in specific macro-adjustments to realize the adjustment goals.

To effectively combine macro-adjustment instruments, the following aspects need to be grasped: (i) The policy instruments available and the strength of their effects should be decided by the characteristics and changing trends of the macroeconomic environment. (ii) When integrating macroeconomic policies, it is necessary to consider that the chosen economic adjustment policy mix must ensure to realization the system of adjustment objectives. (iii) The combination of economic adjustment policies chosen for a given period should be relatively stable. To comprehensively apply economic adjustment policies, attention must be paid to the time lag in the effects of different policies. (iv) The integrated use of economic adjustment policies, like other management activities, requires considering the costs and benefits of the policies in order to maximize the benefits at a fixed cost or minimize the costs at a fixed effect.

11.4.2.1 Matching Fiscal and Monetary Policies in a Loose-Tight Mix

Since the global financial crisis, China has continuously paired proactive fiscal and prudent monetary policies to make timely and appropriate pre- and fine-turning, thus stabilizing development expectations. Regarding proactive fiscal policy, policy measures such as expanding government expenditures, liquidizing surplus budgetary funds, structural tax cuts, and general fee reductions have expanded aggregate demand, eased the burden on enterprises, and better protected expenditures in key areas. Regarding prudent monetary policy, corporate interest rates have been guided downward through repeated reducing reserve requirements and interest rates, as well as the adoption of OMOs such as reverse repurchase, thereby easing the tight liquidity situation in the market and driving up credit demand and investment, which has strongly supported the development of the real economy.

Generally, the joint mechanism of fiscal and monetary policies contains the main elements in the commodity market, such as consumption, investment, output, and price level, reflecting the economy's objective requirements of macro-adjustment under the conditions of a market economy through the role of the market mechanism. The two policies have advantages in macro-adjustment. Fiscal policy has advantages in adjusting the economic structure and developing the economy, but it has an enormous impact based on its administrative nature. However, monetary policy's advantage is more direct in adjusting the total social demand and more prominent in the price level adjustment. However, its effect is less pronounced than fiscal policy regarding structural adjustment and social equity. Concurrently, there are disparities between fiscal and monetary policies regarding adjustment transparency and lag. Fiscal policy has a longer formulating and executing lag and a shorter functioning lag. Conversely, monetary policy has a shorter formulating and executing lag and a longer functioning lag. Implementing fiscal policy affects national income mainly through disposable income, consumer and investment spending. In contrast, implementing monetary policy affects national income through investment changes due to changes in interest rates and price levels. The weak elasticity of interest rates concerning investment and the endogeneity of the price level determine that monetary policy has a weaker and more indirect effect on national income than fiscal policy. Monetary policy directly affects the price level through changing the intermediary variable of money supply. In contrast, fiscal policy affects the price level only through the combined effect of social purchasing power and national income. The endogeneity of national income determines that the effect of fiscal policy on the price level is indirect and lagged.

When implementing an expansionary fiscal policy, an increase in government demand will lead to an increase in total output through the multiplier effect of fiscal policy. In turn, it leads to an increase in the monetary demand. In the absence of any change in the money supply by the central bank, interest rates are bound to rise. In this way, on the one hand, it will offset the increase in the demand for money due to the increase in gross output and, while on the other hand, reduce the investment demand, thus offsetting part of the stimulus to the gross output caused by government purchasing expenditures or tax cuts. If the investment demand is susceptible to interest rates, a rise in interest rates will reduce investment substantially. Conversely, if interest rates do not rise much, or if expansionary fiscal policy has little effect on the interest rate level, the impact of such policy on investment will be small. In this case, expansionary fiscal policy strongly influences aggregate demand. Expansionary monetary policy increases the money supply, whereas contractionary monetary policy decreases it. Suppose expansionary monetary policy decreases interest rates significantly and has a large stimulus effect on investment while increasing the money supply. In that case, it has a significant impact on aggregate demand. If the investment demand is more sensitive to interest rates, a fall in interest rates will lead to a significant increase in investment. If the demand for money is less sensitive to interest rates, an increase in the money supply will lead to a significant fall in interest rates. In both cases, the monetary policy considerably impacts aggregate demand.

Theoretically, the government budget is the difference between government expenditures and tax revenues. If government expenditures exceed tax revenues, the government has a budget deficit. However, if tax revenues exceed government expenditures, the government has a budget surplus. When a government runs a budget deficit, there are generally two ways to keep the balance, either by issuing government bonds or by increasing the money supply, i.e., the government may borrow to generate debt revenue, or it may deal with the deficit by imposing an inflation tax through increasing banknote issuance. Without the cooperation of monetary policy, the fiscal expansion policy can only be maintained by borrowing. If monetary policy is used alone without the cooperation of fiscal policy, the increase in the money supply is precisely equal to the decrease in the number of government bonds in the hands of the public. It can be seen that fiscal and monetary policies are not independent but are objectively required to complement each other.

Practically, fiscal and monetary policies are the central economic policies that governments can adopt in the macroeconomic sphere in a market economy. The commonality of fiscal and monetary policies determines that close coordination between them is an objective requirement. The difference between fiscal and monetary policies, in turn, leads to the possibility of deviations between them in the implementation process. National macroeconomic policies must be coordinated and complemented by fiscal and monetary policies to have the desired effect. Since the various economic policies serve a unified adjustment objective with different mechanisms, only if the various macroeconomic policies achieve scientific coordination and cooperation in terms of the nature and direction of adjustment, can it avoid the choice of policy instruments, the intensity of adjustment, and the timing of the launching of the policies. Only in this way can the time lag between policies be minimized, and the overall economic objective be effectively achieved.

There are four specific cooperation modes between fiscal and monetary policy: (i) double-tightening, i.e., the contractionary fiscal policy in conjunction with contractionary monetary policy; (ii) double-loosening, i.e., the relaxing fiscal policy in conjunction with relaxing monetary policy; (iii) tight fiscal but loose credit, i.e., the contractionary fiscal policy in conjunction with relaxing monetary policy; and (iv) loose fiscal but tight credit, i.e., the relaxing fiscal policy in conjunction with contractionary monetary policy.

These matching models produce different policy effects because of the different directions in which the policies work. A double-loosening or double-tightening policy is characterized by the fact that the instrumental variables of fiscal and monetary policy are adjusted in the same direction. The intermediary variables act on national income and the price level according to the mechanisms common to both policy types. As a result, this type of policy mix has strong effects and low inter-variable friction. Once implemented, it can produce effects quickly with high inertia. The one-loose and one-tight policy mix is characterized by adjusting the instrumental variables of fiscal and monetary policy in opposite directions, thus generating friction between the variables against each other. Since the direction of changing such common variables as investment spending is unclear, the two types of policies under these two cooperation modes tend to have effects only on the variables they can directly affect, with high functionality loss during implementation and weaker acting force. However, the policy effect is more stable without much inertia.

It follows that using policy mixes needs to be judged based on a country's specific economic situation and the strength of its policies. Theoretically, the intensity of policy effects is the basis for judging the choice of different policy-matching programs. In macroeconomic adjustment, the policy coordination should be based on the country's economic realities and scientific decision-making based on scientific evidence. In this way, the chosen policy coordination can produce optimal adjustment effects.

11.4.2.2 Coordination Between Industrial, Regional, Investment, Consumption, and Price Policies

(1) *The coordinating effect of the three major driving forces and innovation-driven*

Under the new economic normal, not only will there be a change in the adjustment objectives, but the macro-adjustment methods should also change accordingly. Macroeconomic analysis usually emphasizes that economic growth should be pulled from the demand side, relying on consumer, investment, and net export demands to solve the problem of insufficient aggregate demand. The synergistic effect of the three major driving forces does not mean that the three demands should contribute equally, but rather, they should coordinately contribute to the needs of healthy macroeconomic development and that the degree of their contribution should differ at different development stages.

For a long time, China's economic growth has been mainly driven by investment and net exports with weak pulling power of consumption. After over 30 years of high-speed growth of nearly 10%, it became the world's second-largest economy in 2010. In 2014, it joined the 10 Trillion Dollars Club with total GDP accounting for 13.3% of the world's economic share. Its annual incremental growth is equivalent to the economic aggregate of a medium-developed country, thus creating a Chinese miracle of economic development. However, at this new historical starting point, the international and domestic conditions faced by China's economic development have undergone fundamental changes, highlighted by changes in the pulling power of the three major demands in the macroeconomy.

As the development space for economic growth driven by the three major driving forces has been significantly reduced, the new growth model emphasizes that the long-term impetus for economic growth lies on the supply side, i.e., the enhancement of labor, capital, and production efficiency, with innovation as its most important source. Therefore, innovation is the first driving force to lead development, so it is necessary to focus the development on innovation, form an institutional structure to promote innovation and shape a leading development relying more on innovation-driven and first-mover advantages. Under this premise, it should further utilize the fundamental role of consumption in growth, the critical role of investment in growth, and the role of exports in promoting economic growth. In other words, it is necessary to unleash new demand and create new supply, promote the flourishing of new technologies, industries, and business forms, and accelerate the transformation of development momentum.

(2) *A new mix of macro-adjustment in the new normal*

Firstly, it should be committed to both ends: demand-side management and supply-side structural reform.

In the past, the main focus was expanding government investment and increasing liquidity to maintain growth, typical of demand-side management. Under the new normal, the role of the three major driving forces of economic growth should also be emphasized to tap constantly the potential of the three major demands, namely investment, consumer, and net export demands. However, simultaneously, it should emphasize more on the supply side and the demand side to expand demand by innovating supply, then force the upgrading of supply by expanding the effectual demand, and ultimately achieve mutual support and co-progress of stable growth and structural adjustments. In contrast, the four key points of structural reform are resolving overcapacity, digesting real estate inventories, lowering enterprise costs, and developing the capital market. The first two points are related to increasing aggregate supply. From demand-side management to supply-side structural reform, China's economic macro-adjustment changes are outlined.

Secondly, it should combine aggregate and structural adjustment. Its fundamental way is to accelerate transforming economic development mode, with the key to deepening the industrial structure's strategic adjustment. It emphasizes improving a policy system relying mainly on fiscal and monetary policy, coordinated with industrial, regional, investment, consumer, and price policies, aiming at enhancing fiscal and monetary policy coordination. In addition, the government supports industrial restructuring through tax and credit policies, guides enterprises to carry out the innovation-driven development strategy, transforms and upgrades traditional manufacturing industries, cultivates and develops strategic emerging industries, accelerates the development of the service industry. These efforts will result in building a new system concerning modern industrial development. Simultaneously, it stimulates residents' demand for consumption to drive the upgrading of the consumption structure by focusing on expanding service consumption.

Chapter 12
Micro-Regulation of the National Economy

The management of the national economy involves both macro-adjustment and micro-regulation. The aim is to realize the government's public policy objectives, ensure the healthy functioning of the national economy, protect the interests of producers and consumers, and safeguard social security. This chapter primarily focuses on analyzing economic and social micro-regulation and exploring strategies for promoting their efficiencies and thus contributing to social welfare through reforming their institutions and improving their systems.

12.1 Micro-Regulation and Its Categorization

12.1.1 Micro-Regulation and Macro-Adjustment

12.1.1.1 Connotation of Micro-Regulation

Micro-regulation is relative to macro-adjustment. Micro-regulation means that, in a market economy, government regulatory agencies restrict, supervise, and standardize the economic or social activities of specific industries, micro-economic behavioral agents, or social subjects by government regulatory agencies. Its aim is to achieve specific economic or social goals based on certain rules through judicial, legislative, administrative, or persuasive means. Micro-regulation is an indispensable institutional arrangement for a modern market economy.

The components of micro-regulation are as follows: (i) The subject of regulation, i.e., the regulator. It mainly refers to the public sector of society, especially the government, acquiring the right to regulate through legislation or other forms. (ii) The object to be regulated. They are mainly market economic players, including enterprises and social subjects, such as individuals and social organizations. (iii) The regulation methods and means. It mainly refers to the specific measures used by

M. Lin and T. Huang, *National Economics*,
https://doi.org/10.1007/978-981-96-9618-5_12

regulators to restrict, supervise, and regulate the behavior of microeconomic players based on specific rules or systems.

12.1.1.2 The Difference Between Micro-Regulation and Macro-Adjustment

There are four main differences: (i) The objectives. The general objectives of macro-adjustment are economic growth, full employment, price stability, and balance of payments. In contrast, those of micro-regulation are economic goals such as efficient resource allocation, fair competition, protection of consumers from monopolistic high prices, improvement of internal efficiency of enterprises, stabilization of enterprise finances, and social goals such as limitation of negative externality activities, protection of rights and interests of the information-disadvantaged party, and enhancement of social security and health. (ii) The objects. The main object of macro-adjustment is generally the macroeconomic aggregates, which focuses on solving problems of macro-failure and under-utilization of resources. By contrast, the object of micro-regulation is the economic or social behaviors of specific industries, micro-economic behavioral agents, or social subjects, which focuses on solving problems of micro-failure and under-optimized resource allocation. (iii) The instruments. The instruments of macro-adjustment mainly include fiscal, monetary, industrial, and international economies. In contrast, micro-regulation instruments mainly include economic regulations such as price ceilings, asymmetric regulations, and incentive regulations, as well as social regulations such as prohibitions, restrictions, standards, and qualifications. (iv) Regulatory characteristics. Macro-adjustment policies are volatile, discretionary, and indirectly guiding. In contrast, micro-regulatory policies are relatively stable, rule-governed, and directly coercive.

12.1.2 Classification and Objectives of Regulation

12.1.2.1 Classification of Regulation

Regulation can be classified into different categories according to different attributes: first, according to whether the regulatory body (i.e., regulator) directly intervenes in the decision-making of economic agents, regulation can be classified into direct and indirect regulations. Direct regulation refers to government intervention directly implemented by the executive branch of government, i.e., directly restraining and regulating economic activities with solid characteristics of public goods and external diseconomies and those seriously affect social benefits. Indirect regulation refers to the regulation of specific behaviors that impede the efficacy of the market mechanism on the premise of safeguarding the free decision-making of market economic agents and indirectly restrains unfair competition and other behaviors. It is implemented mainly based on the anti-monopoly law, commercial law, civil law, and other laws or incentives and disincentives. Second, according to the different nature of regulation objects, regulation can be categorized into economic and social regulation. The following analysis focuses on them.

12.1.2.2 Implications of Regulation

Economic regulation refers to the fact that, in sectors or industries with natural monopoly or asymmetric economic information, the government regulatory agencies employ legal means to standardize and restrict the entry and exit of enterprises and prices, investment, quality, and other related behaviors of products or services. This is done through using licensing and accreditation to prevent inefficiency in the resources allocation and ensure citizens' right of use. The main areas of economic regulation include natural monopolies or industries with asymmetrical economic information, such as public utilities, communications, network transportation, finance, and insurance, while its main methods concern price, entry, exit, investment, quality, and other regulations.

Social regulation is a public one that sets specific standards for the quality of products and services, such as science, education, culture, health, and production activities. It prohibits and restricts specific social behaviors, intending to safeguard workers' and consumers' safety, health, hygiene, environmental protection, and disasters prevention. It focuses on the social effects of government intervention in the market, primarily concerning the hazards and risks that economic and social activities pose to nature and society, thus causing damage to workers' and consumers' safety, health, and hygiene. These concerns have led to the manifestation of social regulation as a major intervention in the following aspects: the way people use nature, the production methods of enterprises, the quality of the production environment, products in science, education, culture, and health, and foodstuffs, the specific behaviors of citizens, and the contracting methods of various transactions by market players (both producers and consumers). These attempts are taken to avoid the unsafe and unhealthy hazards and risks to society that may result from natural, social production, and contracting processes and particular behaviors.

12.1.2.3 Objectives of Economic Regulation

The objectives of economic regulation are fourfold.

The first is efficiently allocating resources. It means that the optimal combination of input factors produces the "optimal" product quantities to minimize costs and maximize returns. In the case of monopoly and monopoly profits, the monopolist can prevent competitors from entering through predatory pricing, cross-subsidization, and other methods. In this case, other resources cannot enter the industry to provide production or services. As a result, the resources cannot be allocated effectively. In areas where there are positive externalities, such as scientific research and development, if measures for economic regulation, such as patent protection, are inadequate, enterprises will not invest in scientific research, thus failing to achieve the purpose of encouraging enterprises to invest economic resources in scientific research and development.

The second is improving the efficiency of social distribution. For the monopoly sector, without effective economic regulation, monopolies will abuse their market power to obtain monopoly profits through monopoly pricing, price discrimination, internal cross-subsidization, and differentiated services to customers. Converting consumer surplus into corporate profits increases the unfairness of social distribution and widening the social income gap. It is necessary to avoid such income redistribution through economic regulation, thus improving the efficiency of social distribution.

The third is improving enterprise internal efficiency. Enterprise internal efficiency generally includes (i) technical efficiency, i.e., efficiency resulting from the optimal combination of input factors of labor, financial, and material resources under the existing technical conditions; (ii) organizational efficiency, i.e., production efficiency produced by organizing production at the optimal production scale; (iii) distribution efficiency, i.e., distribution efficiency from the optimal distribution systems; and (iv) equipment utilization efficiency, i.e., the efficiency of equipment utilization brought about by the highest possible equipment utilization (load rate). Most enterprises subject to economic regulation are those with monopolistic market structures. However, due to their monopolistic characteristics and positions, such enterprises have less external pressure to compete and less incentive to improve their internal efficiency. It is necessary to induce enterprises to improve their internal efficiency through government regulation to increase market competitiveness or incentive regulation.

The fourth is maintaining the potential for enterprises' development. With the development of the national economy, the demand for monopolized industries (e.g., telecommunications) tends to grow at an accelerated rate, requiring the enterprises to operate in these industries to make large-scale investments continuously to increase the market's supply capacity. Therefore, the purpose of regulation is not only to protect the consumers' interests from being infringed upon, but also to maintain the financial stability of enterprises. In this way, they can achieve a balance between income and expenditure, raise a certain amount of internal and external funds to ensure the cost of capital and make the necessary and appropriate investments, thus enabling the enterprises to achieve sustainable development and ensuring continuous supply. Of course, this potential for enterprise development can also be achieved by regulating low prices, but enterprise losses can be covered through government financial subsidies to achieve financial stability.

12.1.2.4 Objectives of Social Regulation

As can be seen from the connotation of social regulation, its significance is to avoid various hazards caused by externalities, internalities, and information asymmetries, such as health and safety problems caused by environmental pollution, natural disasters, and various accidents, the damage to safety and health caused by the quality of food, drugs, and health services, and the economic risks and crises caused by false financial information. The ultimate goal of social regulation is to ensure people's safety and health and improve their quality of life and living standards, including mainly.

The first is to limit negative externality activities and guarantee the sustainable development of human society. In real society, it is mainly the negative impact of people's activities on the natural environment that generates vital global issues, threatening the sustainable development of human society without paying the corresponding price, such as pollution of the natural environment and depletion of natural resources. Since the 1980s, people have become increasingly concerned about environmental and resource problems caused by their destructive behaviors. They have put forward the concept of sustainable development, focusing on the sustainable development of humankind and the natural world. However, protecting the natural environment and realizing sustainable development cannot be solved solely by the market's competitive mechanism or individual behavior. Instead, they must be realized by the government's public regulation, i.e., protecting the environment through legislation, overseeing law enforcement, and raising the people's conscientiousness regarding sustainable development.

The second is to protect the rights and interests of the information-disadvantaged party and improve social security and health. People at both ends of a transaction in economic activities have asymmetric information about the transaction. The information-advantaged party may violate the legitimate rights and interests of the information-disadvantaged party who are out of moral hazard for profit-taking, even posing a threat to them, thereby leading to security and health risks. Therefore, countries across the globe have taken the protection of information-disadvantaged parties' rights and interests as an essential goal of regulation in the process of social control. They have enacted legislation to stipulate the degree of excellent financial assets and advertisements, the quality of food, drugs, and health services, the occupational standards of employees, and the safety standards of workplaces, and the like. The aim is to improve the state of information asymmetric of both transaction parties to ensure the consumers' and producers' safety and health.

The third is to incentivize positive externality activities and exert positive externality effects. There are many positive externalities in social sectors such as science, education, culture, health, and other social undertakings sectors. For example, sectors such as primary education, basic research, scientific and technological innovation, and immunization are usually organized by the government or through social regulation to enhance such positive externalities, because the individual benefits are less than individual costs in the private sector. In contrast, the social benefits outweigh its social costs.

The fourth is to reduce transaction costs and improve the quality of market transactions. According to the Coase Theorem, in market transactions in the modern market, as long as the property rights are clearly defined, the market mechanism will enable both parties to complete the transaction. However, sometimes, the transaction cannot be completed due to the high transaction costs. Transaction costs are various expenses used in transaction activities such as collecting, organizing, and transmitting information, observing and monitoring competitors, inspecting and selecting cooperative partners, advertising, publicity, negotiating and concluding contracts, registering, legal proceedings, and loss of decision-making errors, and the like. Such costs can be summarized into three major categories: information and communication costs, time costs of opportunity, and contracting risk costs. In order to reduce and economize on these transaction costs and lower the risks of market transactions, the government should unify and standardize transaction methods and regulate the contracting process to protect reasonable competition and improve the quality of social transactions by saving transaction costs.

12.2 Economic Regulation

12.2.1 Necessities for Economic Regulation

The movement of NES is based on microeconomy, which needs to be micro-economically regulated to ensure the smooth operation of NES. Specifically, the Necessity of micro-regulation is mainly reflected in the following.

First, it can reduce natural monopolies and monopoly pricing. A natural monopoly usually refers to the ability of a single firm to supply a market at a lower cost than two or more firms when faced with a market demand of a specific size. Typical natural monopoly industries include telecommunications, electric power, railroad transportation, water, and piped gas. The common characteristic of these industries is that it is more efficient for a single firm to provide a particular product or service. Therefore, strictly controlling the number of entering enterprises with entry regulations can reduce duplication construction, avoid unnecessary resource waste, and improve resource allocation efficiency. However, once a monopoly is in a monopoly position and thus possesses a certain degree of market power, it may impose monopoly pricing to make a portion of the consumer surplus become corporate profits and distribute income unfairly. It may also jeopardize efficient resource allocation due to the lack of competitive pressure. Therefore, it is necessary to prevent enterprises from abusing their dominant market position through entry and price regulation to allocate resources efficiently.

Second, it can foster market competition. As the market itself cannot guarantee the free and fair competition, coupled with the existence of natural monopoly and incomplete information, a small number of enterprises have been able to control production and markets by their substantial economic strength, nor can they set monopoly prices using monopoly agreements to restrict competitive behavior within certain market areas. Inadequate market competition will disrupt the survival rules of the fittest, jeopardize the market order of fair competition, and harm consumers' legitimate rights and interests. Moreover, it will undermine the market operation mechanism of optimal resource allocation and ultimately inhibit the dynamic of economic growth. Economic regulation can prevent unfair market competition and ensure an efficient market competition through enacting anti-monopoly and anti-unfair competition laws and intervention in enterprises' investment and pricing activities by civil law. In addition, effective competition can be achieved by relaxing market access and carrying out market-oriented reforms for some competitive businesses in natural monopoly industries.

Third, it can incentivize the internal efficiency of enterprises. In order to address the problem of natural monopoly-type market structures that are not conducive to technological progress and cost reductions for firms, the government can use incentive regulation to ensure that firms' internal efficiency is improved, thus increasing labor productivity and promoting technological progress.

Fourth, it can reduce economic information asymmetry. In finance, insurance, and other sectors, there is generally a more severe economic information asymmetry phenomenon, mainly reflected in the different statuses and abilities in risk identification and avoidance between the financial institutions and the demanders of financial products. Government regulation can more effectively solve the problem of information asymmetry and avoid greater fluctuation in financial operations.

Fifth, it can guarantee universal services. It refers mainly to the state's efforts to safeguard the interests of all citizens by providing access to a service meeting fundamental life needs and development at a generally acceptable price. Universal service mainly involves monopolistic public welfare industries, such as postal services, telecommunications, electricity, and water supply. It concerns universality of service, equality of access, and affordability of users. Since the cost of providing universal services is often high, and the price of services is often subject to government regulation, businesses are less active in providing them. Government regulation is therefore necessary to ensure universal service in specific industries.

12.2.2 Main Elements of Economic Regulation

Economic regulation focuses on the economic effects of government intervention in the market process. It is concerned with the undesirable conditions in the production and market processes, i.e., the formation process of unreasonable market prices, the unreasonable production process of market agents, and the unreasonable distribution process of factor rewards of economic agents. Main elements of economic regulation include.

The first is price regulation. In order to prevent enterprises with market power from setting monopoly prices at the expense of total social welfare, the regulator, based on specific methods, mainly regulations of rate of return on investment (ROI) and price cap, establishes or restricts the prices of products or services in a particular industry or a particular field of business for a certain period, and specifies the periodicity of price adjustments.

The second is entry and exit regulation. In order to maintain scale economies and cost subadditivity in an industry and a rational market structure, regulators need to restrict entering new firms into a particular industry. At the same time, it is also necessary to limit the arbitrary exit of firms from an industry to ensure supply stability. This regulation can be achieved through licensing, vetting-and-approving regimes, or high entry standards.

The third is investment regulation. It mainly refers to the regulator's need to encourage firms to invest in order to not only meet the growing demand for products or services, but also to prevent excessive competition and overlapping investment among firms, as well as to regulate the optimal mix of investment goods in order to ensure the efficiency and effectiveness of investment. It should be noted that there is some crossover between investment regulation and entry and exit regulation in terms of content.

The fourth is quality regulation. It refers mainly to the limitation and restriction of products' or services' quality produced or provided by firms by the regulator through. For example, the setting of quality standards. Quality regulation has developed rapidly after the 1970s. Each country has established its quality regulation system and institutions. However, it is difficult to synthesize these quality elements in regulatory practice, because the quality of many products or services is comprehensive. It is not easy to simply define and intuitively identify. Therefore, in some regulated industries, quality control is often not applied separately but is linked to price regulation, i.e., quality control is included in price regulation. Suppose the regulated firms fail to meet quality standards or have too many consumer complaints about their quality. In that case, the regulator must regulate by lowering the regulated price level or imposing compensatory fines.

Among the four aspects of regulation mentioned above, price and entry regulations are the most fundamental. Since the regulated industries' technical and economic features vary considerably, the same regulatory content varies considerably from industry to industry.

12.2.3 *Main Methods of Economic Regulation*

12.2.3.1 Price Regulation

The first is price level regulation. For natural monopoly industries, if enterprises are allowed to set their prices, profit-maximizing enterprises will set a high monopoly price as per the profit-maximizing principle that marginal benefit equals marginal cost. In order to prevent natural monopolies from utilizing their natural monopoly status to set high monopoly prices, distorting resource allocation and thereby reducing efficiency, it is necessary to impose price regulation on natural monopolies.

A typical method of price level regulation is the ROI regulation. It is a price set by adding a reasonable or "fair" normal profit to cost, which is done as follows. The regulated enterprise first submits to the regulator an application for an increase in price (or ROI). Then the regulatory agencies, after a period of examination, make the necessary adjustments to the price (or ROI) level proposed by the enterprise in the light of changes in factors affecting the price. Finally, it determines the enterprise's return rate on investment, which serves as the basis for pricing by the enterprise in a given period.

Another typical method is price cap regulation. It is an alternative to traditional ROI regulation and is now the most influential incentive-based regulation in national practice. Price cap regulation is analogous to a price change contract between the regulatory agency and the regulated firm. A price cap is imposed so that prices can, in principle, only change under the cap.

Obviously, ROI regulation is quite different from price cap regulation, manifested in terms of the different regulation objects, the cost-effective incentives, the impact on the quality of regulated firms' products, and the time intervals for regulation. However, there are also similarities between the two approaches to price level regulation. First, both aim to prevent the regulated firms from adopting behaviors such as limiting production, raising prices, reducing consumer surplus, and cutting social welfare. Second, both have no substantive differences regarding the factors considered in the price regulation formulation process.

The second is price structure regulation. Large natural monopolies generally deal with different demand groups, even if they produce only one product or provide one single service. These groups form a specific demand structure due to different time, space, consumption, and quality of the products they demand. According to the demand structure, enterprises charge different prices for different needs, and these different price levels constitute the price structure. Differential pricing by firms targeting different groups of consumers captures the lion's share of consumer surplus, thereby severely distorting efficiency of allocation. Therefore, it's necessary to regulate such price structures of natural monopolies. The objective and task of price structure regulation are to formulate a regulated price structure compatible with the demand structure by taking fully into account the impact of the demand structure on the regulated price and accordingly supervise the enterprises to rationally apportion the common costs into products or services to be borne by different users.

If the regulated enterprise produces a range of products rather than a single product, many of the costs incurred in producing the product are common costs. For example, the operating costs of production equipment and pipeline networks in the water industry are of a common cost. For a monopoly producing a series of products, different consumers demand different commodities, whose elasticity of demand varies. In order to obtain more profits, monopolies tend to set prices for products at a high level for consumer goods with low demand elasticity and a low level for consumer goods with high elasticity of demand. This results in irrationality in consumers' sharing of the costs of the enterprise, and thus also deserving of regulation of the price structure.

Ramsey pricing is the method that optimally deviates from marginal cost for firms producing multiple products. It is primarily welfare maximizing under the precondition of break-even, i.e., the price derived when producer and consumer surplus are maximized under the break-even condition of sales revenue equal to total cost and zero profit.

Price structure regulation is selective for several reasons.

First, it aims to increase social welfare. In general, differential pricing in monopolized industries increases total social welfare, i.e., the sum of producer and consumer surplus. However, it is often at the cost of inequitable distribution. Differential pricing in the first and second tiers leads to fully or partially appropriate consumer surplus by producers. However, in the third tier of differential pricing, the increase in the welfare of producers and consumers with high demand elasticity is, in turn, at the expense of the welfare of consumers with low demand elasticity. In this way, the government's regulation of a natural monopoly industry has to make a trade-off between efficiency and equity.

Second, some differential pricing practices in natural monopoly industries are also justified. In the running water industry, for example, scale economies at both the production and transportation stages make it appropriate to set lower price levels for commercial-type users with high usage volumes. In the electricity industry, the price of electricity during peak hours should be increased because the marginal cost of generating electricity during peak hours is much higher than during off-peak periods. Most natural monopolies have enormous fixed costs, for example, the costs of constructing and operating the communication network in the telecommunications industry, the power plants and transmission lines in the electricity industry, and the pipeline networks in the gas and running water industries, all of them are of a common cost, as they can provide products or services for different types of users. Since the needs of different types of users differ, the different costs arise from different needs, so differential pricing by firms is reasonable if it reflects these different costs.

Third, the additional profits monopolies gain through differential pricing can also be used to increase social welfare. Innovation will be encouraged if this increased profit compensates for the costs incurred for new product research and development and productive processes. Similarly, this increased profit will encourage product diversity by compensating for the cost of creating brands. Also, increased profits caused by price differentials will encourage entry and competition by compensating for production's fixed and entry costs.

12.2.3.2 Entry Regulation

Entry regulation means that in monopolized industries, the government allows one or a very few firms to enter the industry or that the government restricts the entry of new firms into the industry from the standpoint of preventing over-competition to strike a balance of supply and demand in the industry as a whole; or that in industries where there is asymmetry of information, the government imposes a restriction on the entry of new firms, including practitioners. The main entry regulation methods include entry licensing, registration, declaration, and asymmetric regulation.

The conventional wisdom argues that a natural monopoly features economies of scale, economies of scope, and network economies, so it is most efficient for a single firm to provide the products or services. In order to ensure that other firms do not enter the industry, the regulatory authority must adopt artificial means to restrict the entry of other firms. However, practice proves that although natural monopolies have significant economies of scale, monopolization by one or a few firms can stifle lively competition. Therefore, a dilemma exists between economies of scale and lively competition in regulating the entry of natural monopolies. The policy framework to resolve this dilemma is to use effective competition, compatible with economies of scale and lively competition, as the main economic basis for the government to formulate entry regulation policies for natural monopolies.

Contestable markets theory argues that within contestable markets, it is not true, as traditional competition theory suggests, that the market mechanism cannot play a competitive role in a market with few vendors. A contestable market is one in which competitive pressures from potential entrants place significant constraints on the behavior of market suppliers. A market is perfectly contestable if there are enough vendors in the market that actual competition is sufficient to ensure market efficiency. If a market is competitive, there must be no enormous obstacles to entry and exit so that potential competition from potential entrants adopting the so-called hit-and-run strategy can play the same role as actual competition. Eventually, it ensures market efficiency by placing forceful constraints on the behavior of the existing players in the market. Therefore, as long as the government relaxes entry regulations, the potential threat of new firms entering the market will naturally force the existing monopolies in the industry to improve their efficiency. Even if there is only one firm, a contestable market will still be able to achieve high economic efficiency.

However, the contestability of a market is based on the following conditions: (i) Free entry and exit. The main sign is that the sunk cost is zero. Potential entrants have no disadvantages relative to incumbents regarding production technology, product quality, and costs. However, in practice, freedom to exit is more important than freedom to enter. Restrictions on exit will discourage entry, thus reducing the competitive threat from potential entrants. (ii) Potential entrants adopting a "hit-and-run" strategy. They evaluate the profitability of entering the market mainly based on the price level of existing firms. Even a short-lived profit opportunity will attract them to enter the market to compete. When the price drops to the point where no profit to be made, they can leave the market with the profit they have already gained, i.e., they can enter and exit the market quickly. More importantly, there is no sunk cost in withdrawing from the market, and thus no obstacle to exiting the market. (iii) Potential entrants with an unrestricted access to the same production technology serving the same market. That is, potential entrants do not have a technological disadvantage and do not have to incur additional entry costs.

Contestable markets theory provides an analytical tool for exploring industrial organization and government regulation issues and has dramatically impacted practice. Governments must consider the following principles and methods in implementing entry regulation policies when implementing entry and deregulation.

The first is making entry and exit from the market as easy as possible. In order to promote the contestability of markets, it is vital to remove laws that prevent potential entrants from entering the market and make potential competition work as much as possible, thereby effectively disciplining the behavior of incumbent firms. Therefore, entry procedures should be transparent, normative, and written, and the entry process should be as short as possible when profit opportunities exist.

The second is utilizing relevant regulatory policies to eliminate the adverse effects of sunk costs. It aims to ensure equal access to sunk equipment at a reasonable price across firms or separate the larger portion of an industry's sunk capital from the contestable portion by imposing regulations on most sunk capital and granting greater entry and pricing freedom to the contestable portion. Simultaneously, it is also possible to reduce the side effect of sunk costs on contestability through institutional innovations that make transferring and selling assets less complicated.

The third is asymmetrically regulating the pre-existing and new firms. It refers mainly to the fact that, in adjusting government entry regulations, as new firms enter a pre-existing natural monopoly sector, the regulatory authority applies differentiated norms and constraints between incumbent firms and new firms designed to support the new entrants. It is because, even if entry is entirely free, the position of potential entrants and incumbents is de facto unequal due to a sort of "first mover advantage" of the incumbent. This inequality would severely undermine the role of potential competition. Thereby, it should be offset by asymmetric regulation of incumbents and entrants. In particular, the incumbent's price response to entry should be dampened while maintaining a degree of "uncertainty" about entry.

The fourth is maintaining the coordination of pricing and entry policies. Under regulatory practices and deregulation, competitiveness can be promoted simply by making entry easier by removing various complex entry restrictions. However, entry policies must be coordinated with other policies, especially price regulation, to improve market efficiency.

12.2.3.3 Incentive Regulation

Given the traditional regulatory system's shortcomings, incentive regulation incentivizes regulated firms to improve their internal efficiency while maintaining the original regulatory framework. The main methods include price cap, licensed bidding competition, interregional comparative competition, and direct competition.

The reason for an inefficient traditional regulatory approaches is that they do not consider the information asymmetry in regulation. For example, while regulating ROI, it is challenging for the regulator to understand the cost information of enterprises and the demand information of the market. Therefore, the price regulation policy can easily make the regulator be bought off. As a result, price regulation serves the producers and is reduced to a means for corporations to chase profits.

Since the 1970s, cutting-edge theories and analytical methods of microeconomics, such as principal-agent theory, game theory, and information economics, have been widely applied to the study of regulatory economics, a new theory of regulation, with incentive regulation as its main content, has emerged. Incentive regulation incorporates the regulation problem into the principal-agent analytical framework and studies how the regulator can design the regulation contract to incentivize the enterprise, aiming to reduce cost and improve social welfare under the information asymmetry between the regulator and the regulated enterprise.

Take the example of the railroads regulation. Their average cost depends on exogenous variables (the adverse selection parameter) and endogenous variables (the moral hazard parameter). The exogenous variables can be understood as the technology that determines the cost. Firms have this information, but the regulator does not, so firms aiming at profit maximization will try to hide their real costs from the regulator. The endogenous variables are the level of firm's effort, which is not observable by the regulator and cannot be written into the regulatory contract. As a result, firms have more freedom to decide on the level of effort, but it may bring about inefficiencies. Incentive regulation is the design of mechanisms to maximize efficiency in the presence of adverse selection and moral hazard.

There are two mechanisms for addressing information asymmetries between regulators and regulated firms: signal transmission and information screening. In the relationship between the regulator and the regulated firms, a frequently used mechanism is information screening. It mainly involves the regulator's use of different contracts to screen proactively for different types of firms, i.e., the regulator offers several contracts (a menu of contracts) for different firms, and different types of firms will choose different contracts. For example, the government offers price-cap and cost-of-service contracts if there are two types of firms: high-cost and low-cost. If the price-cap contract makes the low-cost firm's profit equal to zero or marginal, the inefficient and high-cost firm will not choose the price-cap contract because it will mostly incur a loss in this case. In this regard, it will choose the cost-of-service contract. On the contrary, the efficient and low-cost firm will choose the price-cap contract because it can work hard to earn a profit greater than zero.

In the regulation problem, the regulatory agency and the regulated firm, as agents, do not voluntarily pay a cost to impart the private information they hold. Assuming that the agent receives information rents for concealing information, the principal must compensate the agent accordingly if it wants the agent to impart the information it holds. That is, information rents must also be added to the agent's compensation as an agent, in order for the agent to voluntarily pay the cost of imparting the relevant information to the public and mass market consumers. Only after obtaining the information can the public make decisions on the implementation, reform, and removal of regulation and that the regulated firm's price can be equal to the marginal cost, thus improving the efficiency of resource allocation.

It is thus clear that the essence of incentive regulation is to give enterprises a certain degree of discretion to promote cost reduction, quality improvement, and service improvement and then to induce enterprises to maximize social welfare. Typical incentive regulation methods include price caps, price adjustments, and other methods based on performance indicators. If the introduction of competition is viewed as an extrinsic incentive, incentive regulation also includes franchise bidding, interregional comparative, and direct competition.

Different methods of incentive regulation have higher or lower incentive intensity. High-intensity incentives mean that the firm bears a higher proportion of the cost at the margin. If the firm's actual costs increase by RMB1, the government's total compensation is less than RMB1. However, at the margin, the firm's total monetary compensation barely varies with actual costs so that the firm's actual cost increases are borne only by itself, and vice versa. Profitable cost reductions by the firm is also primarily self-sustaining, thus incentivizing the enterprise to work hard to reduce costs and earn larger profits. Low-intensity incentives mean the firm bears a lower proportion of the cost or does not bear the increased cost at the margin. If the enterprise's actual costs increase by RMB1, the government's total compensation also increases by RMB1. The enterprise's profits are not affected by the cost and other factors, so the enterprise basically cannot get super normal profits (information rent). However, since this incentive does not reduce costs, its incentive strength is feeble.

Many factors affect the intensity of incentives, the main ones being: (i) Product quality. Since high-intensity incentives can lead firms choosing to reduce the quality of their services and products, some certain industries cannot tightly control the quality of their products or services and cannot set quality standards. In this regard, they are better off opting for low-incentive-intensity contracts to ensure the quality of their products. (ii) Regulatory commitments and renegotiation. Regulatory contracts, which are generally less than five years in duration, are subject to renegotiation upon expiration, and renegotiation triggers a ratchet effect, whereby firms that choose to reduce costs throughout a contract period are penalized for better performance by being faced with more onerous contract terms when the contract expires and is modified. In addition, early renegotiation reduces incentive strength. In one case, the firm is highly profitable, and the regulator is pressured to renegotiate early, exacerbating the ratchet effect. In another, renegotiation occurs when the firm loses money or will likely go out of business. In either case, early renegotiation is favorable to inefficiency, so early contract modification reduces the incentive regulation contract's incentive strength. (iii) Regulatory capture. The principal-agent relationship between the public and the regulator makes it possible for the regulator to be bought off by the firm to maximize its interests, high-incentive contracts are more likely to lead to regulatory capture. If the consequences of such capture are grave, the government should adopt regulatory contracts with low incentive intensity.

12.3 Social Regulation

12.3.1 Necessity

Social regulation is a relatively recent and fast-growing phenomenon compared to economic regulation. In the early twentieth century, economically developed countries began to regulate health, safety, and the environment, mainly in the food and pharmaceutical sectors. After the 1970s, social regulation began to expand by establishing social regulatory agencies in various fields. After the 1980s, social regulation developed rapidly. It was further strengthened while economic regulation continued to be relaxed, which resulted primarily from (i) a large number of environmental, health, and social security problems with the rapid development of the economy; (ii) people are increasingly concerned about the value and quality of their lives with the improving living standard. In this regard, more and more people want to regulate behaviors that jeopardize their health and hygiene. The necessity of social regulation is mainly manifested in the following.

12.3.1.1 Information Asymmetry

Due to the division of work and professions, the information collection costs, and technological limitations, the information possessed by different participants in market trading activities is asymmetric. The party with more relevant information is in the superior position, and the opposite, the inferior. For some consideration, the superior party may utilize its information advantage to cause harm to the inferior party. For example, the seller has more knowledge about the cost, quality, and other relevant product information than the buyer. Therefore, they may harm the consumers' rights and interests by concealing the information, setting a high price, and providing poor-quality counterfeit products. Furthermore, information asymmetry can give rise to undesirable consequences such as substandard markets, adverse selection, and moral hazard. Therefore, regulatory agencies need to set an important regulatory objective to protect the rights and interests of the information- disadvantaged party and stipulate by legislation the quality standards of products and services, the occupational standards of employees, the safety standards of workplaces, and other standards to ensure safety, hygiene, and health.

It is worth pointing out that, concerning the quality of products and services, social regulation is mainly aimed at regulating products or services that constitute direct damage to human health, safety, and hygiene or social security, such as food, drugs, education, science, culture, health, and the like. The quality of general products or services belongs to economic regulation, such as manufacturing raw materials, the end product quality, and productive services, including research, development, design, and after-sales service.

12.3.1.2 The Existence of Externalities

An externality is the failure of the normal price system to fully reflect the impact of one economic activist on the well-being of others. It generates non-market-mediated spillover effects from one party to another, essentially due to the absence of property rights and the existence of transaction costs. Specifically, positive externalities bring external benefits, and negative externalities bring external costs. With the continuous progress of production technology and rapid economic and social development, many economic behaviors often generate externalities, resulting in a distorted allocation of resources. For example, enterprises discharge wastewater and waste vapors from the production process into nature without treatment, causing environmental pollution and destruction, thus threatening human health, survival, and development. However, the polluter does not have to pay back the corresponding costs or be penalized accordingly. Therefore, there is a need for regulatory agencies to control them and restrain their negative externalities, thereby guaranteeing humanity's sustainable development. In addition, when an economic agent's activity generates a positive externality, but the costs it pays are not compensated accordingly, it will inevitably affect the motivation of that economic agent. Therefore, the regulatory agencies must include them in the social regulatory objectives to encourage them to continue engaging in activities that generate positive externalities.

12.3.1.3 Existence of Public Resources and Public Property Rights

Public resources are naturally occurring or existing resources, with ownership shared by all society members and providing natural conditions for human survival, development, and enjoyment. However, the existence of public property rights may result in the misuse of public resources. The tragedy of the commons is a case in point. It is precise because each individual's profit from overgrazing is far greater than the cost they bear, and even because they do not bear the cost of degradation of the pastureland, all people in the pastoral area suffer the catastrophic consequence of having no pasture to graze. Therefore, under the condition of public property rights, it is difficult for the market mechanism to maximize social returns, and individual or corporate behavior can easily bring negative externalities to the outside world. In this case, the government must regulate the use of public resources and limit the number of grazing animals through rational programming. In the case of community ownership of communal resources, ownership can be clarified to the individual when conditions permit. In addition, the government can also regulate the reasonable amount of publicly owned resources to be used through taxation to ensure the sustainable development of public resources.

12.3.1.4 Creation of Markets for Non-Value Goods

Competitive markets can achieve an efficient resource allocation for general goods. However, they can also produce undesired products such as drugs, the sex trade, and weapons of mass destruction. These goods, whose production and sale should be restricted or prohibited to a certain extent or entirely in compliance with moral and ethical norms, are called non-value goods. Government regulatory agencies must intervene in their activities by adopting specific policies based on the criteria of fairness and justice or by prohibiting them by law.

12.3.2 *Main Content*

Compared with economic regulation, an important feature of social regulation is its horizontal constraint function, i.e., social regulation does not take specific industries as the object of regulation, but instead, it centers around specific regulatory objectives and implements cross-industry and all-round regulation. It is very rich in content and covers the following four main areas.

12.3.2.1 Ensuring Health and Sanitation

It focuses on the strictest regulation of food, medical drugs, and cosmetics that are directly related to consumers' life and health. The aim is to alleviate information asymmetries in these areas to prevent healthcare accidents and disease epidemics, ensure patient safety, and guarantee that citizens' right to health is not violated.

12.3.2.2 Ensuring Safety

There are two main types of regulations. The first is the standard regulation of facilities. It mainly focuses on the basic and commonly used equipment in the workplace, requiring it to be in a clean and safe working order. The second is the regulation of operational standards. These include health standards, safety standards, and welfare standards, such as regulations on ventilation, temperature, light, and activity space in the workplace.

12.3.2.3 Preventing Public Hazard and Protecting the Environment

Social nuisance and environmental pollution are negative externalities. If the property rights between the perpetrators and the victims are poorly defined, the contractual choices of the two parties may be limited so that the damages caused by the external diseconomies cannot be well resolved. Although theoretically, there are regulatory approaches such as the setting of pollution standards, sewage charges, and emissions trading, in practice, countries tend to use the setting of pollution standards to prevent environmental externalities caused by implementing programming and constructing projects to promote the coordinated development of the economy, society, and the environment.

12.3.2.4 Ensuring the Provision of Education, Culture, and Welfare

Strengthening educational, cultural, and welfare regulations mainly includes improving the quality of education and social welfare and strengthening professional ethics. It is an important means of enhancing positive externalities and promoting social progress. The behavior of teachers, lawyers, and other practitioners determines the extent of positive externalities in these areas, and special legal regulations are needed to ensure that their behavior conforms to professional ethics. In addition, there is a need to enhance the general level of social welfare through cultural protection and improved welfare services.

12.3.3 Main Methods

The nature of social regulation is such that its methods are primarily direct, but there is also a relative degree of indirect regulation. It consists mainly of the following practices.

12.3.3.1 Prohibition of Specific Behaviors

It mainly refers to directly prohibiting social behaviors recognized by society as having the potential to cause harm and adverse consequences through statutes. For example, the law on anesthetics prohibits the arbitrary use of anesthetics. Namely, the statutes on firearms, cannons, knives, and swords strictly limit the scope of their use. As some behaviors that lead to external diseconomies can cause harm to people, they also belong to the list of specific behaviors that are prohibited. For example, enterprises are prohibited from illegally discharging tri-wastes: wastewater, exhaust gas, and residue, and people are prohibited from littering.

12.3.3.2 Restrictions on Business Activities

It mainly refers to restricting social business activities that provide special products and potentially cause harm through the government's authorization and recognition system. For example, business activities related to producing ordnance (public goods), city gas (quasi-public goods), and drugs (non-value goods). They may either be prone to harm or may be prone to external diseconomies that create social harm. For these business activities with unique attributes, the government has to legislate to restrict them and impose social regulations on them by these statutes, i.e., regulate the allocation, authorization, and recognition of these business activities.

12.3.3.3 Occupational Qualification System

It is a system whereby the state recognizes, certifies, and issues occupational certificates for specialized knowledge, experience, and skills of occupational units and individuals engaged in works related to health, safety, and the environment to ensure consumers' interests. The system usually takes three forms: (i) Accreditation of whether certain professionals are professionally qualified in compliance with the characteristics of the profession and the requirements of professional ethics. For example, doctors, lawyers, and accountants can only enter the profession after they are certified to engage in that business. (ii) Accreditation of the conditions and competence of persons managing certain specialized activities in a hazardous, responsible, and challenging nature. For example, the person in charge of safety in the manufacture of high-pressure gas and gunpowder products and the person in charge of operating an atomic reactor are required to have a high level of responsibility, keen observation, and excellent technical skills. (iii) A notarization for a skilled person who has acquired some form of specialized knowledge. For example, it is stipulated that graduates of various specialized schools must be assessed in a certain way before they can be granted specific names and titles, such as information processing technicians or sanitary inspection technicians. The system of professional qualifications is the most common means of restricting specific business activities.

12.3.3.4 Standard Certification and Inspection System

It mainly means that to ensure the safety of products and the safe operation and handling of machinery and equipment, the government should set safety standards for their structure, strength, and performance, particularly assessing their explosive and flammable characteristics. Products not labeled as conforming to the standards or not certified are forbidden from being sold or used. Meanwhile, two inspection systems have been stipulated. The first is an inspection system of obligations for entities and individuals involved in the above activities, which requires them to carry out regular, pre-use, post-use, and other inspections during production and other social activities. The second is the censorship of supervision and accreditation by the regulatory agencies. This system requires regulatory agencies to conduct periodic general surveys or unscheduled random inspections of the above activities to strictly prevent all possibilities of jeopardizing production. For example, it should often censor discharge standards to penalize discharge that exceeds the standards to ensure the environment's safety.

12.3.3.5 Information Disclosure Regime

It mainly refers to the fact that for enterprises or professionals with information asymmetry, the regulatory agencies have the right to require them to disclose to consumers as detailed as possible the business information related to the products or services they provide or information about products and services that the consumer should know and is entitled to request from the seller, in conformity with the law. For example, residents who buy a house ask the real estate company for relevant information, and those who buy food products ask for disclosure of products' ingredients and shelf life.

12.3.3.6 Compensation Fee System

It is primarily a practice of internalizing the damage of externalities. For example, it charges fixed fees like sewage on economic behaviors that can potentially cause fire and environmental damage and resource compensation fees like compensation for mining resources on behaviors to use natural resources. Compensation through fees affects the production enterprises' costs, thus enabling them to minimize damage to the environment and resources.

The first three of the six regime forms mentioned above are considered the primary regulations, whereas the last three complement and concretize the first three.

12.4 Micro-Regulatory Systems and Regulatory Reform

12.4.1 Micro-Regulatory System

In regulatory economics, the government regulatory system refers to the sum of a set of mechanisms and organizational bodies influencing the activities of economic entities or social subjects to achieve the specific economic or social objectives of regulation. It consists of three major systems.

12.4.1.1 Legal System of Micro-Regulation

In a modern market economy, state intervention must be done in compliance with the law. In order to ensure fairness and efficiency, government regulation must use economic, legal, and necessary administrative means for specific implementation based on the law.

The regulatory legal system mainly consists of: (i) The basic laws. They mainly lay the foundations for the regulatory legal system and unify and normalize the regulatory behavior. (ii) Individual law and statute. It is mainly a variety of specific laws and statutes for economic and social regulation. (iii) Detailed rules for enforcing laws. Implementing regulations should be developed on a case-by-case basis to facilitate specific operations, as many problems would be encountered in implementing regulatory laws. (iv) Legal system regulating the government's regulatory behavior. The government's regulatory behavior should also be included in the law to be subject to legal constraints and limitations, i.e., it is necessary to define the rights, standardize the behavior, and clarify the responsibility of the government regulatory agencies by the law. In addition, the legal supervision of regulatory personnel should be improved.

12.4.1.2 Institutional System of Micro-Regulation

The institutional system of micro-regulation mainly consists of: (i) Administrative organs, such as the State Council, functional administrative departments, and local public groups. They mainly regulate market economic entities based on economic laws such as Anti-Monopoly, Anti-Unfair Competition, and Labor Law. (ii) Judicial organs, such as courts and procuratorates. They mainly regulate the behavior of citizens based on civil, criminal, and other laws. (iii) The legislature. It mainly regulates the behavior of administrative organs or SOEs.

In a market economy, regulatory agencies are characterized by the following features: (i) Independence. It mainly refers to implementing policies by people with professional skills without undue outside interference, independent management, and accountability for results following specific operating rules. (ii) Well-targeted. The main point is that the regulatory agencies are organizations set up in response to a specific problem or event, such as establishing the Food Safety Commission of China's State Council. (iii) Statute-based. The main point is that the regulatory agencies must be legally established, and their regulatory behaviors must be supported by legislation. Establishing independent regulatory agencies is not only economically and organizationally rational, but also adapts to the requirements of modern decentralization theory, weakening administrative power.

12.4.1.3 Supervisory System of Micro-Regulation

Regardless of the regulatory system types, there is an established pattern of distributing regulatory power. No matter who is going to regulate or has the right to regulate, the owner of the regulatory power must be supervised. The essence of monitoring the regulator is to "regulate" the regulators, and the ultimate owner of the monitoring power is the public. Public oversight of the regulator means that the public, through its oversight, can limit the regulators' regulatory behavior so that they can perform their duties responsibly and diligently and maximize social welfare through regulation. However, public scrutiny of regulators still suffers from information asymmetry, i.e., the regulator is the party with information superiority, and the public is the party with information inferiority, so it is difficult to judge the regulator's regulatory behavior accurately. Therefore, it is vital to design the monitoring regulation system, which involves checking and balancing each other among the owners of regulatory power and allowing the public to exercise the right to scrutinize the regulators through innovating political system reform.

12.4.2 Micro-Regulation Reform

12.4.2.1 Current Status of Micro-Regulation in China

In the traditional planned economy, government authorities directly regulated all industries. Micro-regulation activities standing in a neutral position did not exist. In the true sense, the regulatory system was gradually established only after the reform and opening up. Although the current regulatory institution and system are imperfect, micro-regulatory activities still have the distinctive characteristics of transition. However, the government's micro-regulatory reform has made considerable progress.

First, the regulator is gradually established. Nowadays, the main regulator in China is the central government. Local governments also implement specific regulations through local legislation and other means, but mainly execute industry-specific regulatory policies under the vertical leadership of the central government. In addition, consumers' micro- subject identity has gradually matured with the improvement of the market economy and begun to play a specific role in promoting regulation.

Second, the behavior of the regulatory object (the regulated) begins to be normalized. The target of regulation mainly refers to enterprises and social organizations. Nowadays, the status of enterprises as market and legal entities is gradually being established, and their adaptability to micro-regulation is increasing.

Third, the regulatory methods are diversified. Since the reform and opening up, significant progress has been made in economic and social regulation. For example, price and entry regulations have been continuously standardized in economic regulation, and incentive regulation has gradually been exercised. In social regulation, the government has done much work regarding food and drug quality, labor safety, and environmental protection.

Fourth, a legal system of regulation is beginning to be established. In recent years, China has made some progress in micro-regulation legislation, and its law enforcement regulation system has been continuously improved.

12.4.2.2 Main Problems of Micro-Regulation in China

First, the regulators are imperfect, and the allocation of regulatory power is unreasonable. It has not formed an independent regulatory agent. Moreover, existing regulatory agencies are often subject to interference in the performance of their functions. The distribution of regulatory powers (e.g., pricing power, standard-setting power, investment approval power, anti-trust investigation power) is too decentralized. It both vertically (between central and local levels) and horizontally (among regulatory agencies) results in policies coming from many departments and each implementing its policy, thus reducing the efficiency of regulation, raising the cost of regulation.

Second, the object of the regulation (the enterprise) has non-market-oriented behavior. At present, many aspects of enterprise behavior still do not meet the requirements of the market economy, exhibiting "non-market economy" characteristics. For example, some enterprises are in disorder in terms of entry, exit, price, competition, and irregular pricing and accounting, while some enterprises have serious negative externalities, and quality and security problems occasionally occur.

Third, methods of regulation are not sufficiently advanced. Whether it is economic or social regulation, there are still many shortcomings in the regulation methodology, resulting in unsatisfactory results.

Fourth, construction of the regulatory legal system is lagging. Insufficient legislation, excessively light legal responsibilities, and lax law enforcement still exist.

Fifth, there is a coexistence of deficient and overstepping regulation. Additionally, overreaching intervention by executive branches and the excessive and abusive administrative approvals still exist.

Bibliography

1. Malthus: "An Essay on the Principle of Population", The Commercial Press, 1969 Edition
2. Marx: "Economic and Philosophic Manuscripts of 1844", "Marx Engels Collected Works", Volume 42, People's Publishing House, 1979 Edition
3. Marx: "Capital", Volume 3, People's Publishing House, 1975 Edition
4. Wang Junhao: "Introduction to Government Regulation Economics", The Commercial Press, 2013 Edition
5. Carl Menger: "Principles of Economics", Shanghai Century Publishing Group, Shanghai People's Publishing House, 2001 Edition
6. Song Zexing: "Socialist Macroeconomics", Liaoning University Publishing House, 1989 Edition
7. Zhang Jinsheng: "Human-Oriented Management: New Developments in Contemporary Management Science", Liaoning University Publishing House, 1999 Edition
8. Zhang Leisheng: "Economic Development of Developing Countries", Higher Education Press, 2002 Edition
9. Lin Muxi, Zhang Jing: "Scientific Development Concept and Discipline Construction of National Economics", Economic Science Press, 2007 Edition
10. Lin Muxi, Huang Taiyan: "National Economics" (First, Second, and Third Editions), Economic Science Press, 2008, 2010, 2018 Editions
11. Lin Muxi, Huang Taiyan: "Dictionary of National Economics", Economic Science Press, 2015 Edition
12. Lin Muxi: "A Dictionary of Modern Economics: Economics Volume", Economic Science Press, 2016 Edition
13. Zhong Maochu: "The Economics of Sustainable Development", Economic Science Press, 2006 Edition
14. Hong Yinxing: "A Dictionary of Modern Economics", Economic Science Press, 2016 Edition
15. Qian Bohai: "National Economics", China Financial & Economic Publishing House, 1986 Edition
16. Wicksell: "Lectures on Political Economics", Shanghai Translation Publishing House, 1983 Edition

M. Lin and T. Huang, *National Economics*, https://doi.org/10.1007/978-981-96-9618-5

MIX
Papier aus verantwortungsvollen Quellen
Paper from responsible sources
FSC® C105338

If you have any concerns about our products,
you can contact us on
ProductSafety@springernature.com

In case Publisher is established outside the EU,
the EU authorized representative is:
Springer Nature Customer Service Center GmbH
Europaplatz 3, 69115 Heidelberg, Germany

Printed by Libri Plureos GmbH
in Hamburg, Germany